Abraham Lincoln in the Post-Heroic Era

Abraham Lincoln in the Post-Heroic Era

*

HISTORY AND MEMORY IN LATE TWENTIETH-CENTURY AMERICA

Barry Schwartz

The University of Chicago Press Chicago and London

BARRY SCHWARTZ is professor emeritus of sociology at the University of Georgia. He is the author of several books, including *Abraham Lincoln and the Forge of National Memory*.

The University of Chicago Press, Chicago 60637
The University of Chicago Press, Ltd., London

Printed in the United States of America

17 16 15 14 13 12 11 10 09 08   1 2 3 4 5

ISBN-13: 978-0-226-74188-8 (cloth)
ISBN-10: 0-226-74188-5 (cloth)

Library of Congress Cataloging-in-Publication Data

Schwartz, Barry, 1938–
Abraham Lincoln in the post-heroic era : history and memory in late twentieth-century America / Barry Schwartz.
p. cm.
Includes bibliographical references and index.
ISBN-13: 978-0-226-74188-8 (cloth : alk. paper)
ISBN-10: 0-226-74188-5 (cloth : alk. paper) 1. Lincoln, Abraham, 1809–1865. 2. Presidents—United States—Biography. 3. Lincoln, Abraham, 1809–1865—Public opinion. 4. Lincoln, Abraham, 1809–1865—Influence. 5. United States—History—20th century. 6. Multiculturalism—United States. I. Title.
E457.2.S383 2008
973.7092—dc22
[B]

2008026876

♾ The paper used in this publication meets the minimum requirements of the American National Standard for Information Sciences—Permanence of Paper for Printed Library Materials, ANSI Z39.48-1992.

To Aaron

Contents

Preface

I cannot imagine a world without heroes, a world without genius and nobility, without exalted enterprise, high purpose and transcendent courage, without risk and suffering. It would be gray and flat and dull. Who would show us the way or set the mark? Who would inspire us and console us? Who would energize us and keep us from the darkness?

Peter C. Gibbon. A *Call to Heroism*

Mr. Smith Goes to Washington was one of the most popular and, by current taste, corny movies of 1939. The plot involves Jefferson Smith, a Boy Scout leader appointed to fill the seat of a suddenly deceased senator. As soon as idealistic Mr. Smith arrives in Washington, he tours its monuments and shrines, making an extended visit to the Lincoln Memorial. He soon discovers that the Senate's men are less than monumental; their work, filled with conniving and graft. When he protests, his colleagues turn against him and manufacture evidence to expel him from the Senate. Utterly disillusioned, he makes a night visit, with suitcase, to the Lincoln Memorial, he gazes again into the countenance of Lincoln, then turns to the Gettysburg Address's last line, carved into the Memorial wall: "that government of the people, for the people, and by the people shall not perish from the earth." He is moved to tears by these words. Clarissa Saunders, his savvy advisor, hears about the senator's debacle and searches for him. "You know, I had a hunch I'd find you here." Smith responds by acknowledging her disdain for his naiveté and idealism:

> I don't know. There are a lot of fancy words around this town. Some of them are carved in stone. Some of 'em, I guess the shysters have put 'em there so suckers like me can read 'em. Then when you find out what men actually do—well, I'm gettin' out of this town so fast and away from all the words and the monuments and the whole rotten show.

Clarissa, inspired by the new senator's predicament, protests, "You did not entrust your faith in the little men of the Senate." She declares:

> You had faith in something bigger than that. You had plain, decent everyday, common rightness. And this country could use some of that. Yeah—so could the whole cockeyed world. A lot of it. Remember the first day you got here? Remember what you said about Mr. Lincoln? You said he was sitting up there waiting for someone to come along. You were right! He was waiting for a man who could see his job and sail into it. That was what he was waiting for. A man who could tear into the [grafters] and root 'em out into the open. I think he was waiting for you, Jeff. He knows you can do it. So do I.

Mr. Smith takes heart from Miss Saunders's words: "Now you're talkin'!" As they leave, he looks up again at the great figure of Lincoln and waves to him.

In Jefferson Smith's life, Abraham Lincoln is much more than a symbol, more than an idea; Abraham Lincoln is a living force. During the first half of the century, artists frequently portrayed ordinary people, like Jefferson Smith, reverently gazing upon Abraham Lincoln seated in his memorial temple. During the second half of the century, Americans were more accustomed to seeing the memorial as a site of public protest. Typical was Martin Luther King Jr.'s "I Have a Dream" speech to 250,000 rallying for jobs and social equality. Men and women from all sectors of society spoke that day, but King's words proved to be the most memorable. The ritual genre was new: speakers stood with their back toward Lincoln, some briefly mentioned him, then spoke about a contemporary issue; the audience, in turn, looked upon the speaker and reacted to the issue, not to Lincoln. To the late twentieth-century mind, the most familiar Lincoln Memorial images are petitioners claiming rights rather than admirers expressing reverence.[1] However, Lincoln has not disappeared. King's agents, after all, chose the Lincoln Memorial, not the Jefferson Memorial or the Washington Monument, as the site for his speech. Lincoln remains an important part of the picture, but he stands in the background.

Throughout the first half of the twentieth century, Abraham Lincoln was a subject of reverence and a symbol of union, equality, and justice. By midcentury, the balance among these ideals shifted as Lincoln became a reminder of the nation's continuing racial discrimination. To place Abraham Lincoln in American memory, then, requires two volumes, because the formation and transformation of his reputation—like the rise and fall of his prestige—occur in different environments.

After Lincoln's assassination, dramatic funeral rites enlarged him, even while funeral eulogists questioned his presidential actions. But over the next four decades his prestige diminished. Not until the turn of the twentieth century did Lincoln emerge as a national idol, surpassing even George Washington. Lincoln's place in American memory grew as Progressive reform democratized urban America and enhanced the average man's well being.

Abraham Lincoln and the Forge of National Memory,[2] the first part of this project, describes the demise of the Civil War generation and the rise of a Progressive Era after the maturing of the Industrial Revolution. Living through World War I and the burgeoning postwar economy, this second generation takes us to the cusp of the Great Depression. *Forge of National Memory* evaluates nineteenth- and early twentieth-century beliefs about Lincoln through the oratory Americans heard; the textbooks, newspapers, and popular magazines they read; the painting, sculpture, and films they viewed. However, the explanation of Lincoln's enlarged place in American memory proved more complex than the theories of our day suggest.

The theory of the politics of memory, which focuses on how beliefs about the past are contested by different communities, makes considerable sense of Lincoln's apotheosis, but this insight alone exaggerates his malleability by making him an object to be fashioned and refashioned as power shifts from one community to another. Lincoln has always been a *lamp* illuminating the ideals of the American people as well as a *mirror* reflecting their interests. *The Forge of National Memory* turns precisely on this distinction. Lincoln's troubles reappear in present predicaments; Lincoln's facing his troubles shows us how to work through our own. Abraham Lincoln in American memory is more than a political asset; he is a moral symbol inspiring and guiding American life.[3]

For those interested in generalizing Lincoln's case, *Forge of National Memory* elaborates a second pair of theoretical concepts: *keying* and *framing*. Keying transforms the meaning of present activities by aligning them to past events. Franklin Roosevelt's death in April 1945, for example, assumes new meaning when keyed to Lincoln's death in April 1865. Keying is more than a new word for analogical thinking, more than a way individuals mentally organize their experience. Keying present-day events to the past is, like any conscious perception, "an act of recognition, a pairing in which an object (or an event, an act, an emotion) is identified by placing it against the background of an appropriate symbol. For more than a century, Lincoln has been an "appropriate symbol," a frame for American values, aspirations, and experience. Abraham Lincoln, thus, *frames* present events when the latter have been convincingly *keyed* to his life.

The diminishing of Lincoln's relevance through eroding symbols and frames is an aspect of postmodernity and multiculturalism, which together constitute the core of the post-heroic era. To track and explain this change will be our concern. The primary condition of Lincoln's apotheosis was the unique fit between his personal traits and the Progressive Era's egalitarian reforms; the primary condition of Lincoln's descent is the fading of the concept of greatness itself. Of this development the diminished renown of other presidents, including George Washington, Franklin Roosevelt, Harry Truman, John Kennedy, and Dwight Eisenhower, is a conspicuous part.

Lincoln rose to prominence during the first three decades of the twentieth century. During the next decade and a half, ending in 1945, his prestige peaked, then, over the next sixty years, declined. Few want to return to the days when Lincoln received his full due, for the conditions maximizing hero worship—crude, ethnic-based nationalism, impermeable social boundaries, and rigid stereotypes—made life miserable for many. As an aspect of America's benign change, Lincoln's decline results from a cultural contradiction: on the one side, self-absoprtion, loss of belief in transcendent entities, resulting from a deepening depravity; on the other side, equality and inclusion and a dissolution of boundaries once separating Americans on the basis of their ethnicity, religion, and race. This book documents Lincoln's transformation and decline but neither calls for the return of his former renown nor expresses admiration for the conditions promoting it. The situation that disenchants Lincoln and induces people to analyze rather than idolize him is also that on which contemporary equality and justice depend. One of the principal questions raised here, in fact, is whether Americans living in a fully integrated society can revere Lincoln as fervently as did their forebears.

If we knew all there is to know about Abraham Lincoln in American memory, the power of his legacy would be obvious. But much remains unknown. In a sequel to this volume, I explore what may well be the most famous event of his presidency and the most effective carrier of his reputation—the Gettysburg Address. During the past twenty-five years, two great books on the Gettysburg Address have appeared, Garry Wills's *Lincoln at Gettysburg* and Gabor Boritt's *The Gettysburg Gospel*. Wills and Boritt approach Lincoln's words from very different standpoints but find in them similar meaning: a reaffirmation of the Emancipation Proclamation. But the Gettysburg Address can also be used as a lens to perform a finer, microscopic examination of the issues addressed in this book. In the process, academic and media professionals making the Gettysburg Address into an addendum of the Emancipation Proclamation and a prologue to twentieth-century civil rights legislation will be challenged. *The New Gettysburg Address* (in preparation) demonstrates what Lincoln meant to say at Gettysburg; what such oft-repeated phrases as "Fourscore and seven years ago," "the proposition that all men are created equal," and "new birth of freedom" meant to his *contemporaries*; why the Gettysburg Address was largely ignored until the twentieth century; how its meaning changed through World War I, the Depression, World War II, the Cold War; and why historians of the post–civil rights generation revised that meaning so radically.

Abraham Lincoln in the Post-Heroic Era prepares the reader to approach critically a body of writings that deemphasize principal elements of Lincoln's legacy: the saving of the Union and, with that, the preservation of the world's only democracy. If reformist writers and artists of the late-twentieth century attracted audiences by molding Lincoln into a racial equality champion, then Americans perceiving him through the entire course of the century provide a reference point for assessing alternative claims about his legacy.

Acknowledgments

Lincoln specialists refer to themselves as "the Lincoln community," and to them and their organizations I owe more than I can repay. They have welcomed me to their meetings and homes; they have taught me most of what I know. They have listened to me with kindness and patience; they have corrected my mistakes without discouraging me. Mainly historians and political scientists, they have never invoked disciplinary privilege to dismiss sociological understandings of Lincoln and his legacy.

I am grateful to Richard Somers and Joseph Garrera for reading and supplying valuable criticism on earlier drafts of this book. The University of Chicago Press's reviewers prompted many fresh ideas and revisions, and I acknowledge their hard work with thanks.

Sociology colleagues working within the field of collective memory have also listened to me talk about Lincoln. To name them all is impossible, but to one person I am especially indebted. One day long ago, Howard Schuman asked me whether it makes sense to describe collective memory solely through texts and symbols while ignoring what ordinary individuals think and feel about the past. No question has done more to change the direction of my work and my understanding. Professor Schuman and I have never totally agreed on how to bring the individual into the analysis of collective memory, but he is right about the necessity of doing so. There is no way to comprehend Abraham Lincoln in American memory without knowing what the American people actually believe about him and how they feel about what they believe. Howard Schuman's counsel applies to and, I think, deepens every sector of collective memory scholarship.

I thank the University of Georgia Senior Faculty Research Grants in the Humanities and Fine Arts, which supported a national survey of beliefs about Abraham Lincoln. Let no one overestimate the thickness of the barrier separating the humanities and social sciences. Paul Roman, director, Center for Research on Deviance, and James J. Bason, director, Survey Research Center, University of Georgia, generously allowed me to add questions to the National Employee Survey. The result is a valuable comparison between two generations of Americans, fifty years apart. I hope the resulting knowledge will justify their kindness.

The Lady Davis Fellowship Trust, Hebrew University of Jerusalem, awarded me a semester to pursue my Lincoln project. This university's willingness to support research on American history in the midst of a national crisis testifies to its universalist devotion to disciplinary rather than topical scholarship.

I have received assistance over the years from graduate students, most recently Michelle Petrie and Lydia Aletraris. Artists and art historian colleagues have helped me utilize paintings, illustrations, and cartoons as evidence on changing generational cultures. Their number defies my wish to name them all.

My final and greatest debt, as always, goes to my wife, Janet. She has read every word I have written and done her best to save me from myself. This master grammarian and critic taught me that faulty prose is a symptom of faulty thinking, that passive voices and expletive patterns are not just ways of writing but ways of describing and explaining the world. I regret that I am not her best student.

Introduction

For in the background figures vague and vast
Of patriarchs and of prophets rose sublime,
And all the great traditions of the Past
They saw reflected in the coming time.
And thus forever with reverted look
The mystic volume of the world they read,
Spelling it backward, like a Hebrew book,
Till life became a Legend of the Dead.
But ah! What once has been shall be no more!
The groaning earth in travail and in pain
Brings forth its races, but does not restore,
And the dead nations never rise again.

Henry Wadsworth Longfellow
"The Jewish Cemetery at Newport"

On the morning of February 12, 1959, Carl Sandburg rose to speak to a joint session of Congress commemorating the 150th anniversary of Abraham Lincoln's birth. The event's significance was marked by the stature of its participants: members of President Eisenhower's cabinet, the chief justice and associate justices of the Supreme Court, the joint chiefs of staff and other military officials, selected ambassadors, and foreign dignitaries. The Army Band and Coast Guard Chorale provided music; actor Frederic March, a dramatic reading of the Gettysburg Address. Carl Sandburg was the star. His account of Lincoln's kindness and love for the people "brought the entire press gallery en bloc to its feet in a demonstration of emotion and applause." Several congressmen wept as he read his speech. Sam Rayburn of Texas, Speaker of the House, thought the ceremony the most memorable he had ever witnessed.[1]

The congressional ceremony, televised live and carried in whole or part (including evening news segments) by at least 4,500 stations, reached 83 percent of America's households. According to media experts, the event's impact was unprecedented. "[T]he immediate influence on the emotions and the thinking of tens of millions of Americans made the Joint Session and the event it commemorated without the shadow of a doubt the most powerfully inspiring educational force in the annals of public ceremonies for exercises of such comparative brevity."[2]

"Brevity," indeed, distinguished the occasion. The Lincoln sesquicentennial was a vastly diminished version of the Lincoln centennial. In 1909, municipal and neighborhood groups, schools, churches, veterans' groups, political clubs, and trade and professional associations organized their own centennial activities. Programs enticed people from private homes into social halls, auditoriums, classrooms, parks, and stadiums. Public events mingled stories of Lincoln (many told in foreign languages) with exotic smells, colorful decorations, chaotic sounds, and dense crowds. Enhancing solemn memories with a touch of disorder and fun, public ritual made the past tangible.

Fifty years later, when the federal sesquicentennial commission requested that state governors establish commissions, only nineteen (all non-Southern) complied. True, many state and local organizations arranged special features to supplement their regular Lincoln Day observance. The federal government added its own touches, including commemorative stamps and a new back for the Lincoln penny. But the public mood, best captured by the U.S. Commission Report's dedication, was muted: in 1959, the "citizens of the United States of America . . . expressed through their Representatives in Congress a desire to commemorate this one hundred fiftieth anniversary of the birth of Abraham Lincoln."[3] Unlike their 1909 predecessors, Americans in 1959 celebrated the sesquicentennial by proxy. The sesquicentennial's structure, like its mood, inverted the centennial's. Because most of the nation's business proceeded as usual, housewives watched the official proceedings on live television; their husbands watched recorded segments in the evening. The sesquicentennial aroused no greater excitement at the local level, however, than it did nationally. New entertainment media cannot explain the difference. No radio or movie theaters competed with the 1909 Lincoln centennial, but in 1932, when these media were expanding in number and influence, the George Washington bicentennial was widely and enthusiastically observed.[4] Compared to the great 1909 and 1932 anniversaries, in both of which every state, including Southern ones, took part, Lincoln's 1959 festivities paled.

Four years after the Lincoln sesquicentennial, President John Kennedy's death powerfully affected the American people. Watching not only the funeral but also one another's reaction to it, America's racial, ethnic, and religious communities seemed to realize with more certainty than ever that they were part of one nation. That the medium did not determine the reaction is certain: everyone remembered the televised Kennedy funeral; few remembered the televised Lincoln sesquicentennial. Was the sesquicentennial forgotten because its rituals moved off the street and into the living room? Because sesquicentennial planning was less extensive than the planning of the centennial? Because state funerals are more dramatic than anniversary events? Because people felt differently about their presidents? About history in general?

No one knows what ordinary Americans think about these matters.

What Americans Believe about Abraham Lincoln

No one knows what ordinary Americans think about Abraham Lincoln. Merrill Peterson's (1994) *Abraham Lincoln in American Memory,* the most comprehensive and authoritative chronicle of Lincoln representations,[5] distills from a 138-year series of Lincoln biographies, monuments, shrines, icons, place names, and ritual observances five distinct images: (1) "Savior of the Union", (2) "Great Emancipator", (3) "Man of the People", (4) "First American" (frontier youth), and (5) "Self-Made Man." Because each image expresses a different pattern of historical writing and commemoration, Lincoln in American memory, as Peterson conceives it, means Lincoln represented by text and symbol rather than Lincoln as individuals think about him. Peterson nowhere denies that Lincoln exists in the minds of individuals, but his account ignores the thinking of individuals almost entirely.

Peterson's vast chronicle of historians, popular writers, painters, sculptors, and monument architects contains good examples of reputational sponsorship and enterprise,[6] that is, repetitive ventures that "form the backbone of collective memories."[7] Peterson's is, in fact, the richest chronicle of Lincoln texts and images ever assembled, but it makes no effort to explain why different agents portray Lincoln in different ways, and whether these portrayals conform to what the average American believes about him. Merrill Peterson's unprecedented account of Lincoln's meaning to America exemplifies "the new structural memory," a theory asserting that memory can be collective only if embodied in symbolic objects existing outside the mind of the individual.[8] Pierre Nora, foreshadowing Peterson, finds collective memory in *lieux de mémoire,*[9] which include all material objects representing France's past, independently of their meaning to individual Frenchmen. Richard Terdiman declares that memory resides "not in perceiving consciousness but in the material [symbolic] objects which do not seem to require either our participation or explicit allegiance."[10] Michael Schudson comes to a similar conclusion: memory consists of the concrete "rules, laws, procedures, precedents, records, files, books, holidays, statues, mementos"[11] of specific institutions—which conforms to Mary Douglas's proposition that *institutions* remember.[12] We thus enter a new age in which archives, statues, and rituals are no longer memory's instruments but its embodiments.[13]

The structural theory of memory is not a methodological artifact, a remnant of earlier days when measures of beliefs and attitudes about Lincoln were unavailable. National surveys have made such measures available for more than a half century. Few collective memory scholars and even fewer Lincoln scholars, however, have shown an interest in pursuing survey evidence. Theoretical perspective, not methodological limits, leads these scholars to emphasize texts and commemorative objects and to deemphasize, even disregard, what ordinary individuals believe about the past.

Beliefs can be examined directly—not instead of, but in addition to the historiographic and symbolic vehicles traditionally comprising collective memory's data. The first set of national survey findings on what Americans believed about Lincoln became available in 1945. By drawing on sample surveys to learn what the American population believes about Lincoln, and how closely these beliefs conform to historians' and commemorative artists' accounts, we move beyond the methodological divide limiting our understanding. Responses to survey questions are no substitute for description of the way Lincoln narratives and symbols frame individual experience,[14] and much of the following analysis uses such qualitative data, particularly works of art, to distinguish the mentality of generations. Properly designed surveys, however, provide complementary evidence of what Americans outside scholarly and artistic circles think about Lincoln.[15]

PRESTIGE AND REPUTATION

Abraham Lincoln's "prestige" and "reputation" must be distinguished in order to assess his historical standing. The word "prestige," referring to emotional and judgmental faculties, derives from the Latin *praestigiae*, a conjuror's trick, and *praestringere*, to tie up, blindfold. Prestige is an aura setting one person apart from another on a scale of esteem—not solely on the basis of rational assessment but also of emotional reaction.

Reputation, on the other hand, refers to personal qualities and character. Derived from the Latin *reputare*, "to reckon up, think over," the word denotes understandings derived cognitively rather than emotionally or morally. Prestige and reputation, together, define Lincoln's "image."

Lincoln's prestige is relatively easy to track. Whether we count articles in newspapers and magazines, Congressional activities, historians' presidential ratings, or the assessments of ordinary Americans, the result is the same: Lincoln has ranked first in presidential greatness since the second decade of the twentieth century when he surpassed George Washington.[16] Traditional portrayals of Lincoln, on the other hand, now seem outlandish. Prior to the mid-twentieth century, biographies verge on hagiography; sermons and essays define Lincoln as the greatest man to walk the Earth since Jesus; neoclassical statues depict him larger than life; state portraits envelope him in the majesty of state power; "grand style" history paintings show him altering the fate of the nation; prints and cartoons depict people looking up to him as a guiding light; ritual observances induce entire communities to suspend their affairs in his memory. Conventional before and during World War II, these forms became almost obsolete by the 1950s.

The more closely representations of Lincoln are traced, the more problematic the relation between heroism and greatness becomes. *Webster's New Collegiate Dictionary* marks the hero with "greatness of ability"; "courage and daring"; "impressive size, power, or effect"; "a man admired for his achievements and qualities"; "the central figure in an event or period." Heroes do extraordinary deeds in many realms of life, including police work, firefighting, military combat, and sports, but they are not necessarily great men. Great men reconstruct the order of their societies and redirect history. Abraham Lincoln's actions are, thus, heroic, but not all heroes are great like Lincoln. Still, the overlap between heroism and greatness is sufficient to allow the two concepts to be used here interchangeably.

That great men are appreciated less in the second half of the twentieth century than at any previous time has been widely noted, discussed every day in political and historical commentary, but never described or explained. Only vaguely can we know when historical greatness began to lose relevance, assess the steepness of its decline, or determine whether that decline differed among different regions of the country, different racial and ethnic communities, social classes, and religious groups. Why some great men lost prestige faster than others or whether the content of their reputation changed as their prestige fell, is also uncertain.

Explanations purporting to account for the fallen stature of American heroes are abundant: the rise of analytic psychology, investigative journalism, deconstructive television and film, a new history emphasizing the achievements of ordinary people and the shortcomings of traditional heroes, fading nationalism, waning belief in the sacred, weakened tradition and authority, erosion of moral values, spreading of doubt, egoism, and cynicism, self-realization replacing commitment to the social good, and lack of critical challenges, including threats to the nation's existence. These explanations all have some ring of truth, but they are all partial, and we cannot tell exactly how they enter into the way men and women think about their nation's past. The consequence of the waning of greatness is even more problematic than its causes. Whether hero worship depends on benign structures to be preserved or malignant ones to be abandoned is rarely considered.

During the second half of the century, Abraham Lincoln remained first among presidents, but the absolute level of his prestige fell. Not only does a declining percentage of Americans consider him the best president; they no longer define "best" to mean "venerable." On the other hand, some insist that Lincoln's prestige has grown, not diminished. They can cite the construction of new Lincoln libraries and museums, the expansion of old ones, the number of hits on Lincoln library and museum Web sites, the sheer number of Lincoln associations, excitement over the discovery of new information about Lincoln's young adulthood and legal career, the large number of recent Lincoln biographies, and the rapidly growing number of Web sites opening Lincoln archives to the public. As the 2009 Lincoln bicentennial approaches, Lincoln remains one of the few historical leaders still respected by the vast majority of American historians.[17] Even so, the quantity of Lincoln scholarship, the vitality of Lincoln associations, and the personal affection of Lincoln experts fail to reflect Lincoln's diminishing place in the imagination of ordinary people. Demonstrating that decline is this book's first objective.

As Lincoln's prestige diminished, his reputation changed. Before the 1960s, most Americans admired Lincoln as Savior of the Union, an ordinary man on whom fate placed a burden heavier than that borne by any other president. Presently, however, Lincoln is a reformer president, a champion of racial justice who drafted the Emancipation Proclamation as soon as the opportunity arose. The Proclamation made abolition of slavery a war goal equal in immediacy to, if not more urgent than, saving the Union, and it set before America the ideal of racial equality. Abraham Lincoln has become a prophet of the civil rights movement. To demonstrate this transformation is the book's second objective.

Three key questions about Abraham Lincoln's changing image must now be posed: (1) Why did his prestige fall so abruptly and so far during the last third of the twentieth century? (2) Why did his reputation change so suddenly and re-center so definitely on emancipation? and (3) Did his falling prestige and changing reputation affect one another, or did both result from a third, more fundamental, condition? Answers to these questions are important not only for what they tell us about people's perception of Lincoln but also for how they clarify the way Americans think about historical greatness in general. Lincoln's diminution is part of a general trend: Christopher Columbus, George Washington, Thomas Jefferson, Andrew Jackson, Theodore Roosevelt, Woodrow Wilson, Franklin Roosevelt—all these men, like Lincoln, were revered more deeply during the first half of the twentieth century than they are today. Lincoln's case is but one instance of a weakening faith in human greatness.

Post-Heroic Era

During the early years of World War II, W. H. Auden published a long poem titled "For the Time Being: A Christmas Oratorio." He wrote the work shortly after converting to Christianity and recognizing signs of an emerging post-heroic culture. In one section of the poem, King Herod debates with himself whether to issue a warrant for the slaughter of the innocents, not because he is inclined to do so but because he fears what the world will look like if the new child-god, humble rather than proud, weak rather than powerful, is allowed to live. Herod has ruled over an orderly kingdom in which everyone knows his place, but he can see the new world's contours:

> One doesn't have to be a prophet to predict the consequences.... Whole cosmogonies will be created out of some forgotten personal resentment, complete epics written in private languages, the daubs of schoolchildren ranked above the greatest masterpieces.... Divine honors will be paid to silver teapots, shallow depressions in the earth, names on maps, domestic pets, ruined windmills, even in extreme cases, which will become increasingly common, to headaches, or malignant tumors, or four o'clock in the afternoon.... The New Aristocracy will consist exclusively of hermits, bums, and permanent invalids. The Rough Diamond, the Consumptive Whore, the bandit who is good to his mother, the epileptic girl who has a way with animals will be the heroes and heroines of the New Tragedy, when the general, the statesman, and the philosopher have become the butt of every farce and satire.[18]

Classic tragedy presents performers of great feats destroyed by their own flaws; in the New Tragedy, insignificant figures enlarge themselves by means of their own problems. Social and moral distinctions disappear; pity replaces justice. Present-day realities with which Audens's words have affinity are not difficult to identify: nonjudgmentalism, victim-centeredness, radical egalitarianism, multiculturalism. The moral and social leveling supporting the most congenial society in history, a society largely free of ethnic and racial hatred, inclusive of all peoples and solicitous of their rights, is precisely the kind of society in which great men and women and their achievements count for less, while the victimized, wounded, handicapped, and oppressed count for more than ever before.

"Heroic eras" refer to periods in history when great deeds performed on the nation's behalf are celebrated. Residents of such ages not only recognize their champions but also identify with them and urge their children to emulate them. Crisis provides the soil for the growth of such cultures. In "post-heroic" eras, epic undertakings are replaced by limited conflicts; democracy is expanded by repudiating inequality and valorizing victimhood above greatness, weakness above strength. In this new society, this post-heroic era, the New Lincoln fits well.

WHY LINCOLN?

Classical notions of greatness refer to leadership of fateful enterprises and movements. The great man is not any leader revered because of his authority or personal qualities, but one who uses both to mobilize society to extend or defend its existing structures.[19] Arduous feats affecting social order and altering history's course objectively define Abraham Lincoln's greatness. But why have the American people, as a whole, lost interest in a Lincoln once deemed so central to national well-being?

Eroding interest in national myths is part of the belief system of a new postindustrial society. "Petit narratives," as Jean-Francois Lyotard defines them, include family and local chronicles as frames for the interpretation of *individual* and *communal* experience; "grand narratives," the frames within which people grasp the meaning of their *national* history and identity. Ours is an era ready to live without grand narratives, an era in which absolutes are local and private rather than collective.[20] The very definition of our "postmodern" time, according to Lyotard, includes incredulity toward grand narratives. Narrative's function, he says, "is losing its functors, its great heroes, its great dangers, its great voyages, its great goal. . . . " Old poles of attraction represented by nation-states, parties, professions, institutions, and historical traditions are losing their attraction" and becoming "delegitimated."[21]

The fading hero is symptomatic of fading confidence in national greatness.[22] Stories of that greatness have not totally disappeared. Historians and biographers continue to cast their subjects in epic form, but they inspire the typical reader less deeply than they did before the middle of the twentieth century. Any one of a number of American heroes could serve as vehicles to explore this claim; Abraham Lincoln is the most appropriate because no American's life has been documented more fully, commemorated more often, and revered more deeply. Because Lincoln, in Clinton Rossiter's opinion, is "the supreme myth, the richest symbol in the American experience," his story becomes an essential part of the story of American "peoplehood."[23] Lincoln personifies the ideals of American political culture: equality, liberty, populism, competitive capitalism, and individualism.[24] If he were removed from this story, its content would remain, but it would be less powerful and moving, its moral essence less compelling.

Lincoln is useful for studying American memory because he is the main character in America's Civil War, the center of what Robert Penn Warren described as the nation's "felt history,"[25] its "reusable past," which successive generations have found directly relevant to their lives[26] and vital to their "civil religion."[27] Garry Wills, in fact, has argued that Lincoln was more than a character in America's story; he single-handedly redefined its plot and laid the foundation of a new society by redefining the ideals of equality and justice.[28] But if the Lincoln story is a grand narrative that sustains America's identity by shaping its citizens' moral character and affecting the way they engage the world, what is to be said of Lincoln's deteriorating prestige and transformed reputation? Do they result from new information about Lincoln or social changes that transcend Lincoln? Are we discovering new facts about a man, or is Christopher Lasch right about our losing our sense of "historical continuity, the sense of belonging to a succession of generations originating in the past and stretching into the future"?[29] Or is America's culture, its indifference if not suspicion of historical greatness, more complex?

GENERATIONS

Changing beliefs about Abraham Lincoln resonate with the worldview and ethos of changing generations. Belonging to the same generation, according to Karl Mannheim, endows members with a common location in the social and historical process, limiting them to a specific range of experience and predisposing them to characteristic modes of thinking and feeling.[30] That beliefs about Lincoln differ across generations is therefore axiomatic.

The span of years from 1930 to present can be partitioned into four generations whose distinguishing conceptions of Lincoln and American history are connected to distinctive economic and political realities. The "G.I. Generation," as many call it, extends from 1930, the beginning of the Great Depression, to 1945, the end of World War II. Those coming of age in this generation are said to be more alive to tradition, more committed to the state and its collective projects, more selfless than its predecessors. The second, "Rights and Justice Generation" occupies a twenty-year period, from 1945 to the mid-1960s—the period of the Truman and Eisenhower presidencies during which a civil rights movement arose and gave minority aspirations unprecedented visibility.[31]

As *duty* drove the G.I. Generation and its predecessors, *rights*—equality and entitlement in the realms of race, class, gender, crime, mental illness, and education—drove the Rights and Justice Generation. Beginning in the mid-1960s, postwar babies came of age, constituting a "Boomer" or, more concretely, "Rebellious Generation"[32] that consolidated the victories of the civil rights movement, on the one hand, and, on the other, proclaimed sexual freedom, contempt for the establishment, opposition to its war in Vietnam, and support for all oppressed minorities. Members of the fourth "Uncommitted Generation," also known as "Generation X," the "Generation After," and "Generation with No Name," came of age in the early 1980s.[33] Where the G.I. Generation is considered the greatest generation, the Uncommitted Generation is the least distinguished. The uncommitted live in a world of eroding authority, loose sexual conventions, deteriorating family structure, and fading of the stigma formerly attached to wrongdoing and failure. "Multiculturalism," with its seemingly infinite tolerance, its celebration of "diversity" and canonization of history's victims, constitutes the Uncommitted Generation's distinctive achievement.[34]

Generations are constituted by people passing through different phases of personal development. Despite their subjective differences, however, those living during the same span of time experience together the same events and participate in the same part of the historical process. Most generation analyses minimize internal diversity and exaggerate differences, but distortions should not cause us to ignore real differences. The Rebellious and Uncommitted Generations, in particular, constitute a post-heroic era that modifies the legacy of earlier generations, rejects their representative men without replacing them and makes their symbolic forms and beliefs appear strange and out of place. This change consists not in the accumulation of new facts but rather in the perspective in which the nation's great men are contemplated. New environments that induce people to see the world differently also induce them to see, or are correlated with their seeing, Abraham Lincoln differently.

Collective Memory: Reality and Construction

Collective memory refers to the distribution throughout society of what individuals believe, feel, and know about the past. Only individuals possess the capacity to contemplate the past, but this does not mean that beliefs originate in the individual alone or can be explained on the basis of unique experience. Individuals do not know the past singly; they know it with and against other individuals situated in different groups and through the knowledge and symbols that predecessors and contemporaries transmit to them.[35] Before this investigation can begin, therefore, certain facts about its subject, Abraham Lincoln, and certain issues concerning their meaning, must be established.

The first issue is whether understandings of Lincoln are always hostage to the problems and needs of the present or whether an objective Lincoln can be known and retrieved. Debates between those emphasizing a constantly reinvented past and those assuming that past realities, with effort, can be known, is lively and consequential. If the past is an invention and Lincoln's legacy is "a living tradition, open to interpretation, so that we may truly claim him as our own,"[36] then others, including racists, hate-mongers, and dictators can claim him as *their* own. Into this controversy the concept of "constructionism" has, unfortunately, been inserted.[37] Lincoln in text and picture is certainly "constructed" in the sense that writers and artists represent him one way rather than another, but to assert that the episodes of his life are no more than "representations" presumes knowledge of how reality differs from appearance. Without such knowledge, one can demonstrate that perceptions of Lincoln change, but one cannot determine which of those changes distort reality and which do not. Without knowing the past as it was, one cannot estimate how significantly perception distorts reality or how it affects Lincoln's place in American memory.

Whether or not we are able to know accurately the historical Lincoln, we make assumptions about him, and those assumptions are typically based on evidence. How far and why our beliefs deviate from such evidence is always in question. However, whether Lincoln was a proto-integrationist, a devout racist freeing African Americans in an effort to save the white man's Union, or a pragmatist whose primary goal was to prevent democracy from perishing for all time, makes a big difference in the way we interpret the vicissitudes in his image.

Five statements summarize the phases of Lincoln's life most often documented between 1930 and the present. Because these statements recapitulate what we know, they provide a tentative benchmark for gauging later exaggeration, understatement, and distortion. If they prove to be unsound, they can be replaced by more satisfactory statements, and the direction of Lincoln portrayals and beliefs can be accordingly reassessed.

1. Lincoln's *social* identity, the way contemporaries and successors have identified him, differs from Lincoln's *personal* identity, the way he defined himself. Politically, Lincoln was an ambitious servant of the people, but no Andrew Jackson populist, no man of the people; he was a Whig aspiring to rise above his class. From the Whigs, he inherited an economic philosophy that grounded America's future in business and industry and depended on the men who could develop these successfully.[38] From George Washington, John Adams, and other high Federalists he inherited a paternalistic political philosophy grounded in the belief that a republic required leadership by its most intelligent and talented men.

2. Lincoln's paternalism manifested itself in an unparalleled compassion for ordinary men and women. Captured in images of his pardoning condemned soldiers, grieving over casualty lists, and visiting the wounded in hospitals, Lincoln's gentleness is the deepest level one can reach in any effort to understand him: "The fatality of it," Max Lerner observed, "that he, with his tenderness for everything living, should become the instrument of death for tens of thousands."[39] Lerner was referring to the death of tens of thousands of soldiers, not slaves. On no project did Lincoln invest more labor than on the defeat of the Confederate army. No aspect of his presidency aged him more or caused him greater misery.

3. Lincoln said so little about the consequences of secession because, like most pro-Unionists, he took them for granted. The interests threatened by secession are rarely discussed in contemporary textbooks or represented in museum exhibits; they are never commemorated by monuments and shrines and iconography, but their importance to Lincoln's contemporaries was immense. When Edward Everett completed his two-hour address at Gettysburg, which included extended remarks about the meaning of secession, Lincoln grasped Everett's hand "with great fervor" and said "I am more than gratified, I am grateful to you."[40] Lincoln's letter to Everett, written the day after they spoke at Gettysburg, refers expressly to his remark about "the national supremacy,"[41] for this matter—whether the national government is an agency of the states or the states constituents of an encompassing nation—defined the meaning of the war. It was Everett, then, not Lincoln, who explained why ferocious battles like Gettysburg had to be fought. To recognize

the independence of the seceding states, Everett told his listeners, would break the Union in two and deprive it of global influence; it would, indeed, make both governments, federal and confederate, vulnerable to foreign nations. Any thoughtful person knew that secession would

> wrest from the Middle and Western States some of their great natural outlets to the sea and of their most important lines of internal communication; deprive the commerce and navigation of the country of two thirds of our sea-coast and the fortresses which protect it; not only so, but would enable each individual state,—some of them with a white population equal to a good-sized Northern county,—or rather the dominant party in each State, to cede its territory, its harbors, its fortresses, the mouths of its rivers to any foreign power.[42]

It cannot be, Everett concluded, that 22 million free and prosperous Americans would consent to this "hideous national suicide."[43] Lincoln, like Everett, believed slavery to be a cause of the war because it had led to secession, but the effect was far worse than the cause: secession meant the diminishing of national wealth and the end of national independence.[44]

3. Lincoln believed that slavery was unjust, that property cultivated through one's own labor is the bulwark of freedom, that the free labor on which a free society is based should never compete with slave labor, and, above all, that slavery had always threatened the integrity of the Union. Lincoln, like most Americans, wished to end the war quickly within the framework of a restored Union. Had eleven states not seceded, he would have never contemplated attacking the South. Had the seceded states been defeated quickly, he would have never contemplated emancipation. Had slavery been the only issue Lincoln faced, he would have never set aside habeus corpus, an act which silenced not the proponents of slavery but the proponents of secession. By taking these and other measures to save the Union, Michael Lind argues, Lincoln intended to preserve democracy in a world in which every previous attempt to establish it had failed.[45]

4. Much recent scholarship focuses on whether Lincoln's motives for emancipation were idealistic, pragmatic, or a combination of both. Less is known about his imagination of black life after emancipation. Lincoln seems to have considered emancipation and racial integration to be separate matters. Realizing in the last years of his life that blacks would remain permanently in America, he favored their having equal political rights, but the prospect of integrating them into society on the basis of complete social equality was to him, as to most Americans of his time, problematic. Given Lincoln's eagerness to reconcile the North

and South, he might not have supported a Fourteenth Amendment if he had known it would someday mean social rather than political equality, the latter understood in the nineteenth century as equal protection to life, liberty, and a pursuit of happiness (through property).[46] Even more problematic is whether he would have supported a Fifteenth Amendment if he had known that its enforcement would alienate white citizens by creating federally protected black legislatures throughout the South.

5. No matter how sympathetic Lincoln might have been toward free blacks or slaves as individuals, no matter how far ahead of his time on race relations issues, his racial attitude was less liberal than those of twenty-first-century proponents of racial equality. Most anti-slavery Republicans, as Eric Foner observed, were racist and, at best, indifferent to the material needs, security, and education of freed slaves. They admired Lincoln's Emancipation Proclamation at a distance. The thing admired, for James G. Randall, "was a generalized rather than particularized freedom. To hold an emancipation meeting furnished a greater thrill than to welcome large numbers of freed Negroes into a Northern community with promises of economic opportunity."[47] Americans wishing to exclude blacks from their communities constituted Lincoln's political base.

The first two of the above statements are documented in the first part of this project, *Abraham Lincoln and the Forge of National Memory*;[48] the remaining three statements are documented throughout James G. Randall's scholarship; in Eric Foner's *Free Soil, Free Men: The Ideology of the Republican Party Before the Civil War*; David Donald's *Lincoln*; John Patrick Diggens's *On Hallowed Ground: Abraham Lincoln and the Foundations of American History*; Edward Ayres's *What Caused the Civil War?* and *In the Presence of Mine Enemies*; along with Michael Lind's *What Abraham Lincoln Believed*.[49] These books afford a rough standard for estimating the historical Lincoln, but those interested solely in tracking Lincoln's image over the decades, or linking his changing image to changing generational circumstances, may choose to ignore their claims.

Argument

Abraham Lincoln was a controversial president from the moment he assumed office. Assassination raised his stature, but throughout the last third of the nineteenth-century the resentments over his waging war diminished his prestige. The American people—Northerners and Southerners, Democrats and Republicans—then embraced George Washington, not Lincoln, as their unifying symbol. Beginning in the Progressive Era, however, Lincoln's prestige rose abruptly, surpassed Washington's, and grew steadily throughout the 1920s. This part of the story appears in *Abraham Lincoln and the Forge of National Memory*.

Two legacies connect *Forge of National Memory* to the present work. Lincoln's legacy for race relations is central to what many if not most Americans believe about him today,[50] but to attend to Lincoln solely on the basis of race relations is to narrow his place in American memory. As the United States industrialized and assumed a key global role in the early twentieth century, Lincoln's striving for North-South reconciliation, his second legacy, became prominent. Because a divided America would wield limited global influence, regional reconciliation became a pivotal goal. Lincoln's second, most general, legacy reflects his effort to transcend the polarities of democratic politics: the tension between right and left, liberty and equality, local and national authority. These ideological tensions framed Lincoln's goals for racial and regional peace. Around racial, regional, and ideological distinctions each chapter of this book is organized.

The opening chapters, "Lincoln in the Depression" and "Lincoln in World War II," show what Abraham Lincoln meant during the twentieth-century's greatest crises. Journalist Tom Brokaw referred to the Depression/World War II generation as the "greatest generation" because its members endured economic catastrophe yet rose to defeat fascism and save democracy for the world.[51] To acknowledge the racial, religious, and ethnic bigotry of this generation takes away nothing from its great achievements. This generation differs from ours in other ways, including its beliefs about greatness itself. Heroes of the past played a role in everyday life they would rarely play again. Among these heroes, Abraham Lincoln stood prominently. His personal suffering, as the Greatest Generation perceived it, made him sympathetic to the suffering of others; and if he failed in many things he remained hardworking, resilient, and persistent. His reputation as Man of the People, First American, and Self-Made Man resonated with the Depression Generation's economic worries. His saving the Union exemplified the cohesion required to face a worldwide military challenge; his emancipation of the slaves symbolized victory over foreign totalitarianism as often as racial integration at home. His identification with the common man modeled the proper relation between the state and its citizens.

The first change in Lincoln's image became noticeable after World War II and unmistakable after the Korean War (1950–53). Midcentury social transformations are known by many names—"Postmodern Turn," "Psychohistorical Dislocation," "Great Disruption"—but all refer to the advent of postindustrial society and a Rights and Justice Generation. The successor to late capitalism (the Progressive Era and its [1900–30] consolidation) and welfare capitalism (the New Deal and emergence of the welfare state [1930–70]), postindustrial society is marked by the expanding role of science and technology, increased wealth, enlarged role of the mass media, meritocracy (with a premium placed on intelligence), expanded civil rights and liberties, widening role of women in the labor force, reduced fertility, and dependence on immigration to fill the resulting labor shortages.[52] These developments would have been impossible, however, without the erosion of traditional authority structures,[53] and such erosion was evident in the frame of mind with which Americans at midcentury understood their past.

While a postindustrial culture formed during the 1950s, Abraham Lincoln's relevance, which had peaked during the late 1930s and early 1940s, leveled. The postwar Rights and Justice Generation, chapter 3 shows, treated its national traditions and heroes respectfully, but something was missing. Lincoln was still the man he had always been, was still admired, but with less fervor than before. Something else changed: Lincoln's reputation—what he stood for—became controversial. Abraham Lincoln saved the Union, but what about emancipation? Was he as determined to free the slaves as he was to restore national unity? And how did the answer to this question bear on the burning issues of racial integration and civil rights?

The relation between the civil rights movement and the imagination of Lincoln is documented in chapter 4, which compares public belief about Lincoln in four national sample surveys ranging from 1945 to 2001. The same images—Savior of the Union, Great Emancipator, Man of the People, First (Frontier) American, and Self-Made Man—appear in the cumulative body of Lincoln books and symbols, but only one of these, the Great Emancipator, is dominant in the minds of individuals. Lincoln's one-dimensional Emancipator image emerges from the multidimensional image crystallized in pre-civil-rights-era history books and commemorative symbolism.

In chapter 5 appears the argument's second element. The Emancipation Proclamation has begun to look like a charter for the civil rights movement, but if race relations were the only factor influencing beliefs about Lincoln, we would be at a loss to understand his diminishing prestige. And that diminution is unquestionable: every indicator, from national surveys and citation counts to memorial visitation statistics and pictorial representations, demonstrates it. The problem is now clear: as the civil rights movement reshaped Abraham Lincoln's reputation, his prestige faded. Did the former somehow cause the latter, or were both related to the same changing circumstances?

In chapter 6, two analytic lenses, the postmodern and the multicultural, are brought to bear on the post-heroic era. Many conservative scholars and commentators have lamented the disappearance of greatness from American culture, but we are living in an unprecedented and complex time. As the lives of the great are cynically scrutinized for cruelty, treachery, prejudice, and egoism, the growth of racial, religious, and ethnic justice, real equality of opportunity, compassion, and the recognition of minority achievement and dignity expands. The weakening of society's time frame and diminishing heroes, thus, go hand in hand with the nation's increasing civility and enlarged awareness of its present faults and their historical sources. Postmodernity and multiculturalism are controversial perspectives, marred by excessive focus on pathology and moral shortcoming rather than moral strength, but, more importantly, they articulate changes that have transformed America.

The discrediting of America's grand narratives is postmodernity's distinctive achievement. Because the key feature of grand narratives is "embodied in a plot line that makes sense to others in terms of socially shared understandings," people require them, collectively as well as individually, to make sense of experience. As postmodernity disparages stories that Americans tell about themselves, the orienting past tense of the individual's life, the bond that once linked men and women to vital symbols of their cultural tradition, is weakened.[54]

Viewed through a second, multicultural, lens, "marginalized" peoples decide on their own historical interpretations and "dominant" groups recognize their right to do so. The multicultural ideal, as understood in the late twentieth century, encourages racial and ethnic groups to cultivate their historical uniqueness and at the same time recognize one another's equal worth. Because historical wrongdoings violate these principles, multicultural elites replace monuments to heroes with monuments to victims; they replace symbols of strength and dignity with symbols of malevolence. Monuments of regret, including Civil War prison camp memorials, Japanese internment camp sites, exhibits, and memorials, Indian massacre sites, civil rights memorials, slavery museums, and lynching exhibits abound as historical texts document America's crimes against its own pluralistic ideal.[55]

The result of these intertwined currents of postmodernity and multiculturalism is the shrinking of American history's triumphs and heroes, including the triumphs of America's sixteenth president, Abraham Lincoln. For the first time in their history, however, Americans can look forward, plausibly, to a world without invidious distinction, a better world in which all men and women are recognized for what they are and are less inclined to yesterday's extremes of disdain and exclusion, reverence and elevation.

However, further questions remain. Is Lincoln less admirable today because Americans find the content of national history irrelevant or because history means more to Americans than ever, so much so that they prefer relevant distortions (Lincoln as civil rights prophet) to less relevant truths (Lincoln as Savior of the Union)? Theories of postmodernity and multiculturalism cannot answer this question plausibly because they explain too much: if Americans were convinced by these theories, their beliefs about Lincoln would be more fickle and negative than they are.

Every society requires a sense of sameness and continuity with what went before, and as historical beliefs outlive societal change, the nation's sense of itself is maintained. Postmodern and multicultural theories fail to explain why so many people continue to revere Lincoln as did their forebears, continue even to model their lives after him, almost as if they are deaf and blind to the post-heroic currents of the era. The seventh and final chapter, "Inertia," attends to the limit below which Lincoln's prestige cannot fall and beyond which his reputation cannot change. This obdurate contradiction–the need for a past at once stately and relevant, and the sense that such a past is no longer relevant—informs Lincoln's place in the American mind.

In every generation since Lincoln's death, Americans have keyed racial and regional reconciliation to Lincoln's life and presidency. For those concerned with race relations, Lincoln's significance inheres largely in his emancipation policy. For those concerned with regional reconciliation, Lincoln's significance inheres in his saving the Union, which includes his understanding of Southerners, the leniency with which he would have administered Reconstruction, and his wish to normalize quickly the relations between the federal and Southern state governments. This project weights both concerns equally. To show that Abraham Lincoln was once symbol of regional unity during decades when race relations did not matter is as necessary as showing him as he is today: a symbol of racial integration when regional goodwill is taken for granted.

NEW LINCOLN

Abraham Lincoln and the Forge of National Memory began with Lincoln's death in 1865 and concluded with the dedication of his national memorial in 1922. As the Great Depression and World War II realigned relationships among the nation's classes, races, and ethnic groups, Americans conception of their own place in the historical scheme changed. During the late twentieth-century expansion of civil rights, Lincoln began to personify the ideal of racial harmony. As egalitarian forces shaped his reputation, however, they also lessened his relevance. Multicultural equality is more complex than the idea of equality before God, to which Americans' were once committed. Multicultural equality requires not only equal rights but also equal recognition and, ironically, encouragement to cultivate separate cultures and identities. Multiculturalism opens a new world that reduces its citizens' sense of obligation to the nation and its traditions as it liberates them from bias and cruelty. The fading of the great man is part of a new moral order at once liberating and just, alienating and shallow. Old beliefs about Abraham Lincoln and the Civil War have been revised, scaled down, and refitted to a post-heroic society based on universal recognition and inclusion. The evidence follows.

* 1 *

Ascension

LINCOLN IN THE GREAT DEPRESSION

"Ascension," the title of this chapter, is a fair but inexact account of Lincoln in the Depression. His prestige had been rising for twenty years before Wall Street crashed, but if every era sees itself in Abraham Lincoln and reveals itself in what it says about him, the Lincoln of the Depression and World War II was unique. This Lincoln was the last of its kind, taking American history's heroic genre as far as it would ever go. He must be the benchmark against which imaginations of subsequent Lincolns are gauged.

If Abraham Lincoln had never been born, the Depression would have felt the same to those who lived through it—although its deprivations, for many, would have been felt differently. If the Depression had never happened, however, Lincoln today would be a different man. The mold of the Lincoln we know today was cast during the 1930s; yet Lincoln could never have been portrayed and perceived then as he is now. One must accept this contradiction in order to grasp what Lincoln meant to the people of that time. If we can penetrate Depression culture, the contradiction will resolve itself.

Prelude

After two decades of Progressive Reform, the1920s seemed ruthless to some, liberating to others. Theodore Roosevelt's and Woodrow Wilson's Progressive presidencies had made their mark, but it was time for new presidents—Warren Harding, Calvin Coolidge, and Herbert Hoover—to champion new ideals. The business of America, Coolidge meant to say, was not just business in the sense of making money, but business as a model for moral virtue and accomplishment. "No longer was the statesman or the priest or the philosopher the spokesman for American society," added author Edmund Stillman, "the businessman . . .

became the self-assured seer." Henry Ford's strong showing in "most admired American" polls, the serious characterization of Moses by Metropolitan Casualty Insurance Company as "one of the greatest salesmen and real-estate promoters that ever lived," and Bruce Barton's 1925–26 bestseller, *The Man Nobody Knows,* depicting Jesus as "the founder of modern business," the public relations go-getter who "recognized the basic principle that all good advertising is news,"[1] make Stillman's point.

Abraham Lincoln, a fusion of potential and achievement, fit this pattern nicely. In 1922, the Lincoln Memorial was dedicated as a monument to America's greatness and a mark of what Lincoln had contributed to it. The memorial was also a sign of what he would become. Nathaniel W. Stephenson's *Lincoln and the Progress of Nationality in the North,* the first biography to emphasize the Civil War's effect on Lincoln's personality, portrays the sixteenth president as nationalistic and authoritarian to the core. "Lincoln was not a friend of the plebiscite or of the referendum." He ignored public clamor over his unpopular arrests. Abraham Lincoln "refused to be the mere spokesman of the people."[2] At the turn of the century, Ida Tarbell had portrayed Lincoln as the ultimate common man; two decades later she wanted everyone to know how uncommon he really was. Her article on "Abraham Lincoln's Money Sense" proved that he was worth $110,000 when he died—almost a millionaire by 1923 standards.[3] His pedigree was as distinguished as his wealth. Although George Washington's refined background was often compared to Lincoln's commonness, "recent historical research," according to Massachusetts representative Frederick Dallinger, "has proved that the English progenitors of Lincoln were fully as high in the social scale as those of Washington."[4]

Carl Sandburg, on the other hand, wrote against the grain of the time, foreshadowing the Lincoln of the 1930s. He was intent on making him an earth god rather than a sky god. His two-volume *The Prairie Years,*[5] completed in 1926, celebrated a man who could not be denied his smallness. Sandburg's Lincoln interacted with the frontier, grew up among people like himself, some better, some worse, all trying to improve themselves. Lincoln also possessed the mind and virtues of the self-starting businessman, but that did not distinguish him. Living in a society of challenges, men on the move, and hardship, Lincoln's vulnerabilities appealed to the struggling people of the Depression.

Lincoln's Decade

The 1930s were at once progressive and tradition-minded, preoccupied with immediate problems and attuned to the past. Federal programs fed the public mood. The Civilian Conservation Corps, whose projects included the reconstruction of historical places; the Works Progress Administration, which compiled local lore and produced state guidebooks; the National Park Service, which administered a wide array of historic sites—these projects democratized tradition by commemorating the lives and concerns of ordinary people.[6]

America's democratic tradition joined the mystique of the land to the memory of the Civil War. By 1920 only half of Americans still lived on rural lands; only a quarter still engaged in agriculture. As urban populations grew, the symbolism of farm life became more prominent.[7] Thoughts of young Lincoln splitting logs on the frontier piqued nostalgia for a lost and seemingly better way of life, a self-reliant life free of futile job hunting and breadlines. Frontier and Civil War nostalgia were interconnected. Because more than half the 1930 population had been born during the nineteenth century, Civil War survivors constituted unique carriers of memory, and they were accorded special significance, no matter what their experience or rank. Lincoln Day issues of Northern newspapers carried stories of these living relics: here, a photograph of two men who had cast their first votes for Lincoln; there, a veteran recalling the Lincoln-Douglas debates at Quincy, Illinois; elsewhere, a gentleman who had witnessed Lincoln speaking against Douglas in Chicago, another who knew Lincoln when he practiced law in Springfield; another who met Lincoln at a White House reception; and yet another whose father had fought with Lincoln during the Blackhawk War. Lincoln remained a living memory.

Worldview

Alfred Kazin included "the passionate addiction to Lincoln" among "the most moving aspects" of the 1930s.[8] For Bernard de Voto, Lincoln was still the nation's savior: at a time when "American democracy has reached a crisis, the American people have invoked the man who . . . in an earlier crisis, best embodied the strength of our democracy."[9] "Crisis," an abstract concept, cannot itself capture Depression realities. Between 1929 and 1932, the year Franklin D. Roosevelt gained the presidency, manufacturing output fell 54 percent; the automobile industry operated at 20 percent of its 1929 capacity; steel plants, at 12 percent capacity. Railroads lost half their freight shipments. As the total volume of American business and wage rates fell 50 percent, national income declined from 85 to 37 billion dollars. More than 5,000 banks closed. A half million families lost their homes. Construction ceased. Many cities and counties could not pay their employees. Unemployment quadrupled. In Cleveland, 50 percent of the workforce was unemployed; in Toledo,

80 percent. In 1931, the Soviet Union advertised in the United States for 6,000 skilled workers and received 100,000 applications. Roosevelt was serious in 1933 when he told reporters "I shall be either America's greatest President or its last."[10]

The Depression crisis meant failure, dislocation, self-contempt, grief. Great disturbances befalling a culturally stable nation, however, can sometimes rouse patriotism and solidarity.[11] The problem that nationalism seeks to resolve is not how to avoid distress but how to make it comprehensible and bearable, to enable the hurt and defeated to relate their personal loss to the pain of the country. The Depression stirred an "upsurge of national awareness," as Harvey Swados[12] called it, a recognition that America was one country; its problems, national problems. That solutions would have to be national was a new idea that stirred the people. "The country is alive again," Louis Adamic said, "painfully so, but alive."[13] Government projects contributed to this rebirth by fusing populism and patriotism, stimulating interest in national achievements and inducing intellectuals, including men of the left, like John Dos Passos, to celebrate *The Ground We Stand On*. Our "sense of continuity with generations gone before," he wrote, "can stretch like a lifeline across the scary present."[14] The Progressive Era, from which Lincoln emerged as a national idol, provided the basis for New Deal reforms by introducing a progressive income tax, workplace regulations, and measures to prevent monopolies and preserve competition. The New Deal, however, was revolutionary in its provision of direct support—food, housing, jobs, old age financial security—to individual citizens.[15] Declaring their countrymen to be entitled to help, New Deal elites conferred upon them a dignity they had never before possessed. Inequalities in wealth, refinement, and achievement remained, but now within an environment of diminished distance between the state and the masses, an environment in which the privileged felt themselves less entitled to deference, indeed rarely demanded it. The least of men, in turn, were freer to express their resentment toward their leaders and their respect for themselves. Although never fully realized, this egalitarian trend made America hospitable to revised memories of Abraham Lincoln.

New Deal egalitarian culture reflected the way intellectuals conceived the nation's problems, but some intellectual currents bore more force than others. Carl Becker was among the first in a field of historians to appreciate the relativity of historical perception. James G. Randall, reflecting his generation's disillusionment with World War I and reacting against the "national" tradition of Civil War history, professionalized Lincoln scholarship and led a Revisionist school to counter the Civil War's romantic legacy. The impact of these new perspectives, however, was accompanied by the emergence of broader, neo-Marxian concepts which influenced the content of high school and university history textbooks.[16] When a California professor of American government asked a class in 1936 to appraise his assignments, one student replied: "Why do you not stress more the economic interpretation of history and politics? After all, you certainly know that entrenched wealth has always ruled this country. . . ." The professor noted that many students were asking this question. Meanwhile, social scientists, already under the influence of economics and sociology, were attributing human actions to impersonal, structural causes.[17] Lincoln's confession—"I claim not to have controlled events, but confess plainly that events have controlled me"[18] —resonated perfectly with this worldview. Ensconced in American soil, social determinism infused young people with optimism rather than resignation. By knowing the iron laws of history, they could manage them. Henry Farnham May, student of American intellectual history, exemplified their ebullient vision of the future as he recalled his undergraduate days at the University of California, Berkeley, noting that "cynicism was regarded as old-fashioned, associated with the bygone and self-indulgent twenties. Hope and even—without its old religious supports—morality were part of being truly modern."[19]

The hopes and moral consciousness of the 1930s caused blacks and whites, men and women, natives and immigrants to draw different but comparable conclusions from what they learned about Abraham Lincoln. Mainline media—magazines, newspapers, films, and drama—presented Lincoln as a means for seeing the world's disappointments, for making its sufferings not so much explicable as meaningful, an aspect of a larger scheme of which one's personal experience was a part. Abraham Lincoln, more urgently than ever before, was "good for thinking,"[20] a guide for living in a troubled world.

SOCIETY OF DEFERENCE

During the 1930s, as during every preceding decade, hierarchy and deference marked the American experience. Societies of deference, in the eighteen-century sense, are "usually conceived of as consisting of an elite and a nonelite, in which the nonelite regard the elite, without too much resentment, as being of superior status and culture to their own, and consider elite leadership in political matters something normal and natural." In England, America, and other societies where power was decentralized, however, recipients of deference maintained their positions not by reducing subordinates to servile roles but by acknowledging their independence and self respect. In such societies, deference was the response of self-reliant men and women to effective and respectful leadership.[21]

The best way to distinguish between deference in traditional and modern societies is to conceive a continuum. In traditional societies, hierarchy is rigid; administration of power is legitimated by custom, behavior is prescribed by status, which is maintained through ritual etiquette and symbolism. In egalitarian societies, hierarchical distinctions are loosely defined, power is legitimated in terms of legal criteria, and deference is attenuated—in some situations almost absent. The Depression generation was located somewhere between these poles: inequalities were economic but not social; power was legitimated by law superimposed upon tradition. The distance between elites and the mass was greatly reduced from what it had been in the late nineteenth century, but not fully bridged. Up to and including World War II, social distance was tutelary and motivating. The great men of the past would remain sources of moral character and guidance only while that distance was preserved.

"WHAT WOULD LINCOLN DO?"

If the rich and poor, powerful and weak, enlightened and ignorant are moved by forces beyond their control, their inequality loses moral significance; success and failure become matters inviting explanation rather than judgment. The hero then becomes the man of compassion rather than the rugged individualist; the protector rather than exploiter of the weak. Given this new conception of man and society, further elevation of Abraham Lincoln seemed inevitable. "A deeper appreciation than mere hero worship was bound to come," Robert Sherwood believed, "when the American people, under the stress of contemporary events, came to a fuller understanding of the ideals for which [Lincoln] fought and died."[22]

Understanding Lincoln required appreciation of a new culture of equality. The political left, preoccupied as always with class struggle and its victims, grew in prominence.[23] Depression media contemporized Lincoln by its stories about his affinity with Franklin Roosevelt, his constituencies, and their values. "How much of Lincoln does Roosevelt have in him?" asked Max Lerner.[24] The answer: plenty. President Roosevelt's own speechwriter, Robert Sherwood, won a Pulitzer Prize for his drama *Abe Lincoln in Illinois*. "Before the end of Franklin Roosevelt's second term," Alfred Haworth Jones recalls, "the image of Abraham Lincoln had emerged as the fulfillment of the search for a usable American past."[25] To assert that Abraham Lincoln somehow "reflected" or "embodied" the Depression generation's consciousness is to express too ambiguous a correspondence between the present condition of a nation and its citizens' perception of the past. Many have made this assertion but never demonstrated precisely how historians, artists, and writers go about the work of making the present historically meaningful. Grasping the perspectives of a generation different from our own, however, is difficult. Without surveys or interviews, we must rely on indirect evidence of how ordinary Americans felt and what they believed.

Titles in major libraries, indicating what Americans read, are one source of evidence. The New York Public Library added 68 new Lincoln books from 1910 to 1919; 84 during the 1920s; and 82 during the 1930s. The Illinois Historical Collection, which includes publications of three pages or more, added 530 new titles from 1910 to 1919; 725 during the 1920s; and 539 during the 1930s.

Citation counts in popular media furnish further evidence of growing interest in Lincoln. The *New York Times* reflected its readers' tastes through the 82 articles it printed in the 1890s, the first full decade prior to the 1909 centennial preparatory activities. During the 1920s and 1930s, the *Times* published 470 and 580 articles respectively. Like other city newspapers, the *Times* included special Lincoln Day sections and well-illustrated Sunday magazine articles on Lincoln. The *Reader's Guide to Periodic Literature* listed 90 articles between 1890 and 1899. From 1922 to 1928, a seven-year period, 141 articles appeared; during the seven and a half years between 1929 and June 1935, there were 135 articles—and this latter figure reflects publishing company failures and downsizing. No one except George Washington, however, even approached this lower volume. The *Congressional Record*'s Lincoln entries numbered 47 during the nineteenth-century's last decade, then increased from 125 to 173 during the 1920s and 1930s.[26] Because every member of the House and Senate had been born in the nineteenth century, they were disposed toward the heroes with whom they had grown up, and their panegyric for Lincoln was dramatic and prolonged. These articles and entries concentrated around the February 12 observance of Lincoln's birth, and they were read in the context of celebration.

"Formative" and "normative" elements comprised the stories that newspapers, magazines, and commemorative symbols communicated about Abraham Lincoln's life. The formative aspect of the stories, as German historian Jan Assman would tell us,[27] consists of their narrative structure; the normative aspect, moral models that connect readers to the history of the nation. To designate Lincoln the greatest American, however, meant something different during the 1930s from what it means today. Ordinary people then believed in greatness and could

FIGURE 1.1. "Awaiting The Man," February 12, 1932, *Chicago Tribune.*

imagine a Lincoln or Washington in their own time (fig. 1.1). The immediately striking feature of the cartoon in figure 1.1 is the size of the great men and the almost ant-like smallness of their admirers. Among these men, only three, Lincoln, Washington, and Grant, are identified. Behind each statue is a curved enclosure, a niche, corresponding to the figure's permanent place in history. The ceiling is high and curved, suggestive of a classic pantheon. The cartoon's focus is on the empty pedestal, expressly reserved for the great man, not yet apparent, who will seize the day and end the nation's strife. In front of this pedestal, ordinary men assemble for a close-up view. Because the hero remains unknown, their hats remain in place, but their very presence at the hall of fame suggests a future when present troubles will be solved and the man responsible for the solution, canonized. The people of the 1930s saw the great man not as a name invoked in speeches, but as a tool for living, an exemplar of what it takes to solve great problems and overcome great obstacles.

Of early twentieth-century leaders using Lincoln to solve problems there is no shortage of examples. When Franklin Roosevelt sought to pack the Supreme Court and neutralize its interference with his legislation, Democratic supporters, in all seriousness, recalled Lincoln's reference to the dangers of judicial oligarchy.[28] However, historical narratives were not always constructed with a view to expanding power; they were also sources of inspiration, moral frames for facing trouble. This is why Lincoln's reference to judicial oligarchy made sense to Roosevelt's supporters in the first place. Indeed, if any leader faced difficulties without reference to the past, he would be viewed as a rare individual, one who engaged his task alone and without experience or hindsight.

Crisis, as Charles Horton Cooley observed in 1901, "by its very difficulty, is likely to call up the thought of some person we have been used to look to as a guide, and the confronting of the two ideas, that of the person and that of the problem, compels us to answer the question, What would he have thought of it."[29] In an article on "Our Appalling Crisis—What Would Lincoln Do?" George Viereck (1932), an anti-Hoover Democrat, writes of falling asleep and dreaming of meeting Abraham Lincoln. He questions Lincoln on matters ranging from unemployment to Prohibition and communism, and he receives answers in Lincoln's own words. "Every word attributed to Abraham Lincoln in this interview," Viereck assures his readers, "is taken verbatim from his letters or speeches, and in the main these extracts are answers to questions or pertain to subjects analogous to those with which they are associated in this interview."[30]

Viereck looked to the past because he needed guidance not to be found in the present, and his questioning, even if partisan, was serious. W. Y. L. Davis, a *Los Angeles Times* commentator, explains further:

> When partisans would support President Hoover for cutting red tape to feed the hungry, Lincoln is cited as the most illustrious example. When any governor or President justifies himself for exercise of the pardoning power, he falls back on the great-hearted Lincoln. . . . "He being dead yet speaketh." He is yet active in the councils of the nation. He is the great contemporary![31]

The *Chicago Tribune* underscored Davis's statement by producing a front-page image of Lincoln in contemporary dress.[32] Beardless, with hair close-cropped and dressed in a modern business suit (fig. 1.2), Lincoln looks natural. He quits history and enters the viewer's world, a world where he belongs and where admirers readily identify with him.[33] He becomes literally "the great contemporary."

"What would Lincoln do?" is an important question because it refers not to a concrete decision or policy but to a guiding pattern defining

FIGURE 1.2
"As He Would Have Looked in Modern Garb," February 12, 1930, *Chicago Tribune.*

(1) goals and purposes, (2) standards of intellectual and moral judgment, (3) values and priorities, (4) strategies of action, and (5) personal dispositions, including honesty, perseverance, resilience. The question "What would Lincoln do?" is, thus, an eminently historical question. Asking "What would Lincoln do?" becomes ahistorical only if posed as a question about specific issues and means. This is what Ida Tarbell, one of Lincoln's most popular biographers, meant when she said: "No one can say what Lincoln would have done about unemployment, relief, war debt, prohibition, Manchuria, inflation." The guiding pattern is what matters. Lincoln's contribution to the solution of a problem depends upon the way Lincoln's emulator "handles his mind and his temper in his attack."[34] No parallel can be drawn between the situation in 1861 and that of 1933, but the fundamental aims Lincoln sought were the same as ours, noted a *New York Times* commentator. "It is the Lincolnian attitude and method that are most pertinent now."[35]

The Depression era's conception of greatness differed from that which most twenty-first- century Americans would understand. With an image of Abraham Lincoln on its cover, the subtitle of Alan Wolfe's *Return to Greatness* (2005) tells the reader that America can recover its grandeur by articulating a meaningful sense of purpose, transforming it into a reality, then protecting it from adversaries.[36] Seventy years earlier, Americans thought differently: they could not afford the luxury of equating greatness with abstract notions of national purpose. They thought of greatness selfishly. They revered Lincoln because he satisfied in his time a need for order they felt in theirs. They revered him not for his preserving and modifying social order as such, but because he had done so in a way that resonated with their own worries and restored their own dignity. Greatness referred to the power of individuals to transform problems into opportunities (again, see fig. 1.1) and to exploit those opportunities for the social good.

Epic Representations

Every generation experiences Lincoln as a model *of* society, reflecting the interests, fears, and aspirations of those who think about him, and a model *for* society, defining people's values and providing the inspiration for realizing them. Invoking the Lincolnian attitude "reflects" reality when people project onto Lincoln their present expectations; invoking the Lincolnian attitude "models" reality when individuals, singly and collectively, find in him a *program* for planning their conduct; a *standard* for gauging its effectiveness and moral qualities, and a *framework* for discerning the meaning of what they think, feel, and do. These aspects, Abraham Lincoln as a mirror and a lamp, are realized in everything said, written, pictured, and thought about him, but they were realized more profoundly during the Depression decade than ever before.

Depression people knew that Lincoln had borne loss and misfortune but had saved the Union, freed the slaves, and made the America they knew. The landscape was full of populist representations that portrayed Lincoln as an ordinary American, a Man of the People. No other president's youth has been more often portrayed in statue, painting, illustration, biography, novel, short story, poem, play, and film (see appendix A). No other president's youth has so fascinated the American people as has Lincoln's. But to portray the greatness in which Americans believed was another matter—a matter necessary to sustain Lincoln as a lamp for the people.

In this regard, *Young Mr. Lincoln* strikes the twenty-first-century viewer as an unbearably mawkish film, but its 1939 viewers took it seriously. Lincoln's concluding words, "I think I'll take a walk up to the mountain," inspired them and captured for them the film's full meaning. As the future president climbs, the storm prophetically gathers, lightning flashes, thunder roars. *Abe Lincoln in Illinois* (1940), too, concludes in high-corn register as Lincoln bids farewell to his friends with a medley

FIGURE 1.3
Grandfather and Grandson at Lincoln Memorial, c.1940. American Railroad poster. The Abraham Lincoln Museum, Harrogate, TN. Photo courtesy of the Abraham Lincoln Museum.

of lines assembled from his most important speeches. The common man is suddenly the strong man battling mighty forces. The train carries him away to Washington to the solemn strain of "The Battle Hymn of the Republic." Preoccupied as they were with deprivation and social upheaval, no people knew better than the people of the Depression how to appreciate this man and the suffering nation over which he presided.

The American Railroad Company captured the public mood in advertisements of its Washington routes: a child and his grandfather are at the Lincoln Memorial, their hats respectfully removed, looking upon the marble statue. To contemporary tourists, among whom dramatic signs of respect have faded, the uncovering gesture is hardly noticed, but it is essential to the meaning of the picture. In his left hand, the elderly man grasps his cane, symbolizing his own lifeline to the Civil War, as he points to Lincoln and explains to his grandson who Lincoln was and what he did (fig. 1.3). This child, like so many Depression children, is connected to the last of Lincoln's own generation. Engraved on the wall behind the seated Lincoln, the last line of the Gettysburg Address: "that government of the people, by the people, for the people shall not perish from the earth," replaces the actual inscription, "In this temple, as in the hearts of the people for whom he saved the Union, the memory

FIGURE 1.4. M. Leone Bracker, *Lincoln's Vision*, 1934. Charcoal drawing by M. Leone Bracker. Courtesy of the Lincoln Museum, Fort Wayne, IN (reference # 1572).

of Abraham Lincoln is enshrined forever." Union is the keystone of Lincoln's legacy, but during national crisis the greatness of the people is more relevant than their union, and it is the people that this Lincoln stands for.

The YMCA also tried to enlarge its membership by coupling a young man, book in hand, with Lincoln's countenance. The point: "Realize Your Better Self." Avoiding one's worst self is demonstrated by an editorial cartoon in which Lincoln looks down on "The Passing Show" of rough-looking men named "Human Greed," "Rascalism," "Human Hate," "Human Avarice," and "Brutality"—men who pass below Lincoln without looking up at him.[37] In an inverted variant, M. Leone Bracker shows Lincoln seated as if he were a neoclassical statue, both arms resting on the chair of state and surrounded by clouds through which a scene of war and death is visible. On the viewer's left is a source of light—a future of peace and justice—and on that light Lincoln's eyes are fixed. He also sees a column of soldiers, the instruments of his will, reappearing in ethereal splendor, reaffirming the great cost of his achievement. On the viewer's right, a contemporary father, mother, and son gaze reverently upon Lincoln, realizing, if they failed to realize before, their own place as beneficiaries of their country's history (fig. 1.4).[38] Such images portray Lincoln not as a common man to admire but as a *paradigm*, an epic model for living.[39]

Pictures of Lincoln's admirers looking up to him are reciprocals of pictures showing Lincoln looking down on his admirers.[40] Each form interprets the significance of the other, and together they express a way of knowing and experiencing moral authority. Logically, they parallel the question, "What Would Lincoln Do Today?" The Lincoln gazed upon by enraptured admirers is no remote and indifferent god, but he is a god nonetheless, a personal god concerned with their troubles. No one is surprised to see young men en mass with Lincoln, moving confidently toward the sunny future (fig. 1.5), or to see Lincoln standing behind a youngster hard at work over a school book, his hand on the boy's shoulder (fig. 1.6).[41] The first picture leaves nothing to the imagination: young Abraham, with ax and book, symbols of the virtues of work and labor, towers over his Lilliputian admirers. They march behind Lincoln, at his sides, and in front of him, but they are guided by his spirit, a kind of invisible gravity that pulls them all in the same direction. The second picture is a more concrete case of the first. To walk among a crowd is one thing; to overcome obstacles is another: the brightness of the future depends on one's will to work to master it. Confronting a problem one cannot immediately solve, as does the sullen-faced boy in this picture, one searches for some reason to try harder, some compelling model to vindicate and guide one's efforts. The viewer knows that the young man will overcome his obstacle, for it is "not wealth, not power, nor rank, nor noble birth; but those whose deeds inspire our youth to greater worth." The inspirer in this case is evident to all: in a simple room, furnished with washbowl and cabinet, table for books, pen, and paper, appears the spirit of Abraham Lincoln. The effects of such representations are difficult to imagine today, but many could not then think of great men portrayed otherwise. These images show people in communion with their past, drawing upon a vital symbol that articulates the experience of their own lives.[42] Such images are benchmarks we will need to gauge the mentality of later generations. Benchmarks are points of reference from which measurements of Lincoln's changing reputation and prestige can be made, but there are as many benchmarks as there are points of view. Three viewpoints— ideological, racial, and regional— organize this investigation and its findings.

Liberal Benchmarks

National symbols are always suffused with political connotation. Accentuated by the threat of fascist tyranny and by persisting racial injustice, economic depression made Lincoln a champion of the needy and a symbol of the broadened responsibility of the state—in short, a hero of the left:

> I heard from a refugee just arrived from Marseilles of the conditions in the prison camps for German and Spanish refugees in France; and then I looked at the obstacles our State Department is placing in

FIGURE 1.5
"His Soul Goes Marching On," c.1932. The Abraham Lincoln Museum, Harrogate, TN. Photo courtesy of the Abraham Lincoln Museum.

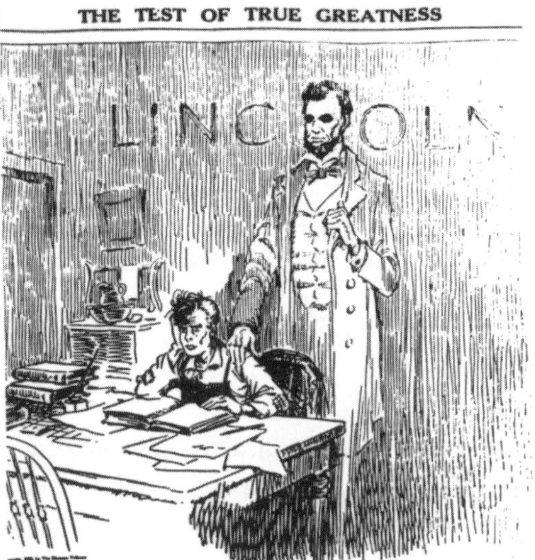

FIGURE 1.6
"The Test of True Greatness," February 12, 1930, *Chicago Tribune*.

> the path of their coming to our country, and I thought of Lincoln. I read Leigh White's account of the butchery of innocent Jews in the slaughterhouses of Bucharest, and then I read the speeches of our appeasers, and I thought of Lincoln. I thought of Ford's fight now against his workers, and of the preparations being made by Bethlehem Steel to fight labor, and I thought of Lincoln. I read of the Jim Crowism still practiced in the American army, and of the fifteen Negro sailors dishonorably discharged from the navy because they had protested against discrimination, and I thought of Lincoln. I had a letter from a brilliant Negro professor who wrote that the vast body of his people saw the need for destroying Nazism: "How grimly ironic therefore that we should have to beg for our chance to help"; and I thought of Lincoln.[43]

Max Lerner spoke for the center of American socialism. He spoke for men and women who admired Lincoln and named their organizations (like the Abraham Lincoln Brigade) after him. He spoke against the antidemocratic snobbery of the radical left, which despised Lincoln because he was so much a part of mainstream America. He spoke for nonsocialist liberals, including Democrats. On many social issues they too thought of Lincoln.

Liberals said little about Lincoln as Savior of the Union and even less about Lincoln as a self-made man. Abraham Lincoln, for them, was the man of compassion and justice. He represented human rights while his Republican successors defended property rights. When President Herbert Hoover's nomination for chief justice of the Supreme Court, Charles Evans Hughes, came before the Senate, Democratic senator Clarence Dill of Washington declared:

> What a coincidence this day presents! The Senate of the United States on the day marking the anniversary of the natal day of Abraham Lincoln, the greatest champion of human rights in the world since Christ walked upon the earth, considers whether or not it shall confirm the appointment of Charles E. Hughes, the greatest champion of property rights of our time, as Chief Justice of the Supreme Court of the United States.[44]

Dill's analogy made rhetorical sense in the 1930s: Hughes was to Lincoln what the Depression was to the Civil War and what slavery was to free labor. At the beginning of the century, suffragists and socialists used the slavery metaphor often, but it did not enter mainstream liberal discourse until the 1930s. Slavery images secured the connection between Lincoln and the little man. Two years after Senator Dill condemned Chief Justice Hughes, he read a poem, "But Slavery Lingers," on the Senate floor. The poem would evoke smirks today, but listeners and readers then took it seriously. What image better defined the day's suffering?

> Would you were living now, old Honest Abe,
> To carry on the mission you began;
> You freed the bonded black, the unborn babe,
> But slavery lingers still to torture man.
>
> Ere you were martyred in an hour of need
> You warned of great monopolies afar,
> Of fetters forged by corporate gold and greed
> More dangerous, you said, than civil war.
>
> You drove slave drivers from the brakes of cane
> And cotton fields, but now, dread aftermath,
> The money changers desecrate your fame
> With none to whip them out in righteous wrath.
>
> If you were here you would emancipate
> Your party from all special privilege
> And striking at new shackles, liberate
> Your land from economic peonage.[45]

If America's workers were wage-slaves,[46] the new Democratic president was their liberator. Two years after Franklin Roosevelt's election, Carl Sandburg defined the National Relief Act as a second Emancipation Proclamation. "Those who live by selling their labor," Sandburg declared, "are having their status changed."[47] In 1936, the year Roosevelt won his first landslide reelection, representative Frank Dorsey, a Pennsylvania Democrat, noted that "Lincoln was the progressive, the New Dealer of his day. If he were alive now he would discern that economic peonage is as terrible a thing as the selling of men on the block."[48] Max Lerner added: "The Civil War, like the Depression, was a struggle between two concepts of labor—free and slave" and a repudiation of the extremist belief that "slavery is the natural condition of the working class."[49]

No one believed that the failing American economy actually depended on slave labor, yet the slavery metaphor influenced readers because it underscored the reality of their lives. Once economic vulnerability is matched to slavery, Lincoln can be invoked as labor's champion. The analogy thus influenced the way liberals conceived Lincoln. When liberal admirers saw a movie, read a book, or looked at Lincoln's picture, they selectively perceived some characteristics and suppressed others, while the realities of Lincoln's life reflected and commented, in turn, on their own predicament. His relevance to the left pivoted mainly on the capacity of his image to mold Depression-era sentiments about labor.[50]

The more effective the metaphor is, the more spheres of activity to which it applies and the wider the range of people who use it. Variously described as "root metaphors" or "conceptual archetypes,"[51] such images become universal. William Allen White, a moderate Republican opposing his party's old guard and seeking positive alternatives to the New Deal, told the Springfield (Illinois) Abraham Lincoln Association:

> How startling is the parallel of our crisis today: Two million slaves in 1850. Ten million idle men today. Ten million men who are dependent upon the whim of government for their food and shelter. These 10,000,000 men are chained to public work which they must take or starve, as the slaves were in bondage to their masters.... The decade of the 1850's, with its slave politics and the decade of the 1930's with its problem of unemployment, present similar, almost parallel, issues in our history.[52]

The slavery metaphor, so rich and appealing, so applicable to political and economic issues, was rooted in reality. That metaphor acted back on Lincoln, transforming him from an emancipator of bondsmen to a helper of the working man. "Truly enough," longtime Democratic representative Emanuel Celler explained, "his whole life was dedicated to an attempt to rescue the American underdog and to pull the poor and lowly from between the upper and nether stones of oppression"[53] Such was the mission of the new liberal elite. Never before or since has a former president figured so directly in debates over current issues as did Lincoln during the Great Depression. Lincoln gives us access to the time because he was made for the time, although not everyone living at the time saw him in the same way.

Conservative Benchmarks

The Depression had nothing to do with slavery, and to cast it as such ignores its origins. However, the liberal establishment of the 1930s, consisting mainly of writers and political leaders, was too ready to transform Lincoln from a war president into a reform president. "Does anyone maintain that the Republican Party from 1868 to 1938 (with the possible exception of a few years under Theodore Roosevelt) was the party of Abraham Lincoln? To claim that is... absurd," said Franklin Roosevelt, answering his own question.[54] Conservatives disagreed. Roosevelt and his friends embracing Lincoln, they said, was a farce because the New Deal's obsession with planning and regulation inclined toward dictatorship, not democracy.[55] No one better justified such worries than

Alexis de Tocqueville. His famous words, first recorded in 1832, must have seemed uncannily appropriate a hundred years later to conservative critics of Roosevelt's administration.

> For [the people's] happiness a government willingly labors, but it chooses to be the sole agent and the only arbiter of that happiness; it provides for their security, foresees and supplies their necessities, facilitates their pleasures, manages their principal concerns, directs their industry, regulates the descent of property, and subdivides their inheritances: what remains but to spare them all the care of thinking and all the trouble of living? . . . The principle of equality has prepared men for these things; it has predisposed men to endure them and often to look on them as benefits. . . . Such a power does not destroy, but it prevents existence; it does not tyrannize, but it compresses, enervates, extinguishes, and stupefies a people, till the nation is reduced to nothing better than a flock of timid and industrious animals, of which the government is the shepherd.[56]

"The Shepherd of the People." Who could deny that Democrats saw Lincoln precisely as such? On the front page of the conservative *Chicago Daily Tribune*, Lincoln with ax and dreamy expression declares: "What a glorious country. No nation offers such opportunity to the humble." Below Lincoln, in the same cartoon, a "WPA career man" leans against a shovel wondering, "What's the use? The government says I haven't a chance in this country until it takes from the "haves" and gives to the "have-nots."—I may as well give up and let the government take care of me."[57]

Republicans, on the other hand, never divorced Lincoln from the individualism he had originally symbolized. On February 12, 1931, as the Depression's grip tightened, President Herbert Hoover addressed the nation by radio from Lincoln's former White House study. Hoover was optimistic, believing economic problems could be overcome by an act of will, and he never doubted that if Lincoln had been forced to give such an address his words would have echoed his own:

> Victory over this depression and over our other difficulties will be won by the resolution of our people to fight their own battles in their own communities, by stimulating their ingenuity to solve their own problems by taking new courage, to be masters of their own destiny in the struggle of life. This is not the easy way but it is the American way. And it was Lincoln's way.[58]

Hoover, like most Republicans, never believed that social problems could be solved by federal reform. Even after eight years of Depression,

Hoover remained steadfast. As a former president, he condemned Roosevelt's New Deal in the same language he spoke while president.[59]

Decades earlier, reactionaries saw reformers as communists seeking to ruin America's economy, but by the 1930s the economy was already in shambles. Moderate Republicans attacked Roosevelt's oligarchy as vigorously as their more conservative colleagues, but they also called for a more flexible, humanized party and a federal response to the Depression. Conservative Republicans never fully understood the popular force behind such reform and responded to it in the only way they knew and with the only vocabulary they possessed. The result was like a broken record. Lincoln Memorial University President John Wesley Hill revealed that "[t]here are over 200 revolutionary publications in this country, which are continually invoking the words of Lincoln in justification of their pernicious cause." Dr. Hill believed a communist revolution was at hand and that Americans could deal with it better if they knew more about Lincoln. If Lincoln were alive, Hill said, he would not tolerate what is happening to the country.[60] The paramount issue was not which party would govern America, but whether America's democratic institutions would endure. Already, "[t]here has been such a socialization of American business as to make the followers of Marxism green with envy."[61]

The deeper problem was that people were questioning traditional beliefs, removing sacred landmarks, disparaging their heritage, and losing confidence in themselves.[62] Meanwhile, liberal demagogues traveled back and forth across the country, stirring up class antagonisms and setting up harmful "experiments." For them Lincoln was great because he "was not afraid to try experiments when old methods failed;"[63] for conservatives, "experiment" was synonymous with "Bolshevism" and New Deal excess. Social experiments differ fundamentally from laboratory experiments, one observer explained, because they inevitably tear down tradition, destroy everything good and worthy in the country.[64] Not new structures but "self-help," President Hoover said, is the answer to the problems of 1931, just as it was to those of Lincoln's day.[65]

Self-help: midstream conservatives connected no theme more often to Lincoln. In a short film titled "He Could Take It," a man considering himself a failure because he could not find a job is inspired after being told of Lincoln's resilience in the face of setbacks. Countless brochures and posters, like "Lincoln Came Through!" (1932)[66] conveyed the same message:

> With the terrible responsibility of War, the long sleepless nights of sorrow, the constant harping of weaker men, proclaiming that all was

FIGURE 1.7 "Guess Abe Was Born a Hundred Years Too Soon," February 12, 1938, *Philadelphia Inquirer.*

lost, and blessed, or cursed, with a soul capable of feeling all human emotions—**Lincoln came through!**

* * *

The world will once again come out from the shadows of gloom—stronger and better. **Will You?**

Readers are invited to identify with Lincoln's self-reliance and persistence. Lincoln came through! Will you? The political implications are plain: government action can solve no one's problems. Under an image of the government asking railsplitter Lincoln "Don't you think I ought to do something for you?" the conservative *Philadelphia Inquirer*'s cartoonist writes his caption: "Guess Abe was born a hundred years too soon" (fig. 1.7). His reaction to big government expresses Lincoln's belief that no man can become a free man without the will to work his own way out of want.

Self-reliance and the New Deal made for a bad fit, and Republicans turned to Lincoln regularly to formulate their impatience with the latter. They saw in the subject of Lincoln's 1837 Lyceum Address—the brilliant leader whose political ambitions are thwarted by democracy—none other than Franklin Roosevelt.[67] Abraham Lincoln celebrated a "government of the people, for the people, by the people"; Franklin Roosevelt, "a people's government for the people's good."[68] Which principle, the commentator asks, inclines toward democracy? Which toward tyranny?[69]

Lincoln was, in truth, beginning to look like Tocqueville's beneficent dictator, not the self-reliant man fighting great odds but the paternalistic man worrying about the people as if they were his children.[70] The Lincoln of the Progressive Era, a period of economic expansion, was the workers' friend; the Lincoln of the Depression, a period of economic collapse, was their guardian. The compassionate Lincoln was the right kind of hero for what political scientist Andrew Polsky called the nationalizing of "public tutelage."[71]

Max Lerner, discerning "a new and revived Lincoln image in the making," saw nothing wrong with public tutelage. In fact, Lincoln was "almost providentially made for the present national crisis." For the majority of Americans, he was a "deeply human being," had a "long tolerance for all modes of belief" and an "unshakable faith in majority rule." He made concessions but fought hard, and after bitter war sought no revenge. Decades of "finance-capitalism" have "wiped the Lincoln image from our minds because Lincoln as democrat, as labor sympathizer, as 'Father Abraham' with his compassion for the suffering of the people, was an inconvenient Lincoln for the plutocrat."[72]

Lerner exaggerated conservatives' influence. True, the new crisis made Lincoln's protective beneficence more relevant than his rugged individualism, but even conservative Republicans, like New York representative Hamilton Fish, found his compassion for the working man inspiring. In the face of an intractable Depression he wanted to restore the reform-mindedness of the Progressive Era: "Let us infuse the spirit of Lincoln and Theodore Roosevelt into a liberalized and humanized Republican Party."[73] Many conservatives wanted to go back further, reinfusing Lincoln with the individualism and self-reliance of the Gilded Age, but they failed.

The liberal-conservative split of the 1930s concerned not only political and economic matters but also residual issues of the Civil War: race relations and regional conflict. On these issues, too, people wanted to know what Lincoln would do.

African American Benchmarks

Because the Depression's archetypal hero was champion of the underdog, nothing was more ironic than Lincoln's place in African American memory. Throughout the 1920s, two pictures of Lincoln had permeated the black press. "The one shows the Immortal Illinoisan as opposed to slavery from an early age and promising to strike a body blow at the inhuman custom should the opportunity ever be his, while the other paints Abe as a friend of slavery and signing the Emancipation Proclamation only as a last resort to keep Negro bondsmen from helping the Confederacy espouse its cause."[74] By the end of the 1920s, many blacks sought to resolve the contradiction by adopting the one conception of Lincoln that placed the least burden on his motives. The *Atlanta Daily World*'s editor took this approach: "[W]hichever picture is true, is of no consequence," since the result of the Proclamation—Freedom—is indisputable.[75] Whether or not this editor convinced himself is uncertain. Three years later, he declared defensively that "Negroes have nothing of which to be ashamed in slavery or Abraham Lincoln"—an unenthusiastic assessment[76] that restated the *New York Amsterdam News*'s view that "Lincoln rests on fame's pedestal more insecurely than he did in years gone by."[77]

The location of fame's pedestal makes a difference. Lincoln's fame seemed far less secure among black elites than among the black masses. Historian Carter G. Woodson marked Negro History Week, 1936, by measuring Lincoln against Elijah Lovejoy, John Brown, Charles Sumner, and Thaddeus Stevens. He concluded:

> Lincoln should be lauded by the Negro, but he has been often overrated as the savior of the race. At best Lincoln was a gradual emancipationist and colonizationist who hoped by methods of compensation to free all Negroes by 1900 and deport them to some neglected part of the earth. He doubted that the two races could dwell together in peace. Lincoln originally had no more idea of issuing the emancipation proclamation than King John had of issuing the Magna Carta. He was forced to this position.[78]

That Confederate victories and progressive men pushed Lincoln along is a recurring theme. Thaddeus Stevens, according to a *New York Age* observer, "made Lincoln's mantle of 'the great Emancipator' and put it upon his shoulders." Lacking Lincoln's "expedient politics" or "oily tongue of diplomacy," Stevens influenced Congress against slavery.[79]

As Depression radicalism spread, Lincoln's critics expressed themselves more angrily. Journalist J. A. Rogers shocked a public meeting at New York's Mother Zion Church by asserting that equality could "never be achieved under the present economic order" and that Lincoln, its great symbol, was a supreme hypocrite.[80] In Boston, journalist

Eugene Gordon dismissed Lincoln as a "clever politician" and "tool of the capitalists."[81]

The African American left's opinion of Lincoln was important, but its influence was limited. The major cause of Lincoln's decline was not a new kind of (Marxist) criticism but the election of a new kind of president—a new emancipator. In the 1932 presidential election, two out of three black voters remained loyal to Abraham Lincoln's Republican party by supporting Hoover over Roosevelt. By 1936 everything changed: more than two out of three blacks voted for Roosevelt. "It was a kind of religion to vote for Roosevelt in '36," reporter Earl Brown remembered. Another reporter observed that in "every black home you went into, you saw a picture of Franklin Roosevelt, *framed*."[82] African Americans were transferring to Roosevelt the reverence they had once reserved for Lincoln.

Roosevelt's undermining of Lincoln's prestige resulted not only from the material benefits he brought to black families throughout the country—benefits that often made the difference between survival and starvation[83]—but also from his policies. As chief executive of a welfare state, Roosevelt did what Lincoln had failed to do: he provided immediate relief, advocated equal economic opportunity regardless of race, and pushed as far as he dared for racial integration. In Roosevelt's shadow, Lincoln shrunk. Harold Rome's "F.D.R. Jones," written for the 1938 Broadway musical *Sing Out the News*, captures the look of the new pantheon:

> Abraham Lincoln Smith, set
> yourself right 'down!
> There's a new hero here,
> He's the man of the year,
> Mr. Franklin D. Roosevelt Jones![84]

By this same year (1938), *Chicago Defender* readers noticed something strange about their Lincoln Day edition. There were fewer articles about Lincoln's birthday than in previous years, and none of them were on the front page. The headlined event of the early thirties had become the back-page news of the late thirties.

Overestimating the influence of black radicals or underestimating Lincoln's prestige would be foolish. To many left-leaning journalists, "capitalist free lancing and individual caprice that produced the cruel profit motive, without limit or curb, enslaving the masses by its dog-eat-dog tactics" seemed to be a fact of life, but they believed that "Lincoln's spirit of give and take will get us along here." In these times, few doubted "that Lincoln who pleaded for fraternal relations with all mankind would be in the middle of the battle for better race relations."[85] Some commentators, in fact, still adored Lincoln: "Night and morning, thank God for Lincoln, the world's ONLY EMANCIPATOR."[86] If a national opinion survey had asked a cross-section of the 1939 black population to list America's two greatest presidents, Roosevelt would have appeared first; Lincoln, second.

Lincoln's image also conveyed changing white attitudes toward minorities. Early in the twentieth century, whites believed African Americans to be unassimilable and a threat to the nation's social fabric. By 1930, European immigration and black migration to the North had practically stopped, and a second generation of children filled the Northern cities. Immigrants and blacks were being seen as victims of the system rather than threats to it. Roosevelt's Commissioner of Immigration and Naturalization declared that "the New Deal means a more sympathetic and humane consideration of [the immigrant's] problems . . . rather than one of antagonism and persecution." The United States Office of Education produced twenty-six radio broadcasts entitled "Americans All," stressing the "rich heritages that have come to us through the many races that make up our population." Hollywood joined radio and government agencies in the campaign against exclusion with a series of films, including *Legion of Terror* and *Black Legion* (the latter distributed for high-school viewing), which condemned racism and nativism.[87] Political, religious, business, and academic organizations, for their part, stressed Lincoln's "tolerance" of all minority groups. Lincoln Day and Race Relations Sunday meetings placed special emphasis on the plight of the African American.[88] Black and white ministers addressing one another's congregations was a Lincoln Day staple among many churches. Bigotry remained more characteristic of America than tolerance, but change was unmistakable.

America's growing antagonism toward fascism boosted the New Deal's inclusive "civic nationalism," distinguished by Gary Gerstle from the exclusive "racial nationalism" of earlier years.[89] The New Deal desegregated no schools or neighborhoods, made employers no less biased, and accommodated the South on all important legislation—including opposition to an anti-lynching bill; but Franklin Roosevelt's support for equal opportunity legislation and appointment of blacks to government positions, along with Eleanor Roosevelt's public statements and actions on behalf of racial justice, led Gunnar Myrdal to conclude, correctly, that "for almost the first time in the history of the nation the state has done something substantial in a social way without excluding the Negro."[90] The new tendency was symbolized by sheet music intended for use by

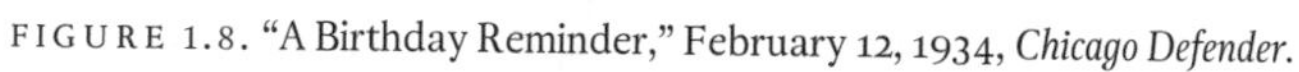

FIGURE 1.8. "A Birthday Reminder," February 12, 1934, *Chicago Defender*.

Democratic party locals. In march tempo, the party faithful attributed to Lincoln the sentiments of their own leadership:

> Now Abe was close to the ground
> Tho' he towered up six foot four (Bare feet!)
> And his heart was big as the whole country
> With room for more (Black Folks too!)[91]

Meanwhile, black protests against segregation replaced accommodative strategies of self-help and racial betterment. The *Chicago Defender*'s 1934 Lincoln Day cartoon, "A Birthday Reminder" (fig. 1.8), depicts Uncle Sam at a desk strewn with documents of lynching, social ostracism, peonage, segregation, Jim Crow law, violation of the Fourteenth and Fifteenth (citizenship and voting rights) Amendments, race hatred, and employment discrimination. As a lynching party, visible through the window, completes it business, Abraham Lincoln's specter confronts Uncle Sam with a scroll bearing words from the Gettysburg Address: "all men are created equal." Earlier *Defender* cartoons showed Lincoln endorsing the ideal of justice; this cartoon shows Lincoln challenging whites to make justice a reality. Lincoln had become a vehicle for black criticism of white society.

Many whites, unemployed or underemployed, and fearful of losing their own status, sympathized with the classes below them,[92] endorsed Roosevelt's race relations policies (at least so long as they posed no threat to their own interests) and, as they projected their mellowing attitudes upon Lincoln, convinced themselves that racial justice was part of his unfinished business and a fulfillment of America's political heritage. This mood is apparent in the *Los Angeles Times* comic section containing a cartoon of a generic white man shining the shoes of a black boy beside a bust of Abraham Lincoln (fig. 1.9)—seemingly the most appropriate symbol to mark racial role reversal.[93] The changing mood is also apparent in the percentage of whites outside the South, 75 percent, who approved of Eleanor Roosevelt's resigning her membership in the all-white Daughters of the American Revolution in response to their denying contralto Marian Anderson the use of their auditorium.[94] That the Lincoln Memorial, dedicated in 1922 as a symbol of North-South reconciliation, seemed to the black arrangements committee and white interior secretary the "most logical" alternative for Anderson's 1938 concert[95] tells much about changing perceptions of Lincoln's legacy.

Political symbols change, according to Karen Cerulo, when their existing "associative connections" are blocked by new ones.[96] That white Americans perceived Lincoln to be Roosevelt's nineteenth-century predecessor is evident in the coupling of race reforms and traditional commemoration. In 1940, the U.S. Supreme Court overturned four black defendants' death sentences based on coerced confessions, and announced its decision on Lincoln's birthday. Also on Lincoln's birthday (1941) the U.S. attorney general abolished the District of Columbia Bar Association's ban on black members. After the "Scottsboro Boys'" first conviction was overturned, an eminent jurist likened their attorney's achievement to "laying a rose on Lincoln's grave."[97] Lincoln's image blocks justification of the old connections between injustice and race.

The significance of these couplings[98] should not be exaggerated. Racial sympathies did not change so much as to suggest an end of segregation; the white people sympathizing with Marian Anderson would not have wanted her living next door. Within and among human consciences there was constant tugging and hauling, one side asserting Lincoln's affinity with social integration, the other side denying it. In

FIGURE 1.9. "He Never Says a Word," February 13, 1935, cartoon by Tish Tash, *Los Angeles Times.*

preparation for the opening of *Abe Lincoln in Illinois,* for example, the RKO Keith Theatre in Washington DC conducted an Abraham Lincoln look-alike contest, announcing a $25 prize to be presented on stage at the film's opening. A forty-seven-year-old attorney, Thomas Bomar, won that contest. He was congratulated by the selection committee and received his award—but not at RKO Keith's. Realizing that the man who most resembled Abraham Lincoln was a light-skinned African American, the sponsor decided to make its payoff privately.[99] A public ceremony would have implied a connection that the theater preferred not to make. The story, however, could not be suppressed. *Time* magazine interviewed "the black Lincoln," and so did the *We the People* radio program. It was wrong to treat a man this way, very wrong; yet, references to Lincoln's "tolerance" in Lincoln Day ceremonies did not mean what they mean today. For Senator Lewis Schwellenbach, liberal Democrat from Washington state, tolerance and justice were indistinguishable. "The majority must recognize the rights of the minority. . . . Otherwise, majority rule becomes merely a form of mob rule." At the same time, "the minority must recognize the right of the majority to govern."[100] There is something peculiar about Senator Schwellenbach's well-meaning statement, for the issue in his day was not minority recognition of majority rights but, plainly, majority indifference to minority rights.

Popular entertainment dramatized the begrudging race tolerance that Lincoln stood for. *Holiday Inn*, a musical with Bing Crosby, Fred Astaire, and Marjorie Reynolds, filmed in 1941 and early 1942, appealed to the Depression generation. One of the songs, "Abraham," represented Lincoln as the Great Emancipator: "That's why we celebrate / This blessed February date." A twenty-first century audience might approve such lyrics but would be astonished by the full script and choreography. Among the singers is an authentically African American mother telling her daughter about the emancipation, but the chorus, led by Bing Crosby, is in blackface. Blond Marjorie Reynolds appears with a black wig, braids standing upright on her head as she sings in a rural black accent. The lyrics tell of "Honest Abe's" humble beginnings, his mother Nancy Hanks, the log cabin, and how he became president and "set the darkeys free."[101] When the chorus mentions the man and his achievement, Bing Crosby asks "Who dah?" The chorus responds: "Abraham." The movie humiliates the African American people, but when shown in 1942 this effect was the last thing the filmmakers had in mind. Like so many aspects of Depression memory, "Abraham" condemns slavery while disparaging the intelligence and dignity of slaves' descendants, deeming them worthy of legal equality, but not dignity.

For whites to recognize seriously the legal equality of blacks in the 1930s was nevertheless a big step. Inclusionist symbolism, including Marian Anderson's concert, solidified racial progress as it made Lincoln a civil rights pioneer. However, there was no such inclusionist *history* of Lincoln. Throughout the thirties and beyond, Carl Sandburg set the tone of popular Lincoln biography, and neither he nor the Lincoln scholars of the day had anything new to say about Lincoln's racial views.[102] Lincoln's emerging role as symbol of racial justice was based on new values, not new facts. Yet, racial justice was by no means Lincoln's only legacy.

Southern Benchmarks

Overestimating African American affection for Lincoln is easier than underestimating it; Southerners' affection for Lincoln, on the other hand,

by knowing Lincoln as a symbol of regional rather than racial unity is a necessary prelude to understanding his place in the mind of the nation. That Lincoln was once a symbol of union when race did not matter is as relevant to us, historically and sociologically, as showing Abraham Lincoln as he is today: a symbol of racial integration in a regionally integrated society.

Long before the Great Depression, influential Southerners praised Lincoln publicly. Henry Grady, editor of the *Atlanta Constitution,* declaring the New South's credo of industrialization, urbanization, education, and national commitment, believed Lincoln embodied both Puritan and Cavalier virtues but transcended both because he was so distinctly American. A decade later, in 1895, Union General Oliver Howard helped to establish Abraham Lincoln University in Tennessee's Cumberland Gap. Besides providing poor mountain people with educational opportunity, this institution stood for Union. The University's main administration building was named Grant-Lee Hall; the school colors, blue and gray.

FRIEND OF THE SOUTH

Lincoln's appeal in the South must be summarized before his Depression persona can be grasped. That Abraham Lincoln would someday emerge as a Southern hero on a par with Robert E. Lee was impossible to imagine during the carnage of civil war. It is difficult for many to imagine today, but facts must be recognized if we are to make sense of memory's ironies. During the Civil War, Henry Watterson, longtime editor of the *Louisville Courier-Journal,* criticized Lincoln severely; after the war, he realized the consequences of his position. If the South had won the war, the result would have been a fragmented nation prey to every foreign power. Lincoln was God's instrument for Union. Had he lived, there would have been no ten-year reconstruction nightmare and national unity would have been achieved more rapidly. His great life melded Northern and Southern virtues into a "common American consciousness." Watterson's paeons to Lincoln, written through the early 1920s, led many Southerners to a pro-Lincoln attitude and converted many hostile Southerners to indifference, if not affection.

More popular than Watterson was former minister, playwright, and novelist Thomas Dixon. His characters were stereotyped, his prose wooden, yet his stories converted proud memories of rebellion into passionate nationalism. He distinguished himself by a series of novels, including *The Clansman,* which D. W. Griffith made into a film, *Birth of a Nation,* the first great full-length photoplay. Condemned today as racist, reactionary, and wrong, *Birth of a Nation* makes the Ku Klux Klan a noble force against crime and violence. The concrete plot, however, is banal. Like scores of 15–20 minute films shown in the back of grocery stores during the first two decades of the century, Griffith's epic involves love interests among the sons and daughters of Northern and Southern families. Against this background, Lincoln's "Great Heart" and affection for the South and its people determines the film's significance. "The rule of the coming nation over individual states" is a motto appearing throughout the film and defining its political message. Senator Austin Stoneman, representing Thaddeus Stevens, perfects the story's irony. His own son and daughter have fallen in love with the daughter and son of the Camerons, a Southern planter family. The final scene, wherein one of the enraptured pairs vows eternal love, fades into the final subtitle—from Daniel Webster: "Liberty and Union, one and inseparable, now and forever!" The conclusion reinforces the film's subtitle: "The agony which the South endured that a nation might be born." However acute its racism, crudity, and hypocrisy, the film's principal theme, reestablishment of Union, is overpowering. That President Woodrow Wilson saw in Griffith's work "history writ with lightning" must not be dismissed because of Wilson's racial views. His metaphor summarizes well the film's pertinence for his generation.

The Southerner: A Romance of Abraham Lincoln, expresses further Dixon's affection for Lincoln, "the supreme American of our history." He dedicates the novel to his college classmate, segregationist Woodrow Wilson, "the first Southern-born president since Abraham Lincoln." In turn, Dixon designates Lincoln (not Lee, Davis, or Jackson) "The Supreme American of our History." In the book's frontispiece, moreover, he attaches a line from Walt Whitman: "Lincoln, though grafted on the West, is essentially, in person and character, a Southern contribution." Dixon's and Whitman's characterizations became more credible to Southern readers as the years passed.

The 1909 centennial celebration of Lincoln's birth heightened his renown in the South. Atlanta's Joel Chandler Harris marked the occasion with "The Kidnapping of President Lincoln" (1909), a short story portraying Lincoln as a Southern man by inclination as well as birth. His kidnapper declares "Down our way they say you're a Yankee, but if that's so the woods are full of Yankees in Georgia." Lincoln replies: "You're paying me the highest compliment in my life." Harris's story ends with Lincoln's safe release.

The scope and quality of Southern participation in the Lincoln centennial is described elsewhere,[106] but the most popular Southern work associated with the celebrations warrants comment: Alabama writer Mary Raymond Shipman Andrews's *The Perfect Tribute.* Andrews writes

had been. In commentator Archibald Rutledge's words, "[M]uch of his secret sorrow and grieving came from a genuine consciousness that the South had been made the pitiful victim of a gigantic and ghastly mistake."[118]

Rutledge's attribution to Lincoln of remorse for his sins probably made sense to many Southern readers, but his view was not the most influential. From the late 1920s to the late 1940s, Southern newspapers continued to publish articles about Lincoln, but most were provided by the Northern news services to which they subscribed.[119] That Northern articles provoked no distress among Southern readers, however, testifies to their growing respect for Lincoln. The importance of this point, bearing on the larger question of the media's role in promoting the integration of society, cannot be overestimated. News services' accounts of Lincoln commemoration appeared on Southern front pages because editors believed they would attract, not repel, readers. Some of this material consisted of tidbits: here, Lincoln opposes wage slavery as well as chattel slavery; there, a beer company uses lines from the Gettysburg Address to advertise its product. In Port Arthur, Texas, a bank closes in observance of Lincoln's Birthday. Henry Fonda had to wear elevator shoes in the film *Young Mr. Lincoln,* Southern readers were told, to match the future president's six feet four inches. But some of this material was serious and conformed to reader opinion: "We may be certain," declares Columbia University's Alan Nevin, that Lincoln "would have opposed all confiscation of southern property, all harsh treatment of former Confederates; that he would have opposed undue prolongation of military government for the south, and that he would have been against the immediate grant of the ballot to all negroes."[120] Nevins's statement, which appeared in newspapers throughout the South, recapitulated the orthodoxy on Lincoln scholarship, then dominated by James G. Randall and his students, whose feelings toward the South, apart from slavery and secessionism, were friendly.

Indigenous commentary was also positive. In *The Cullman (Alabama) Democrat,* Rixford J. Lincoln, member of a prominent New Orleans family (unrelated to the former president), published a poem ending with the familiar question: "Would that you could rule us today / When wracked the world in woe / Oh, guide us from afar, we pray / Wisdom on us bestow."[121] Three years later, a columnist from this same newspaper observed Lincoln's and Washington's birthdays by noting "America at this time can welcome a re-baptism in the clear springs of patriotic memory. . . ."[122] In Congress, too, Southerners praised Lincoln. Democratic senator William Julius Harris of Georgia, after lecturing his colleagues on the great man's qualities, observed: "The blue of the North

TABLE 1.1. American historic and public characters most frequently named by Alabama schoolchildren, 1929

Boys (2,821)		Girls (1,837)	
Name	%	Name	%
George Washington	26	George Washington	20
Charles Lindbergh	22	Clara Bow	11
Abraham Lincoln	5	Charles Lindbergh	9
Robert E. Lee	5	Billie Dove	6
Woodrow Wilson	4	Ruth Elder	6
Babe Ruth	3	Clara Barton	3
Henry Ford	2	Abraham Lincoln	3
Tom Mix	2	Betsy Ross	3
Thomas Jefferson	1	Robert E. Lee	2
Others	30	Others	37

Source: David Spence Hill, "Personification of Ideals by Urban Children," *Journal of Social Psychology* 1 (August 1930): 385, 387.

and the gray of the South are now merged in the khaki of the United States that brought victory to democracy in the [First] World War."[123]

Whether or not positive elite and media commentary could be generalized to public belief is difficult to determine, but the limited survey evidence—a comparison of 1929 and 1945 samples—provides partial answers. David Spence Hill, an educational researcher, questioned 4,658 white boys and girls, ages 6–17, attending school during 1929 in Birmingham, Montgomery, and Mobile, Alabama. He never replicated the study or collected comparable data from non-Southern cities. Hill asked each child: "Of all persons whom you have heard, or read about, or seen, whom would you most care to be like or resemble?" One third of the boys and 60 percent of the girls responded to the question by naming a family member or personal acquaintance. However, table 1.1 shows the students' choices of historic and public characters to be striking. Twenty-six percent of the boys choosing historical figures named George Washington; 5 percent, Abraham Lincoln; 5 percent, Robert E. Lee. The corresponding girls' nominations were Washington, 20 percent; Lincoln, 3 percent; Lee, 2 percent.[124]

Hill's survey shows Lincoln's prestige to have been feeble among school children, but he also documents the decline of the Confederate tradition. That Lincoln and Lee are named by virtually the same small percentage of respondents is surprising, given the belief about the South's lingering resentments. No longer can negative Southern attitudes toward Lincoln be attributed to nostalgia for the Confederacy and its heroes. Moreover, Alabama children were discovering their

Depression people were to contribute to this survival, if they had, indeed, a rendezvous with destiny, they never knew it. They did not, could not, see themselves as a heroic generation. When the Civil War ended, many Union men believed they had achieved something even greater than the Founders, had turned history in a fundamental way, created anew a nation that the Founders had left only half-made, and dedicated thousands of monuments to themselves to mark the event. At the end of World War II, its participants were content to have survived, and they erected few memorials. No member of the breadline generation, idle and dependent on the first welfare state, would have imagined that it would become the "greatest generation."[130] But subsequent generations saw them as such, and no symbol defined their greatness more vividly than Abraham Lincoln.

* 2 *

Apex

LINCOLN IN THE SECOND WORLD WAR

In 1940, the U.S. census showed a population of 132 million, up 7 percent from 1930, the smallest decade increase in history. Ten million Americans were still unemployed, but armaments production had begun to revitalize the economy. Throughout the late 1930s, the prospect of war had been in the air, culminating in Germany's September 1939 invasion of Poland. By the end of 1940 all of Western Europe, including France, had fallen. While Great Britain alone stood against Germany, the vast majority of Americans, well over 70 percent, opposed entering the war. In this same year, Carl Sandburg received the Pulitzer Prize in history for *Abraham Lincoln: The War Years.*

After a German bombing raid on London destroyed part of the House of Commons and the altar of Westminster Abbey, the United States ambassador observed: "Across the street from the wreckage of these two great historic buildings of State and Church, Saint-Gaudens's statue of Abraham Lincoln was still standing." He then alluded subtly to the traditional friendship the Lincoln statue symbolized and to the United States' failure to recognize its moral obligation to come to Great Britain's aid: "I was proud that [Lincoln] was there in all that wreckage as a friend and sentinel of gallant days gone by, and a reminder that in this great battle for freedom he waited quietly for support for those things for which he lived and died."[1] All-out support would be long in coming. Many Americans, in fact, were invoking Lincoln to justify efforts to stay out of war. "We could wish he were around nowadays," announced a critic of Roosevelt's Lend-Lease aid program to Great Britain, "so that the American people could be privileged to hear some of his dry, Midwestern comments on Americans who advocate giving away our shirts to win somebody else's war."[2]

Come, Mr. President" depicts Franklin Roosevelt himself as "Father Franklin D." (recalling "Father Abraham" of the Civil War) and links three generations through three wars—World War II, World War I, and the Civil War: "Our fathers wore the khaki, / our grandfathers wore the gray or blue / and gladly we will do the things / that they once had to do."

That Lincoln was good for thinking about World War II is also evident in his presence in newspapers, magazines, and public ceremony. The *New York Times* printed an annual mean of 26 articles on Lincoln between 1930 and 1934; 43 articles between 1940 and 1944. For the years 1930 to 1934, *Readers Guide* lists an annual average of 17 articles; for 1940–44, 26. The exact same figures appear in the *Congressional Record*.[8] Sheet-music production featuring Lincoln peaked during the war.[9] The autumn 1941 issue of the *Journal of the National Education Association* invited readers to consider the many parallels between Abraham Lincoln and Jesus Christ. Both were born in humble circumstances; both fathers were carpenters; both were men of sorrows, moved by the suffering of the poor and brokenhearted; both were criticized by bigots and extremists; both were of homely physical appearance; both triumphantly entered capitals shortly before suffering violent death; and both died on a Friday.[10]

The convention of asking "What would Lincoln do?" continued throughout the war, His vision was still "needed"; his "prescriptions," still deemed essential.[11] Ten months before America's entry into the war, an editorial writer surmised:

> We would have no right to say that if he could be alive now he would support this or that course of action or this or that party. We do know that he would approach the crisis of our own day, as he approached that of his own day, with a clear and logical mind; that he would distinguish between the essentials and the non-essentials of a proposed solution.
>
> ... We do not know what weapons he would think best to use against Hitler. We do know that he would recognize Hitler and Hitlerism as enemies of every ideal toward which he strove and every truth he cherished.[12]

Americans in crisis have always looked to great figures of the past for inspiration and guidance, but these figures, including George Washington, Thomas Jefferson, Patrick Henry, and Andrew Jackson, have been *in* the past, and as the people invoked them, they knew they were calling upon strangers—great and virtuous, to be sure, but strangers nonetheless. Lincoln alone, although known to be part of the past, seemed contemporary, standing with the people in their struggle. He was the present absent man, the outsider existing inside all; our war, his war; his way, ours.[13] Lincoln remained a living model *for* American society at war.

What made Lincoln so memorable in the early 1940s cannot be determined with certainty. Similarity between World War II and the Civil War is not the answer. World War I furnished much better logistical and technical examples (including air power) than did the Civil War. Most Americans had lived through World War I as children or adults and thought about it constantly throughout the four years of the new war. On the other hand, a 1937 Gallup survey showed that 70 percent of Americans believed that United States participation in World War I was a mistake, while a 1945 NORC survey showed Woodrow Wilson, the World War I president, being named as "one of the two or three greatest Americans" by only 8 percent of the population.[14] World War I was a living memory, not a living frame of reference.

Living frames of reference rest on moral significance, for morality is the "cultural code" to which a historical event must fit rhetorically if it is to become a model for conduct.[15] Civil War memories incorporate the clearest examples of America's moral goals and virtues—the preservation of the Union, emancipation of the slaves, perseverance in the face of overwhelming loss. The Civil War, even more than World War I, embodied these things, furnishing American civil religion with its themes of death, sacrifice, and rebirth.[16] This is why Lincoln's image, not Wilson's, legitimated, oriented, clarified, inspired, and consoled throughout World War II.

To legitimate unpopular wartime measures, orient the people to prolonged sacrifice, clarify the purpose of war, inspire men to fight it in the face of defeat, and console the bereaved were essential to war mobilization. It was not enough for the state to declare war, train an armed force, and orient the economy to war priorities; there also had to be machinery to ensure that individuals were sufficiently motivated to play their parts in the face of hardship and loss.[17] As American society mobilized for war, its media, school, church, and other institutional elites scanned the past and transmitted images defining the war's purpose and sustaining the will to achieve it. This function was performed everywhere, including the Southern states, whose newspapers carried the same Lincoln references and illustrations appearing in newspapers outside the South. But the parallel was imperfect. The Southern press, with its long tradition of legitimating segregation by invoking Lincoln, tried to instill in African American readers the will to fight, while openly recognizing the injustice under which they labored.[18] For its part, the African American press devoted many pages to the black community's contribution to the war against fascism, but rarely did it associate this topic with Lincoln's legacy, which was confined largely to emancipation.

the desire to find a better way out."[26] For wartime dissenters who went too far in their search for a better way out, Roosevelt sought criminal prosecution. Attorney general Francis Biddle, a staunch defender of civil liberties, declared that it would be almost impossible to get convictions on dissent alone, but Roosevelt, according to a reliable witness, was sure Biddle could find a way to succeed. The president explained that "when Lincoln's Attorney General would not proceed against Vallandigham [the Ohio Copperhead], Lincoln declared martial law in that county and then had Vallandigham tried by a drum-head court-martial."[27] Stimson and Roosevelt alike believed that Americans did not understand what it meant to be at war, and that no words or actions could give them a better explanation than Lincoln's.

Roosevelt's and Stimson's audience saw Lincoln's conception of what it would take to win the Civil War for what it was: a model *for* the present—another version of "What would Lincoln do?"—not a "high resolution" model to be mimicked or literally applied to the current situation, but a "low resolution" model to be used as a guideline for the molding of attitude and motivation.[28]

These guidelines, so often applied by the administration to motivate civil society, were applied, in turn, to the administration itself. "Lincoln, faced with a tragic war and difficult home front, divided his time between them" to keep political corruption and war profiteering in check. Roosevelt, according to Athens, Alabama, *Limestone Democrat*'s editor, must do the same.[29]

CLARIFICATION

Invoking Lincoln's memory helped legitimate Roosevelt's assumption of emergency powers and provide orientation on how to fight the war. These two functions—legitimation and orientation—key present to past situations through two discourses. Legitimation discourse is about presidential rights in national emergency. Orientation discourse is about long-term military and homefront strategies. Legitimation and orientation discourses concern action; clarification discourse, on the other hand, is a hybrid concerning action and values, a cultural discourse defining the values on which coordinated political, economic, and integrative activities feed.

Abraham Lincoln's image symbolized many values justifying the war, but the most important were democracy and the dignity of the common people. Discourse and symbolism of the common man were found everywhere—in legislatures, city halls, factories, schools, churches, newspapers, radio, and film.[30] The year before Americans heard Bing Crosby sing "Abraham" in blackface, they listened to the song "Nancy Hanks:

FIGURE 2.1
A Scout Is Loyal, 1942. Calendar illustration by Norman Rockwell. Art from the Archives of Brown & Bigelow, Inc., and with permission from the Boy Scouts of America. Photo courtesy of Brown & Bigelow.

Abraham Lincoln's Mother" (from a 1933 poem by Rosemarie and Stephen Vincent Benét).[31] Nancy returns from the past wondering "What's happened to Abe?"—a question made meaningful by the fact that everyone knew the answer. He had become president but remained the plain young man she had reared. A 1942 poem, "The Lincoln Penny," printed in *Collier's*, revealed that "Lincoln loved the plain things / He was called to Gettysburg! / The dead could hear him say / Something about 'the people' / That's good down to this day!"[32]

In war as in economic depression, pictorial representations of Lincoln made democratic ideals tangible. Norman Rockwell's *A Scout is Loyal* (fig. 2.1), produced as a 1942 calendar illustration before being reprinted in Boy Scout magazines, personified America's new generation. A lad in mid-adolescence appears in scout uniform, traditionally associated with the leveling of class differences, cohesion, and militancy.[33] At his feet lay knapsack and shovel, standard equipment of the soldier. Behind him stand George Washington and Abraham Lincoln. Appearing after fourteen months of war, the background of eagle and flag communicates redundantly the meaning of the painting's theme: loyalty. The scout's

FIGURE 2.4. "As in 1865—So in 1943," February 12, 1943, *Philadelphia Record.*

a giant-size Abraham Lincoln (Daniel Chester French's statue) looks down on a sword-wielding yet puny Adolph Hitler. The inset compares Hitler's demand for territorial concessions to American slaveholders' demand for the extension of slavery. World War II is thus seen as a continuation of the Civil War. This key was used time and again. Here, in a newspaper, Lincoln stands behind Roosevelt and rests his hand on his shoulder above the caption, "You have a greater task than I had. Slavery must be removed from the whole earth." There, in a train station, an OWI poster shows Lincoln's countenance below the famous line from his "House Divided" speech: "This World Cannot Exist Half Slave and Half Free"; elsewhere, in a factory cafeteria, another poster uses the same words to interpret a vivid scene of Nazi brutality. Along this same line, a *Philadelphia Record* front-page Lincoln Day cartoon (fig. 2.4) keys fascism to slaveholding: Lincoln's emblem, the ax, splits a swastika above the great summons (taken from Lincoln's second inaugural address): "Let Us Strive to Finish the Work We Are In." The caption: "As in 1865—So in 1943." Next year, 1944, in an (Athens) *Alabama Courier* cartoon, Lincoln stands behind the words he uttered to an Ohio Regiment in August 1864: "It is not merely for today but for all time to come, that we should perpetuate for our children's children that great and free government which we have enjoyed all our lives."[37]

As a frame for interpreting World War II, images from the Civil War were reinforced by images from the American Revolution. In one cartoon, Lincoln's countenance is associated with two revolutionary war scenes: George Washington crossing the Delaware and George Washington at the Battle of Monmouth. The written message, "Adolph, Have You Ever Read American History?" refers (through time-phased pictures of Washington and Lincoln) to the American people's traditional readiness to fight. In another illustration, silhouetted profiles of George Washington, Abraham Lincoln, and Thomas Jefferson are set against a background of bombers flying off on a mission. The illustration's title, "From Every Mountain Side Let Freedom Ring," formulates the bombing mission's ultimate purpose (fig. 2.5).

State and media iconography in a pluralistic society reminded all Americans of their shared values. Recurrently, the word "liberty" appeared. Liberty did not need to be defined. Its power was in its ambiguity,

FIGURE 2.5
Let Freedom Ring, 1944. The Abraham Lincoln Museum, Harrogate, TN. Photo courtesy of the Abraham Lincoln Museum.

But there was no news of victory, only disaster, and it was in the context of disaster that the first Lincoln Day of the war was observed. Foreign recognition strengthened Lincoln's symbolic wartime role. Nine weeks after the president's December 8, 1941, declaration of war, Lord Halifax, new British ambassador to the United States, traveled to Springfield, Illinois, to lay a wreath at Lincoln's tomb.[40] At the same time, Lord Lytton, highly regarded among British foreign officers, addressed an American audience by radio from London to extol Lincoln's achievements. In England itself, Lincoln's birthday was celebrated at Westminster Abbey, after which a wreath was placed at the base of his statue.[41]

In Washington, federal information offices seeking to put early military losses into perspective, asked composers to write patriotic songs to boost morale. To know what must be done, concretely, to accomplish this end is to know how to formulate the purposes and emotions of war. Some composers knew better than others. Jerome Kern and Oscar Hammerstein's "Abe Lincoln Had Just One Country" had little impact on the public mood. Aaron Copland's *Lincoln Portrait*, on the other hand, was one of the most popular wartime musical productions. Inspired by *Requiem Suggested by the Gettysburg Address*, written by his teacher Rubin Goldmark during World War I, Copland's thirteen-minute orchestral piece includes a speaker reciting various passages from Lincoln's speeches. From Cincinnati, where it was first performed, a journalist reported that "I have not seen so excited an audience as this Cincinnati one upon the completion of Copland's Lincoln. . . ." From several other cities came reports that "audiences get all excited by it."[42] *Lincoln Portrait* aroused audiences because it made early 1942 battle losses comprehensible and manageable by placing them in the perspective of Lincoln's war goal (preservation of the Union) and Lincoln's strategy (perseverance in the face of successive military calamities).

In July 1942, amid still discouraging news from the war front, conductor Andre Kostelanetz performed *Lincoln Portrait* (with Carl Sandburg as reader) before a crowd gathered near the Lincoln Memorial. "After the concert," Copland recalled, "Andre told me that he felt Lincoln's words 'with a terrible new clarity,' and we both knew the audience felt it also."[43] Copland's comment on Lincoln's words having the same effect on Kostelanetz as on the people who heard them reflects the familiarity of the patriotic symbols his music communicated. Copland had composed his piece by invoking these symbols, not exploiting them. An exploited audience must, by definition, hold values different from those its manipulator wishes to impose. Copland's task (like Roosevelt's

FIGURE 2.8. *Lincoln Park in Wartime,* 1942, photo appearing in personal scrapbook. The Abraham Lincoln Museum, Harrogate, TN. Photo courtesy of the Abraham Lincoln Museum.

and OWI's) was to invigorate, not change, the public's conceptions—to reaffirm beliefs and feelings that he and his audience shared.

People, however, do not always know what ideas they share with others. Commemorative ritual as well as commemorative music makes implicit consensus explicit. Thus, on February 12, 1942, Chicago servicemen, amid news of astonishing German and Japanese victories, invoked the narrative of the Civil War at Augustus Saint-Gaudens's statue in the presence of a Lincoln Park crowd (fig. 2.8). New York veterans and Boy Scouts conducted their ceremony at Henry Kirk Brown's statue of

FIGURE 2.9. "Courage!" February 12, 1942. Used with permission of the *Philadelphia Inquirer*.

"Americans Will *Always* Defend Liberty," reiterates the point as it emphasizes national endurance.

Lincoln's response to defeat was an essential part of this narrative. In the winter of 1942, the *Philadelphia Inquirer* shows him placing an encouraging hand on the shoulder of a despondent Uncle Sam, wincing at the latest war news (fig. 2.9). One week earlier, in the Senate, Alexander Wiley of Wisconsin entered into the *Congressional Record* a script of a recently aired Madison, Wisconsin, radio program. "In the dark hours when we have heard so many disheartening reports of the campaign in the Far East, we do well to recall Lincoln's words: "Let us not be oversanguine of a speedy final triumph. Let us be quite sober . . . never doubting that a just God, in His own good time, will give us the rightful result."[50] Through the summer of 1942, as German and Japanese forces continued to advance, *New York Times Magazine* published "He,

Too, Had Dark Days," a story by one of Lincoln's secretaries, William Stoddard, retold by his son. The story follows Lincoln after his army's disastrous defeat at Chancellorsville and shows how he looked beyond it: on the very night of the calamity he wrote out military orders setting the stage for victory at Gettysburg.[51] The reprinting of Stoddard's article expresses a powerful theme in the culture of war. Armies that win battles effortlessly require no memories to sustain their morale, while spectacular victories of the past are useless models in a hard-fought war marked by costly defeats.[52]

CONSOLATION

Throughout World War II, Lincoln images operated as vehicles for conception—"programs" (as Clifford Geertz would call them) controlling ideas and feelings about the war.[53] Lincoln images were powerful programs not only because of their capacity to motivate men to fight but also because they made sense of suffering and death.

People who live through a war costing 350,000 lives and a million injuries need more than inspiration. They need a theodicy. The discourses of theodicy and inspiration are comparable: both enable people to work together effectively in the face of loss. Theodicy discourse is formulated to make the ultimate loss, death, meaningful and, thus, bearable. Two documents of the Civil War performed these functions best. Lincoln wrote the first document, the Gettysburg Address (part of the "New Testament" of "civil scripture"),[54] for the dedication of a new military cemetery, but its substance is generalizable. "In this tremendous war, whose every day adds to the number of our dead," wrote a *New York Times* editor, "Mr. Lincoln's words of eighty years ago are as strong, inspiring and immediate as if they were heard today for the first time."[55] The *Statesville (NC) Daily Record*, under the heading "Lincoln never died," made the point tangible: "We should again resolve that our dead shall not have died in vain—nor have lost their lives needlessly because we here at home did not help with all our resources. . . . If we do that, the faith in freedom that was Lincoln's can never die." At the bottom of the announcement was a War Bond appeal (fig. 2.10). The back of the *Philadelphia Inquirer*'s Sunday supplement shows a soldier in full battle gear lying face up, dead (fig. 2.11). He appears in the picture's foreground, directly in front of the viewer. In the background, elevated above the fallen soldier, is Daniel Chester French's statue of Lincoln. Lincoln looks down upon the soldier, and both are illuminated by the same mysterious light. On the viewer's left, between Lincoln's statue and the soldier's body, is an excerpt from the Gettysburg Address: "That We Here Highly Resolve That These Dead Shall Not Have Died in Vain."

The Weatherhead Company of Cleveland, Ohio, offered a free replica of the Bixby Letter to all bereaved parents. The letter, as advertised (fig. 2.12), omits Lincoln's first sentence, which refers specifically to the Bixby boys; beginning at the second sentence it refers to any boy. The Weatherhead Company profited by war contracts, as the inset shows, but its gift was nonetheless a gift of meaning because it drew a familiar and powerful sign, an image of Abraham Lincoln, and matched it against the catastrophic effects of war in such a way as to make the latter comprehensible. To place a soldier's name on some casualty list is to make his death a point of information. To connect that name with Lincoln's is to sanctify it. Asserting an identity of purpose between nation and family, the Bixby letter communicated an ideal that no other relic could so effectively convey.

As fatalities increased, the Bixby letter became more prominent. Calling attention to Nelson Craig of Indianapolis, who had lost three sons, former journalist and Indiana Democratic representative Louis L. Ludlow said he could not think of his constituent's grief without also thinking of Abraham Lincoln's letter: "I pray that our Heavenly Father may assuage the anguish of your bereavement, and leave you only the

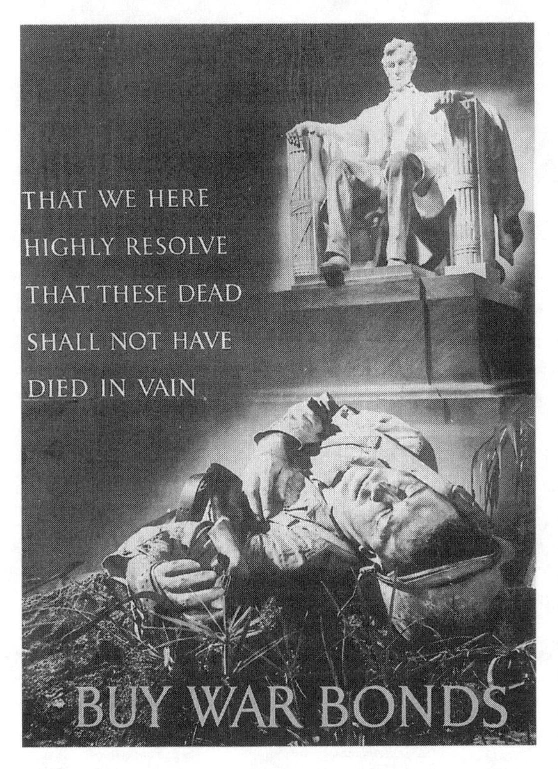

FIGURE 2.11
"That These Dead Shall Not Have Died in Vain," U.S. Office of War Information poster, WWII.

FIGURE 2.12. *To Those Whose Sons Have Died in Battle*, c. 1943. Weatherhead Company announcement. The Abraham Lincoln Museum, Harrogate, TN. Photo courtesy of the Abraham Lincoln Museum.

cherished memory of the loved and lost, and the solemn pride that must be yours to have laid so costly a sacrifice upon the altar of freedom."[56] Abraham Lincoln gave to stricken Americans in the 1940s a vocabulary by which they could realize the full depth of their private distress yet relate it to the transcendent good of the nation.

RETURN OF THE MAN OF SORROWS

Racine, Wisconsin, dedicated Frederick Hibbard's statue of Abraham Lincoln on July 4, 1943. After the usual preliminaries, the veil was lifted and the people saw Lincoln seated on a simple upholstered chair with a shawl over his lap and his wife standing beside him, her left hand placed upon his right (fig. 2.13). The statue's domestic mien and its location in a small residential-area park seemed appropriate. Reminding people of the intense fighting taking place on that day, one of the speakers pictured Lincoln as a "brooding" family man for whom casualty lists were not "unintelligible figures," but rosters of homesick boys who knew nothing of war but were determined to do their best.[57] To the wooden frame houses behind the monument some of these homesick boys hoped to return.

Lincoln's sympathy for the casualties of war defined a key facet of his identity. As one of the *New York Times* editors put it, his distin-

FIGURE 2.13. *Mary Todd and Abraham.* Statue by Frederick Hubbard. Dedicated July 4, 1945. Photo courtesy of Racine (WI) Heritage Museum.

guishing wartime emotion "was pity, from which no wounded soldier, no bereaved or afflicted family, North or South, was excluded."[58] Accordingly, Oswald Garrison Villard, editor of the *Nation*, had no trouble imagining what Lincoln would do if alive on February 12, 1944:

> Can anyone doubt that if Lincoln were here those heavy lines in his so troubled face would be deeper than ever, the inner glow in his moving eyes more intense, his whole aspect more tragic? . . . Where have we a leader today similarly bowed down by the weight of an overwhelming responsibility, by the insupportable duty of decisions which may mean one hundred thousand, two hundred thousand, three hundred thousand young American lives? Where is there an outstanding American politician who has voiced one single word of compassion, of grief, of inner suffering for the bereavements on every hand?[59]

Villard recovered for the nation at war an image that had become powerful during the Great Depression: Lincoln, the compassionate Man of the People.

World War II ended in August 1945, but moving from war to peace, in certain respects, is as difficult as mobilizing a peacetime society for war. It is hard to stop fighting, hard to stop thinking about survival and begin thinking about living, for war fastens all material and psychological resources on one point: the enemy and the necessity of defeating him. Yet, commitment to war must give way to civil pursuits if victory is to have meaning. In 1945, new images of Abraham Lincoln framed demobilization. One of these pictures (which evokes a sense of the sacred by its resemblance to an illuminated manuscript) reproduces the last sentence of Lincoln's second inaugural address, which concludes with the call to "bind up the nation's wounds; to care for him who shall have borne the battle, and for his widow and his orphan—to do all which may achieve and cherish a just and a lasting peace, among ourselves, and with all nations" (fig. 2.14). The word "victory" on the print's left margin is interpreted by highly detailed integrative symbolism: insignias of the various military services, flags of the allies, emblems of Christianity and Judaism. On the lower right, four fighting men, including a wounded soldier on crutches, salute the slogan "Peace on earth to men of good will," to which an angel of peace adds "and all good people everywhere." In the extreme lower right-hand corner appears a widow with black armband and fatherless children. On the upper left, diagonally opposite the widow and orphans, is the encompassing visage of Abraham Lincoln.[60]

Lincoln's image tells viewers how to feel about the war's ending, how to make sense of its outcome, how to come to terms with it. Many who

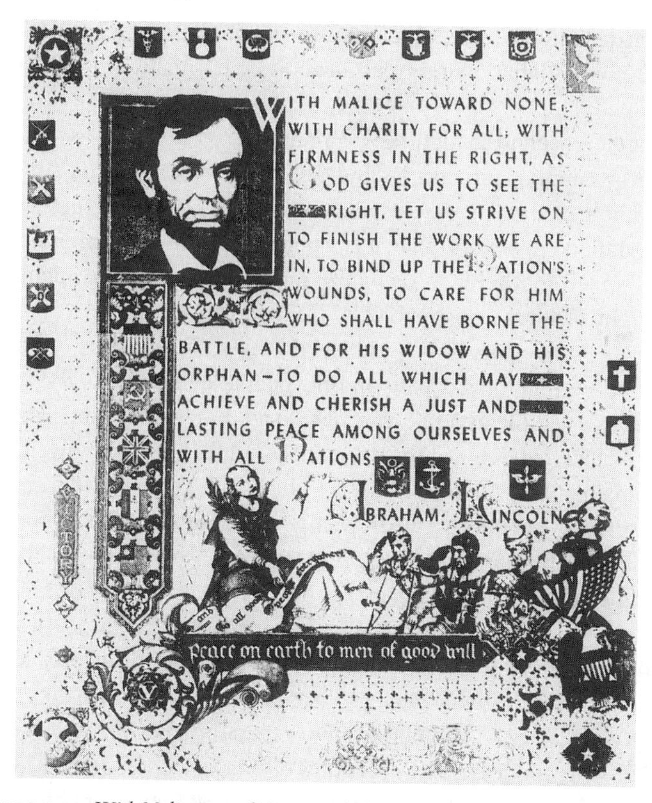

FIGURE 2.14. *With Malice toward None,* 1945 The Abraham Lincoln Museum, Harrogate, TN. Photo courtesy of the Abraham Lincoln Museum.

cherish peace also crave, at some fundamental level, to go on fighting until all motives for fighting are exhausted. On Lincoln is projected the mixed feelings, the ambivalence, for all to see and, by seeing, to resolve. Abraham Lincoln's determination to save the nation and wish to heal the nation modeled the transition from the emotional simplicity of war to the complex realities of peace.

Many thought about this moral and emotional transition and adopted Lincoln to proclaim it. On February 23, 1945, the churches of Statesville, North Carolina, placed an announcement, sponsored by ten local businesses, in the *Statesville Daily Record:*

> Forgiveness is not a matter of easy sentimentalism, or appeasement of evil minded aggressors or men of violence, but neither is it a matter of vindictiveness or violence. . . . Lincoln expressed the spirit of it beautifully and efficiently in his great postwar message of 'malice toward none,' but Lincoln was a realist who never compromised with what he considered to be wrong.[61]

Lincoln delivered his second inaugural message while fighting still raged, but his point is what matters: preparation for normalcy is as difficult as it is essential.

Lincoln's second inaugural was remembered not only as a call for the forgiveness of adversaries but also compassion for the suffering of all one's countrymen. Compassion, however, is more than a wish to alleviate compatriots' pain; it is a political sentiment, different from pity. To pity another is to recognize misfortune, as a king might ease the plight of his poorest subjects. Compassion, as its derivation implies (< L *com*—together + *pati*—to feel, suffer) means "to suffer together"—something a king and his people cannot do. "The nobleman," observed Alexis de Tocqueville, "held that his duty and his honor required him to defend, at the risk of his own life, those who dwelt upon his domains," but "he held himself to be a different nature from that of his serfs. . . . Aristocrats acknowledge none but the members of their own caste to be like themselves."[62] Democratic societies are different: "servants are not only equal among themselves, but it may be said that they are, in some sort, the equals of their masters."[63] In politics, too, democratic elites recognize the suffering of their constituents by identifying with them. Nothing conveys Tocqueville's insights into the culture of postwar American democracy better than the Man of Sorrows—the head of state mourning the casualties of battle. Depression and world war made the compassion of the state more real than ever before, and in this context Lincoln's compassion had emerged as his relevant trait, transcending his role as Savior of the Union and Emancipator. As Lincoln's compassion and toughness fused, Carl Sandburg saw the man of "steel and velvet, hard as rock and soft as drifting fog, who holds in his heart and mind the paradox of terrible storm and peace unspeakable and perfect."[64]

DYING IN LINCOLN'S SHADOW

The people of America need a leader for present and past alike.[65] Franklin Roosevelt was the newest leader, and it seemed natural to connect his death to Lincoln's. Roosevelt had so often invoked Lincoln, was so often coupled with him by artists and commentators, that the two began to merge. In spring 1945, Roosevelt died, and Archibald MacLeish threaded the two losses together:

> Now there is another April. Now there is new grief and new remembrance. Now it is not to the old that the lilacs speak in the April dooryards: not to the old alone. Each of us has his image of this other April—the messenger's face in the office door with the frightened eyes

> behind the spectacles, every feature remembered forever; the terrible, not to be forgotten words. . . . We remember the marching troops in the streets beneath the new-leaved trees, the caisson with its folded flag, the music dying out, the silence. We will think of these things for a long time. Those who are children now will remember this.
>
> We did not know we would weep so for him. We did not know we would stand in the spring sun or at evening by the railroad tracks or along the streets where they would bring him. We did not know we would sit in our chairs, at our desks, our hands still. There were many who loved him, but even those who loved him did not know.[66]

April 1865. April 1945. Everyone saw the connection. Letters to the editors described it[67] and officials brooded over it. Commemorating the anniversary of Lincoln's death, Dr. M. L. Wilson of the Agriculture Department delivered a memorial address at Ford's Theater, where Lincoln was shot. Abraham Lincoln and Franklin Roosevelt alike, he said, overcame severe handicaps: Roosevelt conquered paralysis; Lincoln, poverty. Their manner of service revealed a common and "deep sympathy for humanity, for all humanity, regardless of race, creed, or color." Dr. Wilson emphasized his point. "I think both men were in this respect different from most men . . . they were always ready with understanding sympathy to assist the troubled, the sick, and the insecure."[68] Wilson's words extended beyond Lincoln and Roosevelt. In the aftermath of economic depression and world war, something new had occurred: compassion for all people became the defining quality of presidential greatness—a new way of thinking about past as well as future presidents. Had Roosevelt lived until Japan surrendered, the (Alabama) *Cullman Banner*'s editor believed, he would have delivered a new version of Lincoln's second inaugural address, written "with malice toward none, with charity for all."[69]

LINCOLN AND WASHINGTON

Franklin Roosevelt was elected president four times. He led the country through a decade-long depression, a world war, and he enlarged the government. Roosevelt was the first man in the public mind to equal Lincoln and Washington, but he could never stand with one apart from the other. Washington and Lincoln were then too closely connected. Ten days after the British honored Lincoln near Westminster Abbey in London, they honored Washington at his ancestral home in Sulgrave. Ten days after New York City veterans formed around the Union Square statue of Lincoln, they reassembled around the statue of Washington near Wall Street. Ten days after President Franklin Roosevelt placed a wreath at the Lincoln Memorial, he placed another at the Washington Monument or at Washington's Mount Vernon tomb.

Throughout the war, Washington and Lincoln were central characters in America's story,[70] but their significance differed. Given the war's exigencies, many Americans believed that Washington, not Lincoln, should be the nation's model. Several weeks after Pearl Harbor, Thomas C. Hart, distinguished admiral and future Connecticut Republican senator, contemplated General Washington's eight years as commander in chief, his defiance of a powerful enemy, his fortitude in the face of terrible defeats. The admiral concluded: "in its dark hours a nation needs most the old-fashioned qualities of honesty and integrity, courage and self-control, industry and perseverance, simplicity of mind and heart. We have need today of a return to a simpler, sterner way of life."[71] Washington's wartime responsibilities might well have been more demanding than Lincoln's, but Admiral Hart was projecting eighteenth-century military values upon mid-twentieth-century culture. The Gallup Poll, on February 3–8, 1945, asked a national sample "Who do you think was the greater—George Washington or Abraham Lincoln?" Twenty-eight percent believed the two men were equally great; 42 percent believed Lincoln was the greater; 22 percent, Washington.[72] Patriotic music-writers produced far more songs about Lincoln than about Washington, while OWI posters and illustrations invoked Lincoln more often than Washington.[73]

The more egalitarian American culture became, the more George Washington's admirers began to talk about his concern for the well being of the common people. Washington's "democratization" had in fact proceeded steadily through the late nineteenth and early twentieth centuries,[74] but by 1945 new attitudes were ascribed to him, notably a compassion for wounded soldiers and hatred of racial and religious bigotry. A significant turnabout had occurred. In the mid-nineteenth century, Lincoln's admirers ascribed to him Washington's traits; in the mid-twentieth century, Washington's admirers looked to their hero and found Lincoln.

CLOSING RANKS

As the fight against Germany and Japan intensified, political power became more centralized and the presidency evolved from an executive agency into an almost ethereal office; the image of its incumbent, Franklin Roosevelt, assumed new dimensions for his admirers. "The World may sleep but God will keep him safe when the shadows fall," assured the lyrics of "God Bless Our President" (1942).[75] "God will keep him safe" is the presidency's ultimate legitimation. The presidency grew amid invocations of tradition, including patriot songs whose sheet-music covers feature Franklin Roosevelt's countenance backgrounded by George Washington's and Abraham Lincoln's. According to one such song, "Washington and Lincoln would tell us what to do. They would say: Protect the freedom we made possible for you."[76] Matching Roosevelt's image with Lincoln's and Washington's formed an ideal wherein people and state become two aspects of the same reality.[77]

The people and the state summoned Lincoln to justify war policy, inspire solidarity against powerful enemies, sanctify the war dead, and assuage grief. This Lincoln, however, differed from the Lincoln that Americans once knew. From 1865 to 1930 there had always been two sides to him: a history-making man who saved the Union and freed the slaves, and a self-made frontier-bred man of the people. By the end of World War II, the two lineaments remained, but their dualism had begun to disappear. Lincoln's gentleness assumed epic dimensions as it humanized his historic achievements.

It seemed inevitable, in hindsight, that a man of steel and velvet should loom larger during America's most critical years. The Depression raised the question of whether American capitalism would survive; German and Japanese military challenges raised the question of whether American democracy would survive. Roosevelt was aware of the "calamity howlers," "fear mongers," and "appeasers" who believed that democracy was "outworn," "decadent," and "effete,"[78] but he consistently invoked the most resilient symbol of democracy, Lincoln, to answer their claims. Roosevelt was no different from hundreds of other leaders who told stories about Lincoln during these days. Doing so, he raised Lincoln's prestige to its apogee. The salutary influence of national calamity, Emile Durkheim said, "is due not to the crisis but to the struggles it occasions. As they force men to close ranks and confront the common danger, the individual thinks less of himself and more of the common cause."[79] It must be emphasized that the war did not cause people to agree on Lincoln's greatness. The 1945 NORC survey (appendix B) shows no more agreement on Lincoln along the lines of race, education, region, and party identification during the war than afterward (as later surveys will show); however, the wartime Lincoln never symbolized these divisions; competing parties and interests never used him to reinforce their position or to gain advantage over opponents, as they did in the 1930s and would again in the early 1950s. Depression-era Republicans rarely assumed that Lincoln stood for the same things as Roosevelt; during World War II, they found this assumption was more plausible—or, at least, less objectionable. In short, Americans turned to Lincoln in time of war because of their attachment to the values he symbolized. Lincoln's invocation did not create but presupposed this agreement. His prestige, although differing across the nation, expressed a consensus forged by shared trauma and aspiration. Americans at war reached back to Lincoln to grasp the meaning of the most tremendous undertaking in history. That undertaking ended, however, in August 1945. Never would Americans feel so deeply about Lincoln again. The last heroic generation was about to pass into history.

* 3 *

Transition

COLD WAR, RACIAL CONFLICT, AND CONTESTED IMAGES OF LINCOLN

As Adolph Hitler armed Germany, anthropologist Roger Callois pondered the nature of the war that he and his French countrymen awaited. It would be like a primitive festival, he thought, when the society assembles for a *corrobori*. In its effervescence, people become delirious, know holiness, and see god. The festival, in Callois's words, is the paroxysm of primitive society. In modern societies, many events simulate the festival's convulsive effect, but only war can duplicate it. War is the paroxysm of modernity. Psychologically, festival and war make for an opposition as absolute as joy and terror; sociologically, they express one and the same state. "War, no less than festival," said Callois, "is a sacred time, the period of divine epiphany."[1] Observing Newburyport, Massachusetts, during World War II, American anthropologist Lloyd Warner concluded on an equally positive note: many people derive more satisfaction from war than any other national event. War—all-out war—makes everyone a participant in history and produces "a feeling of unconscious well being—a euphoria—because everyone [is] doing something to help in the common desperate enterprise."[2]

War crystallizes national identity by stimulating the production of national symbols. After 1918, when the divine epiphany of World War I ended, American cities erected monuments to their sons who had served and died. The war itself was fought against a background of intense nationalism, at a time when "Hyphenated Americanism" was condemned and "One Hundred Percent Americanism," pure patriotism, demanded. As assimilated second-generation immigrants replaced their forebears before World War II, such sentiments waned. The binge of monument-making that followed World War I did not repeat itself after World War II. Moreover, the patriotic feeling once associated with Lincoln became free-floating, reattaching itself to contemporary entertainers, athletes, politicians, and presidents. Rather than a liberation from feeling, the inability to focus feeling on any but immediately present objects marked a new era and a new way of thinking about the past.

In 1950, eighty-five years after his death, Abraham Lincoln was still present; but he had changed. What was said and not said about him bespoke a new kind of depthlessness, for the larger, transcendent reality Lincoln once embodied had shrunk as Lincoln himself assumed a new mien.

No depthlessness, no shrinkages, no change in the old mien could be discerned on the surface. New events had in fact made Lincoln almost as visible as he had been during World War II. Just as anti-segregation measures were associated with Lincoln's memory during the late 1930s and early 1940s, civil rights activists of the 1950s and early 1960s invoked Lincoln to articulate the full significance of the 1954 *Brown vs. Board of Education* decision. For the South, the African American, and the nation as a whole, this Supreme Court ruling was the most important event since the Emancipation Proclamation.[3] Lincoln's name attached itself to innumerable civil rights events across the land. After the formal announcement of the *Brown* decision, African Americans joined together at the Lincoln Memorial for a rally of thanksgiving. On May 16, 1957, Martin Luther King, still a Montgomery, Alabama, pastor, appeared at the Lincoln Memorial to speak to an integration rally. In Hammond, Indiana, the annual high school oratory contest was won by a student who argued persuasively that the Emancipation Proclamation was a precursor to racial integration.[4] Three years later, for Emancipation Day, King prepared a statement declaring that the Gods of Justice had given President John Kennedy the duty to end segregation.[5] Lincoln's connection to the contemporary meaning of civil rights was in the air.

The average white American may or may not have seen Lincoln's freeing the slaves as a warrant for racial integration, but integration talk somehow reminded them of Lincoln, and the volume of statistical indicators attesting to his prestige was thick and consistent. The number of Lincoln articles listed in the *Readers Guide* was almost the same in the period 1945–61 (25 per year) as it had been in 1941–45 (26 per year). Between 1940 and 1944, the *Times* printed an average of 43 Lincoln articles per year; between 1945 and 1959, also 43 articles. The *Congressional Record* shows a definite increase in Lincoln entries—from 27 per year between 1940 and 1944 to 44 per year between 1945 and 1959. In magazines, newspapers, and Congressional references, Lincoln receives a constant or increasing amount of attention.[6]

Lincoln's standing was also evidenced by the Gallup Poll. In 1948, Gallup asked a national sample, "With which person in American history would you pick to sit down and have a talk?" Twenty-nine percent selected Lincoln, 12 percent Franklin Roosevelt, and 11 percent George Washington.[7] A year later, Gallup asked a comparable sample, "Who would you say was the greatest statesman, or political figure, in United States history—past or present?" Franklin Roosevelt was selected by 29 percent of the respondents, Abraham Lincoln by 25 percent, George Washington (again the third-place choice) by 7 percent.[8] In 1951, Gallup sampled people listed in *Who's Who in America*: "From your own personal point of view, which president of the United States would you regard as the greatest?" Most respondents—45 percent—named Lincoln; 19 percent named Washington; 7 percent, Roosevelt.[9]

At the end of Eisenhower's first term in office (1956), the Gallup Poll asked Americans to name the three greatest presidents in history. Lincoln was placed among the top three by 62 percent of the respondents, Franklin Roosevelt by 64 percent, and George Washington by 47 percent. The popular incumbent, Dwight Eisenhower, named by 34 percent of the sample, occupied fourth place.[10] In the late 1950s, the Gallup Poll asked a nationwide sample of adults: "If you could invite any three famous persons in history—from the present or past—to your home for dinner, which three would you most like to have?" The first choice, according to frequency of mention, was Abraham Lincoln; second, Franklin Roosevelt; third, Dwight Eisenhower; and fourth, George Washington.[11]

Two exceptions to Lincoln's high repute, however, must be noted. People were not reading Lincoln books as often as they used to. According to WorldCat, Lincoln book production dropped from an annual 153 books during the 1930s and 155 during the first half of the 1940s (World War II) to 133 during the last half of the 1940s and 131 during the 1950s. Jay Monaghan's Lincoln bibliography, drawn from the Illinois State Historical Library, also shows a post–World War II decline in the publication of Lincoln books. Since Monaghan includes very short publications, typically eulogies, there can be no precise comparison between his and the WorldCat collection, but the trend lines are similar. The New York Public Library's Lincoln collection, however, conforms to WorldCat, showing a reduced volume of academic Lincoln publications after World War II. When grouped into five-year intervals, 42 and 39 publications appear for 1930–34 and 1935–39 respectively. Between 1940 and 1944 the number of books acquired was 42. In the postwar years a sharp drop occurs: 29 publications between 1945 and 1949; 28 and 27 between 1950–54 and 1955–59 respectively.[12]

Secondly, Lincoln's visual portrayal indicated his diminished stature. Images common during the first half of the century—pictures of people looking up at pictures of Lincoln, or Lincoln looking down upon the people as a source of guidance and inspiration—are seldom to be found. Rarely does Lincoln's picture appear on the front page of February 12 newspaper editions. The rich iconography of the Depression and World War II disappears after 1945 and never reappears—not even during the Korean War. Unlike the "chambered nautilus," that snail-like creature in whose successively outgrown and discarded shells Oliver Wendell Holmes saw the ennobling of his own soul, Abraham Lincoln's commemoration has become successively narrower, mundane, cramped, and common—like a shell still intact after being washed ashore, but emptied of its living contents. When individuals no longer seize upon images of Lincoln to adorn the walls of their home, no longer place them in their family Bibles and in scrapbooks, no longer see them featured in newspapers, magazines, stage, and screen, we know something has changed.

Postwar Lincoln legacies were continuations of threads laid down during the Progressive Era and New Deal, but temporarily broken during World War II. Blacks and whites had always seen Lincoln differently, but now that difference was accompanied by a massive civil rights movement with which a large portion of the white population sympathized. Conservatives and liberals had always seen Lincoln differently, but now that difference was accompanied by a New Deal legacy of regulation and centralized government, not to mention aggressive socialist states threatening to bury the capitalist order that made Lincoln's self-reliance so relevant for so long. Southerners and non-Southerners had always seen Lincoln differently, but now that difference was intensified by movement against a Jim Crow caste system that had been in place for more than sixty years. The postwar Lincoln thus embodied the amplification of prewar tensions whose reconciliation had become imperative. Race relations and segregation had moved beyond the talking point; the merit of free markets, under domestic criticism and foreign reproach, could no longer be taken for granted. Never before had Lincoln been used so transparently for so many self-serving purposes. Earlier generations keyed their interests and their conduct to Lincoln unwittingly because they identified with him; this generation did so deliberately for the sake of utilitarian advantage.

Crisis

Fear of the annihilation of the world, police actions abroad, and a civil rights movement and internal fragmentation at home—these provided new contexts for thinking about Lincoln. Times of "unbelief, distress, perplexity" were, for Thomas Carlyle, like "dry, dead fuel, waiting for the lightning out of Heaven that shall kindle it. The great man, with his free force directly out of God's hand, is the lightning."[13] World War II was undoubtedly a time of "unbelief, distress, perplexity," but could the same be said for postwar struggles?

"I cannot tell you when or where the [nuclear] attack will come or that it will come at all," announced President Harry Truman. "I can only remind you that we must be ready when it does come."[14] In 1955, two years after Truman left office, almost 75 percent of Gallup poll respondents believed another war would probably occur during their lifetimes, and if it should be nuclear, 27 percent believed, the world would be destroyed.[15] Soviet power made calamity plausible. Four out of five Americans believed that Russian leaders wished to conquer the world and that no peace treaty would inhibit them. Three Americans out of five believed that Communists were trying to infiltrate the United States government and subvert it from within.[16] The postwar years and cold war years were among the most frightening in American history.[17]

Cold war fears[18] kept alive World War II moods and memories. "[P]atriotism was basically 'in' and cynicism was 'out,'" according to Michael Kammen, "for more than fifteen years following the end of [World War II]."[19] During these years, history textbook prefaces commonly made known their authors' love for the "American way of life." Visits to historical shrines increased (see chapter 5), and the word "pilgrimage" was commonly used to describe them. For those who could not get away, the Freedom Train (expressly designed as a bulwark against Soviet communism) carried throughout the land sacred relics of the nation's past. The federal government enlarged its role as superintendent of national memory, and the phrase "Our American Heritage" came into common usage.

To characterize the mood of the country solely by its trepidations and nationalistic impulses is to produce an incomplete picture. Amid fears of war with the Soviet Union,[20] two ideological forces existed: a negative one resulting from intellectuals' suspicion of the masses, the state, and the corporations exploiting them, and a positive belief, exemplified by conservative spokesmen like Henry Luce, founder and publisher of *Time, Life,* and *Fortune* magazines, that America's unique mission is to be a moral force for the world. "The American Century," ushered in by victory over fascism, "must be a sharing with all people of our Bill of Rights, our Declaration of Independence, our Constitution, our magnificent industrial products, our technical skill. . . . Our vision of America as a world power includes a passionate devotion to great American ideals, a love of freedom, a feeling for the equality of opportunity, a tradition of self-reliance and independence."[21]

Boosted by a late 1940s and early 1950s economic expansion that justified Luce's statement,[22] Lincoln Day turned evangelical: during every celebration, American offices abroad conducted ceremonies, presented films and lectures, and held receptions in host countries. These presentations of our national identity made Lincoln, for the first time, a major political export. The Abraham Lincoln Sesquicentennial Commission's Committee on International Participation sent Lincoln scholars on lecture tours around the world and distributed *The Collected Works of Abraham Lincoln* to every nation "so that his philosophy and ideas might be better understood and remembered."[23] The United States Information Agency, Voice of America, and Radio Free Europe helped to spread the word. In the Commission's last act, chairman John Sherman Cooper reported to Congress: "Lincoln is truly the symbol of the Free Man and as you read these pages, I am sure, you will be aware of his world-wide influence on freedom-loving peoples everywhere."[24]

Believing that Lincoln's prestige was growing abroad, Americans grew more confident in their ability to win the war for men's minds. They knew that any nation admiring Lincoln was out of communism's reach. This is why representative Clyde Doyle, California Democrat, made such a fuss over an Ecuadorian foundation's presenting a bust of Lincoln to the Lincoln Museum of Washington DC,[25] and why newspapers and magazines gave such generous coverage to the dedication of statues and naming of streets for Lincoln in foreign countries.[26] Such events may seem trivial today, but in the middle of the cold war Lincoln's image was a tracking device marking progress in the ideological struggle against the Soviet Union. Thus, Herbert Mitgang performed a great service by informing the public that Sun Yat-sen, first president of modern China, used the Gettysburg Address to formulate his theory of government, that President Sukarno of Indonesia declared Lincoln to be one of his major teachers, and in the midst of his country's revolt against the Soviet Union a Hungarian freedom fighter read the Gettysburg Address over the radio.[27]

President Eisenhower, as if to underscore Mitgang's observations, began his Lincoln sesquicentennial speech by asserting that the Great Emancipator "belongs to all humanity." Indian Prime Minister Nehru, he revealed, keeps a casting of Lincoln's hand on his desk; the city of New Delhi, India, made plans to establish a museum in Lincoln's honor; students of a Tokyo, Japan, high school ranked him the most admirable national leader.[28] During this same sesquicentennial, Carl Sandburg told Congress that "The people of many other countries take Lincoln now for their own."[29] Newspapers reported that other countries were, indeed, making commemorative stamps, busts, and statuettes, planting trees, and laying wreaths in honor of the sesquicentennial. No one did more to clarify the solemnity of these events than West Berlin mayor Willy Brandt. Standing in front of a poster bearing Lincoln's slogan, "A House Divided against Itself Cannot Stand," he recognized the sesquicentennial's global significance. The "truths which Lincoln spoke here in Springfield," Brandt said, are "even more applicable to the present situation of the German people than to the one he faced." He noted that Berlin, like the United States in 1861–65, was divided; he drew quotations from the Gettysburg Address to justify sacrifice for the sake of freedom.[30] The cold war, he implied, might turn hot.

Through the early 1960s, federal officials, still concerned about the country's influence abroad, measured it by reactions to Lincoln. He was a light to a world menaced by communism. Secretary of state Dean Rusk noted that the Vatican's delegate to the United States had described Lincoln's Gettysburg address as "one of the greatest documents ever issued by man." Visitors to the Lincoln Memorial, he added, include "tens of thousands from abroad. . . . Thus Lincoln is a worldwide symbol of freedom and democracy."[31] Republican representative Usher Burdick of North Dakota, a local historian and "Prairie Populist," explained that "The name of Lincoln did not dim at territorial lines, but went on and on throughout the world where people were struggling for freedom."[32] Who else but Lincoln, asked businessman Herman Blum, could persuade Gandhi to oppose British tyranny, or inspire revolts against dictators Rhee in Korea and Menderes in Turkey?[33] Never before had Lincoln's international image been attributed so much influence.

Communism, Free Markets, and "Slavery"

On November 19, 1960, about halfway between the ending of the Lincoln sesquicentennial and beginning of the Civil War centennial, Mrs. H. B. Sancomb wrote a letter to General Ulysses Grant III, chairman of the Centennial Commission. She wanted him to know about the day her mother met Abraham Lincoln:

> Although my married name is Sancomb, I like it particularly because it was my mother's, also. At the age of fifteen, her father, Charles Sancomb, took her to Plattsburgh or Ogdensburgh (I never knew which or I must have forgotten which it was) to see the [future] President who was due to stop there. Looking at the black-haired girl who held my grandfather's hand, he spoke. Mother could remember only ONE thing regarding that day . . . President Lincoln placed a big, boney hand on her head! To her dying day she said she could feel it stroking her hair![34]

Assuming a birth date of 1870 (when her mother was thirty years old), Mrs. Sancomb must have been near ninety when she wrote her letter. As one of the last survivors of the generation that had shaped Lincoln's image for the twentieth century, her death would symbolize a break with the past. Through family stories, Mrs. Sancomb's grandchildren might know something of the world she knew, but not so vividly as her own children. Her great-grandchildren would know it only from their history books. Since life expectancy makes grandparents the oldest predecessors with whom most people have sustained contact, their gradual passing during the late 1940s and 1950s constituted a generational break: afterward no one could claim a family member or friend to have been a contemporary of Lincoln. The Lincoln text had replaced the Lincoln oral tradition.

Nevertheless, new political realities gave Lincoln a cast reminiscent of the decade following World War I. Conservatives successfully used Lincoln in the political realm to support military strength and limits on central government; in the economic realm to support the free market over the regulated market; in the social realm to support states rights as prior to, but not necessarily inconsistent with, civil rights; and in the international realm to support democracy over totalitarian communism.[35] Thus, the Lincoln of the transition years, 1945 to 1960, differed from the Lincoln of the 1930s and early 1940s. Conflicts about Lincoln's historical role began to permeate public discourse. The people and their representatives showed unprecedented interest in his emancipation policy while the soft parts of his folk image—homely background and identification with common people—lost some of their resonance. The internationally oriented, conservative-leaning Lincoln of the fifties differed from the domestically oriented, liberal-leaning Lincoln of the thirties.

In the struggle against the Soviet Union, conservative politicians and commentators redefined many symbols with which Lincoln had been connected. During World War II, Polish patriot Thaddeus Kosciusko and Abraham Lincoln symbolized together the Polish community's fight against fascism; during the 1950s Kosciusko and Lincoln symbolized the resistance of Poland's people to Soviet tyranny.[36] As American conflicts with the Soviet Union widened, old slogans acquired new subjects. In one newspaper cartoon, Stalin, replacing Hitler, reads Lincoln's alleged caution, "You can't fool all of the people all of the time;"[37] in another, Lincoln frowns upon the communist bully, no different from his Nazi predecessor, who covers the eyes of a chained captive to prevent his seeing the Great Emancipator (fig. 3.1).[38] On the Asian front, Lincoln's presence justifies the 7th Fleet positioning itself in the Taiwan Straits after

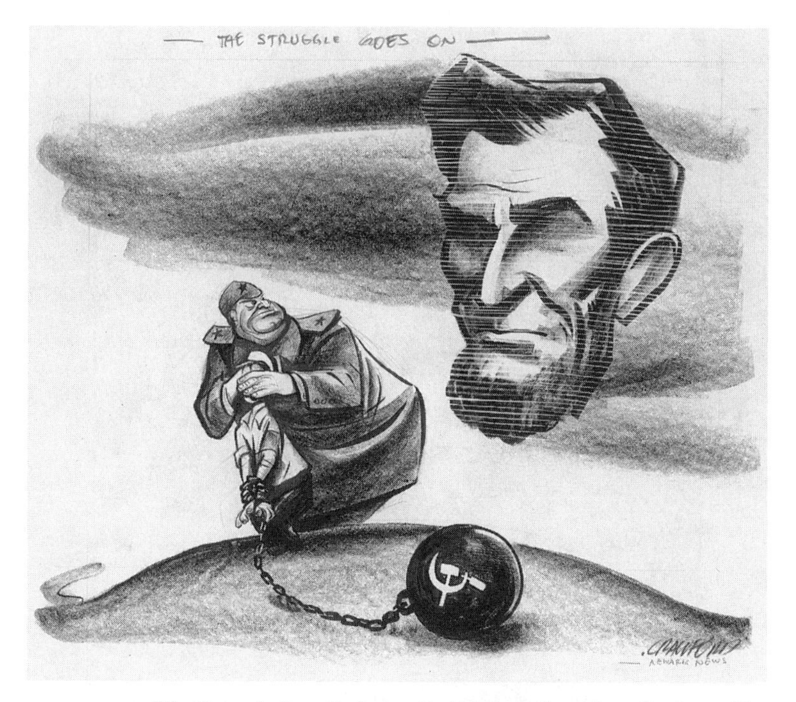

FIGURE 3.1. "The Struggle Goes On," 1955, *Newark News*. From the collections of the Library of Congress.

China's 1954–55 shelling of Quemoy and Matsu. His words: "Freedom Shall Not Perish from This Earth!" (fig. 3.2).

The making of Lincoln into an anti-communist accompanied his new relationship to slavery and emancipation. As early as the Progressive Era, chattel slavery was a metaphor for the oppression of labor and women; during the cold war, a metaphor for Soviet occupation of Eastern Europe. Wisconsin republican Senator Alexander Wiley, a member of the Committee on Foreign Relations, believed Lincoln had asked "Can *mankind* endure half slave and half free?" and he found distinct contemporary parallels:

> We will never be silent in the face of slavery.
> Abraham Lincoln pointed out in the course of his great career that to be silent in the face of evil is to take part in that evil.
> Wherever there is slavery, that is where the conscience of America asks for freedom.
> As once the North could not ignore the moans and suffering of the enslaved Negroes of the South, so today, the peoples of the free world hear the moans and groans from the concentration camps of Siberia,

FREEDOM SHALL NOT PERISH FROM THIS EARTH !

FIGURE 3.2. "Freedom Shall Not Perish from This Earth!" February 12, 1955, *Lowell (MA) Sun/Donald Stone.*

> the forced labor camps everywhere behind the Iron Curtain. We can see in our mind's eye the persecution, the suffering, the torment of the enslaved hundreds of millions.
>
> We will never acquiesce to their permanent enslavement.
>
> As a matter of fact, we oppose slavery in every shape, manner or form—political slavery; economic slavery, intellectual slavery; military slavery.[39]

In his many references to persecution and suffering, however, Senator Wiley never included the burning issue of the day: American racial segregation.

That capitalism and competitive individualism are slavery's solvents was forgotten during the New Deal but recalled after World War II. Senator Wiley's comment on "economic slavery," after all, referred to welfare excesses inhibiting minority progress. New Deal liberals worked hard during the 1930s to portray Lincoln as a friend of the weak and vulnerable, but Lincoln's association with the Republican Party remained strong. In the 1945 NORC survey, 70 percent of Republicans and 53 percent of Democrats named Lincoln as one of the greatest Americans in history. In 1956, 71 percent of Republicans named Lincoln among America's three greatest presidents, compared to 55 percent of Democrats—a difference that cannot be explained by the preferences of Southern Democrats. (See appendix I.)

Conservatives routinely exploited Lincoln's compatibility with the Republican Party's rising fortune. Daniel Reed of New York, toward the end of his forty-one years of continuous service in the House of Representatives, produced a series of vignettes in which Lincoln, George Washington, Thomas Jefferson, and Andrew Jackson meet to discuss the nation's ills. "It seems to me that our people have gone soft since you and I lived on earth," says Lincoln to Washington. "I hope that when the politicians [utter] resounding phrases in our honor that they will remember that we believed in deeds, not talk; in work, not idleness; in self-reliance, not dependency." The focus of Lincoln's complaint is New Deal liberalism; its object, the New Deal network—"the power-mad groups who [*sic*] are striving to make this great free nation a fear-ridden, subservient, dependent-upon-Government mass of cringing, spineless, individuals."[40] The welfare state was not Lincoln's way, and The *Altoona (PA) Tribune* editor went out of his way to prove it by publishing the wise precepts of a self-made man:

> You cannot help the poor by destroying the rich.
> You cannot help the wage earner by pulling down the wage payer.
> You cannot establish sound security on borrowed money.
> You cannot keep out of trouble by spending more than you earn.
> You cannot build character and courage by taking away a man's initiative and his independence.[41]

Lincoln never made these statements,[42] but the editor and his readers believed he did, and their conviction conformed to what they knew about their nation's troubles. Lincoln's cautions against borrowing, as the context of the quote makes clear, apply not only to individuals and households but also to states. And his warnings against attacking the wealthy are meant to preserve national as well as individual freedom, for it is the prospect of becoming rich that makes men self-reliant and ready to oppose tyranny.[43] The free market makes communism tremble because it transforms free men, like Lincoln, into great men. Vice president Richard Nixon thought so. He adored Lincoln. On his thirteenth birthday, his mother gave him a picture of Abraham Lincoln along with a verse from Longfellow about the legacy of great men: "Lives of great men all remind us / We can make our lives sublime, / And, departing, leave behind us / Footprints on the sands of time."[44] Lincoln's legacy was permanent. On February 12, 1956, Nixon extolled Lincoln by condemning the liberals' "obsession for the common and the average" which "must lead the nation to uniformity and mediocrity."[45]

Antistatism and Equality

Sometimes the mediocre man must put the superior man in his place. President Harry S. Truman had brooded long over what to do about his uncontrollable Korean War commander, Douglas MacArthur. MacArthur believed the United States could win the war only by attacking China, and he said so publicly—which reminded Truman of an old Lincoln story about a saddled horse that broke loose, kicked up, and accidentally stuck a foot through its own stirrup. "If you are going to get on," the rider (Lincoln) said (to the horse), "I will get off." The horse was general George McClellan, who believed the president of the United States had no right to give him orders. Truman told the story often to explain the constitutional separation of military and civil powers and to justify his decision to replace MacArthur:

> Lincoln was patient, for that was his nature, but at long last he was compelled to relieve the Union Army's principal commander. And although I gave this difficulty with MacArthur much wearisome thought, I realized that I would have no other choice myself but to relieve the nation's top field commander. . . .[46]

For history-conscious Truman the parallel ran deep. He considered his firing of MacArthur a twentieth-century reenactment of Lincoln's firing of McClellan. For Truman's admirers, too, the parallel was evident. In fact, they regarded Lincoln himself as "Trumanesque."[47]

ABE AND IKE

MacArthur met his second defeat at the hands of Dwight Eisenhower. Military heroes in the same war, Eisenhower and MacArthur had led the list of "America's Most Admired Men" in the late 1940s and were Republican presidential candidates in the same election year (1952). When the Gallup Poll asked Americans to choose between these men for the presidency, however, almost two-thirds chose Eisenhower. Eisenhower, as one observer explained, "is a direct, unpretentious speaker with none of the spur-jangling rhetoric of MacArthur."[48] Like his ideological forebear McClellan, MacArthur seemed "an autocrat born to the purple." Eisenhower not only seemed to others a man of the people; he felt like one himself. Shortly after his election, he painted a portrait of Abraham Lincoln, photographed it, and gave copies to friends as Christmas gifts. By the end of his first presidential term, his friends saw him as the personification of Lincoln.[49]

Eisenhower's populist traits were apparent even in wartime. When militarily threatened, democratic states centralize in order to protect themselves. Administered by egalitarian leaders, however, the centralized state's threat to democracy is diminished. When Eisenhower took control of the allied army in Europe during World War II, people were pleased because he was portrayed as the very model of the ordinary citizen. Stories circulated about the "G.I.'s General" visiting with "the boys" on the evening before the D-Day invasion. Although he commanded "the whole shebang," "Ike" was still the epitome of the common man.[50] "He talked to people like a friend," declared a former soldier under his command. He "was willing to get out and shake hands and talk to soldiers as an equal and a person."[51]

Journalists traced the roots of Eisenhower's egalitarian ways to "pioneer traits" reflecting "his upbringing in rural Kansas." They found "Ike in Abilene and Abilene in Ike." "What Ike is," stated *Time*, "derives from his boyhood in the Abilene, Kansas, of the 1890s" and qualifies him for "a kinship with millions."[52] Symbolically, Abilene was to Eisenhower what Little Pigeon Creek, Indiana, was to Lincoln. When Eisenhower died, it seemed fitting that he be carried from Washington on a funeral train reminiscent of Lincoln's and laid to rest in Abilene, near the modest white frame house where he had spent his childhood. The funeral rhetoric was as plain as the nickname by which Americans knew him. The "last farm boy to rise to national heights," the symbol of a simpler age and of the frontier had come home: "home to the Heartland." "Ike returns to the Heart of America."[53]

Whether Lincoln's life in the Heartland, including his birth in a humble log cabin, his Kentucky childhood, or his fourteen years growing up in Indiana, prepared him for the presidency cannot be known, but these experiences were thought to be necessary to his success.[54] The hard aspects of Lincoln's folk image—self-reliance and individualism—became dominant throughout the 1950s and reinforced Republicans' renewal of their ownership of Lincoln's memory. In one editorial cartoon, the Democratic donkey seems no longer to recognize Lincoln as the rugged individualist; in another, Lincoln exudes the Republican virtues of self-reliance, determination, and the will to succeed. But in other respects, Lincoln was changing.

Since free markets thrive best where power is diffused, conservatives portrayed Lincoln as the ultimate anti-authoritarian. Domestic developments coupled with memories of the war against fascism backgrounded this revision. Shortly after World War II ended, Robert Penn Warren's *All the King's Men*[55] probed the specter of political power gone awry. Social scientists Erich Fromm[56] and Theodore Adorno[57] warned about the psychological bases of deference to all-powerful leaders. Fearing in retrospect Franklin Roosevelt's Depression and wartime power, Americans in 1951 approved the Twenty-Second Amendment, which limited to two the number of terms a president could serve.

Cares about abuse of power determined not only the kinds of virtues Americans attributed to their president, Dwight Eisenhower, but also the values Eisenhower himself publicly embraced. In *Reader's Digest*, he warned against "any needless concentration of power" because it is "a menace to freedom" and, in what was perhaps an obliquely diffident reference to his own stature, he warned against letting "yourself be persuaded [by] any Great Man."[58] While president of Columbia University, Eisenhower expressed the same point in a speech about Abraham Lincoln to high school students. To Lincoln he attributed "the proper attitude toward power":

> [T]here is nothing in Lincoln's writings that could lead any of us to believe that he recognized or believed that he himself was a source of power. He was a director of power, a man who might give it its trend to go somewhere, but he had no ambition to associate the source of power with himself and, thereby, rule others. He served others.[59]

LINCOLN AND LIBERTARIANISM

Although Eisenhower defended the welfare state against conservative extremists, he found the centralized New Deal distasteful and sought to undermine Roosevelt's statist legacy. He had plenty of support. Most conservatives bent Lincoln in the antistatist direction. Political virtue, as they saw it, resides in pluralism: the separation of state, local authority, and market forces. To this code, according to Czechoslovakia-born Karl Stefan, a Nebraska House Republican, Lincoln conformed and, by conforming to it, sustained its legitimacy:

> Lincoln never envisioned farmers being dictated to by Washington bureaucrats.
> Lincoln did not approve of teachers being told what to teach by Washington.
> Lincoln did not advocate telling the people of Nebraska how to run their State, county, and community governments.
> Lincoln did not propose the enslavement of physicians.

> Lincoln did not stand for the binding of merchants by coils of red-tape regulations.
> Lincoln did not support the idea of sending snoopers to pry into the private lives of law-aiding citizens.
> He believed—and he repeated over and over—that the best Federal Government was the least necessary Federal Government.[60]

To turn Lincoln, the nation's strongest president, into a libertarian was a continuing struggle to which conservatives creatively pressed the metaphor of slavery. They discovered how well slavery, which paralleled the condition of Soviet-occupied Europe, applied to the legacy of the New Deal. In a 1946 speech on "Lincoln and the New Slaves," longtime Republican representative and senator Frank Carlson of Kansas asserted, in words reminiscent of Alexis de Tocqueville, that "A type of slavery is returning to the United States in a bloodless revolution, and those who accept dependence upon government and become subservient to governmental dictates are wearing chains of their own forging."[61] Eleven years later, during the early years of the civil rights movement, Karl Mundt found in the Emancipation Proclamation, which "freed men from the shackles of human slavery," the seeds of the modern Republican Party, which "continues the mission of expanding human liberty and of freeing our citizens from the shackles of political power and the exalted, all-embracive centralized government."[62]

Dwight Eisenhower was thinking about the New Deal when he concluded his 1959 sesquicentennial address by quoting Lincoln's strictures against "undue" state expansion.[63] But how are "due" and "undue" expansions to be distinguished in terms of civil rights? Eisenhower faced this issue at Little Rock by forcing the integration of its schools, but he faced it out of obligation, not conviction. His reluctance to intervene against racial segregation, a state matter, reflected the attitude of a large constituency, but did he also represent Lincoln's attitude? The answer to this question is not straightforward, but it will help us clarify Lincoln's transfiguration from a savior of the Union, common man, and emancipator into a civil rights champion.

Civil Rights: Whose Side Was He On?

While civil rights conflicts grew more heated and news of them spread around the world, opinion leaders invoked Lincoln to convey the impression that Americans were living up to their own ideals. This was especially evident during the 1950s, when twenty years of Democratic hegemony ended, and Republican forces, led by moderate Dwight Eisenhower, assumed greater influence. Significant progress in racial equality accompanied by renewed waves of conservatism, fueled in part by the cold war, crystallized new perceptions of Lincoln.

No series of events did more to change Americans' perception of Lincoln and the Civil War than the civil rights movement. President Truman's decision to make civil rights a 1948 campaign issue and President Eisenhower's enforcement of Supreme Court–ordered school integration in Little Rock reflected an inexorable transformation of American life. The South, where modern industry had begun to dominate a heretofore impoverished and oppressive rural society, felt the change acutely. In the 1950s, the first decade in Southern history in which manufacturing employment exceeded agricultural employment, the standard of living increased significantly. Southern family income was one-half the national average in 1940; by the end of the 1950s it had risen to 75 percent and was still growing. In the generation following World War II, the percentage of Southerners living on rural land fell from 55 percent to 15 percent; Two million black Southerners and one and a half million white Southerners left the region for good.[64] As the formerly solid, homogeneous South became a combination of rural and urban culture, of modernity and tradition,[65] existing images of Lincoln as champion of segregation remained relevant but were less persuasive.

Increased education, rising income, and a rising standard of living were equally evident among African Americans. Between 1940 and 1970, the percentage of African Americans in white-collar occupations rose from 5 to 22 percent among men, and 6 to 36 percent among women. Between 1940 and 1960, black poverty dropped from 87 to 47 percent. Professional sports, schools, and the armed forces rapidly integrated. The percentage of Southern blacks registered to vote between 1940 and 1960 rose from 3 to 30 percent; by 1970 it reached 67 percent.[66] The percentage of white people favoring racial integration of schools increased 32 to 65 percent from 1942 to 1963; equal job opportunity, 45 to 85 percent from 1944 to 1963; integrated public transportation, 46 to 79 percent from1942 to 1963. White people who thought blacks should be allowed to live in white neighborhoods also increased significantly.[67] White attitudes changed as hundreds of thousands of African Americans migrated from rural into urban areas, doubling the black population of America's largest cities.

The civil rights revolution drew attention to what has always been the most problematic aspect of Abraham Lincoln's personality—his racial views. Those views had rarely been debated publicly outside the black press, neo-Confederate circles, and the academy, but the widening relevance of race affected the way future generations would think about Lincoln.

Liberals asserted that Lincoln personally favored racial equality, as understood in the late twentieth century. "I am certain," declared Illinois Democrat Charles Melvin Price in the House of Representatives, "that if Lincoln were serving in this body today he would be aligned on the side of the progressive, liberal men who believe in the supremacy of human rights."[68] "Lincoln cannot be quoted on both sides of any question touching humanity," said House Democrat Helen Gehagan Douglas in her comments about racial discrimination, "since we know so clearly where he stood."[69] Carl Sandburg, singing and speaking on Lincoln Day to a sold-out Milwaukee auditorium, criticized Arkansas governor Orval Faubus. The United States, he said, is now a real Union. Governor Faubus doesn't know that yet. "But he's gonna know it."[70]

Mainstream Republicans felt almost the same. When a Miami, Florida, hotel owner refused to accommodate twenty-five blacks at the 1955 state Republican Lincoln Day dinner, 125 white diners walked out. Some remained, but most agreed with the state chairman that "Lincoln would turn over in his grave" if he could have seen what had happened.[71] The chairman's statement implied no preference for total integration but reflected a mellowing of racial attitudes. In Lincoln's day, whites and blacks conducted no party business together, but separatist traditions become more difficult to maintain as racial justice becomes more imperative. After the Supreme Court invalidated school segregation (*Brown vs. the Topeka Board of Education*, decided in 1954 after three years of deliberation), Republicans claimed that the Court's decision would win votes for Eisenhower. Accordingly, vice president Richard Nixon used his 1956 Lincoln Day address to brag that chief justice Earl Warren, the decision's engineer, was an Eisenhower appointee.[72] Doing so, Nixon assumed that Lincoln would have supported the court's decision. That assumption is contestable, but never before, Nixon said, did the Republican party have a better cause to present to the American people. Nixon was probably sincere, for he told a colleague during his presidency that whenever he was faced with a difficult decision, he sat at the table where Lincoln signed the Emancipation Proclamation and prayed for guidance.[73] Richard Nixon's name is not associated with racial justice, as is Lyndon Johnson's or John F. Kennedy's, but his words reflected the views of many Americans who, although unfriendly toward African Americans, embraced the principle upheld in ending segregation.

Yet many moderate Republicans believed the Supreme Court had acted too hastily, and they summoned Lincoln to explain their belief. Moderate Vermont senator George Aiken told his 1956 Lincoln's birthday audience in Ford's Theater that Lincoln "hated slavery but was loath to take drastic action to achieve its end." Senator Clifford Case of

New Jersey, one of the Senate's most progressive Republicans, saw Lincoln in himself. Citing Lincoln's belief in human dignity, he condemned the University of Alabama's rejection of African American students and Virginia's effort to bypass the Supreme Court's *Brown* decision. But Case did not "mean to imply that the problems involved in assuring equality of educational opportunity, equality before the law, equality of economic opportunity are easy and can be solved overnight by the stroke of a pen."[74] Racial segregation, he thought, must be brought to a gradual demise. Aiken, for his part, warned that precipitous action "may conceivably result in greater evils than the one [integrationists] seek to correct."[75] Most Americans probably shared Aiken's and Cases's gradualist views.[76]

Southern Democrats, on the other hand, quoted Lincoln often to legitimate defiance of the Supreme Court's integration order. In particular, governor Orville Faubus of Arkansas and senator Robert Byrd of West Virginia remembered Lincoln's determination to resist the *Dred Scott* decision. That ruling, as Southern leaders recalled it in the late fifties, defined slaves as property of their masters, even when taken into free territories. Lincoln asserted publicly that the decision was wrong, that the Supreme Court is not a sacred institution, and that citizens should challenge its decisions when they consider them unjust. So compelling was the logic of the Southern argument that the *Washington Post*'s editorial writer felt obligated to defer to it, but other liberal commentators reminded Southerners that Lincoln's criticism included a clear statement on the people's obligation to obey court rulings.[77] Such a nicety missed the point. Many Southern leaders who had fought Franklin Roosevelt's battles against the Supreme Court were still active in the 1950s. The passage of time, they believed, had vindicated Roosevelt's contention that the Court was out of step with public opinion, and they were proud that they had supported his efforts to pack it with sympathetic justices. These men and their younger colleagues felt the same way about the *Brown* decision: to oppose *Brown* was in line with American tradition from Lincoln down to Roosevelt.[78]

However, the line separating Republican moderates and Southern Democrats was unambiguous. Southerners believed segregation to be right; they never tired of quoting from Lincoln's fourth debate against Stephen Douglas: "I will say then that I am not, nor ever have been, in favor of bringing about in any way the social and political equality of the white and black races." As Georgia representative Elijah Forrester put it, "Mr. Lincoln was a segregationist, no matter what any wild-eyed leftwinger says."[79] When the Baptist Convention of Texas called on Lincoln to justify its vote to abide by the Supreme Court's decision and integrate the state's schools, opponents explained that Lincoln believed in emancipation, not amalgamation (which was deemed the inevitable consequence of integration).[80] The Capital Citizens Committee of Little Rock, Arkansas, likewise distributed brochures indicating what Lincoln had said about the necessity of segregation.[81] In this connection, governor James Byrnes of South Carolina, speaking to the Illinois Bar Association, recognized segregationists' stake in the revelation of Lincoln's real racial views but was even more impressed by Lincoln's beliefs about the role of majority opinion. He reminded his audience that whether segregation, in Lincoln's words, "accords with justice and sound judgment is not the sole question, if indeed it was any part of it. Universal feeling, whether well or ill founded cannot be safely disregarded." In other words, Lincoln would see segregation retained if the majority of whites wanted it.[82]

Southern newspapers expressed themselves even more bluntly. After federal courts began to enforce school integration in Virginia, the *Richmond News Leader* recalled:

> In one of his many comments in support of Negro colonization, Mr. Lincoln said this: 'There is no room for two distinct races of white men in America, much less for two distinct races of whites and blacks. . . . I can conceive of no greater calamity than the assimilation of the Negro into our social and political life as our equal. . . . We can never attain the ideal union our fathers dreamed, with millions of an alien, inferior race among us, whose assimilation is neither possible nor desirable.'

The *News Leader*'s editor had, in fact, taken this fictional passage from Thomas Dixon's *The Clansman*.[83]

The cold war inflamed passions aroused by civil rights issues. Reactionaries associated civil rights reform with communism and state tyranny. Would it not be a supreme irony, Minnesota Republican, former journalist, Baptist minister, and Kellogg executive August Johansen asked, "if, under the guise of creating alleged social rights, we were to so centralize government . . . that the security of all liberties, including those guaranteed by the Constitution, would be in jeopardy?"[84] Johansen had addressed his rhetorical question to "Illinois's conservative spokesman," Noah Mason. The Wales-born Midwesterner responded affirmatively: this was precisely what was happening in the nation.

Assertions about civil rights leading to tyranny seem outrageous today, but many took them seriously during the cold war. It was not as if a communist takeover was a remote possibility. And who would be in favor of the bill proposing a Federal Equal Opportunity Commission to ensure that government jobs be made available to minorities? Would it not be the liberals and communists, whose causes the black man and the Jew so earnestly embrace? Representative John Elliott Rankin of Mississippi thought so, and while many people dismissed him as a madman, others found truth in his words: "If Abraham Lincoln could come back and read that communistic monstrosity (the Equal Opportunity Commission Bill) . . . and hear his name used in their arguments for its support, he would spurn such a proposition with utter contempt."[85]

Segregationists did not need political extremists to express their understanding of Lincoln; their claims about his racial attitudes were perfectly consistent with postwar historiography. Benjamin Thomas, Donald Riddle, and Reinhard Luthin saw Lincoln not as a moral hero but as a politician who used the slavery issue to enhance his political fortune. James G. Randall, the most influential Lincoln scholar, believed that Lincoln had more in common with Northern Democrats and moderate Southerners than with abolitionists, but was forced into war by his party's radicals.[86] None of these historians endorsed segregation, but their evidence divorced Lincoln from the pro-integration views that race-relations reformists had ascribed to him.[87]

Such claims could not be casually dismissed. In 1952, the Ford Foundation, in an effort to strengthen the moral fiber of the American people in their war against communism, sponsored a series of popular television programs broadcast by CBS under the title of *Omnibus*. James Agee, a lifelong socialist, agreed to write a five-part series on Abraham Lincoln. Agee wrote at the dawn of the Eisenhower era and resurgence of conservativism, a time in which New Deal liberalism struggled to shake off its Depression-era communist and socialist remnants. His Lincoln seems to have reflected this mood, appealing to those who opposed race relations reform as much as to those who supported it. His script, the most beautiful of any Lincoln television drama, contains no reference to race. A proponent of racial justice and writing on the very eve of the civil rights movement, Agee is silent about Lincoln's hatred of slavery. In one scene, in fact, he has Lincoln questioning his teacher: "Who is more unfortunate, the Negra or the Injun?" The teacher responds, "Indians," without correcting Lincoln's pronunciation of Negro. Abe wants a chance to debate the question. He has studied the matter, he explains, and is ready to argue either side of the case.[88]

Former socialist Carl Sandburg also pleased segregationists when he stated that Lincoln's Gettysburg Address was dedicated to Confederate as well as Union soldiers, that Southern soldiers showed great valor, that many Northerners—perhaps 25 percent—agreed with the Confederate cause, that Lincoln realized blacks needed education and believed only intelligent blacks should be allowed to vote.[89] Sandburg made these comments in his 1959 Lincoln sesquicentennial address to a joint session of Congress.

Midcentury Stature

From 1945 through the 1950s a vast change occurred in Lincoln's reputation—from the uncommon common man to the emancipator, the main issue being how, if at all, his emancipation policy foreshadowed the struggle for racial integration in the mid-twentieth century. That the Lincoln of the 1950s was attributed opinions deemed conservative today is less important than the relevance of his racial views growing more important and his prestige diminishing.

In many respects, Americans were saying the same things about Lincoln during the 1950s as they were during the early 1940s, but with different feelings and for different purposes. During World War II, the threat of external enemies muted racial, ethnic, and class divisions. When the war ended, racial and ethnic conflicts resurfaced; so did resentments over the New Deal, fears of an intrusive federal government, and hatred of communism. The new age of disunity led to new uses of history. To assert that Lincoln was more frequently "used" than "invoked" during the cold war–civil rights era captures the essence of two underlying attitudes toward the past. The person who *invokes* Lincoln seeks to affirm the values he shares with his audience. The person who *uses* Lincoln seeks to change the view of an audience whose values differ from his own. During World War II, leaders who believed the same as their followers about their country invoked the same Lincoln. In the fragmented cold war environment, leaders holding different ideas about America used different conceptions of Lincoln to make their arguments. Advocates of strong and weak government, foreign-policy hawks and doves, supporters and opponents of efforts to root out domestic communism, proponents of segregation and members of the civil rights movement—all pressed Lincoln's image to the service of their cause. Cynicism abounded as various constituencies threw Lincoln in one another's faces.

The mood of the World War II years, when people felt a personal stake in the outcome of a struggle that transcended their own interests, could not be revived during the Korean War. Its scale was too small, its setting too international, its stakes too uncertain. Lincoln images saturated February war bond advertisements in the early forties; few appeared during the "police action" of the early fifties. The "forgotten war," as later generations called the Korean War, had no legacy or precedent; that is to say, no past war framed it; none defined its meaning.

Americans who lived through the cold war years encountered a Lincoln as familiar as before and as relevant to the major conflicts of the time, but he embodied more vaguely than ever the sentiments that once unified the American people. No single event captures his diminishing cohesive power as well as the sesquicentennial of his birth. In December 1958, the White House declared 1959 to be "Lincoln Year," while Congress, prodded by the Lincoln Group of the District of Columbia, set up a Sesquicentennial Commission. Chaired by senator John Sherman Cooper and located in the National Archives building, the commission elected William Baringer of the University of Florida its executive director. In consultation with its public relations firm, the commission established contact with such organizations as the National Federation of Republican Women, National Cartoonists Society, National Council of Negro Women, and business organizations such as the John Hancock Mutual Life Insurance Company, American Association of Railroads, International Harvester Company, and National Retail Merchants Association. In every sphere of its work the commission provided a wide range of materials, from "line-a-day fillers" for newspapers to license-plate ideas and materials to aid civic celebration and instruction. The less-than-spectacular festivities culminated in a televised joint session of Congress.[90]

The seven members of Congress's organizing commission, in separate responses to the press, revealed that Lincoln Day 1959 was a "success" because (1) the "warm, all-pervading glow" of Lincoln warmed the people of America and the world; (2) the joint session itself arrested the nation's attention; (3) Carl Sandburg, as a person rather than a writer, pleased everyone; (4) Frederic March gripped his audience with his reading of the Gettysburg Address; (5) the ceremony was carried out with precision and appropriateness; (6) the media covered the event with astounding skill; and (7) radio and television, working together, gave the world a panorama of America and of Lincoln. The commission's idea of why everything went well is worth noting. Two of the seven members referred to the mass media; two referred to the celebrities participating in the affair; two, to the observance itself. One of the seven referred to Lincoln.

The shift from the *invocation* to the *use* of Lincoln manifests itself in the erosion of traditional commemoration. Before the fifteen-year period (1945–59) ending with the sesquicentennial, Lincoln was idealized through rhetorical excess: prints and cartoons depicted Lincoln holding Theodore Roosevelt's hand and pointing him in the true direction, hovering in ethereal splendor behind Woodrow Wilson as he contemplated matters of war and peace, placing his hand on Franklin Roosevelt's shoulder—these forms were conventional before and during World War II. By the end of the 1950s they all but disappeared—not only the forms themselves, but the ideas and emotion associated with them. Postwar observances recognized greatness without revering it, and transformed great men into objects to be contemplated, not embraced; learned about and understood, but not emulated.

Moral Mediocrity

Hero worship arises during times of moral passion and diminishes during times of "moral mediocrity."[91] Members of morally mediocre generations confine themselves to their private worlds, are less mindful of the larger society, feel less of a stake in its past and its future. Every society moves alternately from one phase to another, from moral passion to moral mediocrity, from eras of "collective effervescence" wherein the nation's sacredness is felt and its myths and symbols reaffirmed, to eras in which the presence of sacred myths and symbols recedes. During the 1950s, the United States found itself somewhere between these two states: morally passionate, but less so than it had been; morally mediocre, but less so than it would become.

The cold war kept Lincoln on the commemorative scene: for some he was a nineteenth-century version of Harry Truman and Dwight Eisenhower; for others, Truman and Eisenhower were twentieth-century versions of Lincoln; for most, however, the cold war, although potentially more perilous than World War II, did not promote the kind of crises from which great men arise. World War II, the most cataclysmic of all wars, made the coupling of Lincoln and Roosevelt seem natural; the Korean "police action" and danger of nuclear exchange made the coupling of Lincoln, Truman, and Eisenhower more difficult. War seemed to have lost its capacity to fascinate and enthrall. To reenact Pickett's Charge or watch D-Day on screen was one thing; to contemplate nuclear destruction, another.

Lincoln's presence was felt in new ways because he was represented for new purposes, including the struggle against communism for men's minds. Might his export have been a part of the incipient globalization of postwar societies? If Lincoln, in fact, belongs to the world, can he belong uniquely to America, and if he is not uniquely American can he remain America's emblem?

Domestic forces, too, undermined Lincoln's aura. With the advent of motion pictures, then television, celebrities began to replace great men.[92] Mark Reinhard lists for the 1950s no fewer than twenty-two television dramas in which Lincoln plays an important role,[93] but he does not indicate the number of programs with which these competed. That television has brought into prominence entertainers and athletes whose celebrity has overwhelmed the public's interest in the great figures of history is certain. These celebrities, in many ways inferior to their audience, do the opposite of what great men did. "The celebrity cult," Orrin Klapp observed in 1962, "celebrates the triumph of ordinariness—charm without character, showmanship without ability, bodies without minds, information without wisdom. Hero-worship looks horizontally, even downward, to a 'man like myself.'"[94] Heroes, as Klapp defines them, are no longer great men.

When Klapp asked his respondents to record derisive terms that seemed applicable to Lincoln or which they had heard assigned to Lincoln, they listed: crusader, hayseed, character, do-gooder, roughneck, wisecracker. (To George Washington, in contrast, the terms highbrow, superpatriot, crusader, blue-nose, boy scout, do-gooder were applied. For Franklin Roosevelt, do-gooder, bureaucrat, crusader, glory-hog, bigwig, braintruster, highbrow, diehard, spellbinder.) Everyone was able to assign comic and derisive traits to every great American.[95] The debunking of great men is not an idiosyncratic act; it is a collective act that appears in spurts reflecting vicissitudes in the state of the society. If World War II was the last incarnation of the unity of nation, state, and society, as the previous chapter suggested, the present chapter shows the first stage of breakdown. The era's political fissures are the results, not the causes, of a fraying cultural fabric. The next four chapters show national and state symbols to be receding further from consciousness, not disappearing, but possessing less capacity to articulate the shared experience of the nation, and being called on less often to do so.

* 4 *

Transfiguration

CIVIL RIGHTS MOVEMENT, VANISHING SAVIOR OF THE UNION

With Howard Schuman

No historical reputation fades before the generation exploiting it passes on; no new reputation appears until it becomes relevant to a new generation's concerns. By the turn of the twenty-first century, Abraham Lincoln was a transfigured man. The new Lincoln, champion of racial justice, appeared in textbooks and the media as the civil rights movement formed and matured through the second half of the twentieth century. Securing justice in every sphere of life, from education and employment to housing and use of public facilities, was part of a comprehensive minority rights movement including not only African Americans but also Native Americans, Asians, Hispanics, women, and other groups previously excluded from the full rights of citizenship. These movements prompted formal state and church apologies for wrongdoing, the erection of monuments to victims, and the devotion of textbook space to national crimes against minorities. All these developments provide a context for the emergence of the Lincoln we know today.

History, Commemoration, and Belief

The concept of "reception," applied to collective memory, reflects the way individuals process historical and commemorative statements. "Whether the general run of people read history books or not," Carl Becker observes, "they inevitably picture the past in some fashion or other."[1] Becker's point reiterates Charles Horton Cooley's dictum: the "imaginations which people have of one another are the solid facts of society."[2] The solid facts of memory, likewise, are the imaginations people have of historical events and actors.

Connecting historical texts and commemorative symbols ("facts of representation") to individual understandings of Lincoln's life ("facts of reception"[3]) raises four questions never before posed or addressed: (1) How far, if at all, do individual beliefs about Lincoln deviate from what historians write about him and how artists and ritual organizers represent him? (2) Do these historical and commemorative contents change at the same rate and in the same direction as individual beliefs? (3) How and to what extent do individual beliefs, historical texts, and commemorative representations affect one another? That late twentieth-century social reform affected Lincoln's reputation is widely known. But how and when this transformation occurred, whether or not it was more evident in some parts of the society than others, is less understood. In the present chapter, we measure the amount and quality of change in Lincoln's *reputation*; Chapter 5 deals with the nature and extent of changes in his *prestige*. Chapter 6 explains these changes by showing them to be constituents (not causes or effects) of a cultural transformation in which the commemorative space devoted to ordinary men and women, celebrities, and victims replaces that reserved for great men, and why Lincoln exemplifies this process.

FIVE LINCOLNS

That Merrill Peterson's (1994) *Abraham Lincoln in American Memory* is the most comprehensive chronicle of Lincoln texts and symbolism bears repeating. Incorporating but transcending typologies formed independently by Roy Basler, Dixon Wector, David Donald, and David Potter,[4] Peterson identifies five Lincoln images:

1. "Savior of the Union" refers to actions expressing Lincoln's belief in the indivisibility of the Union.
2. "The Great Emancipator" represents Lincoln's efforts to abolish slavery.
3. "Man of the People" consists of writings and symbols depicting Lincoln's identification with ordinary Americans.
4. "The First American" is Lincoln the frontier youth, symbolized by log cabins and axes, and a personality combining folksiness with dignity, vulgarity with kindness.
5. "The Self-Made Man" shows Lincoln as the exemplification of upward mobility.

Peterson's five Lincolns manifest what Kerwin Klein calls a "structural" perspective on collective memory.[5] Because each image expresses a specific pattern of historical writing and commemoration, Peterson depicts the way generations of historians, commentators, and artists represented Lincoln, not how ordinary individuals thought about him.

Thus, we stand at a turning point. Will our knowledge of Lincoln in American memory be based solely on how historians and artists portray him or will we break through to a new level of inquiry that includes the beliefs of nonscholars. Put differently, will we know Lincoln solely in terms of the "New Structural Memory"—a perspective based on historical texts and commemorative objects—or will we also know him in the minds of average Americans?

LINCOLN IN THE AMERICAN MIND

Popular beliefs about Lincoln reflect the content of texts and commemorative symbols, but popular beliefs also reinterpret texts and reinvigorate symbols. Because responses to questions about Lincoln can be interpreted differently depending on how the questions are framed, more than one approach to measuring beliefs must be taken. The first inquiry will ask a sample of American adults to evaluate Lincoln as a president; the second will ask what they think of Lincoln as a person, including reactions to his pre-presidential life; the third and fourth, how different generations have compared him to another great president. Each inquiry, regardless of differences in question-wording, elicits comparable perceptions.[6] Because these surveys form the basis of understanding beliefs about Lincoln, and because belief is a key element in analyzing Lincoln in American memory—and collective memory more generally—a short discussion of the survey is necessary.

On several occasions beginning in 1956, the Gallup Poll posed the same presidential preference question—"Which three United States presidents do you regard as the greatest?" Gallup's question was also included in a 1999 National Omnibus Random Digit Dial telephone survey carried out through the University of Maryland Survey Research Center. Lincoln was named most often, by 40 percent of the sample.[7] Kennedy was second (35 percent), and the other runners-up were Reagan (25 percent), Washington (24 percent), Franklin Roosevelt (24 percent), and Clinton (22 percent). The naming of further presidents then drops off sharply, with Truman next at 10 percent.

The next step was to assess the primary content of Lincoln's reputation. Five genres of reputation—Savior of the Union, Great Emancipator, Man of the People, First American, and Self-Made Man—have endured since Lincoln's death, but because Peterson did not trace their changing relevance, they must be assumed equal at any given time. To test this null hypothesis, the Maryland sample was divided into those who named Lincoln a great president and those who did not. Interviewers asked the former "Why do you think Abraham Lincoln was one of America's three greatest presidents?" To those who did not name

Lincoln a great president, interviewers asked a parallel question: "Although you did not mention Abraham Lincoln as one of the three greatest presidents, we would like to know what comes to mind when you think of Abraham Lincoln." Both questions included nondirective follow-up probes ("Can you say a little more about that?") to encourage fuller replies. Before combining the two sets of very similar responses,[8] up to two responses to the original questions and up to two follow-up probes were coded, with 40 percent of the respondents providing more than one distinguishable type of response.

In a second survey, carried out through Knowledge Networks between July 13–17, 2001, we asked a different question about what Americans think of Lincoln: "Suppose a nephew or niece about twelve years old had just heard some mention of Abraham Lincoln and asked you to explain what Abraham Lincoln had done. What would you say?" This question is especially appropriate for investigating collective memory because it focuses on what adults recall as most important about Lincoln to communicate to a younger generation. For each respondent, one to three themes were coded.

In sum, respondents answered open questions, expressed their beliefs about Lincoln in their own words, with their responses coded into the categories shown in table 4.1. The two surveys, referred to below as the Maryland and Knowledge surveys, were different in the questions they asked, one focusing on the man and the other on what he had done (with the Maryland survey using two slightly different questions depending on whether Lincoln was initially named or not named as great); in their modes of administration (telephone vs. Internet); in their sample response rates and likely sources of sample bias; in their dates; and in the organizations administering them (appendix C). These differences in question form and sampling, expected to produce some differences in results, showed significant consistencies.

The initial categories were designed to fit the five Peterson themes, but additional categories accommodated other reasons appearing in a preliminary subsample of responses. The "first mentions" columns in table 4.1 report the initial responses given in each survey. Since such answers are mutually exclusive, they add to 100 percent when the miscellaneous "other positive beliefs" are included. The "any mentions" columns allow for coding multiple responses given to a question and thus use all the answers; they are not mutually exclusive because a respondent may have mentioned several codable themes. The two types of coding yield similar patterns, not surprising since the bulk of the "any mentions" are first mentions. "Any mentions" is the focus of discussion below.

TABLE 4.1. Major attributions to Lincoln in two surveys[1]

	Maryland Survey				Knowledge Networks Survey			
	First mention		Any mention[2]		First mention		Any mention[3]	
	N	%	N	%	N	%	N	%
Peterson categories								
1a. Great Emancipator	259	31.8	375	46.1	384	43.9	578	66.3
1b. Equal rights	51	6.3	93	11.4	33	3.7	75	8.6
2. Savior of the Union	26	3.2	54	6.6	72	8.3	124	14.2
3. Folk themes	16	1.9	39	4.8	22	2.5	36	4.1
Additional categories								
4. Moral traits	91	11.1	156	19.2	39	4.5	89	10.2
5. Leadership	48	5.9	79	9.7	47	5.4	89	10.2
6. Negative beliefs	17	2.1	29	3.5	25	2.9	37	4.2
7. Other positive beliefs	307	37.7	-	-	251	28.8	-	-
N	814	100			873	100		

[1] The "don't know" category contained 132 responses in the Knowledge survey and sixty-five cases in the Maryland survey.

[2] The base N for each percentage in the Knowledge survey is 873.

[3] The base N for each percentage in the Maryland survey is 814; in addition, 122 respondents who could not name any president as great were not asked an open question about Lincoln.

Epic Hero. Peterson's five Lincolns constitute "social types"[9] because they are shared through common but not necessarily extensive educational experience. History books and biographies convey full accounts of Lincoln's life and achievements, but few people have the time to develop a full understanding of Lincoln; they carry within their mind fragments of information not complete in themselves let alone well integrated. What is striking about these fragments is that so many people possess the same ones, that they are organized in different minds in similar, coherent, and recognizable ways, and that they vary among different groups meaningfully, according to their respective values and interests.[10]

Before conducting the surveys it seemed the first type, Savior of the Union, would be mentioned most often. Secession is the greatest threat to Union, and no emancipation could occur without successful resistance to secession. Yet, only 6.6 percent and 14.2 percent of the Maryland and Knowledge samples mentioned Lincoln as Savior of the Union. Respondents' phrasing varied. Some said Lincoln saved the Union by preventing its disintegration: "His sole purpose was to preserve the Union"; "He was the only man that held the country together." Others believe Lincoln restored a Union that had already disintegrated: "He united a broken country"; "He brought the divided nation back together again." These are all aspects of "saving the Union."

If Lincoln had freed the slaves without restoring the Union, he would have crippled the country. If he had saved the Union without freeing the slaves (which a prompt Union victory would have ensured), he would have achieved his and his party's war goal. Lincoln preferred the latter outcome, but his army failed him. His Emancipation Proclamation was, in his own words, a "military necessity" following a series of military defeats. Nevertheless, the single most frequent explanation of Lincoln's greatness—46.1 percent in the Maryland survey and 66.3 percent in the Knowledge survey—casts Lincoln as the Great Emancipator. The most common statement is the simplest: "He freed the slaves," with variants ranging from "Slavery was wrong; he got rid of it" and "He fought for the slaves" to "He stuck out his neck to free the slaves."

Coding such "emancipation" responses was straightforward, but many respondents gave answers that went well beyond emancipation, and these called for a separate code, labeled "equal rights." These respondents—11.4 and 8.6 percent in the Maryland and Knowledge surveys respectively—described Lincoln as prophet of contemporary ideals of racial equality, although evidence for Lincoln's embracing such ideals is almost entirely lacking, and considerable evidence exists to the contrary.[11] Typical responses in this category include: "He was somewhat the father of equal rights" and "[h]e tried to ban racism." In some cases this meant the achievement of a universal value—"He fought for civil rights, human rights"; "He realized it wasn't the color of the skin that mattered"—in other cases, a particular value—"He gave equal rights to minorities, specifically the African Americans"; "He addressed black civil rights." Furthermore, if both emancipation and equal rights responses are considered together, fully 57.5 percent of the Maryland survey respondents and 74.9 percent of the Knowledge Network respondents gave one or both as a reason for Lincoln's greatness.

That emancipation, including or excluding the equal rights response, ranks so highly in both the Maryland and Knowledge Network surveys suggests that question wording (emphasizing greatness in the former and how Lincoln acted in the latter) played a minor role in producing the result. Also, question wording cannot explain why, within each survey, the same wording yielded such a great difference in Union and emancipation responses.

Presidential leadership is the other Lincoln attribute commonly linked to epic achievement. In a few cases, this attribute referred to his restoring the Union, but its stress was on Lincoln's leadership skills. "He led the country through difficult times," remarked one respondent. "He understood the big picture," said another. "He had to deal with the worst war the world has ever had." His "vision and knowledge" won the war. Almost 10 percent of the respondents in both the Maryland and Knowledge surveys attributed these qualities to Lincoln. Leadership is associated positively with Savior of the Union in both the Maryland and Knowledge surveys, negatively with the Great Emancipator in the Maryland survey, and essentially zero in the Knowledge survey.[12] Freeing the slaves evidently reflected traits—perhaps moral qualities rather than tactical skills—perceived as having nothing to do with leadership. Even if the leadership and Savior of the Union categories are combined, yielding totals for the Maryland and Knowledge samples of 16.3 percent and 24.2 percent, the percentage in both samples mentioning the Great Emancipator would still be almost three to four times as great. In other words, leadership responses are not given at the expense of Savior of the Union responses.

Folk Hero. Lincoln's earthiness has led some Americans to see his presidential greatness in terms of traits they think he shared with the common people. Their responses reflect the biography and commemorative symbolism of: (1) Man of the People: "He was a common person"; "He understood the people and he was not a rich man. He was poor"; "He was solid, down to earth." (2) First American: "He grew up in a log cabin"; "He would write with charcoal on the floor." (3) Self-Made Man: "He was self-taught"; "He came from the log cabin to the presidency."

Few people answered questions about Lincoln in these terms. If the three sets of answers are combined into a single category called "Folk Image," only 4.8 percent of the Maryland respondents and 4.1 percent of the Knowledge respondents, as table 4.1 shows, fall into it. Perhaps many respondents do think of Lincoln in these terms but do not see them as reasons for "greatness," even when encouraged to give multiple responses. If this were so, however, one would expect a higher percentage of folk responses in the Knowledge Survey, which innocuously asks the respondent to indicate what Lincoln had done, than in the Maryland survey, which specifically asks why Lincoln was great. This was not the case. Edwin Markham's early twentieth-century observation that "[t]he color of the ground was in him, the red earth; / The smack and tang of elemental things" may well have been more meaningful to earlier generations than it is to ours.[13]

Moral Character. Another aspect of reputation, one based on five types of moral attribution, appeared among the responses: (1) honesty; (2)

compassion; (3) bravery; (4) religiosity, and (5) other moral qualities, including fairness, virtue, and strong convictions. These five attributions are infrequent when taken individually, but at least one of the five is mentioned by 19.2 percent of the Maryland respondents and 10.2 percent of the Knowledge respondents. They are not mentioned, however, as a major theme by Peterson.

The last category in table 4.1, "other positive beliefs," includes a wide range of responses, the most common of which are ambiguous phrases including "Civil War" and vague positive responses such as "one of our great presidents," "great man," "decent man," "did important things." Other responses concerned physical appearance, assassination and martyrdom, visual images (painting, statues, profile on the penny), monuments, school lessons, Gettysburg Address, and a few that were wrong but positive (e.g., "father of our country").[14]

In contrast to the volume of positive beliefs about Lincoln, 3.5 percent of the Maryland respondents (entirely from those who had not named Lincoln great) and 4.2 percent of the Knowledge Network respondents expressed negative beliefs about his dishonesty, supposed extramarital sex, indifference to slavery, and the meaninglessness of his Emancipation Proclamation.

HISTORICAL PERIOD

The Maryland and Knowledge Network data reflect American experience at one time, but beliefs change as time passes. Without data from an earlier period one cannot be certain whether the Great Emancipator is more prominent now than before. Since the Maryland and Knowledge Network surveys were administered when minority rights were foremost in the public's mind, we want to know whether different results obtain from surveys administered when racial justice and minority rights were not major public issues.

Respondents from Gallup's wartime survey of January 1945 and from the National Employee Survey carried out shortly after September 11, 2001, provide us with a means of comparison.[15] Lincoln in a racially segregated society can be compared to Lincoln in an integrated society. Eliminating nonemployees from the Gallup survey produced two closely matching samples with no retirees, fulltime housewives, or unemployed. To the 2001 National Employee Survey are attached the two questions posed by Gallup's 1945 interviewers: "Who do you think was the greater man, George Washington or Abraham Lincoln?" and "Why?" The Employee Survey reasons for ranking Lincoln above Washington are coded into categories comparable to those reported by Gallup. (See appendix

D for verbatim description of the Gallup and Employee Survey response codes.)

When the Gallup Poll asked the 1945 sample "Who was the greater president: George Washington or Abraham Lincoln?" 42 percent of the respondents named Lincoln. In 2001, 51 percent of the Employee Survey respondents named Lincoln. In 1945, 22.7 percent named Washington; in 2001, 21.3 percent. The percentage naming both equal in 1945 and 2001 were 27.2 and 20.8 percent.[16] Because Lincoln and Washington have long symbolized the ideals of equality and liberty respectively,[17] the increase in Lincoln's prestige relative to Washington's suggests an expansion of egalitarianism relative to libertarianism in American society.[18]

Between 1945 and 2001, Americans gave different reasons for their rankings, and these enable comparison of the relevance of Merrill Peterson's five Lincolns by historical period. From the 1945 survey only first mentions are available; these are compared to the 2001 first mentions. (For a comparable table showing Employee Survey "any mentions," see appendix E). Like their 1999 Maryland and 2001 Knowledge Network counterparts, the National Employee Survey's 2001 respondents named Lincoln the Great Emancipator (31 percent) more often than Savior of the Union (4.8 percent), and another 5.9 percent mentioned equal rights (table 4.2, note 2). Thus, based on a third sample of contemporary Americans and still different questions about Lincoln, the Employee Survey findings provide further evidence of the Great Emancipator's current cultural power.

The 1945 Gallup survey coded Union and emancipation responses into a single category (possibly because the 1945 coders took for granted the connection between Emancipation and Union). To make the 2001 Employee Survey's Great Emancipator and Savior of the Union responses comparable to Gallup's, they had to be combined into a single category also. Into this combined category, 26.1 percent of the earlier Gallup respondents and 41.7 percent of the Employee Survey respondents fell (table 4.2). In 1945, this combined category probably contained more Union than Great Emancipator responses, but even if the 26.1 percent falling into Gallup's category contained only Emancipator mentions, there would still be fewer such mentions in 1945 than in 2001, when 31 percent named Lincoln the Great Emancipator (table 4.2, note 2). When racial equality responses are included in the 2001 emancipation category (the only category in which they could possibly fit in 1945), the Great Emancipator figure becomes 36.9 percent. If the ratio of emancipation to Union responses were the *same* in 1945 as in 2001, emancipation would have contributed 22 percent to the 1945 total

TABLE 4.2. Reasons for designating Lincoln greater than Washington: Gallup Poll (1945) and National Employee Surveys (2001)[1]

	Gallup Poll 1945 n = 906	National Employee Survey 2001 n = 1366
1. Emancipation, saving the Union[2]	26.1	41.7
2. Humanitarianism, people's president	26.3	4.4
3. Self-made man	23.3	3.1
4. Honesty	1.7	2.0
5. Greater statesman	2.1	11.8
6. Greater problems	7.4	8.4
7. Great communicator	2.1	1.6
8. Washington's shortcomings	1.0	1.4
9. Miscellaneous	10.0	26.0
Total	100.0	100.0

[1] The 1945 percentages are based on an N of 906, which excludes 23 nonresponses. The 2001 percentages are based on an N of 1378, with 104 nonresponses and 45 uninterpretable responses excluded. The numbers in each column add to 100 percent because the Gallup survey data provide one response; the NES results are calculated on first response only. See appendix C for the codes included under the "miscellaneous" category. The Gallup "miscellaneous" codes are unknown.

[2] In the 2001 Employee survey, this category consisted of three separately coded components: saving the Union = 4.8 percent; emancipation = 31.0 percent; equal rights = 5.9 percent.

of 26.1 percent. If the ratio of emancipation to Union responses were *lower* in 1945, which, as the next section will show, is most probable, the difference between the percentage of emancipation responses in 1945 and 2001 would be even more pronounced.

From 1945 to the present, the substance of Lincoln's reputation changed in other, equally important, ways. In the 1999 Maryland and 2001 Knowledge Network samples, few saw Lincoln as a folk hero. The 2001 Employee Survey sample also shows few Folk Hero mentions: only 4.4 percent identified Lincoln as a humanitarian People's President comparable to Peterson's Man of the People; 3.1 percent as a Self-Made Man. In 1945, however, 26.3 percent saw Lincoln as a humanitarian People's President; 23.3 percent identified him as a Self-Made Man.[19] These differences, including differences in Union and emancipation responses, appear in all categories of age, education, gender, race, region, and ideology, and they correspond to distinct differences in generational experience.

As we move backward in time from our environment, one highly sensitive to civil rights, to the 1945 environment, which was not, fewer people saw Lincoln's greatness residing in his emancipator role. Almost all of Gallup's 1945 respondents were born before 1925, when more than half of America's population resided in nonurban places, and more than 25 percent of the labor force was agricultural.[20] One-third of this population was born and reared in the early Jim Crow era—the end of the nineteenth century; most of the rest were their children. Gallup's white forty-five year olds, born in 1900, can be thought of as having participated in the segregated 1909 Lincoln centennial celebrations, learned about Lincoln from Ida Tarbell's populist biographies, admired Lincoln's freeing the slaves but never associated Emancipation with racial equality, and were cheering twenty-two year olds when President Harding dedicated the Lincoln Memorial expressly to North-South—not white-black—reconciliation.

Reared in a society still suffused with the values of the farm and small town, living through a severe, decade-long depression and a world war, people in 1945 saw in Lincoln a multidimensional man—a Savior of the Union and, yes, paternalistic Emancipator, but even more a compassionate Man of the People and Self-Made Man. The 1945 Gallup Poll thus captured the Lincoln of 1930s film, poetry, statuary, and biography (appendix A)—the tough but gentle man, the ordinary man performing extraordinary deeds.

Present perceptions of Lincoln as Emancipator and champion of racial justice differ from perceptions of 1945, but when did the transformation begin? Do data on individual beliefs answer this question differently from historical and commemorative archives? How do new understandings about America's minorities affect ways of seeing Lincoln?

CIVIL WAR, CIVIL RIGHTS, AND THE FIVE LINCOLNS

Three surveys—Maryland, Knowledge Network, and National Employee—present Lincoln as a man whose greatest achievement was not so much to make the nation stronger and greater as to redeem its sins, protect the weakest of its citizens, and change its racial attitudes. In America, white racial attitudes have been moving in a positive direction since World War II,[21] and this shift has aided public acceptance of changes initiated by the courts, the government, and even private organizations like baseball teams. Late twentieth-century minority rights revolutions and race pride movements have accelerated these trends.[22]

A new culture of inclusion, whose emergence most white Americans experienced as a crisis and later accepted ambivalently, coincided with new feelings about America's past and new interpretations of Abraham Lincoln. To find legitimation for the late twentieth-century civil rights revolution, many historians have imposed on Lincoln's Civil War policy a character it never possessed.[23] As a good Republican, Lincoln needed no lessons on the sanctity of freedom; but if he were as progressive, as close to Republican radicals on racial equality as some would like to believe, then these same radicals would have grieved rather than thanked God when the assassin removed him from office.

The new Lincoln is not so much forced upon us from without as demanded from within. "The mind," observed sociologist Charles Horton Cooley, "having energy, must work and requires a guide, a form of thought, to facilitate its working."[24] Abraham Lincoln was "the thought form" facilitating new ways of conceiving equality. In some instances, this new form led to new truths. On February 9, 1960, Illinois representative Roman Pucinski invoked the name of Thaddeus Kosciusko, the Polish officer who fought with Americans in their battle for independence from Great Britain. Because Kosciusko was born on February 12, his name was commonly mentioned on Lincoln Day, but during the civil rights era a new side of his life became relevant. Representative Pucinski explained that Kosciusko abhorred slavery and gave to then president Thomas Jefferson a considerable sum of money to build a school for black children and to buy their freedom.[25]

Emancipation's relevance for progressive politics became apparent during the 1961–65 Civil War centennial. Backgrounded by fierce civil rights struggles in the South, participants in the 1963 Gettysburg Address observance transformed Lincoln's 1863 eulogy for fallen Union soldiers into a plea for racial integration.[26] By the end of the decade, Lincoln had come into view as racial integration's prophet. In a 1968 Star Trek episode, Lincoln's spirit boards a spacecraft and greets its "charming Negress" cordially, comments on the status of blacks during his lifetime, and apologizes to her for "the foolishness of my century." Coincidences of tragedy added successive layers of meaning to Lincoln's new image. *Abraham, Martin and John,* a popular song, first appeared under a sheet-music cover picturing four faces on Mount Rushmore. Abraham Lincoln's face remains on the mountain, but John Kennedy has replaced George Washington while Robert Kennedy and Martin Luther King appear in place of Thomas Jefferson and Theodore Roosevelt (fig. 4.1).[27] Lincoln's martyr image, revitalized by the assassination of progressive leaders—John Kennedy, Robert Kennedy, and Martin Luther King—merged the issues of racial and economic equality. Thus, George McGovern campaigned against Richard Nixon with advertisements showing Lincoln's countenance above the statement: "If he'd known what the GOP would have become, would he have started it?" The GOP had become the party "that virtually no Black American would vote for" and one that "would freeze the wages of the

FIGURE 4.1. *Abraham, Martin and John.* Sam DeVincent Collection of Illustrated American Sheet Music, Archives Center, National Museum of American History, Behring Center, Smithsonian Institution.

average working person while causing business profits to go to record highs."[28] New York governor Mario Cuomo could then claim that "Lincoln's work is not yet done. A century after Lincoln preached his answer of equality and mutual respect, some discrimination—of class or race or sex or ethnicity—as a bar to full participation in America still remains." Unpleasant reminders of earlier times do persist, but McGovern and Cuomo imply that Lincoln, during the heat of war, found time to concern himself with such matters.[29] Two years later, a new television documentary on Lincoln's presidency, *New Birth of Freedom*, narrated by Atlanta mayor Andrew Young, made the same point. Lincoln's war aims, in fact, included neither a poverty-free nor multiracial society, but in the late twentieth century many historians and artists claimed just that. Fourteen years later, Cuomo magnified his initial views in *Why Lincoln Matters*, which ascribes to the sixteenth president definite positions on issues ranging from preemptive war, unilateral political actions, hunger and homelessness, the plight of needy in foreign lands, and a host of other twenty-first-century problems. The measures Lincoln would have adopted in these cases, Cuomo explains, differ vastly from those of sitting president, George W. Bush.

Mario Cuomo's academic admirers do not always welcome challenges to their presentist standpoint. Michael Lind's *What Lincoln Believed: The Values and Convictions of America's Greatest President*, for example, documents Abraham Lincoln's awareness of the many failed attempts to establish democracy in Europe, of the United States' being the only democratic nation in the world, and how Confederate victory would end America's democratic "experiment." Lind argues, further, that Lincoln's conception of emancipation gave black Americans no right to attend the same schools or to live near whites or work next to them; he believed that only black war veterans and intelligent black men deserved the right to vote. Arguing that Abraham Lincoln was no twenty-first-century civil rights advocate, Lind nevertheless believed him to be The Great Democrat. Not only did reviewers attack Lind for failing to recognize Lincoln's radically benign views on racial justice; prominent scholar Richard Norton Smith, then director of the Abraham Lincoln Museum, after declaring that the museum must be judged in terms of its effect on race relations, ordered the bookstore manager to cancel not only Lind's book-signing but also the order for Lind's book.[30]

Smith's and others' reactions to Lynd have been so harsh not because Lynd diminishes Lincoln; on the contrary, the very subtitle of his book defines him as America's greatest president. The problem is that the grounds for greatness, as Lind defines them, are not what twenty-first-century emancipationists consider them to be. In the conventional biography, Lincoln's many unkind references to African Americans are deemed responses to external pressures, including racist beliefs that he must accommodate in order to win office. His sympathetic references and beneficent actions, including emancipation, on the other hand, are said to reflect inner convictions. Lincoln's essence is his love of racial justice; his willingness to subordinate justice to the demands of Union is coincidence. If he were not fundamentally, from the very beginning, a friend of the African American people, he could not symbolize America's heritage of equality.[31]

Lincoln's alleged belief in a colorblind society is presently reinforced by a culture of victimhood and grievance. Just as the unfinished work of the Civil War includes the ending of poverty and lifting of all who despair, the Civil War's primary achievement, freeing the slaves, is now the first stage of the twentieth-century civil rights movement.

Revisions of American history during the civil rights revolution conform to Charles Horton Cooley's dictum: "the function of the great and famous man is to be a symbol," and the real question in other minds is "How far can you help me develop my own inclinations?"[32] The inclinations toward Union that Lincoln once symbolized, however, are no longer deeply felt. New needs have arisen to take their place.

GROWING RELEVANCE OF SLAVERY AND EMANCIPATION

Don Fehrenbacher, writing in 1968, was among the first to observe the civil rights movement draw scholarly attention to slavery, but he had no idea how intense this new focus would become. Before the 1960s, slavery and emancipation interested few Americans and rarely appeared in their newspapers and magazines. In the WorldCat collection, books listed under the keyword "emancipation" numbered 4.3 per year during the 1930s. During the 1940s and 1950s, there were 3 and 2 emancipation books per year. Over the 1960s, 1970s, and 1980s, the annual volumes increased to 10, 19, and 19 respectively. The end of the century brought faster growth: 27 books per year during the 1990s and 39 from 2000 to 2005. When "slavery" replaced the keyword "emancipation," the annual volumes trace a similar trend.[33]

In the *New York Times Index* the number of slavery entries (relating to America) recorded for the first year of each decade from 1910 to 1980 never exceeded more than 2 articles. The production of slavery articles rose abruptly, however, from 4 in 1990 and 1992 to 28 in 1998, 61 in 2000, and 80 in 2001. Similar trends appear in *Readers' Guide to Periodical Literature* and *American Book Publishing Record*. The steepest rise in slavery writing appears at the end of the twentieth century.[34]

The new spate of writings contain common topics: the underground railroad, Thomas Jefferson and Sally Heming, the revolt aboard the *Amistad*, debates over the quality of slave life, and the role of various historical figures and groups in the slave trade. Policy topics include reparations to descendants of slaves, the disposition of slave artifacts and burial grounds, President Clinton in Africa confessing to American offenses against the continent, and the making of the summer retreat where Lincoln drafted the Emancipation Proclamation into a national monument. Ironically, many men and women presently writing about slavery believe that Americans have no wish to know about it, that the topic challenges cherished assumptions about the past and is something everyone wants to forget. We now know that Americans questioned in national surveys attribute Lincoln's greatness to emancipation. So do surveys about university students' historical beliefs. Asked to name

American history's major sources of dishonor, disgrace, and shame, slavery is mentioned more often than any other wrong doing.[35]

Many slavery topics are unrelated to the Civil War, but Americans' interest in them expresses beliefs about slavery's relevance for contemporary race relations. Ira Berlin's recent essay on "Coming to Terms with Slavery in Twenty-First-Century America" declares: "There is a general, if inchoate, understanding that any attempt to address the question of race in the present must also address slavery in the past. Slavery is ground zero of race relations."[36] The first generation of civil rights leaders, including Martin Luther King Jr., never saw such a connection. They struggled over fundamental rights—jobs, housing, education, voting. They never believed the achievement of these rights required agreement on the meaning of slavery. Nor did they associate Lincoln with a particular interpretation of slavery's consequences. For the members of the Justice and Equality Generation, Abraham Lincoln's legacy concerned constitutional rights, and they turned to the courts to uphold them. Yet, issues and conditions change together. Within academia, the business world, and part of the black press, issues of race no longer bear on fundamental political entitlements; they are about recruitment, work quotas, affirmative action, commemorative displays, recognition, and other matters having to do with identity politics. To twist a phrase from Richard Rorty, "cultural protest," concerned with identity politics, has replaced "reform protest," concerned with rights, jobs, and food.[37] In this context, slavery assumes unprecedented importance, and Lincoln's relationship to slavery becomes a topic of scholarly and public interest.[38] As a symbol of racial justice, then, Abraham Lincoln means something different at the turn of the twenty-first century than he meant during the beginning of the civil rights movement.

In 1999, with public interest in slavery rising, the House of Representatives Committee of Conference directed the Department of Interior to encourage Civil War battle site superintendents to "recognize and include in all of their public displays and multimedia educational presentations the unique role that slavery played in causing the Civil War and its role, if any, at the individual battle sites."[39] At stake for us is not the merit of the directive itself but what it tells about commemoration bending history. The phrase "unique role" echoes Lincoln's belief that "slavery was somehow the cause of the war."[40] Lincoln meant that slavery was a necessary but not sufficient cause. Without slavery there would have been no secession and no war; but secession would have led to war with or without slavery. Secession was the war's necessary *and* sufficient cause. The House bill, however, put the power of the state behind the emancipationists. Prior to the bill's passage, U.S. representative

Jesse Jackson Jr. explained to a National Park Service symposium on historical interpretation that African Americans rarely visit Civil War battlefield sites because "there is nothing there for them." He declared that "race is the central factor in American history. Race is the lens through which I view American history." Jackson's statement reflected growing pressure from African American organizations to represent the Civil War as a fight to end slavery and the growing belief throughout American society that such a representation is valid.[41]

No one knows when the public began to identify Lincoln so exclusively with emancipation. We do know, and will now demonstrate, when textbook writers began to do so.

HISTORY TEXTS: UNION AND EMANCIPATION

The public's growing interest in slavery corresponds to historians' reinterpretation of the Civil War. During the 1920s and 1930s, leading historians believed the Civil War resulted from extremist agitation in the North and South, that emancipation failed to affect the lives of the black masses, that the war's horrendous costs could never be justified.[42] Present-day historians are more inclined to consider the war inevitable and morally just, to sympathize with abolitionists and radical Republicans, to judge emancipation and reconstruction more important than North-South reconciliation, and to include extremists—John Brown, William Lloyd Garrison, and Thaddeus Stevens—among the war's heroes. The Savior of the Union and Man of the People resonate with David Blight's "reconciliationist memory" of the Civil War, which assumes that decent men from the North and South fought gallantly for their respective beliefs and should respect one another's heritage. The new Lincoln—the Great Emancipator—resonates with Blight's "emancipationist memory," which defines the war's essence as a struggle for racial justice and reduces reconciliation efforts, which excluded African Americans, to their racist elements. We are now in the midst of the first great surge of emancipationist memory.

Before the mid-1960s, most textbook writers defined the saving of the Union as Lincoln's major goal; since then, an unprecedented number of scholars believe that Northern Republicans supported the war to restore the Union, but gradually saw emancipation as its major purpose and justification. This development is apparent in a review of forty high school textbooks—three to seven texts for each decade between 1920 and 1999; two for the year 2000 (appendix F).[43] All books published during or prior to the 1970s were sampled from Frances Fitzgerald's bibliography of widely used history texts.[44] Those published after 1980 were selected from the library of a highly reputable school of education.

Because the textbooks were written by different generations of authors for different generations of students, they indicate the changing relevance of Union, emancipation, and democracy. As such, they approximate the turning point in Lincoln's reputation—the last third of the twentieth century—during which the relevance of the Great Emancipator began to supercede that of the Savior of the Union, Man of the People, First American, and Self-Made Man.

Textbooks: 1920–44. Between 1915 and 1944, when most members of Gallup's 1945 sample were educated, textbook writers described slavery as a moral wrong, but defined emancipation as an instrument of Union victory, not an end in itself. The rationale for emancipation was to weaken the South's labor force, augment the Union's manpower, and prevent European governments from recognizing the Confederacy. The narrative, centering on the state and its salvation, is textured with pictures of military and political scenes, monuments, memorials, statues, and portraits of leading generals and statesmen. Representations of slavery are sparse. Slavery is represented as a philosophical rather than humanitarian evil, not so much a source of concrete suffering as a violation of the principles of free labor, sanctity of private property, and individual liberty. Authors deem emancipation a restoration of such principles, but they never connect it to the matter of racial segregation or imply through it an endorsement of racial integration. The Great Emancipator is recognized but not connected to issues of contemporary racial justice.

Almost all pre-1945 textbooks cover extensively Abraham Lincoln's pre-presidential life, his being born in poverty, reared on the frontier, and achieving the presidency by hard work. They describe the log cabin where he was born, his simple manner, and show pictures of his chopping wood and reading books. Civil War–era women, in the little space devoted to them, appear as housewives and supportive mothers. These themes endure through the 1970s, but less conspicuously after 1945 than before.

Textbooks: 1945 to Present. Textbook contents between 1945 and 2001 move in the same direction as changes evidenced in the Gallup and National Employee surveys. Against the background of World War II, the cold war, Soviet condemnation of American racial segregation, and, above all, the growing fury of Southern black protest (1945–64), roughly when the Justice and Equality Generation's members came of age, textbook writers devote more space to emancipation, but continue to see the Union's preservation as Lincoln's goal. In texts published after

1965, however, commitment to social reform becomes more prominent. That emancipation widened the war's purpose, an assertion characteristic of the earliest textbooks, is reiterated, but some writers in the late 1960s and 1970s[45] begin to assert that moderate Americans—not just abolitionists—perceived emancipation as the primary war goal rather than an instrument for winning the war. In the 1980s, too, historians like Melvin Schwartz and John O'Connor explain: "People in the North had felt they were fighting to keep the Union together," but emphasize that "Now they also felt they were fighting to free the slaves."[46] Winthrop Jordan, Miriam Greenblatt, and John Bowes went further: "The Emancipation Proclamation gave the Northerners the weight of a moral crusade and began to replace Union as the war goal."[47]

During the late 1980s and 1990s, as slavery themes multiplied in the mass media and book publications, the emancipation theme became more prominent. The Northern population, according to Henry Bragdon, Samuel McCutchen, and Donald Ritchie, could never justify the war's carnage by mere restoration of the Union;[48] but the Emancipation Proclamation "aroused a renewed spirit in the North" and strengthened the will to win the war.[49] Since slavery was the war's only moral issue, Joanne Buggey and Gerald Danzer explain, emancipation was the cement that held the North together.[50] Thus, at Gettysburg, according to Paul Boyer, Lewis Todd, and Merle Curti, Lincoln "announced to the world that the abolition of slavery had become a major purpose of the Civil War." The death of so many men would have meaning only if the country remained "dedicated . . . to the unfinished work which they who fought here have thus far so nobly advanced." This unfinished work was not the saving of the Union but "the movement to free the slaves and an enduring commitment to racial justice."[51] "Commitment to racial justice": not only do text authors detach emancipation from the saving of the Union, they transform the meaning of emancipation itself. What was once a violation of libertarian principle is now a precursor to racial integration.

As post-1965 texts reinterpret the relationship between emancipation and Union, they discuss it in new formats redefining the war's meaning. Centering on liberation, the narrative is filled with representations of the African American experience. "Until the mid-sixties," Frances Fitzgerald observes, "black Americans had hardly entered the textbooks at all."[52] After the mid-sixties, textbook authors make up in intensity what their forebears ignored. They name slavery an evil, define its psychological effects, display pictures of human neck yokes, slaves being auctioned and laboring in the field, runaways being captured, black citizens being brutalized during Reconstruction. They discuss black contributions to the war effort and show pictures of black soldiers individually and in action against the enemy. In addition, they discuss the wartime fight in the North against discrimination toward free blacks in work, schools, and local places. They relate information about the Underground Railroad, depict John Brown's martyrdom, draw liberally on slave narratives, and consider the fate of blacks after emancipation. Lincoln's benign racial attitudes, his concern for the well being of emancipated slaves, and the accomplishments of African American leaders are common topics. Teacher guides recommend connecting the wartime situation of blacks to present civil rights issues. During the last third of the twentieth century, then, textbooks reconfigure Lincoln's place in history by devoting more space to slavery and emancipation.

Multiculturalism, with its characteristic preoccupation with minorities, enhances emancipationist memory. Textbooks, for example, devote unprecedented attention to the role of women. They identify white women in espionage and combat roles, working in factories, managing homes, farms, and plantations in their husbands' absence, and they provide information on black and white women administering medical care, nursing, teaching, mobilizing drives for reading materials, food, and other support. Irish, German, and Native American contributions are also discussed in the Civil War chapters, although more briefly than those of African Americans. To emphasize "history from below" is logically unrelated to the war's purpose, but by recognizing minority experience, writers make emancipation morally plausible as a primary war goal, and transform the Civil War from a tragic to a necessary struggle.

Table 4.3 summarizes the main axes of difference between early and later American history textbooks. All textbooks describe emancipation's purpose, institutionalization, and consequence. Reading across the table's eight rows, these topics converge on the Union's relevance becoming subordinated to slavery's. The priority of emancipation over Union is conveyed by multicultural symbols replacing symbols of the strong state, of a social-equality champion replacing a folk hero. The way we think about Lincoln and the way we perceive the Civil War, table 4.3 shows, are aspects of the same perspective.

HISTORY, COMMEMORATION, AND BELIEF

Differences between history texts written before and after World War II are considerable, but no one-to-one relation exists between their contents and their influence. If understanding individual beliefs about Lincoln depended solely on textbook content, we would, in fact, vastly underestimate the increase of emancipation's relevance between 1945 and

TABLE 4.3. Characteristic features of Civil War chapters in American history texts published before and after 1965

Topic	Before 1965	After 1965
1. Purpose of war after Emancipation Proclamation	Save Union; free slaves	Save Union; free slaves
2. Function of Emancipation	Instrumental (weakens Confederacy)	Moral (justifies war)
3. Key Problem	Unity of states	Institution of Slavery
4. Priority	Union > Emancipation	Emancipation > Union
5. Illustrations and examples accompanying text	Symbols of strong state and dominant political culture: history paintings, statues of military and political men, monuments, shrines	Multicultural symbols: representations of the slave experience, pictures and stories of African American soldiers, political figures, women, Native Americans, immigrants
6. Representations of equality	Pictures of young Lincoln; log cabin; accounts of Lincoln's social background and ambition; vertical mobility as symbol of equality	Freed slaves; assimilated but culturally distinct minorities as symbols of equality
7. Primary image of Lincoln	Epic hero (Savior of the Union) and folk hero	Epic hero (Great Emancipator) and champion of social equality

2001. No contemporary historian, not even the most radical, asserts that Lincoln would have initiated a war to free the slaves if eleven Southern states had not seceded from the Union. In the Maryland and Knowledge Network data, however, 46 percent and 66 percent respectively mention emancipation, compared to 7 percent and 14 percent mentioning the preservation of Union, as Lincoln's greatest accomplishment. Likewise, Lincoln the Folk Hero is mentioned by approximately one-quarter of late twentieth-century textbooks, but by only 5 percent and 4 percent of the Maryland and Knowledge Network survey respondents. In the Gallup–National Employee Survey comparison, moreover, the humanitarian People's President drops from 26.3 percent to 4.4 percent; the Self-Made Man from 23.3 percent to 3.1 percent respectively (table 4.2).

When commemorative and survey trends are compared, the problem of ignoring individual belief becomes even more apparent. Although textbooks are written annually, the production of monumental symbolism peaks in definite decades, then ceases. Most prominent Lincoln icons, monuments, shrines, and place names were dedicated before 1950; since then, their number has remained steady while beliefs about Lincoln have changed dramatically. Since changing beliefs are occurring against a relatively fixed commemorative backdrop, Lincoln monuments are more likely than texts to be screens on which new beliefs are projected.

HISTORY OF MEMORY AS A SUPPLEMENT TO COLLECTIVE MEMORY

Historical figures resonate with contemporary experience when their personalities and achievements engage the presuppositions of the people encountering them. Since these presuppositions are patterned by generational experience, we expect some analogy between the present analysis of collective memory, based on beliefs individuals take from history books and commemorative symbolism, and reader-reaction studies, which ask individuals what they get from novels and other popular books or how reviewers in different countries react to identical novels.[53] Like these reactions, individual beliefs about Lincoln are not passive end-links on some chain of causation; on the contrary, they reinforce or modify the texts and symbols they consume. The succession of historical perceptions is mediated by the interaction of authors, artists, and other producers, on the one hand, and, on the other, students, general viewers, readers, and other consumers. When analysis of collective memory is grounded in consumption, the producer's dependence on consumer reaction comes more fully into view, as does the latter's role in generating collective memory's content. "Culture creation" and "culture reception" are inseparable,[54] but we can only explore this connection if we know what and how individuals, as cultural consumers, actually believe.

Surveys assess individual beliefs as outcomes, but they cannot capture the process leading to them. We can *imagine* teachers in 1945 telling their students that Lincoln at Gettysburg praised the soldiers who died to save democracy; parents at Lincoln's Springfield home telling their children, "Here lived the poor, common man who made himself president by hard work"; tourists visiting the Lincoln Memorial, gazing at its powerful inscriptions about Union. We can *test* hypotheses about contemporaries' reaction to these objects, however, by combining qualitative and survey methods. As Lincoln appears against a changing "horizon of expectations"[55] based more on equality than unity, focus groups, depth interviews, direct observations, and on-site interviews can reveal a mnemonic resocialization process[56] beyond the reach of surveys:

teachers telling their students that Lincoln at Gettysburg praised the soldiers who died to bring about racial justice; parents now waiting to enter the Lincoln home telling their children, "Here lived the man who freed the slaves"; tourists visiting the Lincoln Memorial admiring the statue of the Great Emancipator, ignoring its declaration of gratitude to the Union's Savior.

Aggregation of individual beliefs, however measured, reacts upon the environment from which the beliefs emerged. As this environment's horizon of expectation becomes emancipationist, it inspires and welcomes the modification of old structures, like the Lincoln Memorial plaque that commemorates Martin Luther King Jr.'s "I Have a Dream" speech; or it promotes the canonization of old structures, including the placement of the long-forgotten Soldiers' Home, where Lincoln drafted the Emancipation Proclamation, into the National Historical Registry; and it influences the policy of new organizations, including the Abraham Lincoln Bicentennial Commission, which has adopted the premise that the Emancipation Proclamation redefined the Civil War, "changing it from a war for Union to a war for human freedom," and has explicitly made Lincoln's significance for racial equality its major focus.[57] From its initial Web site layout to its most recent reports, the Abraham Lincoln Bicentennial Commission's purpose has been unambiguous: "It is especially important to the Commission that the Bicentennial involve and engage *diverse perspectives on Lincoln, specifically African-American and multi-cultural perspectives*" (emphasis in the original). The report goes on to explain that "race relations and human and civil rights" constitute America's greatest challenges, that Lincoln experts must be recruited "to explain Lincoln's legacy as it relates to race relations" and that key African American organizations (NAACP, Urban League, etc.) be singled out and invited to participate.[58] Such an invitation would have been unimaginable during the 1909 Lincoln centennial, when African Americans in most places were forbidden to participate in official events. Not a new Bicentennial Commission but a new society with a new horizon of expectations makes the difference.

Those whose job is to represent Lincoln are often uncertain as to whether they are shaping public belief or reflecting it. The National Park Service's March 2000 Report to Congress titled *Interpretation at Civil War Sites*, for example, insists that "[H]istory needs to be based on solid and current research and interpretation needs to accurately and sensitively reflect the research." At the same time, and in the same document, readers are told that "Interpreters must meet visitors on their own terms and be prepared to work with multiple points of view. When we succeed, we facilitate a connection between the interests of the visitor and the meanings of the park." This is because history "does not possess only one truth, but many truths—and we contribute to the public's knowledge about history . . . by presenting a past with multiple voices, multiple views, and differing, even conflicting interpretations." In fact, the Park Service would never present reconciliation viewpoints, let alone neo-Confederate or even Southern heritage ones, as sympathetically as it would present the emancipationist interpretations preferred by African Americans. Since the Park Service is responding to a House of Representatives directive attached to its budget, and since that directive, according to one of its authors, reflects "the will of the people," there can be no doubt that the Park Service reflects more than it shapes the contemporary horizon of expectations. This is even more evident in the reading list from which the Park Service draws its inspiration and makes recommendations to the public. The great classics of Lincoln scholarship, beginning with the work of James G. Randall, are missing from this list. No conservative or even neutral accounts are included—only those texts which see the war from the emancipationist standpoint.[59]

The National Park Service's new horizon of expectations, reflecting the public's, transcends battlefield sites. The Lincoln Memorial, according to its interpreters, was originally designed and dedicated as a monument to Union, but they also assert, baldly, that its creators distorted history while the present generation is correcting their errors: "Perhaps it should come as little surprise that the predominantly white, classically minded and university educated architects and engineers that built the Lincoln Memorial would stress the theme of National Unity over that of Social Justice." It remains for the present generation "to restore the balance to the twin themes of National Unity and Social Justice. Architect Henry Bacon and sculptor Daniel Chester French actually designed a commemorative monument that the Lincoln Memorial (McMillan) Commission, representing the tastes of the American people, would recognize and accept as fitting. Above all, the Memorial's architecture, despite its engraved reference to Lincoln as Savior of the Union, does not deny a connection between Lincoln and social justice. The very same monument that President Harding defined as a celebration of Union is widely regarded now as a symbol of racial equality. The active agent in this case of commemoration, as in all others, is the consumer, not the producer.

The seriousness with which any writer or artist assumes his audience's perspective, reflected in beliefs about Lincoln arrayed in tables 4.1 and 4.2, is a measure of that audience's power to affect academic and popular media. However, we will never know about the climate of public belief to which historians and artists adapt if we fail to assess it. The history of memory (trends in individual belief) affects the structure of memory (textual and symbolic patterns) because the former provides the context for the latter's persistence and change. Belief is both a source and product of Lincoln representation.

WHO BELIEVES WHAT ABOUT LINCOLN?

To assert that the Lincoln Memorial is "widely regarded now as a symbol of racial equality " is a statement about consensus, and consensus is to be demonstrated, not assumed. Compelling evidence of consensus is easier to assemble through individual beliefs than through texts and commemorative symbols, and so we must turn again to our survey results. Consensus about Lincoln means that respondent characteristics are weakly correlated with questions about him. True, some people answer such questions the same way for different reasons; some disagree about Lincoln for similar reasons, but these problems must not prevent us from addressing the issue.

Consensus can never be perfect. Lincoln appears different, very different, today in text and symbol than he did yesterday, but different segments of any generation, although recognizing the same man, cannot see him identically. That emancipation is Lincoln's greatest achievement and racial integration his legacy became evident to the general population by the turn of the twenty-first century, yet some sectors have been more receptive than others to emancipationist assertions. The Knowledge Network Survey shows non-Southerners, Democrats, and self-defined liberals mention emancipation more often than do Southerners, Republicans, and conservatives. Democrats and liberals are most inclined to name equal rights as a Lincoln legacy; whites and Republicans are most likely to choose Savior of the Union (table 4.4).

The University of Maryland survey shows a similar pattern.[60] Non-Southerners, blacks, and Democrats are more likely than Southerners, whites, and Republicans to attribute Lincoln's greatness to emancipation. Non-Southerners are more likely to recognize Lincoln's moral traits. Whites and Republicans choose Savior of the Union most often; whites are also most likely to attribute to Lincoln folk and moral traits, and superior leadership. In both surveys, Southerners are most likely to judge Lincoln negatively (table 4.5).

The slight peaks and troughs of a very high mountain—minor variations on the grand theme of emancipation. Within every category of region, race, party preference, and ideology, emancipation stands far above every other reason for Lincoln's greatness.[61]

TABLE 4.4. Major attributions to Abraham Lincoln in Knowledge Network survey, by region, race, political-party preference, and ideology (any mentions)*

	Non-South (N=574)	South (N=301)	White (N=640)	Black (N=80)	Democrat (N=421)	Independent (N=149)	Republican (N=283)	Liberal (N=158)	Moderate (N=402)	Conservative (N=204)
Peterson categories										
1a. Great emancipator	68.2	63.0	67.3	63.3	69.8	61.7	62.9	73.4	66.3	63.2
1b. Equal rights	10.0	8.0	8.3	2.5	11.9	5.4	5.7	13.3	8.2	6.0
2. Savior of the Union	16.1	11.6	15.9	8.8	11.2	17.4	17.7	15.5	13.9	18.8
3. Folk themes	4.6	4.7	3.4	2.5	4.5	2.7	3.5	7.1	3.7	3.6
Additional categories										
4. Moral traits	11.5	8.3	10.8	8.8	7.1	13.4	13.0	11.0	9.7	12.8
5. Leadership	10.9	9.0	10.6	6.3	7.8	11.3	13.4	11.8	10.7	12.9
6. Negative beliefs	3.2	6.3	2.3	13.9	5.5	3.3	2.8	5.8	3.5	6.7

*Excludes respondents declining to name a characteristic trait or achievement (nonresponses) and miscellaneous responses. Column percentages add to more or less than 100 depending on number of attributions made, nonrespondents, and miscellaneous responses.

TABLE 4.5. Major attributions to Abraham Lincoln in University of Maryland survey, by region, race, and political-party preference (any mentions)*

	Non-South (N=524)	South (N=290)	White (N=661)	Black (N=104)	Democrat (N=272)	Independent (N=250)	Republican (N=239)
Peterson categories							
1a. Great emancipator	51.0	39.1	45.0	50.0	50.4	48.4	44.4
1b. Equal rights	11.3	11.8	11.4	9.6	8.1	11.6	12.6
2. Savior of the Union	6.5	7.6	7.4	1.9	5.1	5.6	8.8
3. Folk themes	5.9	3.4	5.2	1.0	4.4	7.2	3.8
Additional categories							
4. Moral traits	21.5	14.9	20.7	9.6	20.6	16.4	20.9
5. Leadership	9.3	11.0	11.2	1.0	9.6	10.4	9.6
6. Negative beliefs	2.1	6.9	3.0	5.8	5.5	3.2	2.5

*See note, table 4.4.

To these findings the 2001 National Employee Survey adds nothing. The National Employee Survey is limited to working people and lacks a measure of political preference; nevertheless, the findings are similar. Southerners name emancipation, but not racial equality, as often as non-Southerners; African Americans name emancipation, but not racial equality, more often than whites. Admiration for Lincoln as a folk hero, on the other hand, is limited to whites. The highly educated is the only group more likely than average to mention Lincoln's role in saving the Union. Most of these correlations are weakly correlated with respondent characteristics, while emancipation, within each racial, regional, educational, and other demographic category, is the dominant reason for Lincoln's greatness.

What, then, is to be said of the real Lincoln and how Lincoln will appear in future days? Changing interpretations of Lincoln may bring him closer to or further from reality, but because every generation believes its own image of him to be the truest, the last thing its members consider is how future generations will regard him. Whereas the Union's permanence can be taken for granted today, future generations taking racial harmony for granted might find Lincoln's views on slavery and race irrelevant to their concerns. Social movements that have formed these concerns must eventually reach completeness, and when they do, the ground supporting them will lose its resonance with life.

CONCLUSION

The New Structural Memory contributes rich insights into the workings of Lincoln's biography and commemoration, but it ignores the question of how individuals think about him. Merrill Peterson's five Abraham

Lincolns—Savior of the Union, Great Emancipator, Man of the People, First American, and Self-Made Man—exemplify this point. There is no way to determine from a cumulative body of texts and symbols which of the five Lincolns is most relevant today. Only when individuals are asked about Lincoln's greatness, what comes to mind when they think of him, why he was a greater president than another, do we realize the importance they place on emancipation and, beyond that, on his imagined commitment to civil rights as presently understood. When recent surveys are compared to Gallup's earlier evidence, we know that the one-sided imagination of Lincoln as emancipator was alien to the American mind of the mid-1940s, but that emancipator imagery now typifies individual beliefs even more than history texts and symbols.

That the civil rights movement affected Lincoln scholarship has been well known, but hardly investigated, so that we had little idea of when this change began, how far our historians have exaggerated, underestimated, or ignored the different lineaments of Lincoln's life and presidency, and whether collective belief lagged or led historiography. Current portrayals of Lincoln, as we now know, contradict in several ways the Lincoln of the early twentieth century. Not only do historians place greater emphasis on emancipation and slavery; they also write for a highly receptive audience that exaggerates their exaggerations. These same historians de-emphasize and their readers seem to have forgotten the traditional Lincoln—Ida Tarbell's and Carl Sandburg's Lincoln—the common, self-reliant man who raised himself by his own bootstraps.

In this chapter's opening pages, four interrelated questions were posed. The first question asked "How far, if at all, do individual beliefs deviate from historical and commemorative statements?" Textbooks still affirm Union's importance, but place far more emphasis on emancipation during the last third of the twentieth century than before. Among the individuals we surveyed, however, this emphasis is magnified: the Great Emancipator has for the most part swallowed up the Savior of the Union and marginalized the Folk Hero.

The second question was "Do historical and commemorative statements change at the same rate and in the same direction as individual beliefs?" Comparison of the 1945, 1999, and two 2001 surveys shows that the importance of saving the Union and of folk themes, relative to emancipation, diminished more quickly within the public than among history-book writers. The Humane People's President was mentioned in surveys more than six times as often in 1945 as in 2001; the Self-Made Man, more than four times as often; the Emancipator, about half as often.

Any answer to the third question, "How and to what extent do beliefs, historical texts, and commemorative representations affect one another?" must be tentative. Comparing 1945 and 2001 shows that a population believing in Lincoln as Great Emancipator not only produces writers and artists who define him as such but also provides these writers and artists with an appreciative audience. Lincoln's memory, then, is embodied not in a succession of books and symbols consumed passively, but a succession of books and symbols actively embraced, rejected, and thus shaped, by their consumers.

"Which aspects of late twentieth century American society do [Lincoln] representations symbolize?" was the fourth question. The primary social fact of the late twentieth century, the revolution in race relations, frames all findings about Lincoln. Despite continuing debate about "states' rights," virtually all Americans take the permanence of Union for granted, and Lincoln's rescuing it is one of the last things about him that comes to mind. The Civil War makes sense today as a struggle for racial equality, and the Great Emancipator explicates the meaning of this new interpretation, puts definite constructions on the events associated with it, gets the connotation of those events into the open where people can see it and grasp it in a collective as well as personal way. Specifically, the disadvantage of contemporary African Americans seems more understandable as a product of slavery, while slavery itself seems less relevant apart from its legacy of affliction.

Recognition of history's victims is one of the mechanisms transforming American memory. Revisionist historians, to take one example, freely describe Columbus's crimes against native peoples, and Columbus Day now generates protest as well as celebration. Several national surveys, however, show beliefs about Columbus to be almost uniformly positive.[62] Revisionists have been less than successful partly because the Indians whom Columbus is perceived as having oppressed are a smaller and less vivid presence than African Americans, whom Lincoln is perceived as having freed.

The Columbus and Lincoln cases are part of a broader pattern. George Washington's presidential policy toward Indians was highly conciliatory, but today he is more distinguished by his status as slave holder.[63] President Andrew Jackson's atrocity against the Cherokees is less known today than Thomas Jefferson's alleged sexual liaison with his slave; but if the target of Jackson's offenses had been African Americans, his reputation would be badly tarnished. The public's affection for Franklin Roosevelt would likewise lessen if he had approved the internment of African Americans rather than Asian Americans. Given Lincoln's reputation as a friend of oppressed minorities, his remarks about the social inferiority of African Americans and Native Americans rarely appear in textbooks and media, and they seem incongruent when they do. That his prestige would be lower had he espoused the interests of Indians rather than African Americans follows from a horizon of expectations defined by the African American civil rights movement. This new horizon shapes the reception of Columbus, Washington, Jefferson, Jackson, and Roosevelt as well as Lincoln.

The fading of the Union's Savior and Folk Hero, like the rise of the Great Emancipator, is symptomatic of a widening, compassion-centered frame of memory. "Regret," Jeffrey Olick observes, "as a sine qua non of post-conflict peace building is a preeminently modern phenomenon." Perhaps "postmodern" would be the more precise definition, for negative events did not induce widespread guilt until the last quarter of the twentieth century, when minority entitlement gripped the collective conscience. The obverse side of the politics of regret is the public confession, now a stock feature of collective identity. Bernhard Giesen provides rich detail, but his topic, *Triumph and Trauma*, or, more precisely, "The Triumph *of* Trauma," thrives in an age where the victim gains political as well as moral victory. Abraham Lincoln cannot avoid these cultural currents. In a society whose past is a moral burden as well as a source of inspiration, where the duty to remember applies as much to atrocity as to heroic achievement,[64] the Great Emancipator is more relevant by far than the Savior of the Union.

Accordingly, no longer is there a prominent place for the down-to-earth people's president sitting beside a cracker barrel peeling an apple and telling jokes, nor even for the gentle president brooding over casualty figures and visiting wounded soldiers, including Confederates. The beneficiaries of this kind of humanitarianism have always been white men. Less relevant, even, than the kindly Man of the People is the Self-Made Man, the dynamo who relies on his own will and wit to rise from log cabin to White House. When linked, these last two images, rooted in the nineteenth-century world of the frontier and free market, a world in which minorities were despised, fail to inspire the best in modern leaders determined to bring all people together. The individualist ideal of hard work remains important today, but social equality is more relevant. Bill Clinton, John Edwards, and Dennis Kucinich have worked as hard to achieve their stature as Colin Powell, Condoleezza Rice, and Joseph Lieberman, but the latter's minority status gives their success greater moral resonance.[65] Reason leads inexorably to a reconception of the past: the slaveholder is no longer the self-made, although morally imperfect, man; no longer the contradiction of free labor, self-reliance, and perseverance; he is the epitome of evil and the contradiction of every human virtue.

Since preoccupation with past discrimination and sympathy for the wronged are part of the present horizon of expectations, they affect what people learn when they read biographies, look upon statues, and visit shrines.[66] No horizon of expectation, however, can be totally new, totally devoid of tradition's traces. Even now, many people think of Lincoln as did his contemporaries, for today's Lincoln, "our Lincoln," is largely constituted by the Lincoln of yesterday. Those who assume that changing historical reputations are necessarily congruent with the changing tastes and expectations of society therefore face a dilemma: if the significance of historical figures inheres in their transcending the mores of their own time, why should they not transcend the mores of ours? This is why traditional Lincoln themes cannot resist new ones, and why the latter cannot entirely replace the former. Most respondents associate Lincoln with emancipation and racial justice, but the number associating him with the preservation of the Union, identifying him with the common man, the frontier, and self-reliance, although small, is significant, and these themes remain available for exploitation (or rejection) by future generations.

Given the place of reception in collective memory, what is to be said about the New Structural Memory? Merrill Peterson's *Abraham Lincoln in American Memory* exemplifies the structural perspective because it portrays the past largely as material artifact. The Savior of the Union, Man of the People, First American, and Self-Made Man—the Lincoln of Ida Tarbell, Carl Sandburg, and Robert Sherwood—live still, and their prominence, as Peterson conceives it, is equivalent in print, canvas, and stone. At the turn of the twenty-first century, however, the image of the Great Emancipator appears most relevant to most Americans.

Measuring belief apart from texts and symbols would be unnecessary if belief could be inferred from them. Since this is not always the case, individual men and women must be brought into our understanding. On the other hand, Lincoln in American memory does not consist of individual beliefs alone. Bringing men and women into collective-memory scholarship widens, not narrows, its scope. Abraham Lincoln in American memory refers neither to history, commemoration, nor individual belief, but to the relations among them.

* 5 *

Erosion

FADING PRESTIGE, BENIGN RIDICULE

In spring 1930, Edgar Lee Masters's *Lincoln the Man* stunned Abraham Lincoln's admirers. The famous poet claimed that Lincoln was lazy, dishonest, stupid, ambitious, immoral, a war monger; his presidency, a disaster to the country. Reactions to Masters's biography ranged from contempt to outrage. Republican representative Joe Crail of California introduced a bill to bar the "scurrilous and unprincipled" book from the mails. Vice president of the United States, Charles Curtis, denounced it. Newspaper editors outside the South condemned it. "Masters's muck is almost universally received with ridicule or disgust." He is the literary politician who would "gather in a few shekels by attacking Abraham Lincoln and Christianity, which are synonymous."[1] Many Americans probably took that last phrase seriously.

Seventy years later, Lerone Bennett, editor of *Ebony* magazine, published *Forced into Glory: Abraham Lincoln's White Dream*. Resonating as it does with "wet dream," Bennett's subtitle, in effect, depicts Lincoln's view of a land without black people as a pleasant fantasy. For five hundred pages he skewers Lincoln the racist, but his book provoked milder reactions than did Masters's. Some reviewers commented positively, some negatively, but none dismissed Bennett as scurrilous or unprincipled. Television interviewers politely allowed him to explain himself. At the 2002 Lincoln Forum, the largest annual gathering of Lincoln scholars and admirers, critical questioners politely raised matters of evidence, then bid him farewell with a hearty round of applause.

Two days after Bennett spoke, the Lincoln Forum gave its 2002 award for the best college-student essay to "Abraham Lincoln: Emancipator or Racist?" The paper, read in full to the audience, concluded that Lincoln was emancipator and racist. He hated slavery, but like other men and women of his generation he never imagined whites and blacks mingling as social equals.

The Lincoln Forum's openness to unflattering commentary on Abraham Lincoln has not been coerced by the accumulation of new facts; it is symptomatic of a diminishing of its own members' emotional attachment to Lincoln. Between 1930 and 2001, something had changed. Edgar Lee Masters or Lerone Bennett walking away unscathed from a 1930 variant of the Lincoln Forum is difficult to imagine. The erosion of Lincoln's renown manifests the uniqueness of today's perspectives, particularly the welcoming of criticism towards all traditional heroes, no matter how narrow minded or outrageous. The anti-Lincoln literature has not caused Lincoln's prestige to fall; the falling of his prestige makes anti-Lincoln literature "interesting" as an "alternative perspective" adding to the "diversity" of Lincoln interpretations that "mature" readers demand.

Counts

No single source of information provides an adequate measure of Abraham Lincoln's prestige. National opinion surveys show how respondents rate Lincoln in comparison with other presidents, but since the surveys were taken on an irregular basis they can only approximate the time when his prestige began to fade. The first nationwide survey, taken in July 1945 by the National Research Opinion Center (NORC), showed 57 percent of respondents naming Lincoln "one of the two or three greatest Americans."[2] In 1956, the Gallup Poll conducted the first of a series of surveys on presidential distinction. Each survey asked respondents to name the *three* greatest American *presidents*. In 1956, 62 percent of the respondents named Lincoln. By the time of the next survey (1975), this figure had fallen to 49 percent. In the 1985 survey it fell further to 47 percent, and in the January 1991 survey, it dropped to 43 percent. In 1999, 40 percent of the respondents of a University of Maryland national sample named Lincoln among the top three presidents. From 1956 to 1999 Lincoln ranked first or second in presidential greatness, but the percentage naming him great fell by more than a third.

Since the Gallup Poll asks respondents to name no fewer than three presidents, prestige deterioration manifests itself in diffused preferences. In 1956, two of the three top-rated presidents—Roosevelt and Lincoln—were named by more than 60 percent of the respondents; one of the three, Washington, was named by almost 50 percent. By the end of 1999, the highest rated presidents—Lincoln and Kennedy—were named by only 40 and 35 percent respectively; Roosevelt placed third

TABLE 5.1. Percentage of respondents designating Lincoln and other selected presidents as one of America's three greatest presidents

	July 1956	November 1975	June 1985	February 1991	May 1999
N	1,385	1,507	1,540	1,013	1,001
Lincoln	62	49	47	44	40
Kennedy	–	52	57	49	35
Roosevelt	64	45	41	28	24
Washington	47	25	25	24	24
Truman	22	37	27	20	10
Eisenhower	38	24	17	12	8

at 29 percent. Recent presidents receive nominations the most popular presidents have lost. Lincoln's descent, however, does not result from the increasing number of presidential choices. His early twentieth-century reputation, as will be shown, rose as presidents succeeded one another; and his late twentieth-century fall, like that of all popular presidents, was abrupt, not gradual, as the presidential succession hypothesis leads one to expect.

Lincoln's declining prestige is apparent in every demographic category—among whites and blacks; Southerners and non-Southerners; Republicans, Democrats, and Independents; the most and least educated; male and female; young and old; city and small-town dwellers; rich and poor. Because some of the categories in table 5.2 contain a very small number of cases, some chance fluctuations are inevitable. On the full pattern of findings, however—Lincoln's losing prestige everywhere—we are confident. In every nook and crevice of the land, Lincoln's aura has faded.

Significantly, most of the decline in Lincoln's rating occurred between 1956 and 1975, the period during which a veritable revolution in values—the so-called postmodern turn—is supposed to have occurred. George Washington, Franklin Roosevelt, and Dwight Eisenhower lost most of their prestige during this period, and after 1975 they lost even more. Harry Truman's prestige, at its low point during Eisenhower's presidency, rose from 1956 to 1975, but afterward fell precipitously. The postmodern era is, plainly, a post-heroic era.

Annual citation counts do not measure Lincoln's prestige as directly as do sporadic surveys, but they are useful supplements. The phrase opening many Lincoln books and articles, after all, is "More has been written about Abraham Lincoln than any other American." If the sheer number of writings indicates Lincoln's stature, then variations in this number must be important to us. Entries from the *New York Times Index*,

TABLE 5.2. Decline in the percentage of respondents designating Abraham Lincoln one of America's "three greatest presidents," by race, region, party, education, sex, age, residence, and income (number of cases in parentheses)

	Year					Absolute decline*	Percent decline
	1956 (1,385)	1975 (1,507)	1985 (1,540)	1991 (1,013)	1999 (1,001)	(1956–1999)	(A.D./1956)
Race							
White	64	50	48	47	41	23	36
Black	48	37	45	35	35	13	27
Region							
East	66	54	44	46	38	28	42
Midwest	70	49	52	49	43	27	39
South	45	42	37	36	36	9	20
West	72	48	52	55	44	28	39
Party							
Republican	71	57	53	54	48	23	32
Democrat	55	41	42	36	42	13	24
Independent	68	53	49	47	33	35	51
Education							
0–11 grade	52	34	32	19	27	25	48
H.S. grad	69	48	43	35	33	36	52
Any college	80	62	60	57	49	31	39
Sex							
Male	61	48	46	47	41	20	33
Female	63	49	49	43	38	25	40
Age							
<20	–	53	54	36	53	0	0
20s	69	60	57	50	49	20	29
30s	68	51	56	53	44	24	35
40s	64	44	51	50	39	25	39
50s	54	44	43	37	38	16	30
60s	53	38	39	38	28	25	47
70+	53	41	28	28	31	22	42
Residence							
<2,500	60	48	41	–	–	19	32
2,500–99,999	70	47	48	–	–	22	31
100,000–499,999	59	47	47	–	–	12	20
500,000+	63	51	51	–	–	12	19
Income							
<10,000	–	41	33	39	–	2	5
10,000–14,999	–	49	39	38	*	11	22
15,000–19,999	–	52	46	42	–	10	19
20,000+	–	59	46	49	**	10	17

* Absolute decline (A.D.).

TABLE 5.3. Entries per year for Abraham Lincoln in *Readers' Guide*, 1941–2002

Year	Average/year
1941–51	25
1951–61	25
1961–70	14
1970–80	7
1980–89	8
1990–99	11
2000–2002	8

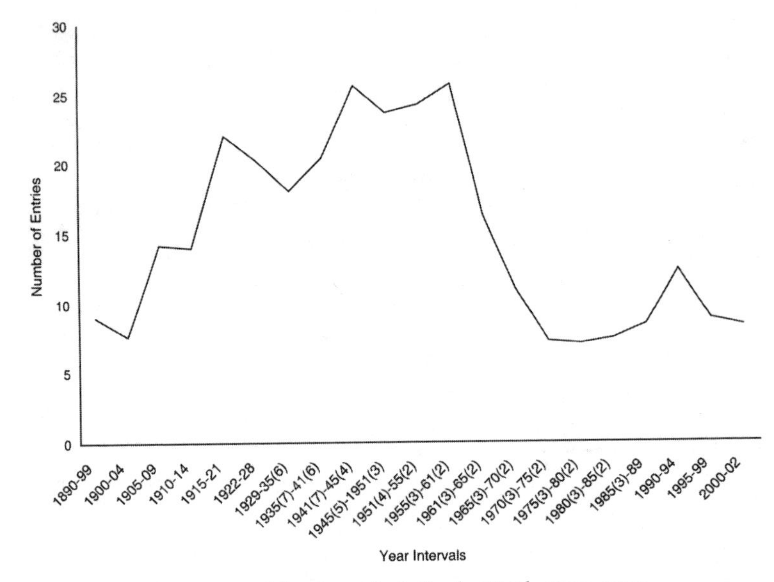

FIGURE 5.1. Lincoln entries in *Readers' Guide*, 1890–2002.

Readers' Guide to Periodical Literature, and *Congressional Record* are relevant to Lincoln's changing stature because they reflect the demands of a general reading audience and the commemorative activities of the U.S. Congress. All three trends show that interest in Lincoln rose abruptly during the Progressive Era but declined abruptly during and after the 1960s.[3] Diminishing interest in America's greatest men is characteristic of its post-heroic era. On this count, the evidence leaves little to the imagination. *Readers' Guide* articles rose from 1910 (following the 1909 centennial of Lincoln's birth) to 1960—a fifty-year period—then dropped sharply (fig. 5.1). During the peak of the trend, the 1930s, 1940s and 1950s, an annual mean of 22 articles on Lincoln appeared. During the 1960s, table 5.3 shows, the mean dropped to 14 articles; during the 1970s

TABLE 5.4. Entries per year for Abraham Lincoln in *New York Times* and *Congressional Record*, 1940–2002

Year	*New York Times*	*Congressional Record*
1940–49	42	23
1950–59	52	29
1960–69	26	41
1970–79	10	12
1980–89	7	12
1990–99	7	8
2000–2002	2	8

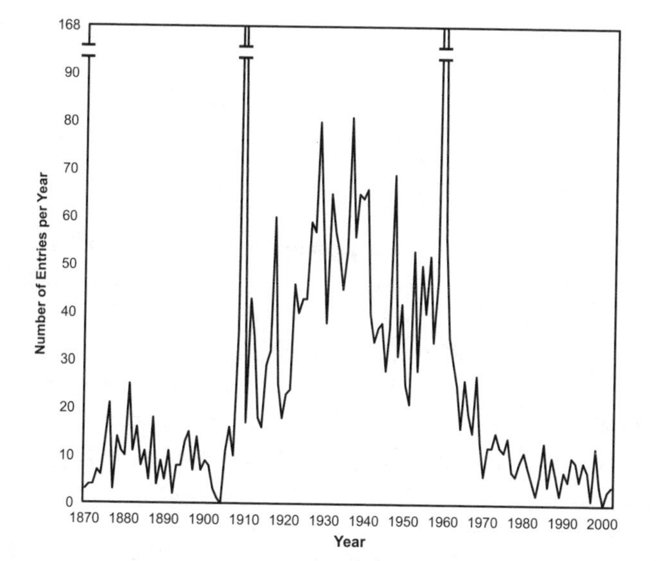

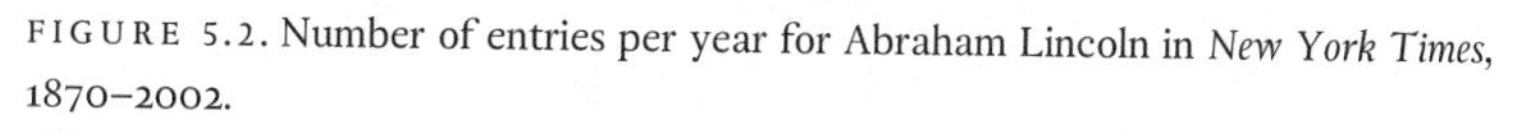

FIGURE 5.2. Number of entries per year for Abraham Lincoln in *New York Times*, 1870–2002.

and 1980s, it fell to 7 and 8 articles, remaining essentially unchanged at 11 articles from 1990 to 1999, and 8 articles from 2000 to 2002.

New York Times articles on Lincoln increased from the 1909 centennial to the 1959 sesquicentennial, then, after 1960, fell suddenly and far (fig. 5.2). The *Times* printed a yearly mean of 58 articles on Lincoln during the 1930s, 42 articles during the 1940s, and 52 during the 1950s. The mean number of articles published yearly during the 1960s, 1970s, and 1980s dropped to 26, 10, and 7 respectively. From 1990 to 1999 the volume remained at 7, then fell to 2 from 2000 to 2002.

Congressional Record's Lincoln entries, like the *Readers' Guides*' and the *Times*', rose rapidly from 1910 through the 1920s (fig. 5.3). The volume of entries increased from 17 to 23 and 29 during the 1930s, 1940s, and

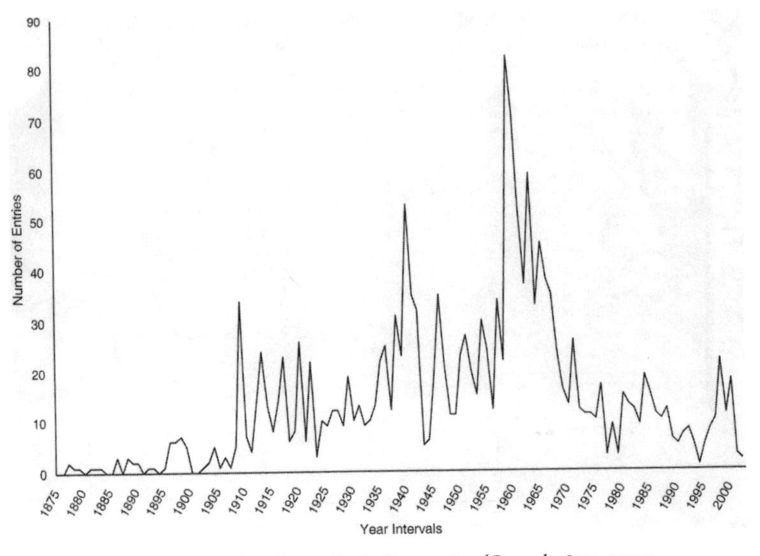

FIGURE 5.3. Lincoln entries in *Congressional Record*, 1875–2002.

1950s; afterward, there is one deviation from the *Readers' Guide* and *Times* pattern: the *Congressional Record*'s entries on Lincoln maintained their peak during the 1960s because they included reports on 1961–65 Civil War centennial activity, which stirred little interest among most newspaper and magazine editors. The yearly mean of 41 entries appearing in the *Record* through the 1960s, however, fell to 12 during the seventies and eighties and to 8 through 1990–99 and 2000–2002 (see table 5.4 above).

These three trends are based on unlike publications. The wide range of *Readers' Guide* coverage suggests its contents are highly representative of American readers' preferences. The *Congressional Record*, publishing local editorials and constituents' articles inserted by senators and representatives to honor Lincoln's Birthday is also a source of data on what ordinary Americans think about Lincoln. The *New York Times*, in contrast, reflects the views of better educated and more affluent readers. Yet all three sources yield approximately the same pattern of change. Lincoln's appeal remains as the Rebellious Generation of the 1960s transforms the American cultural scene, then abruptly declines, as if the country had its moral supports pulled out from under it.

Even the slight rise in Lincoln books during the last twenty-five years occurs against a background of long-term decline. The *American Book Publishing Record* covers major publishers, and its criterion for inclusion is constant, despite the low volume of books indexed; therefore, its trend may be representative. Between 1980 and 1999, new Lincoln books

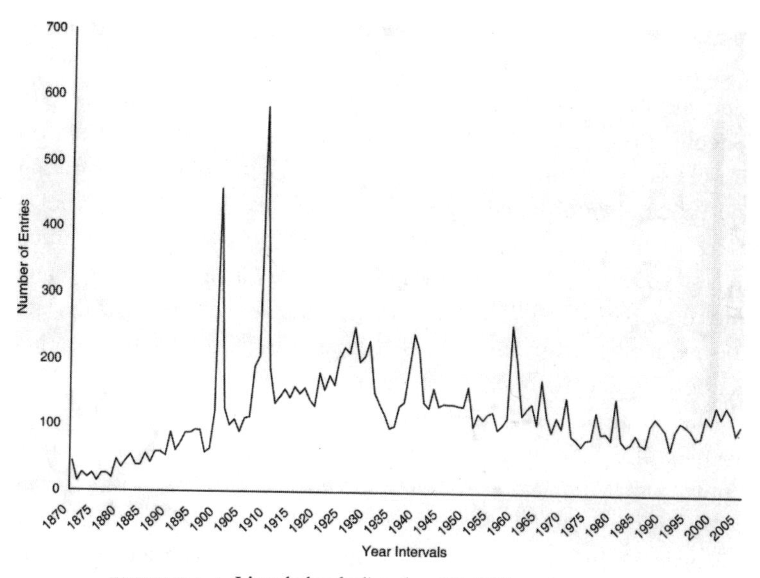

FIGURE 5.4. Lincoln books listed on WorldCat, 1870–2005.

increased from nine to nineteen. If the *American Book Publishing Record* is too exclusive, the WorldCat—a worldwide inventory of books in print by year—is too inclusive because it contains works that do not name him in the title. Assuming the percentage of books with Lincoln in the title to be constant, however, one can use the trend as an estimate of changing production. The annual number of such books changed from 94 during the 1980s to 97 during the 1990s, then rose slightly to 117 between 2000 and 2005. Seen in the context of a 135-year trend, however, the decline in Lincoln book output is evident—especially when the fin-de-siècle (1900) and Lincoln Centennial (1909) peaks are included.[4]

During heroic eras, when the great dead continue to be revered, people eagerly visit their shrines and monuments. Nothing retains their memory better than the physical stuff they have sanctified by their touch and use, or by the fabulous monuments that celebrate their accomplishments. Visits to Lincoln's shrines and monuments, however, either leveled or diminished during and after the 1960s. This information is summarized graphically in appendix G, but can be readily detailed. The numbers, in the aggregate, might be tedious, but their implication for Lincoln's renown is significant because they refer to behavior—trends in the way people act in relation to Lincoln's greatness rather than what they believe about it.

Visitation to Lincoln's Springfield home dropped from more than 650,000 per year during the last half of the 1960s to 427,000 per year during the late 1990s, and to 393,000 from 2000 to 2003. From 1993 to 2002, Lincoln-Herndon Law Office visitors remained constant in the low 40,000s. (By the late 1980s, street signs directing visitors to Lincoln "shrines" had been replaced by new signs directing them to Lincoln "sites.") Lincoln's tomb in Springfield, Illinois, drew 508,000 visitors yearly during the 1950s, peaked at 676,000 per year during the 1960s, then dropped through the next three decades. By 2000–2002, the annual number of visitors had fallen to 300,000. Visitation to New Salem, a town near Springfield where Lincoln spent his young adulthood, traces a different pattern, peaking above a million in the late 1960s, moving erratically through the next three decades, then settling at about 550,000 by the turn of the century.

The Springfield visitation picture, however, is complicated by the opening of the Abraham Lincoln Presidential Library and Museum in April 2005. Within less than two years, this museum drew its one millionth visitor—the fastest any presidential museum has reached the million mark. Because this new museum has provided an economic gain to the entire city, one might expect a resurrection of interest in Lincoln, marked by an increase in the number of visitors to other Lincoln sites in Springfield. This is not the case. Visitation to Lincoln's Springfield home declined from 419,552 in 2005 to 388, 887 in 2006. New Salem also experienced declining visitation: 510,024 in 2005 to 466,554 in 2006. Lincoln-Herndon Law Office visits increased slightly from 36,351 to 37,267 in 2005 and 2006 respectively. Visitors to Lincoln's tomb dropped from 415,478 in 2005 to 348,624 in 2006. These figures suggest the Presidential Library and Museum is competing with, rather than feeding, the city's traditional Lincoln sites,[5] and the museum, although less authentic, is designed to be more entertaining. This does not mean it is nothing but a source of fun; however, it competes successfully with other attractions for visitors' limited time. When one imagines this highly engaging museum located in Washington DC, for example, one infers declining Lincoln Memorial visitation.

The long-term visitation trend outside Springfield is almost everywhere downward. Lincoln's (Kentucky) birthplace visitation rose steadily from 245,000 per year during the fifties to more than 400,000 during the early 1970s, then fell to the present level of 309,000. The annual number of visitors to Lincoln's boyhood home in Gentryville, Indiana, grew from 146,000 in the 1960s to 180,000 and 215,000 in the next two decades, then diminished to 172,000 during the 1990s and 142,000 during 2000–2002.

The greatest of all Lincoln monuments, the Lincoln Memorial, attracted 1.9 million visitors per year during the fifties, 3.5 million during the sixties, and 3.1 million in the 1970s and 1980s; after restoration during the 1990s annual visits to the memorial rose to 3.8 million (2000–2002), but in no recent year did the memorial approach the 1987 high of 4.3 million visits. (Visitation rates leveled off well before the Vietnam Veterans Memorial, Holocaust Museum, Korean War Veterans Memorial, FDR Memorial, World War II Memorial, and other competing sites were erected.) Only one Lincoln site, Ford's Theater, has enjoyed continual growth in visitation, rising from more than a half million annual visits during the 1950s to one million during the 1990s and the first three years of the twenty-first century. In a way, Ford's Theater is the Washington site most similar to Springfield's Lincoln Museum. The carefully preserved scene of one of the most famous murders in American history, Ford's Theater, which contains its own museum, possesses a drawing power traditional Lincoln shrines cannot match.

Because different site superintendents use different methods of counting visitors, the trends are erratic; the overall pattern, however, is uniform. Except for Ford's Theater, which may not have peaked, visitation trends for all Lincoln sites reach their high point in the late 1960s or early 1970s, then level off or decline.[6] These trends, which appear at George Washington as well as Abraham Lincoln sites, occur in a nation that has added more than 130 million citizens from 1950 to 2000—an increase of 87 percent. In the Midwestern states closest to most Lincoln sites, the corresponding increase has been 45 percent. If we confine our analysis from 1980 to present, when all sites began using a uniform data collection protocol,[7] the conclusion remains the same: visitation generally levels or declines while the post-1980 population increases (24 percent for the nation; 9.4 percent for the Midwest).

Statue production, another measure of Lincoln renown, also traces a decidedly diminishing trend. Frederic Bullard's *Lincoln in Marble and Bronze,* supplemented by the *Bulletin of the Lincoln National Life Foundation,* shows eleven full-size outdoor statues of Lincoln in place at the turn of the twentieth century. Between 1900 and 1909, five additional statues were erected. Between 1910 and 1919, seventeen statues appeared, followed by eleven more during the 1920s and fifteen more during the 1930s. Suddenly, statue production slackened: five statues appeared during the 1940s, but only four more during the entire second half of the twentieth century. What is important about this trend is not the slowdown of Lincoln statue creation, which is inevitable, but its timing. Statue dedications diminish most sharply as Lincoln's prestige falls.[8]

Film production is another indicator of public interest in Lincoln. *The Civil War in Motion Pictures* lists Lincoln's as the leading role in ten films during the 1950s (mostly for school rather than mass audiences).[9] Only one Lincoln film was listed for the 1960s and none was listed after

1970. Television programs featuring Abraham Lincoln, as reported by *Variety Television Reviews*, declined more gradually, but the trend is unmistakable: from thirteen features during the 1950s to two during the 1980s. Mark Reinhard's *Abraham Lincoln: A Filmography* provides the best annotated list of Lincoln films, television dramas, documentaries, and home videos. During the period 1945 to 1959, according to Reinhard, five films and twenty television programs were devoted to Lincoln or included Lincoln in a significant role. Between 1960 and 1989, when most American homes had television sets, the number of Lincoln television programs decreased slightly. After 1990, thirty-seven videos and television programs included Lincoln centrally or marginally, not much greater than the number of films and television programs including Lincoln during the 1945–59 period.

Mass Media

Surveys, as well as counts of citations, visitors, and films, indicate Lincoln's changing visibility but fail to capture the quality of his appeal or convey what he means to Americans. They fail to explain why Americans watch Lincoln documentaries, read about him, and visit his shrines in the first place or what they think about what they read and see. For all their uses, quantitative indicators fail to capture Lincoln as concretely as the popular writers and artists who represent him.

Abraham Lincoln's reputation peaked in a cultural environment the present generation would find strange and amid traumas it never experienced. That the Lincoln images of that environment are unique is evident now that they are obsolete, or, at least, have lost their original meaning. No longer are the primary features of these images inspiration and uplift.

"Mr. Lisa Goes to Washington," a *Simpsons* parody of *Mr. Smith Goes to Washington* (1939), illustrates how thoroughly Lincoln's moral and emotional significance has waned. Jefferson Smith (played by James Stewart), the main character of Frank Capra's film, is a Boy's Club advocate who can "recite George Washington and Abraham Lincoln at the drop of a hat." Appointed to complete the term of a deceased senator, Mr. Smith is awed by his new position, and when he arrives in Washington, his patriotism is so aroused that he abandons his new colleagues and visits the city's monuments. In travelogue format, familiar sites are flashed on the screen to the accompaniment of patriotic music. "When Johnny Comes Marching Home" and "Taps" attend vistas of Civil War statuary, the Tomb of the Unknown Soldier, the graves at Arlington Cemetery, and, finally and climactically, the Lincoln Memorial. Full shots of Mr.

Smith's face reveal how moved he is by what he is seeing. He is no tourist taking in the sights but a man in communion with his country's past. His pilgrimage frames the rest of the story. When the new senator catches up with his party, he tells everyone about "Mr. Lincoln." "He's just lookin' straight at ya as you come up those steps. Just sittin' there like he was waitin' for somebody to come along." To this same monument Mr. Smith returns when his illusions about politics are shattered.

Mr. Smith visited the memorial for inspiration and guidance in his crusade against corruption. Lisa, fifty-five years later, noticing a congressman taking a bribe, tears up her "Roots of Democracy" essay. She is disillusioned. Searching for guidance, she heads for the Lincoln Memorial:

Lisa: [over the strains of the "Battle Hymn of the Republic," sees the Lincoln Memorial in the reflecting pool]
Honest Abe, he'll show me the way.
[goes to the Memorial]
Mr. Lincoln?

Man 1: Mr. Lincoln, I need your advice. What can I do to make this a better country?

Woman: Is this a good time to buy a house?

Man 2: Would I look good with a moustache?

Old Man: [takes off his hat, revealing his bald pate]
So I tried some turpentine, but that just made it worse.[10]

Plainly, the primary feature of Frank Capra's *Mr. Smith*, from a late twentieth-century point of view, is its corniness. Corny things are distinguished by exaggerated theatricality and threadbare moralizing; they are backward, banal, stereotyped, boorish, bromidic, unoriginal.[11] Corny representations suffer from the contradiction of lofty goals pursued by low and unskillful means; they try to inspire and uplift in a world no longer seeking either.

Corniness is also evident in relevant problems resistant to solution. The *Weekly World News*, a tabloid sold at the nation's supermarket checkout counters, informs its readers that the spirits of Abraham Lincoln, Martin Luther King Jr., and John F. Kennedy have joined forces to eliminate hate crimes throughout the United States. Reverend Josiah Adams was present when a group of ten skinheads lit torches to burn down his church.

> With a wave of his hand, Mr. Lincoln made the torches go cold, recalls Adams. Then Dr. King said, 'Hate is never the answer. Look into your hearts for the love and peace that dwells within.' The ten men stared

> wide-eyed for a moment, then ran down the road as fast as their legs could carry them. It was a genuine miracle![12]

The icy sarcasm is easy to recognize, but of the infinity of corny stories the *Weekly World News* could conceive and publicize, why was this particular story, involving Lincoln and a not-so-subtle texture of ridicule among them?[13]

BENIGN RIDICULE

Abraham Lincoln has always been a target for varying styles of humor. Between 1925 and 2004, *New Yorker* magazine published forty-three cartoons including Lincoln, usually as primary subject. Half these cartoons appeared between 1960 and 1979, about twice the number expected if the images had been randomly distributed across seventy-nine years. The form was typical of most *New Yorker* art: subtle, gentle pokes at tradition and authority, but nothing demeaning. A 1965 cartoon shows Lincoln calling up to his wife: "Mary, is the twelfth of February George Washington's birthday or is it mine?" The cartoonist is commenting on the public mood, not Lincoln: many Americans are unaware of the difference between Washington's and Lincoln's birthday.[14] In a 1976 comment on the upcoming presidential election debates, a candidate asks his manager: "Just one thing more. If *he* invokes Lincoln before I invoke Lincoln, who the hell do *I* invoke?" Lincoln is thus reduced to his use-value. In the same national bicentennial year, Lincoln appears as a leprechaun passing two fellow leprechauns sitting beneath a mushroom: "And yet *another* Bicentennial hype." Seven years later, use-value passes to absurdity as an end in itself: the sixteenth president, feathers and stovepipe hat, stands on the perch of his log cabin birdhouse.[15]

Other artists represent Lincoln in more striking ways. Here Lincoln wears a party hat and blows a whistle to mark a bank's anniversary; there he plays a saxophone to announce a rock concert. The most amusing images, however, began to appear in the 1990s. On a 1994 cover of *Scientific American* (fig. 5.5) Lincoln walks arm in arm with Marilyn Monroe. The designer, modifying old photographs to advertise the power of digital forgery, makes Lincoln appear prudish and stuffy beside the vivacious Marilyn.

In the logo for the film *Senior Trip,* Lincoln appears on his memorial chair of state grasping a can of beer, wearing sunglasses and an anti-Dole button. Behind his statue, the actual inscription to the Savior of the Union is changed to a parody of the opening lines of the Gettysburg Address: "Four Score and Seven Beers Ago. . . . " The story line, dimwitted high school students visiting Washington DC, is sustained by our

FIGURE 5.5. *Marilyn and Abe*, February 1994 cover illustration, *Scientific American*. Digital image by Visual Logic. Courtesy of Jack Harris, Visual Logic.

era's comedic conventions: vomiting, flatulence, urinating, drunkenness, teachers copulating with students.

Abraham Lincoln in kitsch advertisement reflects a new way of experiencing the world. Jon Stewart, late-night television comedian, talk-show host, sometime actor, and "Sultan of Savvy" exploits the new worldview by choosing Lincoln to advertise his *Naked Pictures of Famous People* (fig. 5.6). None of Stewart's eighteen satirical chapters, including "Princess Diana Writes Mother Teresa" and "Martha Stewart's Vagina," has anything to do with Lincoln, but he is pictured naked on the cover wearing his high hat, his two hands covering his genitals. Stewart needs a ridiculously modest Lincoln to affirm, through contrast, the new sexual freedom.

The new status of homosexuals in society is another variation on the new Lincoln theme. Gay activist Larry Kramer, lecturing on "Our Gay President" to a University of Wisconsin conference, claimed to have documentary evidence that Lincoln and his friend Joshua Speed were

FIGURE 5.6
Cover image for *Naked Pictures of Famous People,* a book by satirist Jon Stewart.

FIGURE 5.7
Gay Lincoln, 1999. *Salon.* Photo courtesy of Jeff Crosby.

homosexual partners. Kramer's statement, first published in the online magazine *Salon* (fig. 5.7), caused a stir.[16] In a serious variation on this theme, one of the participants in San Francisco's 2004 gay marriage festival placed in the crook of the arm of Haig Patigian's statue of Lincoln a sign declaring "We All Deserve the Freedom to Marry" (fig. 5.8). The gesture would not have worked if large numbers of gay Americans did not believe that Abraham Lincoln had engaged in homosexual relations. The protestors' decision to exploit Lincoln's supposed homosexuality and the public outrage accompanying the press's insinuating that Lincoln may actually have been gay, stemmed from the same source, namely, a cultural revolution seeking to widen the definition of normal sexuality.

Not only homosexuality but any variant of conventional sexuality was pressed to the service of questioning Lincoln's moral life. The newspaper that told the world that Abraham Lincoln was in truth a woman named Abigail Lincoln (fig. 5.9) later published an article headlined "Abe Lincoln's Private Porn Collection Found," revealing that an eleven-man team of historians authenticated the discovery of "fourscore and seven pictures of scantily clad or naked women," one of which is Mary, her private parts covered by a silk handkerchief. This cache proves that Lincoln, deemed "a champion of human rights, viewed women as second-class citizens and mere sex objects."[17]

The Secret Diary of Desmond Pfeiffer, a 1998 television comedy, depicts Lincoln in like manner: an oafish player of telegraph sex, attracted not only to his gorgeous intern but also to unshirted Union troops at work outside the White House. Significantly, the show was canceled after a few episodes not for its characterization of Lincoln's sexual preferences (which commented on President Clinton's "inappropriate relationship"), but for its failure to treat slavery with sufficient disdain.[18] C. A. Tripp, on the other hand, did not allow the slavery issue to interfere with his account of Lincoln's homosexuality. His *Intimate World of Abraham Lincoln*, which describes his relation with a guard at the Soldier Home, has been widely publicized and taken seriously by many.

Whether depicted as gay or transvestite, Lincoln adds weight to a new openness toward alternative sexual lifestyles. Sometimes, however, he is invoked for no reason at all, like a postmodern version of a nonsense syllable. In a *Saturday Night Live* skit based on *Godzilla*, Lincoln arises from his memorial chair and goes beserk after learning about the Republicans closing the government over a budget disagreement. He eats people and knocks down buildings. Thomas Jefferson arises and knocks down Lincoln, who is skewered on the Washington Monument as he falls. He dies, and his spirit returns to the Lincoln Memorial. *Mad* magazine, for its part, presents Alfred Newman throwing a snowball at Lincoln's hat.

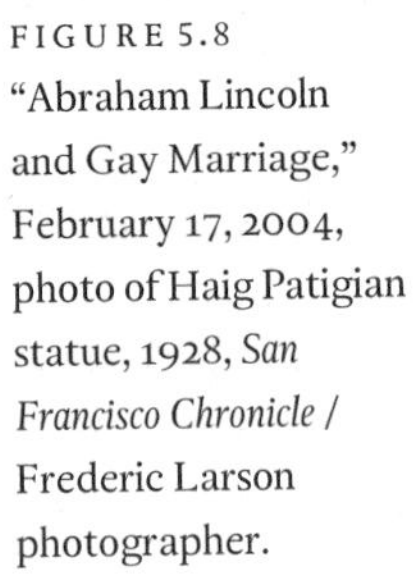

FIGURE 5.8
"Abraham Lincoln and Gay Marriage," February 17, 2004, photo of Haig Patigian statue, 1928, *San Francisco Chronicle* / Frederic Larson photographer.

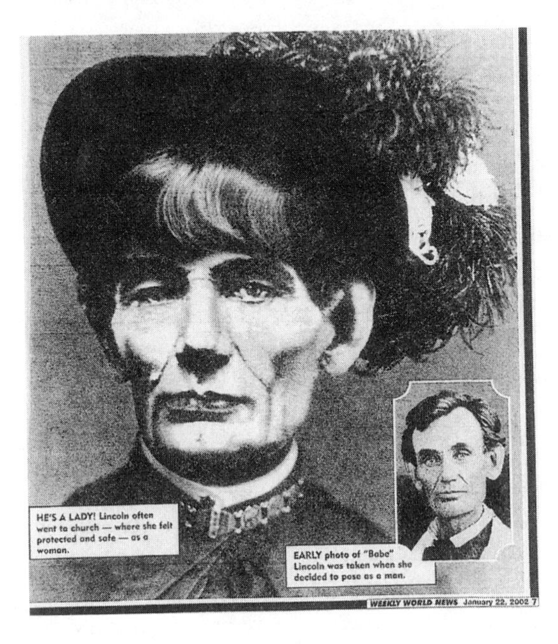

FIGURE 5.9
February 2002 photo, *Weekly World News*.

FIGURE 5.10 *Hard Drinkin' Lincoln,* 2000. Courtesy Icebox.com.

One of the characters in the 1993 film *Dazed and Confused* senses for a split second that she is having sex with Abraham Lincoln; in another film, *Happy Gilmore,* Lincoln appears for three seconds in a cloud with the protagonist's dead golf teacher and a crocodile. In yet another appearance, Lincoln pitches a baseball to Babe Ruth, who homers with the bat that Lincoln made for him. Lincoln looks into the camera and states "That's the Babe for ya," and the original story line continues. In *Honest Abe and Popular Steve,* a thirty-minute television comedy, Lincoln gives a rubdown to a famous rock 'n' roll star. The new Lincoln portrait exploits celebrity as a source of absurdist comedy.

The Internet affords the most striking novelties. *Hard-Drinkin' Lincoln,* a fourteen-episode (Icebox.com) series, unveils "the real Honest Abe: a loud, lewd, obnoxious guy in a big hat—the kind of guy you sit behind in a theater and just want to shoot." The episodes follow a common thread, beginning with the theme song about "The Great Emancipator," a chronic drunkard, an "irritator," and "public masturbator" (fig. 5.10). In stories ranging from "Abezilla" to "The Play's the Thing," Abe, belching constantly, makes unkind remarks about his wife ("a nattering scoop of lard" who would never win a wet t-shirt contest), requests sexual favors from beautiful young women ("How about if I put my log into your cabin?"), and reminds Frederick Douglass that "I freed your black asses." Abe is so obnoxious that the audience applauds when John Wilkes Booth shoots him.

That *Hard Drinkin' Lincoln,* which shares its Web site with an equally transgressive series about *Jesus and His Three Brothers,*[19] might someday become corny is doubtful. These narratives are devoid of everything that makes for corn, including sentimentality, overestimation of worth, saccharine motives, and mindless commitments.

One of the newest sources of Lincoln representation is the "YouTube" Web site, where anyone can upload a self-made video. Many have chosen to make skits about Lincoln. Some of these videos, including Gabor Boritt on Lincoln's relevance to the free world, Robert Willard's money-raising walk for the Abraham Lincoln Institute, and actor Jeff Daniels reading the Gettysburg Address, are serious documentaries. The vast majority of items, however, are produced by adolescents, sometimes for fun, most as high school assignments. The length of the videos runs from five seconds to thirty minutes or more; their coherence is equally variable. The filming site is sometimes a monumental or historical place; usually it is inside the producer's home or backyard. The story contents are broad: assassination comedies, Lincoln walking up and down walls, shopping in a supermarket, appearing before his audience with spinning head, singing the song "Crazy," acting out a foot fetish. Humorous interviewers question the gay Lincoln. The stoned Lincoln dances in front of a marijuana plant. For those who like their stories spiced with sexual content, there is "Abraham Lincoln: Unauthorized Biography." The Savior of the Union approaches Robert E. Lee's wife in bed: "I don't care about America," he confesses. "All I care about is sex, booze, and pills. Damn this country and everyone in it." "Baboon Torture Division" is slightly more kinky, with bondage, blood, and sex. A sadist thinks of Lincoln with bleeding head as he has sex with a bound lady.

The Gettysburg Address is among the most popular topics. In one situation, Abraham Lincoln loses control of his bowels while delivering the address. (The producer informs his viewers that he made the video while hopped up on Vicodin.) In another place, Lincoln wears a modern suit and tie and delivers his eulogy in computer monotone. Lincoln also appears as a still photograph with moving lips enunciating the address.

One of the more interesting categories consists of semi-serious documentaries. Larry Dortch, for example, goes to the Lincoln Memorial, reads the inscriptions, asserts that all is a lie. The Great Emancipator freed the slaves for strategic reasons. In another video, *Abe Day*, an admirer tries but fails to interest people in the fact it is Lincoln's birthday.

These videos are seen by a small percentage of the population, although many high school students may look at them for ideas for their own Lincoln video projects. For the most part, they reflect the vanishing solemnity of Lincoln's image in American memory. That high school skits rarely even strive to be serious is especially noteworthy in view of the many serious Lincoln plays written and performed by students during the first half of the twentieth century.

Juxtaposing greatness and grossness, although *uncharacteristic* of present Lincoln portrayals, *distinguishes* them from earlier ones. New

FIGURE 5.11
The Coolest Guy in the World, 1989 advertisement. Department of Commerce and Community Affairs, Office of Tourism, Springfield, Illinois.

portrayals depict nothing in the way of a bond between Lincoln and his admirers, evoke no moral sentiment, make no reference to what is lacking in ourselves. These are pictures one expects to see in a disenchanted world where "the ultimate and most sublime values have retreated from public life,"[20] a world whose monuments lack heroes, a world that has lost the pneuma, that breath of life which once welded together fragmented communities to face and conquer great dangers. Inhabitants of this world, we recognize vaguely what some of the older Lincoln images symbolize; we know they are authentic, even vaguely heroic, yet they seem alien. We can see them but cannot see ourselves in them. In some inexpressible way, the newer Lincoln images put us into closer contact with ourselves. In a 1989 Springfield, Illinois, tourism advertisement (fig. 5.11), Lincoln is said to be heroic because he delivered the Gettysburg Address without saying "like"; he is also approachable and, above all, cool—the coolest guy in the world. No longer the remote hero for adolescents to emulate, he is an adolescent himself. Wearing the newest in sunglasses, he can "relate" to students on their Springfield trip.

None of the new portrayals disparage Lincoln; all exploit his image for amusement or advertising because he symbolizes what is most conventional in our culture. But it is one thing to depict America's icon as an object to be looked upon and revered; another, as a source of distraction. How seriously, then, should we take Abraham Lincoln? Is he still Savior of the Union? Great Emancipator? Man of the People? Yes, but we still can have some fun with him. The question is who is having the most fun. Which part of the population is playing with Lincoln; which is hostile toward him? Indices of Lincoln's decline are ubiquitous, but they combine uniquely with the experiences of different sectors of American society. How American communities de-traditionalize and disenchant themselves is an old question, but hardly explored.

African American Impressions

Many communities during the last half of the twentieth century have proven themselves indifferent to the nation's past. Black communities have proven increasingly hostile to it and to Lincoln's particular role in it, partly because their alienation from the larger society has already made them receptive to criticism of its heroes.

From the time of Abraham Lincoln's death to the early 1930s, he was the African American community's champion. To no other white American did blacks feel more gratitude. Yet, one sector of the black population, the academic and political left, always looked on Lincoln suspiciously. Lincoln Day issues of African American newspapers almost always carried critical remarks amid effusive praise, and from the New Deal forward this criticism grew. Toward the end of the twentieth century, while whites were losing interest in Lincoln and using his reputation as an instrument for lighthearted parody, black critics took him seriously. They found nothing funny about him. Julius Lester was typical: "The South was fighting to take slavery out of the Union," whereas "the North [under Lincoln] was fighting to keep it in the Union."[21] Dick Gregory, too, dismissed "the myth of emancipation" as one of America's great lies.[22] Lerone Bennett expressed the radical viewpoint more effectively than anyone. His 1968 *Ebony* article, "Was Abe Lincoln a White Supremacist?" rejected the assumption of Lincoln's hostility to slavery. Only as war crippled slavery did he decide on emancipation, making a virtue out of a necessity. Bennett also concretized moral reservations about Lincoln by revealing Lincoln's fondness for the word "nigger."[23] In black newspapers everywhere, editors and commentators congratulated Bennett for his careful research and endorsed his conclusions. The *Chicago Defender* noted sorrowfully, "The Negro and a large body of the American people have been deceived" about Lincoln. Belief in "'Father Abraham' as a labor sympathizer with his compassion for the suffering of black slaves is being wiped out."[24]

Thirteen years later, Vincent Harding enlarged Bennett's argument. Lincoln, according to Harding, never freed the slaves—the slaves had taken history into their own hands:

> "the heart of the matter was this: while the concrete historical realities of the time testified to the costly, daring, courageous activities of hundreds of thousands of black people breaking loose from slavery and setting themselves free, the myth gave the credit to a white Republican president . . . [who] dreamed of a Haitian island and of Central American colonies to rid the country of the constantly accusing, constantly challenging black presence."[25]

In the 1980s, Lincoln-bashing turned crude. In one example, *I'm Gonna Get Ya Sucka*, a 1988 stage play, the protagonist pays a visit to Brothers Against the Man, a revolutionary organization whose leader beams with pride as his son recites the story of Abraham Lincoln:

> Abraham Lincoln was born in a log cabin in Illinois. This poor white trash went on to become the president of the United States. Once in office, this white capitalist swine manipulated the freedom of the black man for his own political career until another piece of poor white trash shot him in the head. The end.[26]

Such language must have offended many blacks, but the verdict on Lincoln, even for the conservative *Atlanta Daily World*, remained mixed. He "was not actually interested in saving the Negro." For him, personal friendship with blacks was impossible, "but the fact that he could go against the majority feeling to offer freedom . . . to ignorant slaves, places him far above the average human being."[27]

In recent years, the growing number of African Americans assuming political power has been restrained in its criticism of traditional heroes; yet, with the exception of conservatives, African American leaders have been equally restrained in their praise. Despite his admiration for Lincoln, Senator Barack Obama declared: "I cannot swallow whole the view of Lincoln as the 'Great Emancipator.' As a law professor and civil rights lawyer and as an African American, I am fully aware of his limited views on race. Anyone who actually reads the Emancipation Proclamation knows it was more a military document than a clarion call for justice." Jesse Jackson Jr. believes that "Lincoln valued the Union above all, but he knew the result of saving the Union was emancipation for the slaves"—in short, emancipation was a random act of beneficence. Louis Farrakhan greeted his Million Man March audience by publicly recognizing Lincoln as "Our Supposed Deliverer," and made explicit mention of his cruelest public statements about blacks.[28]

Based on the historical record alone, Abraham Lincoln could be admired, but not revered. He could be the Great Emancipator, to be sure, but also the Reluctant Emancipator, the eager colonizer, the bigot whose highest aspiration was to keep whites safe from the presence of blacks. Beneath every media affirmation of Lincoln's sympathy for America's black people lurks the nagging evidence of Lincoln's contempt.

Nationwide surveys provide the best information on Lincoln's comparative standing. When the National Opinion Research Corporation (NORC) asked a 1945 sample to name the "two or three greatest men who have ever lived in this country," 57 percent of the white respondents, compared to 52 percent of black respondents, named Lincoln. Between 1956 and 1999, black ratings of Lincoln declined at a significantly lower rate (27 percent) than white ratings (36 percent), but they also display consistently a lower regard for him (see table 5.2). In 1956, the approximate beginning of the Southern civil rights crisis, the Gallup Poll asked "Who do you think were America's three greatest Presidents?" Almost two-thirds—64 percent—of white respondents named Lincoln, compared to 48 percent of black respondents—a sixteen-point difference. In 1975, 50 percent of whites and 37 percent of blacks answering the same question named Lincoln;[29] in 1985, the difference narrowed—almost certainly by sampling error—to five points (48 and 43 percent), but in 1991, a wide difference reappeared, with 47 percent of whites naming Lincoln; 35 percent of blacks.[30] In 1999 the percentages were 47 and 28, with whites, again, naming Lincoln more often than blacks (table 5.5). The robustness of race difference in attitude towards Lincoln is evident in appendix I, which compares black and white responses in the years 1956, 1975, 1985, 1991, and 1999 within different categories of education, gender, age, residence, and religion inside and outside the South. In every single year and in every category where the number of African Americans is large enough for meaningful comparison (in no survey does the total number exceed 200), a higher percentage of whites place Lincoln among the greatest presidents.

Race differences are also evident in comparative presidential rankings. Whites have ranked Lincoln the best president in every Gallup survey but one (1975, when they placed him three points behind Kennedy). Blacks have assigned him distant second and third ranks: 29 points behind Roosevelt in 1956; 49 points behind Kennedy in 1975; 36 and 26 points behind Kennedy in 1985 and 1991 respectively; 13 points behind Kennedy in 1999 (table 5.5). During the last third of the twentieth century, John F. Kennedy replaced Franklin Delano Roosevelt as the liberator of the African American community.

TABLE 5.5. Percentage of respondents designating Lincoln and other selected presidents as one of America's "three greatest presidents," by race

	Year									
	1956		1975		1985		1991		1999	
President	White (n=1218)	Black (n=151)	White (n=1362)	Black (n=151)	White (n=1359)	Black (n=181)	White (n=857)	Black (n=147)	White (n=779)	Black (n=119)
Lincoln	64	48	50	37	48	43	47	35	42	28
Kennedy			48	86	51	79	45	61	32	41
Roosevelt	63	77	45	48	45	42	32	16	29	13
Truman	9	42	38	21	29	15	19	8	15	1
Washington	50	22	26	22	27	17	26	22	27	10
Eisenhower	33	38	25	14	16	9	14	10	10	8

Source: Gallup Polls, January 6–11, 1956; November 21–24, 1975; June 7–10, 1985; February 7–10, 1991; University of Maryland survey, May 1999. Differences in data collection methods and coding for race in Gallup and University of Maryland surveys are discussed in appendix C.

At question is whether respondents reacted to Lincoln or expressed the general inclination, common among people who came of age during the 1960s, to denounce all traditional heroes. Both factors are at play. Black ratings of every president have fallen as steeply as they have for Lincoln (see table 5.5). In 1936, for example, black voters shifted from Lincoln's Republican Party to Roosevelt's Democratic Party, and when Gallup took a poll twenty years later, in 1956, he found 77 percent of black respondents still naming Roosevelt a great president. In 1975, 48 percent considered Roosevelt among the three greatest, compared to 86 percent for Kennedy. By 1999 only 13 percent of African Americans named Roosevelt, while Kennedy nominations dropped to 41 percent; Lincoln, to 28 percent—far below Kennedy. Yet, within any given age group in any year (appendix H), African Americans are less inclined toward Lincoln than whites.

Education is an important part of the context affecting Lincoln's standing. The handing down of values, beliefs, and moral judgments, including information about the national heroes embodying them, is one of education's key functions. However, many blacks are alienated from the culture into which educational institutions try to integrate them. Among whites, appendix I shows, education increases Lincoln's greatness rating sharply and consistently; among blacks this relation is weak and inconsistent. The number of percentage points by which whites exceed blacks in naming Lincoln a great president is less than 1 percent for people with less than twelve years of education; among high school graduates, 7.6 percent; for those with one or more years of college,

17.8 percent. Education does not lessen regard for Lincoln among African Americans but greatly enhances it among whites. On the other hand, the percentage naming Lincoln a great president declines equally fast for whites and for blacks with high school and college education.

Weakening belief in Lincoln's greatness differs within and outside the South. From 1956–99, the percentage of Southern blacks recognizing Lincoln's greatness diminished by 21 percent; outside the South, it fell 49 percent. Comparable rates of decline for Southern and non-Southern whites were 17 percent and 34 percent respectively (appendix I). The pattern conforms to an old observation about rising expectations: where racial justice is best established and living standards and aspirations are highest, frustrations are greatest and the prestige of traditional heroes lowest.

The late twentieth-century decline of Lincoln's prestige, then, has only partly to do with race. The previous chapter shows that blacks believe Lincoln's freeing the slaves was his greatest achievement, regardless of whether or not they named him a great president (tables 4.4 and 4.5). Because this same chapter shows only a small percentage of black respondents describing Lincoln negatively, race differences can be ascribed to indifference rather than hostility. As generations pass, new presidents sympathetic to civil rights, namely Roosevelt and Kennedy, become more relevant than an old president who opposed slavery. Whites also admired these new presidents, but to a lesser extent than African Americans. Thus, while academics debate Lincoln's racism and his motivation for drafting and signing the Emancipation Proclamation, ordinary black citizens believe Lincoln's antislavery sentiments were genuine but consider them less relevant than the antisegregation sentiments of more recent presidents whom, ironically, they revere in smaller numbers over time. African Americans seem to be affected by the same cynical mood, to be assessed in the next chapter, that affects whites.

In speculating why Lincoln has lost his exalted place among African Americans, one realizes that contemporary culture has raised expectations for equality of condition. To his own generation of beneficiaries, Lincoln seemed a true savior, yet later generations, including our own, have demanded more. Accordingly, the same egalitarian trends that heightened the historical relevance of Lincoln's Emancipation Proclamation made most of its beneficiaries indifferent to it.[31]

Southern Impressions

If feelings about Lincoln were the same now as they were one hundred years ago, African American complaints would be overwhelmed by praise and gratitude—not only for the Great Emancipator but for the Savior of that Union without whom emancipation would have been impossible. White Southern praise, on the other hand, would be accompanied by hatred. Every generation, however, has its own way of coming to terms with Lincoln.

South Carolina democrat Joseph R. Bryson, in 1946, alive to the stirrings of black discontent, quoted a poem to the U.S. House of Representatives: "In the dark days, when the South in her grief / Needed a Lincoln to lend her relief / From carpetbaggers' and free negroes' scorns / Scalawags scourged her and crowned her with thorns."[32] Historian Richard Harwell, like Senator Bryson, considered Lincoln an ally. "Southern antipathy for Abraham Lincoln," he observed in 1952, is gone. Lincoln "has taken his place in the hearts of Southerners as in those of all Americans, as a national hero along with Washington and, in the South at least, along with Lee."[33] But as civil rights activities intensified, consensus on Lincoln's pro-South credentials weakened. Shortly before the Montgomery boycott, an *Atlanta Constitution*'s editor recognized Lincoln's birthday while noting that Lincoln was "not our greatest American."[34] On the other hand, vestiges of the segregationist Lincoln remained. When Senator Everett Dirksen of Illinois told the United States Senate that Lincoln believed Negroes were entitled to the same right to life, liberty, and the pursuit of happiness as whites, South Carolina's Olin D. T. Johnston, known as "the Senator for the South,"[35] protested the "present civil rights holocaust" and efforts to "force a new reconstruction," and reminded his colleagues that the Illinois senator omitted from his remarks Lincoln's belief in the natural superiority of the white race.[36]

Southerners' perception of Lincoln reflected their relationship to the rest of the country. In 1961, during John Kennedy's first year in office, no one doubted Southerners' patriotism, for they had willingly fought and died in two world wars and in the recent Korean War. The question was whether Southerners' hostility toward their nation's enemies could be matched by solidarity with its black and non-Southern citizens—whether they could now feel part of the country they had helped defend. Never was this issue more problematic than when the Lincoln sesquicentennial, the Civil War centennial, and the civil rights movement collided.

Southern participation in Lincoln's 1909 centennial was limited, yet every city made some effort to join in. The 1959 sesquicentennial was different. Congressional festivities reached the South by television, but locally sponsored events were virtually nonexistent. The Sesquicentennial

Commission's final report, in fact, did not mention a single Southern event in its formal summary.[37] The South never showed up for Lincoln's one hundred and fiftieth birthday party.[38] In the (1961–65) Civil War centennial, the South played an active but negative role. From the first, Southerners welcomed the centennial, but they seemed eager to participate not *with* other states but *against* them.[39] Ralph McGill, the *Atlanta Constitution* editor, had anticipated the split even before the centennial began. Since Southern moderates chose not to express themselves in the civil rights crisis, he said, "the myth of state sovereignty" has reemerged.[40] Governor Ross Barnett of Mississippi proved McGill right when he said to a Civil War centennial audience: "Among the cherished traditions which Southern men and women have always supported is local control of local affairs."[41] South Carolina senator Strom Thurmond agreed. The Confederacy's cause, he said, is "a living cause today—the right of self-determination."[42] But if the "Confederacy's cause is a living cause," what is to be made of Lincoln? Southerners, even in the border states, never knew how to answer that question directly. "Lincoln's bronze statue is the largest in the rotunda of our State Capital," Kentucky centennial commissioner G. M. Pedley declared. "Kentucky did not secede from the Union, furnished more fighting men to the North than to the South, but today is largely pro-Southern, in sentiment, at least."[43]

Commissioner Pedley's use of the word "but" reflects the new antinomy between recognition of Lincoln and support for segregation. Northern states made the Emancipation Proclamation a Civil War centennial highlight;[44] Southern commissions ignored the Proclamation and urged the National Commission to dissociate itself from it. The Commission could not go that far, but its arrangement committee did try to exclude black speakers from the Emancipation Proclamation program at the Lincoln Memorial. Although quickly overruled, the Commission's plan reveals how much Lincoln's symbolic connection with black interests (despite black ambivalence toward Lincoln) troubled Southern officials.

Southerners' beliefs about Lincoln, expressed in national opinion surveys, were more positive than those of Southern officials. Asked in 1945 to name the two or three greatest Americans, 61 percent of NORC's non-Southerners named Lincoln, compared to 46 percent—almost half—of the Southerners. In 1956, two years after the U.S. Supreme Court desegregated the nation's public schools and one year before President Eisenhower met the Court's first major challenge in Little Rock, Gallup asked a national sample of 1,385 adults for their choice of the three greatest American presidents. Sixty-nine percent of white Northerners named Lincoln compared to 44 percent of white Southern respondents—a

25 percentage-point difference. In 1956, as in 1945, almost half the Southern respondents named Lincoln, but the gap between Southern and non-Southern samples, as appendix I shows, appears in every subsequent survey year—1975, 1985, 1991, and 1999—and in every population group: small town and big city, Republicans and Democrats, rich and poor, college-educated and non-college-educated, young and old, men and women. This gap does not indicate dislike of Lincoln in the South. Not only do half the Southern respondents name him one of the great presidents—a number that remains almost the same in 1975; Lincoln's rank, compared to that of George Washington, also changes dramatically from 1956, where the two receive approximately the same percentage of Southern votes, to 1975, where Lincoln is 17 points above Washington and within 5 points of Roosevelt and Kennedy. Table 5.6 also shows the regional difference shrinking from 25 percentage points in 1956 (Southern compared to non-Southern states) to 8 points in 1999. The convergence does not mean that Southerners learned to love Lincoln more since 1956 but that non-Southerners, as noted, loved him much less.

Appendix I allows for more detailed comparison. Southern whites display more positive attitudes toward Lincoln than Southern blacks in four of the five years in which they are compared. In three of these five years, Southern whites display equal or more positive attitudes toward Lincoln than non-Southern blacks.

Survey figures hardly tell the whole story. Many Southerners who think Lincoln a great president would be totally unwilling to erect a statue of him in their town, observe a holiday in his memory, build him a monument, or even name a major street after him. Historian Avery Craven, writing in 1942, considered these symbolic elements unimportant. The South, he claimed, has merged into the life of the nation. Old men and women continued to resent Lincoln, but "the younger generation . . . accepted him from the first as a national hero, less than Washington because they attended school on [Lincoln's] birthday, but, nevertheless, a great figure. . . . His greatness is now the Southern boy's heritage."[45] That Lincoln was "less than Washington" because there was no Lincoln school holiday meant to Craven that his reputation was theoretically equal to Washington's. The Gallup survey taken three years after Craven wrote his article proved him at least partially right. Forty-three percent of Southern respondents, as noted, named George Washington as one of the two or three greatest men in American history; 46 percent named Lincoln.

However, Washington and Lincoln occupied different places in Southern and non-Southern culture. That all Southern children attended

TABLE 5.6. Percentage of respondents designating Lincoln and other selected presidents as one of America's "three greatest presidents," by region

	Year									
	1956		1975		1985		1991		1999	
President	Non-South (n=1004)	South (n=381)	Non-South (n=1192)	South (n=335)	Non-South (n=1265)	South (n=275)	Non-South (n=711)	South (n=302)	Non-South (n=622)	South (n=379)
Lincoln	69	44	50	42	50	37	49	35	44	36
Kennedy			53	46	54	53	48	47	36	34
Roosevelt	64	67	44	47	44	44	31	26	29	23
Truman	12	16	38	31	26	31	17	19	12	13
Washington	47	47	25	25	26	26	27	21	24	26
Eisenhower	31	40	23	31	15	17	12	16	9	8

Source: Gallup Polls, January 6–11, 1956; November 21–24, 1975; June 7–10, 1985; February 7–10, 1991; University of Maryland Survey, May 1999.

school on Lincoln's birthday, few on Washington's, may have had limited bearing on Lincoln's standing in Southern opinion polls, but it went to the core of his place in the symbolic life of the South. Lincoln preserved the Union and destroyed slavery at the expense of more than 250,000 Southern lives—25 percent of the South's military-age male population. He unleashed a wave of destruction against Georgia civilians by allowing one of his armies, unopposed, to burn and pillage from Atlanta through Charleston; he allowed another army to do the same across Virginia's Shenandoah. Given the magnitude of its losses, the South could have built monuments to Lincoln only if its whites first renounced their own sense of themselves.

Nevertheless, at the turn of the present century, the United States Historical Society, a private, nonprofit, Richmond-based organization directed by former Illinois resident Robert Klein, persuaded the U.S. Park Service to allow it to erect on federally leased land in the former Confederate capital, Richmond, a statue commemorating Lincoln's April 1865 visit.[46] Neo-Confederate petitioners opposed its placement: to rub the nose of the South in its own defeat would be "a slap in the face of the brave men and women who went through four years of unbelievable hell fighting an invasion of Virginia led by President Lincoln."[47] Resistance grew fierce as the date for the statue's dedication approached but died down soon afterward. At question is how receptive other Southern cities would be to such a symbol. Because the Richmond city council was 67 percent black and contributed $40,000 toward site-preparation costs, and because the controversy took place against the background of Black History Month replacing Confederate History and Heritage Month in the school and community ritual calendar, one is entitled to ask whether the white Southerner, notwithstanding his positive beliefs about Lincoln, is as eager to commemorate him as a predominantly black city council. The question will be pursued further in chapter 7.

Conservative Impressions

Racial, regional, and ideological supports for Lincoln must be distinguished. Willmoore Kendall set the reactionary agenda when he said that Lincoln falsified history by designating the Declaration of Independence as America's founding charter and by replacing liberty with equality as its founding ethos.[48] Adopting this theme, which many Lincoln scholars believe to be true, conservative M. E. Bradford attacked Lincoln fiercely. His was a "religion of Union," to be sure, but a "religion of Union *in* equality." The politics of the left, Bradford believed, is rooted in "the Lincoln precedent."[49] Thomas Fleming, as editor of

Chronicles, elaborated Bradford's complaint. Lincoln is the inspiration and the model for "the New Deal, with its labyrinth of welfare entitlements, and the civil-rights revolution which now extends the status of privileged minority to fully three-fourths of the population: women, blacks, atheists, Hispanics, and . . . the lame, the halt, the blind, and the perverse."[50]

Thomas DiLorenzo, a libertarian rather than traditional conservative scholar, attacks Lincoln as the Great Centralizer, the statist who took the nation to war to advance his own and his party's interests, to diminish if not abolish the Jeffersonian principle of state's rights, local autonomy, limited government, and free trade. *The Real Lincoln: A New Look at Abraham Lincoln, His Agenda, and an Unnecessary War* is no defense of the Old South's oppressive institutions and traditions, but it does attack Lincoln as a tyrant. Lincoln's and his party's flaws were coextensive, with protective tariffs, centralized banking—the whole Hamiltonian model that Jefferson despised. Lincoln's administration was the forerunner of Big Government.[51]

Such a reading of Lincoln's legacy is limited to the extreme right; most American conservatives consider Lincoln a man who would share and sympathize with their views. They see in him no big-government tyrant, but an egalitarian who believed in a fair chance for everyone. They also sense what Lincoln would be against: "If Lincoln lived today," announced *U.S. News and World Report*,[52] he would not be as successful as he was, for the Great Society's welfare programs would have deprived him of the challenges that built his character and made him great. "What did Lincoln stand for?" He stood for competition, not leveling, Ralph McGinnis (1979) told the Illinois legislature. Lincoln believed in the "natural processes of production and distribution." He was not ashamed to admit that he was once a poor man, and he was in favor of everyone's having the chance to improve his situation. In short, "He stood for economic free enterprise."[53] Nicolai Lenin, in this regard, was the favorite foil. Lenin, like Lincoln, understood the poor, but Lenin's sympathy was destructive. He "spent his whole life setting class against class," whereas Lincoln realized "You cannot help the poor by attempting to destroy the rich."[54] The analogy is there for anyone willing to see: Lincoln is to Lenin what free enterprise is to the welfare state.[55] Given his appreciation of free enterprise, Lincoln's personal efforts to overcome poverty reflected the kind of character that made him a successful president. In short, nostalgia for Lincoln's frontier means opposition to the welfare state. The frontier attracts because it invigorates and makes for self-reliance; the welfare state repels because it enervates and makes for dependency.

Conservative intellectuals, like Steven Hayward, believe that the ideological right has abandoned Lincoln to the left,[56] but Hayward never asks why it has done so, whether rank-and-file conservatives have followed its lead, or why the left has succeeded in appropriating Lincoln—at least in its public discourse. Lincoln's appreciation of free enterprise, although based on a moral principle of individual freedom, never distinguished him historically. His rags-to-riches story never gave meaning to war, death, or misfortune. The conservative Lincoln is the most authentic and the most compatible with the ideology of competitive individualism, but this Lincoln cannot reach people in their profoundest moments of need. As grassroots conservatives continued to revere Lincoln as the embodiment of honest work leading from rags to riches, liberals continue to see his supreme gentleness, compassion, and kindness.

Lincoln once pulled in two directions, not one. Gallup surveys from 1945 to 1991 show more Republicans than Democrats naming Lincoln among the three greatest presidents (table 5.2), while the 1991 survey, the only survey to ask respondents for both political ideology and party affiliation, shows that liberals and middle-of-the-roaders, regardless of party preference, are more likely than conservatives to name Lincoln a great president. Because Southern Democrats, as well as Republicans, are likely to be conservative, however, ideology is correlated with party identification less closely in Southern than in non-Southern states. Therefore, a comparison within regions is necessary (appendix J). Outside the South and among Democrats within the South, liberals and Republicans, independently of one another, are most likely to name Lincoln a great president. However, Lincoln's affinity with the Republican party is stronger by far than his affinity with ideology. The ideological right, as Steven Hayward suggests, may have abandoned Lincoln to the ideological left: the mass media's affection for Lincoln and certain federal efforts to align him with liberal causes suggests as much.[57] But if Lincoln "belonged" to anyone in 1991, it was to the American Republican mainstream. (See also table 5.2 above.)

As the 1990s progressed, however, Abraham Lincoln became dissociated from the Republican party. As table 5.2 shows, the difference between Republicans' and Democrats' beliefs about Lincoln averaged seventeen points between 1945 and 1991; in 1999 it is a negligible six points. On the other hand, if Lincoln now symbolizes Republican and Democratic values alike, a smaller percentage of both Democrats and Republicans consider him the greatest president as the decades pass (table 5.2).

Because different communities bring unique experiences and presuppositions to representations of the past, they perceive it differently. This is why vast revisions of the historical record often have limited influence on the public. The rise in Alexander Hamilton's prestige among Progressive Era ideologues never rubbed off on the people at large. Thirty-five years of presidential-greatness surveys indicate that revisionist views of John Adams and Thomas Jefferson have failed to change their place in the public's prestige-ranking. Likewise, the absolute level of books and scholarly articles about Abraham Lincoln has remained high during the last twenty-five years, but his prestige in American popular culture has not risen.[58] In fact, Lincoln's prestige, as table 5.1 shows, has declined since the mid-1970s. African Americans, once the most fervent admirers of Lincoln, are no exception to this trend. Paradoxically, the personification of egalitarianism and racial justice loses prestige as racial justice becomes secure and multiculturalism grows.

In America, as elsewhere,[59] the post–World War II peace has been associated with a lessening stake in the past:

> A situation has developed which is quite paradoxical in human terms: The barriers of the past have been pushed back as never before; our knowledge of the history of man and the universe has been enlarged on a scale and to a degree not dreamed of by previous generations. At the same time, the sense of identity and continuity with the past, whether our own or history's, has gradually and steadily declined. Previous generations *knew* much less about the past than we do, but perhaps *felt* a much greater sense of identity and continuity with it. . . ."[60]

The paradoxical "situation" to which Hans Meyerhoff alludes has afflicted different generations in different ways. For the twenty-five years preceding the Civil War, usually defined as the antebellum era (1835–60), Americans recognized no heroes of their own, but adored the Revolutionary generation. Since the 1960s decade, the postbellum era of the twentieth century, greatness itself has lost much of its reality.

The feeling of men and women toward political and moral heroes, once similar to their worship of the idealized characters of religious narratives, was a form of religion; religion, a form of hero-worship, when most people still believed that God intervened in the affairs of man and chose America's great leaders, from George Washington to Abraham Lincoln, to direct His favored nation on the right path. In those times, political leaders and clergymen regularly compared Abraham Lincoln's life to Christ's. As religion loses relevance and gods become objects of analysis rather than devotion, however, political heroes lose their aura, and the myths enveloping them grow stale. This does not mean, however, that heroes become villains, or even disliked; they are simply contemplated with less emotion and moral fervor. American civil religion and its history have become secularized. But why and how?

* 6 *

Post-Heroic Era

ACIDS OF EQUALITY AND THE WANING OF GREATNESS

How could Lincoln's great stature diminish? "The Lincoln establishment," with its thousands of partisan curators, collectors, biographers, historians, textbook writers, and antiquarians, was more powerful at the end of the twentieth century than the beginning, outgrowing Lincoln himself. Today, the Lincoln commemorative community remains the largest of any in America.[1] "As the twentieth century drew to a close," Merrill Peterson observed, "no other famous American had such a large scholarly complement as Lincoln, so many organizations, publications, and activities devoted to cultivating this resource."[2]

Abraham Lincoln's story is preserved by organizations conveying information about the Civil War through meetings, journals, and magazine articles, and special-purpose organizations conveying information about Lincoln. The latter organizations, which number about one thousand, form an inverted pyramid. At the apex are a small number of large organizations producing, preserving, and distributing information about Lincoln's life. Headquartered in the national center of Lincoln specialization, Springfield, Illinois, is the Abraham Lincoln Association. The Abraham Lincoln Library and Museum in Springfield, Illinois, is the nation's largest repository of information on Lincoln, and it contains the newest and most popular exhibits. Moving away from Springfield are smaller Lincoln libraries and museums with paid administrative officers and staffs, including the Lincoln Museum (of the Lincoln Memorial University, Harrogate, Tennessee), the Lincoln Library at Lincoln College (Lincoln, Illinois), and the Lincoln Museum of Fort Wayne, Indiana. The John Hay Library at Brown and the Huntington Library house large quantities of Lincoln documents and relics. The Surrat Society cultivates interest in Lincoln's assassination. Newsletters and journals, especially the *Journal of the Abraham Lincoln Association*, *Lincoln Herald*, and *Lincoln Lore* disseminate current scholarship.

Toward the base of the triangle are Lincoln organizations conducting important but limited activities. In the typical organization, chief executive officers serve as volunteers, do not devote themselves full-time to their work, and the administrative staff, if paid, consists of one or two persons. The Lincoln Forum, a Gettysburg-based organization drawing its members from nearby states, is the largest of the regional organizations. The Lincoln Fellowship of Pennsylvania sponsors important events at Gettysburg, the Abraham Lincoln Institute meets in the Washington DC area, and Lincoln groups and Lincoln fellowships of various states are administered for the benefit of local Lincoln scholars and admirers.

Forming the base of this organizational triangle are hundreds of Civil War roundtables, heritage groups, and other organizations located in cities and towns throughout the United States. Such groups also disseminate information on Lincoln through newsletters and meetings, but their focus tends to be on events of local rather than national significance.[3]

Given such massive historical and commemorative activity, why has Abraham Lincoln's prestige eroded? The simplest and most direct explanations are unfortunately the weakest.

Decline

New populations, the emergence of new presidents, new political-party alignments, and new biographies constitute the first explanation of Lincoln's diminishing place in American memory. During the early twentieth century, European immigrants took to Lincoln quickly and warmly, but since 1970 most of the more than twenty million immigrants entering the United States are Asians and Hispanics who feel less affinity with white Anglo-Saxon presidents, present or past. Moreover, the public-education sectors committed to multiculturalism encourage immigrants to cultivate their own heritage at least as fervently as they adopt America's. The increased number of Asian and Latin American immigrants, however, cannot explain Lincoln's declining prestige because their number, although increasing, amounts to a small percentage of the American population (0.8 to 8.6 percent from 1960 to 2000).[4] Although no presidential greatness comparisons by ethnicity are available, the Knowledge Network survey contains a sample of Hispanic and other (mainly Asian) respondents large enough to make a tentative comparison with white and black respondents naming Lincoln as Great Emancipator, Savior of the Union, Folk Hero, or belonging to one of the other four categories reported in chapter 4. Most Hispanic and Asian respondents are probably native born, but on average they are newer citizens, and their responses provide some indication of immigrant beliefs. No significant ethnic difference exists in any one of the seven reputation categories.[5]

Has Lincoln's prestige diminished because another president more representative of the era has arisen? This "Substitution Effect" is a more plausible explanation. Two bodies of evidence suggest that John F. Kennedy substituted, in some degree, for Lincoln. First, the Gallup surveys (table 5.1) show Kennedy rated three percentage points higher than Lincoln in 1975 and ten and five percentage points higher in 1985 and 1991, before falling slightly below Lincoln in 1999. Second, the printed media and Congress paid less attention to Lincoln immediately after Kennedy's 1963 assassination than before. From the periods 1960–64 to 1965–69, the mean annual number of *New York Times* articles on Lincoln dropped from 32 to 20; the number of *Congressional Record* entries, from 50 to 31; and the number of *Readers' Guide* articles from 16 per year (1961–65) to 11 per year (1965–70).

John Kennedy was well suited to the visual culture of the late twentieth century, an electronic culture where physical attractiveness and articulateness yielded unprecedented dividends.[6] His death and funeral, moreover, constituted the first presidential "media event." But these factors cannot explain why his own presidential greatness rating fell as Lincoln's did, or why Lincoln's rating in the Gallup survey failed to recover from its 1956–75 decline. They cannot explain why Lincoln entries in the *New York Times*, *Readers' Guide*, and *Congressional Record* fell continuously throughout the 1970s and 1980s, long after Kennedy's ratings fell below Lincoln's. They cannot explain why Lincoln film and stage production virtually vanished after the 1950s. Diminishing regard for Lincoln may have been precipitated by Kennedy's martyrdom and explained to some extent by Kennedy's absorbing part of Lincoln's prestige, but its major cause must reside elsewhere.

Since Lincoln's prestige depends on the efforts of admirers, it must diminish as writers, artists, organizations, and other "reputational entrepreneurs," as Gary Fine calls them, lose their motivation to work on his behalf.[7] Traditionally, the Republican Party has been the most important source of Lincoln support. Lincoln's declining appeal during the 1960s corresponds to the Republican party's turn to the political right and adoption of a Southern strategy for which Lincoln's image was less useful.[8] However, if Lincoln's prestige ebbed and flowed with changing Republican political aims, there would be no way to understand his steady rise in prominence during the first half of the twentieth century, through progressive (Roosevelt, Taft) to conservative (Harding, Coolidge, Hoover) and moderate (Landon, Willkie, Dewey, Eisenhower) Republican eras, or why Lincoln's most articulate admirers were Democrats Woodrow Wilson and Franklin Roosevelt, or why the number of *Congressional Record* entries rises for fifty years among Congresses of vastly different political and ideological composition. Also, Republican party officials' interest in Lincoln may or may not have lagged as they courted the South, but the gap between the percentage of Northerners and Southerners naming Lincoln a great president was only a third as great in 1999 as it was in 1956 (table 5.2).

The Republican party, as shown in the previous chapter, remained the party of Lincoln until the very end of the twentieth century. However, post–World War II weakening of the party system and party discipline, reassertion of Congressional prerogatives, and the growing influence of Political Action Committees—all well advanced by the 1970s—weakened the presidency. Lincoln's prestige began falling during this period, but because it failed to rise again as the balance of power shifted from the Congress to the presidency after Ronald Reagan's 1980 election, it could not have been totally dependent on the vicissitudes of presidential power.

Marc Landy and Sidney Milkis concede that changes in the political environment, including the lessened significance of political parties, the growth and intrusiveness of the mass media, and a more demanding public undermine presidential effectiveness and prestige; however, they assert that Americans still yearn for effective leadership in crisis. Since Franklin Roosevelt died, no president has met this need. Lyndon B. Johnson and Ronald Reagan had moved to the cusp of greatness, only to fail by seeking to achieve too much (Johnson) or too little (Reagan). Because good men, subtle in their sense of the power of the office, might, in principle, achieve greatness, new political and media structures cannot explain Lincoln's diminishing prestige.[9]

Did Lincoln's prestige shrink because biographers and historians discovered new information and wrote more critically about him in the late twentieth century? More writers, in fact, portrayed Lincoln unkindly after the 1960s than before. Liberals and radicals of the civil rights era criticized Lincoln for his reluctance to free the slaves and for his lifelong desire to induce them to leave the United States.[10]

"Psychohistorians" treated Lincoln worse, asserting that he took the country to war in order to satisfy his neurotic drive for recognition. Edmund Wilson, a literary critic, set the stage in *Patriotic Gore* (1962): when Lincoln warned his Springfield Lyceum audience against men of towering genius who cannot stay on the beaten path but seek instead dictatorial power, he was unconsciously describing himself. Seventeen years later, George Forgie argued that Lincoln resented the Founding Fathers because they stood in the way of his own thirst for fame. Projecting his personal aspiration upon Stephen Douglas and the leaders of the South, Lincoln took his country to war. Dwight Anderson's *Abraham Lincoln: The Quest for Immortality* (1982) also sees in Lincoln's ambition the primary source of the war. Charles Stozier's work—*The Public and Private Lincoln* (1979)—provides useful psychological insights on Lincoln's private life, but he, too, attributes Lincoln's decision for war to personal ambition rather than national interests. Less portentous but still controversial is Michael Burlingame's *The Inner World of Abraham Lincoln,* which explores the sixteenth president's idiosyncratic early life without insinuations about its major role in the causes of the Civil War. Most Lincoln scholars find these psychobiographies, in the aggregate, controversial at their best, nonsense at their worst. The most notorious, which claim Lincoln's psychological problems prompted him to wage war, are roundly rejected.

Historical fiction, more popular than the psychobiographies, include William Safire's *Freedom* (1987), an otherwise sympathetic novel emphasizing Lincoln's problematic civil liberties record, and Gore Vidal's *Lincoln* (1984) which portrays the sixteenth president as scheming rather than ideologically driven. In contrast, Donald T. Philips's *Lincoln on Leadership* (1992), a self-help manual, trivializes Lincoln by casting him in the mold of the ideal business administrator, as was common during the 1920s.[11] These writers, like the psychohistorians, provide new slants on Lincoln's career, and although their portrayals are partly if not totally positive, they have had relatively little influence on popular conceptions.

The most influential scholarship on Lincoln's life is the most complimentary. Harry Jaffa's *Crisis of the House Divided* (1959) is a philosophical study affirming Lincoln's political egalitarianism, while Don Fehrenbacher's *Prelude to Greatness* (1962) reveals the depth of his antislavery convictions. Later, Peyton McCrary's *Abraham Lincoln and Reconstruction* (1978) and LaWanda Cox's *Lincoln and Black Freedom* (1981) carry forward Fehrenbacher's and Jaffa's vision of Lincoln's idealism. These books are important, but their readers are mainly confined to the academy. The bestsellers included Carl Sandburg's biographies, *The Prairie Years* (1926, two volumes) and *The War Years* (1939, four volumes), which depict Lincoln as a homespun all-American and dominated popular biography from the mid-1920s to the late 1970s. *The War Years* alone sold six million copies and won the Pulitzer Prize. Stephen Oates's *With Malice Toward None* (1977), the most widely read biography of the late 1970s and 1980s, is highly flattering. In a related work, Oates (1984) adores Lincoln openly, defends him against criticism, and condemns the government for not making his birthday a national holiday.[12] David Herbert Donald's *Lincoln* (1995) tells a prize-winning and best-selling story of Lincoln's presidential virtues. Equally complimentary are the more recent writings of Alan Guelzo, John Patrick Diggins, William Lee Miller, Harold Holzer, Mark Neeley, Dorothy Kearns Goodwin, and John Cawardine.[13] Joshua Shenk's *Lincoln's Melancholy*, unlike earlier psychobiographies, is an inspirational book that compellingly relates Lincoln's presidential greatness to his depression, not his political envy.[14] In short, disparaging accounts of Lincoln have been either ignored, effectively challenged, or overwhelmed by the reception of positive Lincoln biographies.

History textbooks, too, are powerful vehicles of grand narrative, but their way of telling the story differs. Biographies interpret events of the day from the standpoint of their subject; textbooks turn biography inside out by incorporating the subject into the sweep of history. The forty high school texts discussed in chapter 4[15] reveal most of what Americans learned about Lincoln's historical role.[16] Texts written before 1960 are author-centered and uncritical. Their stated goal is to socialize readers by setting before them "noble examples" from the past.[17] To make explicit America's merits, not its failures and moral shortcomings, is their concern. History is justified, in Lewis Paul Todd and Merle Curti's view, by "the need for all citizens to understand and appreciate the American way of life."[18] Everett Augsperger and Richard McLemore "start out with certain basic ideas which we think will be most valuable to you. For one thing we love our country and are proud of it and we want to increase your love of it and pride in it."[19] Affirmative history made Lincoln colorful, exaggerating his every identifying mark: he was the "greatest democrat of his time." As commander in chief, he was unbeatable, and as a statesman "none threw a greater shadow than he." Like the prophets of old, Abraham Lincoln stamped society with his own values. "He voiced ideals that have become part of our national heritage."[20]

Post-1960 texts are "reader-centered," inviting students to assess history critically and draw their own conclusions about the past and "alternative futures."[21] Such texts are more probing than earlier ones, but they also differ substantively, devoting more space to blacks, women, and other minorities, and less space to white men competing against one another. The new Lincoln of the new history is hardly a disparaged man; he is described from a new, race-conscious standpoint emphasizing his views on slavery and defining emancipation as the principal achievement of his presidency. Uniform depictions of John Wilkes Booth as "half-crazed," "mentally sick," "unstable," "fanatic," and "mad" uphold Lincoln's epic role. Given the animosities engendered by four years of war and hundreds of thousands of Southern deaths, a conspiracy to assassinate Lincoln can be defined as madness only if the victim's greatness and benevolence are deemed universal.

Historians also magnify Lincoln's greatness in their treatments of Reconstruction. If Lincoln had lived, he *would* have or at least *might* have reconciled North and South without the unpleasantness of military occupation. Not one writer is willing even to suggest that excessive leniency might have damaged Lincoln's presidency, let alone resulted in his own rather than Andrew Johnson's impeachment. Portraying Lincoln as the man who would have successfully placated the South, writers take Johnson's incompetence as a matter of fact. His failure to implement Lincoln's policy, they explain, stemmed not from radical Republican opposition but from personal flaws: meanness, crudity, pettiness, inflexibility, vindictiveness, and inability to get along with anyone who disagreed with him. Beside this hopelessly inept man, Abraham Lincoln's greatness shines.[22] Attached to all sides, concerned even with the well being of his enemies, Lincoln appears superhuman. Authors praise the "sad-eyed," "sad-faced" president, explain how four years of care wrinkled his young face and show prewar and late-war photographs to prove it.[23] He grew old loving everyone.

That historians depicted Lincoln in the same heroic light after the 1960s as before, and rated him first or second in their presidential greatness polls,[24] that biographers wrote flattering accounts of his life throughout the late twentieth century, means that his declining prestige cannot be explained by change in what we know about him. The explanation resides in how we feel about what we know. And this feeling has little or nothing to do with Lincoln himself; it results from the context in which biographical facts are interpreted. If this feeling is to be understood, we must move beyond Lincoln and the way people think about him. He may personify the national myth as certainly as ever and the factual content of that myth may be as credible as ever, but why is his image less magnetic? Why does it no longer solidify and inspire? The first answer must be based on an understanding of the era in which Lincoln's prestige begins to decline; the second must match this era's characteristics with the traits and achievements it associates with Lincoln.

Post-Heroic Era

Demographic change, substitution effects, reputational enterprise, and critical information about Abraham Lincoln cannot account for late twentieth-century change in his image. They fail to distinguish early generations that revere Lincoln from recent ones that merely respect him. They cannot portray the context within which the relevance of Lincoln's identity diminishes or the universe within which Lincoln is a symbol. Determining what Lincoln means to a given era is essential to understanding his fate. No one can grasp the post-heroic era's effect on Lincoln's image, however, without knowing that era independently of the image itself.

The term "post-heroic" is an imprecise concept, for we recognize many heroes in our time: military, civic (including police and firemen), and sports heroes stand out in the public mind—and justly so. But the term as used here is a variation on historian George Forgie's original formulation. Characteristic of the antebellum mind, according to Forgie, was the tendency to divide American history into two stages: an extraordinary, heroic period of creation by the Founding Fathers, and an ordinary, "post-heroic" era of preservation and consolidation.[25] Heroic generations are remembered not only for their achievement but also for providing frames of reference for moral and practical judgment. In 1825, Daniel Webster declared that his generation was born too late to be great. "Our fathers," he said, have given us a nation and all that remains is the "great duty of defense and preservation."[26] The era of which Webster spoke, a time of relative peace, expansion, and prosperity, was characterized by its critics as an age of "ennui,"[27] a "prosaic epoch," a "prosperous forcing house of mediocrity,"[28] a time of "microscopic realities" representing the clearest possible evidence of spiritual deterioration, "a lamentable degeneration from that sublime political morality which characterized our ancestors."[29]

The decades of the late twentieth and early twenty-first centuries are post-heroic in a different sense. No feeling of having descended from a higher state of political morality, no nostalgic yearning for a sublime period in which great men walked the earth, no belief in, let alone effort to restore, earlier periods of epic heroism defines it. In this generation the very notion of greatness has eroded.

Fading of great men is evident in the diminished scale of the monuments which once commemorated them. Traditional monuments to human greatness celebrated individual triumph in the service of a national cause. From this heroic ideal no specific design can be inferred, but the ideal itself can be described: a statement engraved on the monument describing the cause for which it was built, idealistic human representation, larger-than-life physical dimensions, vertical preeminence, centrality and prominence of placement, lightness of color, grandness of size, prominence of national symbolism. No monument need incorporate all these features, or even a set combination of them, to qualify as a heroic design, but at least some of them are required. The most widely known American examples are Washington DC's Jefferson Memorial, Lincoln Memorial, and Washington Monument. Many similar structures built throughout the country in the early twentieth century could be named. Post-heroic monuments, on the other hand, are distinguished by absent or ambiguous statements about cause, abstractness of representation, horizontal lines (often walls hugging the ground or placed below ground), inconspicuous placement, darkness of color, smallness of size, want of national symbolism. Such monuments, exemplified by the many versions of the Vietnam Veterans Memorial and, to a lesser extent, the Franklin Delano Roosevelt Memorial, Korean War Veterans Memorial (although designed expressly to contrast with the Vietnam Memorial), and the World War II Memorial, exemplify the monumental in a world without greatness. The Iwo Jima Monument was perhaps the last classical monument erected before the post-heroic era, and its gigantic lines, condemned by some as "triumphal," are unknown in today's memorials to America's great men.

The point must not be exaggerated. Great men have not been universally dismissed, but for most people the prevailing attitude is one of dispassionate respect. Whatever the founders and preservers did is simply less relevant now than before, and there is no replacing them with better leaders, for there is nothing anyone can do to distinguish himself in the eyes of a generation that no longer recognizes greatness. A stable, post-industrial democracy no longer requires great men and women to revere, no longer inspires their appreciation, no longer can find a place for them. Weakened social attachments,[30] cynicism toward cultural ideals, radically new conceptions of equality, eager recognition of historical wrongs—these are aspects of a postindustrial culture wherein Lincoln appears less imposing. The post-heroic mentality and the diminishing aura of Abraham Lincoln reinforce one another.

The post-heroic era is benign. No political order has ever been more determined to respect the dignity of the individual, protect his rights, maintain his well being. No society has ever been more respectful of diversity, more determined to abolish invidious distinctions based on race, religion, ethnicity, gender. No polity has been more sensitive to victimhood and its own history of wrongdoing. Few members of such a society want to return to former times when dividing lines were clearer and more vigorously enforced. Less than a century ago, America's great cities consisted of tight, ethnic enclaves whose members, as in medieval days, worked in a public marketplace, but returned home to their exclusive worlds. Here, tradition and its carriers kept communities segregated, families together, inhibited destructive impulses, enforced commitment and loyalty by stigmatizing their violation, protected its members from the influence of strangers, defended the boundaries between right and wrong—as locally conceived. Such enclaves have loosened their hold on their members.

On the plane of interpersonal relations, this change is evident in the content of stereotyping. Stereotyping is a process by which people (1) identify a category of persons, including heroes and villains, by agreeing on the characteristics to be attributed to them, and (2) attribute such characteristics to any person belonging to the category. Stereotyping, as is well known, enables us to make a complicated world semi-predictable. But the content of stereotypes and their relation to one another is variable, and this variation mediates new social structures, like postindustrialism, and new value systems, like multiculturalism, and the perception of persons living and dead.

In 1932, the percentage of Princeton students describing Americans as "industrious," "intelligent," and "progressive" was 48, 47, and 27 respectively; in 1967, these percentages decreased to 23, 20, and 17. In 1932, exactly 33 percent described Americans as "materialistic" and "ambitious"; in 1967, these figures had increased to 67 and 42. In other words, the stereotype of the American became more negative over the thirty-five years studied. Stereotypes of African Americans changed in the opposite direction. In 1932, the percentage of blacks deemed "superstitious," "lazy," "happy-go-lucky," and "ignorant" was 84, 75, 38, and 38; in 1968, after the Southern phase of the civil rights movement ended, the corresponding percentages were 13, 26, 27, and 11.[31] African Americans were regarded more positively at the 1968 peak of the sixties cultural revolution than they were in 1932.[32]

That the prestige of Abraham Lincoln and other American heroes falls during a period when Americans become more open minded about their own shortcomings and more skeptical about the negative traits ascribed to blacks and other minorities cannot be a coincidence. To revel in the existence of gifted and morally superior men who stand above the masses of their countrymen is to believe in the existence of inferior men whose talents and morals place them in permanent mediocrity. Nationalism, racism, and belief in the importance of great men are all rooted in the same social condition: a clearly bounded world in which the lines dividing nations, racial, class, and religious communities within nations, and individuals within communities, are clear and invidious. The nostalgia for the "old days," when people knew the difference between right and wrong, is understandable, for negative stereotyping is a social and psychological advantage in communities detached from or threatened by their neighbors. One need not ridicule moral certainty to appreciate its costs: injustice, bigotry, deprivation of rights, conflict and resentment, and the economic and social inefficiencies that invariably accompany a social system where merit is subordinated to color, creed, and ethnicity. The appreciation of great men thrives in precisely such settings.

The very conditions that promote equal rights and make society more just and decent reduce Lincoln's stature by undermining tradition, authority, and social boundaries. "Nothing," said Emile Durkheim, "is good indefinitely and to an unlimited extent. The authority which the moral conscience enjoys must not be excessive; otherwise no one would dare criticize it, and it would too easily congeal into an immutable form." Durkheim recognizes an essential polarity of every social order, a moral dualism admitting of no resolution. Idealism and depravity alike are conditions of progress. The imagination, however idealistic or depraved, must be able to express itself if society is to advance. "In order that the originality of the idealist whose dreams transcend his century may find expression, it is necessary that the originality of the criminal, who is below the level of his time, shall also be possible. One does not occur without the other."[33] The corollary is straightforward: doubting virtue and greatness and tolerating evil and failure go together. The same generation that scoffs at an "axis of virtue" or "virtuous republic" rejects the notion of an "axis of evil" or "evil empire." Deteriorating values and traditions, however, are manifest not only in criminality, vulgarity, coarseness, diminished standards, and alienation, but also in respect for human rights and decency; not only in declining renown of the historically great to whom society owes its existence and well being, but also in unprecedented recognition of the contributions and sacrifices of ordinary men and women.

Lincoln's decline is part of a larger cultural pattern that involves (1) a new openness and acceptance of all peoples, regardless of race, religion, and ethnicity, and (2) deterioration and coarsening of traditional symbols and practices. Reading table 6.1 columns alternately from top to bottom summarizes this contradiction. The world in which Lincoln and other great presidents have lost their aura, as the table's first column asserts, is one of unprecedented social progress, a world in which all individuals gain dignity and inclusion through equal economic, political, and social opportunity, a world in which minority accomplishments are acknowledged as invidious boundaries and stereotypes diminish. In this world, the historical figures most admired include champions of the disdained, the excluded, the oppressed. This same world, as the second column asserts, is awash in obscene vulgarity, incapable of recognizing

TABLE 6.1. Late twentieth-century culture: erosion of social boundaries, social structures, and traditional norms

Positive effects of boundary erosion	Negative effects of boundary erosion
1. Enhanced dignity of the individual	1. Diffusion of vulgarity and obscenity
2. Equality of political, economic, and social opportunity	2. Waning of belief in the sacred and sublime
3. Acceptance and social inclusion of minorities	3. Weakened commitment to individuals and civil institutions (including family and church)
4. Clarification of legitimate and illegitimate inequalities	4. Weakened identification with nation and state
5. Recognition of minority accomplishments	5. Erosion of institutional authority
6. Increased rates of ethnic, religious, and racial intermarriage	6. Rise of the celebrity
7. Dissolution of gender distinctions	7. Diminished recognition of human greatness and historic exemplars
8. Relaxing of obsolete cultural restraints	8. Fading vocabulary of good and evil

let alone embracing sanctity. As time passes, its inhabitants become less committed to nation, community, and family. The great men that once represented these establishments are replaced by a vulgar subset of celebrities whose major achievement is to have distracted rather than restored and refreshed society. Thus, the world that recognizes Abraham Lincoln as an emancipator is liberated enough to recognize him, but too liberated, too uncommitted, to maintain his prestige.

Plainly, Lincoln's decline does not reflect a demoralization of the society; it is part of a social and cultural revolution, a postmodern turn, that has led to both desirable reform and undesirable excess. The same process that destroys stereotypes belittling religious and racial groups also destroys stereotypes distinguishing the great man from the ordinary.

Postmodern culture links Abraham Lincoln's changing reputation and prestige to the development of postindustrial society. Nowhere is this change more evident than in the lessening credibility of the nation's "grand narratives." Ours is an age ready to live without triumphal doctrine, an age in which absolutes are local and private rather than national, a post-heroic age in which national greatness is the epitome of the naive and outmoded.[34]

PSYCHO-HISTORICAL DISLOCATION

"All the armies of Europe, Asia, and Africa combined," said Lincoln, "could not by force take a drink from the Ohio or make a track on the Blue Ridge in a thousand years." The danger to America is internal dissension. "If destruction be our lot, we must ourselves be its author and finisher." This argument from Lincoln's 1828 Springfield Lyceum address on "The Perpetuation of Our Political Institutions"[35] may be applied to the perpetuation of his own renown, lessened not by hostile debunkers but by exhaustion of the cultural values that once led people to revere him. The object of the argument, Lincoln's changing prestige and reputation, are constituents, not products, of post-heroic culture. "Reasons" for Lincoln's changing image must inhere in his changing meaning, and the latter cannot be known without continually moving back and forth between the experience of Lincoln and the makeup of the world, and doing so without highlighting one over the other. That more people began to see Lincoln as a Great Emancipator at the very time fewer considered him (or anyone else) worthy of the dramatic veneration of earlier days, is a puzzle solved only when seen as part of a cultural irony.

Exhausted reverence is distinctive of egalitarian eras, but its roots reside in the soil of democracy. "Democratic philosophy," Alexis de Tocqueville noted, "submits all things to scrutiny of individual judgment. No tradition is immune to critical inquiry, no great man remains above the suspicion of the masses.... They do not recognize any signs of incontestable greatness or superiority in any of their fellows."[36] For more than a century after Tocqueville's visit to America, however, heroic tradition limited democracy's critical potential. From George Washington's era to Franklin Roosevelt's, examples of great men reinforced ideals; for people who might otherwise fail to understand, they explained why some aspects of history were desirable or repulsive, significant or trivial. Admiration of greatness was based on respect for the lines dividing oneself from one's betters, but during the twentieth century's closing decades these lines blurred.

Seymour M. Lipset and William Schneider's surveys document massive decline of trust in government and its leaders from the mid-1960s through the 1980s, with no visible end to "the series of events that create and sustain the confidence gap."[37] Just as Lincoln's early twentieth-century stature rose with the rising authority of the state,[38] his late twentieth-century stature diminished as the dignity of the state fell.

Among the events sustaining the late twentieth-century confidence gap are a string of political scandals. Watergate, Irangate, the Clinton-Lewinsky affair, exemplify these transgressions, but there are so many others that it would take an entire section even to list them. Scandals, according to John B. Thompson, "are struggles over symbolic power in which reputation and trust are at stake."[39] By reputation, Thompson refers to the esteem accorded by others—a conception presently used

TABLE 6.2. Assumed effects of media scrutiny on the perceived greatness of six presidents (in percentages), by race and region*

	Lincoln	Kennedy	Roosevelt	Washington	Truman	Eisenhower
			White			
Number	(341)	(259)	(233)	(217)	(119)	(80)
Equally great	39	43	36	43	45	48
Not as great	52	50	58	51	46	50
			Black			
Number	(35)	(51)	(16)	(12)	(1)	(0)
Equally great	37	45	19	25		
Not as great	51	51	81	58		
			Non-South			
Number	(276)	(221)	(178)	(152)	(72)	(55)
Equally great	40	43	39	43	47	53
Not as great	51	51	55	49	46	44
			South			
Number	(137)	(127)	(86)	(98)	(50)	(30)
Equally great	39	46	25	43	42	37
Not as great	50	50	69	53	48	60

* "Don't know" responses excluded.

to denote "prestige." By symbolic power, he refers to the ability to affect the outcome of events and influence beliefs. Scandals can thus harm the institutions in which they occur. Political parties and elected offices are particularly vulnerable when scandals violate the trust on which government by consent depends. Presidential scandals have varied in their effects, but they have all contributed to undermining the presidency.

Not only do scholars like Thompson believe that scandals jeopardize the public's reverence for national leaders; the public is itself aware of the media's effect on its judgments. In the University of Maryland survey of presidential greatness (chapter 4) the following question appeared: "If the great American presidents of the past were subject to the same intense television and other media coverage as occurs today, would they be considered (1) equally great or (2) not so great?" Forty-two percent of those responding believed that all presidents would be considered equally great, regardless of media scrutiny; 50 percent, not so great. Eight percent were uncertain.[40] Table 6.2, based on those ascribing greatness to one or more presidents, demonstrates this pattern to be as coherent inside the South as outside; among African Americans as among whites; as true for Washington, Roosevelt, Eisenhower, Truman, and Kennedy as for Lincoln.

For those naming Lincoln a great president, fifty percent or more of whites, blacks, and non-Southerners believe that more media attention would have lessened his renown. Everywhere, then, most individuals naming him a great president are ambivalent, recognizing that their choices might have been less positive if the media had been as intrusive when he was in office as they are today. In the post-heroic era, Americans look around at their own leaders, then look to the past and conclude that history's heroes could never have been as great as they seem.

Simultaneously, the intellectual, once the state's ally, became its critic; his method, a constant search for "the telltale sign that will reduce the stature of the great."[41] Diminishing regard for Lincoln reflects the mentality of a "Destructive Generation" whose inchoate assaults on tradition and indiscriminate maulings of centers of authority, according to Peter Collier and David Horowitz, have weakened America's "immune system"—its capacity to fight off nihilistic and anti-American ideologies, especially those of the radical Left.[42] "Our case is astounding," wrote liberal Paul Goodman. "For the first time in recorded history, the mention of country, community, place has lost its power to animate."[43]

Weakened institutional authority reduces the capacity as well as the inclination to admire. Three-quarters of a century ago, it seemed only natural for Henry N. Couden, chaplain of the House of Representatives, to rise on Lincoln's birthday and pray to God: "May we cherish his memory, emulate his virtues, tell his story round the fireside, in the schools, churches, and in all public places to coming generations; to the honor and glory of thy name. Amen."[44] On that same day Illinois's Democratic senator James Lewis, although Southern-born and Southern-reared, emphasized Lincoln's Christ-like qualities and explained how Lincoln's successors, Theodore Roosevelt and Woodrow Wilson, had achieved greatness by carrying forward his ideals.[45] Couden's and Lewis's words seem peculiar today, for skepticism and ridicule have eaten away much of the institutional basis on which heroic stature depends.[46] How many schools now convey traditions sanctifying Lincoln's memory? And if it is to the honor and glory of God's name that Lincoln must be remembered, what is to become of Lincoln as God's name, too, loses authority?[47] Heroic narratives lose relevance as their "foundational" principles—values, beliefs, and norms assumed true beyond mere demonstration—dissolve. Lincoln's fall, an aspect of the 1960s cultural revolution, was symptomatic of the belief among many young adults that their country, for the first time since the Depression, was on the verge of disintegration.[48] Erosion was manifest in the demystification of the world—the feeling, which for Hans Koning and others became stronger during the 1960s, that "all the clichés, platitudes, and myths of our public life . . . were suddenly seen as such, and not just by a handful of lefties in small magazines, but by the people at large, many of them."[49] The basic content of America's grand narrative—liberation, equality, and progress—seemed a lie. As respect for America's representative men waned, patriotism faded, and the popularity of elected officials, including presidents, invariably diminished during their second terms in office.[50] Lincoln's fall is an aspect of this development, this "Age of Crisis," this weakening of civic tradition connecting the citizen to his political legacy, this breakdown of consensus in beliefs about the past.[51]

Strong forces caused this breakdown. In 1968, peak year of the 1960s cultural revolution, R. J. Lifton observed that absurdity and mockery had become part of the post–World War II life style. Modern "protean" man takes nothing seriously; "everything he touches he mocks"; everything, present and past, he ridicules.[52] The stature of Washington, Lincoln, Wilson, and Franklin Roosevelt was once morally imposing, Robert Nisbet said, "but great as these individuals were, they had *audiences* of greatness, that is, individuals in large number still capable of being enchanted. How, in all truth, in an age when parody, self-parody, and caricature is the best we have in literature, could any of the above names rise to greatness? . . . The instinct to mock the great, the good, and the wise is built into this age."[53] Nisbet was a conservative scholar, but his observations transcend ideology. Liberal scholar Andrew Delbanco, too, observes that Americans now believe that "national pride is no longer appropriate. In both popular and elite culture, most descriptions of what America will be like in the twenty-first century are written in tones either of self-mockery or disgust."[54]

TARNISHED IDOLS

Postindustrial environments not only render primordial (racial, religious, and ethnic) boundaries obsolete; they also narrow the gap that traditionally distinguished the great man from the common man. The aura once concentrated at the center of society, where great men resided, has been diffused. The presidency's diminishing dignity is but one aspect of this diffusion process.

Presidents' Day: Ritual Erosion in the Post-Heroic Era. During the first half of the twentieth century, two major holidays, Abraham Lincoln's birthday and George Washington's birthday, broke up the month of February. These were big days: newspapers placed Lincoln's and Washington's picture on their front page and supplied information on where different business, civic, and religious organizations would meet to celebrate. Stories of Lincoln's and Washington's exploits abounded. Valentine's Day was celebrated in February, too, but it was mainly an amusing day when adults exchanged frilly cards, candy makers put their products in

FIGURE 6.1
"The Biggest Day of the Month," *New Yorker* 1988 cover illustration, Condé Nast Publications, New York, NY.

special wrappers, a few adults went to a movie or dinner, but little more. Certainly there was no consumer frenzy, no fleets of flower trucks making their rounds throughout the city. There was also a Negro History Week, but few whites knew anything about it. Minority ethnic and racial communities observed national events separately. Today, the pattern is reversed: *New Yorker*'s February 1988 cover shows Washington and Lincoln exchanging Valentine cards, conceding that the commemoration of their births is no longer as important as Valentine's Day (fig. 6.1). In schools and media, too, Lincoln and Washington occupy a diminished place. Black History Month, successor to Negro History Week, and January's commemoration of Martin Luther King Jr., receive as much or more media attention as do the nation's founder and savior. In major newspapers, Lincoln and Washington are as often as not unmentioned on either their traditional birthdays or on Presidents' Day.

America's greatest presidents will continue to be remembered in future decades; the question is what will be the tone and texture of their remembrance. The 1968 Uniform Holiday Act—also known as the Monday Holiday Act—more than any other cultural event assures that that tone will be muted; that texture, vague. Holidays, in the words of Amitai Etzioni, are "seedbeds of virtue,"[55] but whether America's most peculiar and confusing holiday is a seedbed of anything, let alone national virtue, is questionable.

Congress gave five reasons for changing traditional holidays to Monday: (1) provide new jobs in the U.S. travel industry; (2) generate local tax revenues through increased tourism; (3) slash absenteeism by preventing workers from adding a day or two to midweek holidays; (4) eliminate the problem of schools and businesses making costly midweek shutdowns and startups; and (5) expand the do-it-yourself home repair industry. Patriotic organizations opposed the bill because they felt it would diminish the significance of relocated holidays; churches opposed it because it would cut down Sunday church and Sunday school attendance; public safety lobbies opposed it because of the prospect of more auto traffic and higher accident rates. The congressional proposals, however, received overwhelming support: The Air Transport Association, American Hotel and Motel Association, American Petroleum Institute, Chamber of Commerce of the United States, AFL-CIO, National Recreation and Park Association—these and scores of other organizations supported the bill, and their combined influence overwhelmed all opposition.

The original bill provided that existing Memorial Day, July 4th, Columbus Day, Veterans Day, and Thanksgiving dates be changed to the nearest Monday, and that Washington's birthday be abolished and replaced by Presidents' Day. Congress flatly rejected the proposed changes for July 4th and Presidents' Day. It rejected the Thanksgiving proposal partly because it would interrupt the pre-Christmas retail cycle, but it did change the observance of Washington's birthday from February 22 to the third Monday of the month. Memorial Day and Veterans Day, too, became Monday holidays. Columbus Day, observed in many states, would become a federal holiday observed on the first Monday of October.[56]

Two-thirds of a national sample interviewed by the 1968 Harris Survey wanted the traditional holiday dates to remain, and the *Christian Science Monitor*'s editor spoke for this majority when he said that date-switching weakens the holidays' "intrinsic meaning."[57] The bill's supporters, however, prevailed, and The Uniform Holiday Bill, so named in wishful thinking that the states would follow the federal example, was signed into law by Lyndon Johnson on June 28, 1968 (highpoint of the decade's civil disorders), and scheduled to go into effect in 1971.

Although rejected by Congress, twenty-three states (as of 2004) formally adopted Presidents' Day. When debated in Congress, however, no one knew for sure what Presidents' Day referred to. Some believed it was a time to honor all American presidents; others assumed that it merged Lincoln's and Washington's irthdays—a view reinforced by the choice of the third rather than fourth Monday of February, which guarantees that Presidents' Day would never fall on either Lincoln's or Washington's original birthday.[58]

The Uniform Holiday Act now means different things in different states and to different organizations and different people within each state.[59] In Michigan, Presidents' Day alone is a legal holiday, but were it not for the state Web site, one would never know that it refers to Lincoln and Washington. Illinois observes Lincoln's and Washington's birthdays in addition to Presidents' Day, which can only mean that the latter honors all presidents in addition to Lincoln and Washington. Arizona names the third Monday of February Washington/Lincoln/Presidents' Day. Texas officially observes Presidents' Day but does so "in honor of George Washington." California also observes Presidents' Day, but in alternate years recognizes Abraham Lincoln's birthday, which means that the presidential pantheon changes from year to year. Eighteen states, most in the West, have holiday calendars providing no hint as to what Presidents' Day celebrates. There are other ambiguities. The United States Postal Service officially declares Washington's birthday as its employee holiday but refers to it in local post offices as Presidents' Day. Banks in many states, including those which do not recognize Presidents' Day, close on what they choose to name Presidents' Day. Many department stores remain open for Presidents' Day sales. Thus, even in states where no Presidents' Day exists, most people believe they are observing it.

Throughout the 1970s, the law's opponents sought its repeal. The *New York Times*, which endorsed the bill in 1968, said in 1971 that the price of new holiday benefits "is one more sacrifice of tradition at a time when that commodity is in seriously short supply."[60] President Gerald Ford had already returned Veterans Day, observed on the last Monday of November, to its original date, the old Armistice Day, November 11. Five years later, during the 1976 bicentennial, journalist Sean O'Gara wrote about George Washington's place in the new holiday calendar: "This subtle disparaging of Washington as the father figure supreme of our country . . . is a blatant indication that the actions of our forefathers and the lessons of the past are insignificant in today's America." O'Gara was doubtlessly thinking of Lincoln also when he recalled bitterly:

> In 1941, when our nation was endangered, we reached down into our well of national heroes and resurrected them selfishly and possessively, because we needed them, and we used them shamelessly to buoy our hopes in that time of travail; now, with danger apparently passed, we are discarding them by relegating them to secondary memory.[61]

Supporters denied that the bill encouraged ingratitude let alone denigration of America's traditions. After all, the old holiday dates were arbitrary. Washington's birthday was February 11 on the Julian calendar in use when he was born in 1732; Memorial Day had no historical affinity with the date on which it was celebrated; Veterans Day, which covers all wars, bore no necessary relation to the World War I November 11 armistice. Since several days passed before all delegates signed the Declaration of Independence, there was no reason to be sentimental about July 4th. The historical basis for a Thursday Thanksgiving was even shakier. Supporters of the holiday bill argued very much like postmodern theorists seeking to demonstrate the essential arbitrariness of social institutions and conventions.

Congress can shatter the fixations of tradition, can reshuffle the national patrimony, but only the people can make a holiday. The *New York Times* editor said as much in October 1971.[62] He was predicting that the people would take back their old Lincoln and Washington birthday dates. He was wrong: the public quickly got used to Presidents' Day and the long weekend. In fits and starts, congressional opponents[63] tried but failed to rescind the new holidays.

Because Lincoln's birthday was never a federal holiday, the emergence of Presidents' Day enhanced his prestige relative to Washington's; but in absolute terms Lincoln lost more than he gained. The cost to him of being featured on Presidents' Day is the lessened integrity of state-celebrated and locally celebrated Lincoln Day. "Communities of memory," as Philip Rieff would later observe, "are a therapeutic and professional abstraction without doxologies of observance. . . . Even the mythic hero of my youth, Lincoln, no longer has a birthday to celebrate publicly."

Rieff goes further, condemning Presidents' Day as a "deathwork"—which he defines as "an all-out assault upon something vital in the established culture." He believes Lincoln to be the last, if not the only, "sacred messenger" in American history, and the abolition of Lincoln's sacred day is part of the assault against what he represents. "Sacred messenger" rings strange to the twenty-first century ear, but, then, Philip Rieff, born in 1922, was no twenty-first-century man, and he was educated during the pinnacle of Lincoln's renown. Because Lincoln delivered sacred messages to earlier American generations, Rieff believes he is deliberately targeted for "scourging." In fact, Lincoln is at worst simply ignored.[64]

Presidents' Day is thus a peculiar holiday possessing no creedal content, no ritual, no affective core, offering dates to be recognized, not embraced—abortive holidays standing for nothing, inspiring nothing.

In his 2001 comments on "Shrinking Lincoln," Little Rock, Arkansas's columnist Paul Greenberg notes:

> Presidents' Day. That's what happens to the mythic after it has been safely shrunk and bubble-wrapped. If you do manage to unwrap it, there's nothing inside. It's how the system is programmed, how the product is packaged now. Each generation makes its own accounting with the past; ours just tends to be blank at the moment.[65]

To blame the Monday Holiday Bill for the blankness of the past, however, would be a mistake. The Bill itself did not weaken the presidency and national legacy; it was a symptom of a presidency and a legacy that had already deteriorated. By 1968, the holidays reserved for Monday celebration were for the most part unobserved to begin with.

Presidents' Day expresses the kind of society we have become. The people of our society retain a residue of their tradition, memories, and customs.[66] They still preserve historical sites and presidential papers. But our society—a postmodern society, as it is called—tends toward a traditionless state where practices are assessed legally and rationally, a state where historical beliefs are dissected rather than embraced.[67] Traditionlessness—the loss of continuity between past and present—is evident in the triviality, pointlessness, and moral emptiness of America's newly conceived Presidents' Day.

Losing the Center. The signing into law of the Uniform Holiday Bill was one of the most definite indicators of Abraham Lincoln's as well as George Washington's fading renown. The question is whether these developments, the Holiday Bill and the diminished prestige of the presidents, is to be attributed to critical events rather than the emerging of a new worldview and ethos.

Could Lincoln's fall be attributed to the major political crises of the time: the Vietnam War, Watergate, and the civil rights movement? Probably not. Americans became disillusioned over the Vietnam War because of the military's failure to win it quickly and at an acceptable cost;[68] the rejection of President Richard Nixon resulted from indisputable evidence of unconstitutional activity; reaction against segregation and injustice throughout the South resulted from dramatic demonstrations, transmitted by television, of segregationist brutality. But needless war, presidential wrongdoing, and racial injustice would have been less alienating if located in a different historical period. Criticism of slavery and racial segregation appeared long before federal and state courts made them illegal; the War of 1812 split the nation more sharply than did the Vietnam War, and the abuses of Ulysses Grant's administration revolted

Americans long before Watergate. Whether these nineteenth-century events were more or less harmful than comparable events in the late twentieth century, critics had not used them to challenge their society's historical foundations. They rather attacked their government by invoking the past; they held up its great men as models defining what present leaders and their policies had betrayed.[69] Since culture shapes public reaction to events, their intrinsic harmfulness cannot explain all criticism. No civil rights movement, unpopular war, or major political scandal plagued Europe during the 1960s, but disillusionment and disorder were no less acute there—especially in France and Germany—than in the United States.

Americans revered and emulated Abraham Lincoln as long as they could agree on what he stood for, but this agreement had weakened during the 1950s and 1960s. In the pre–World War II decades, Americans gathered around Lincoln to express their solidarity; in the postwar decades they used him to support claims against one another. For the first time, Lincoln's image articulated America's divisions more often and more clearly than its unity. To justify their cause, Vietnam War protesters recalled Lincoln's opposition to the Mexican War. Lincoln remained firm in his own antiwar conviction, they said, even though it cost him the nomination for a second term in the U.S. House of Representatives.[70] War resisters also inscribed Lincoln's words on their posters: "It is a sin to be silent when it is your duty to protest."[71] War resisters, however, felt no special affection for Lincoln, felt nothing resembling what their grandparents in Depression and wartime felt; indeed, they would not have invoked him except to express their antiwar sentiments. In contrast, war supporters acknowledged Lincoln's Mexican War position, but saw nothing in common between Lincoln and Vietnam War critics. Once men were in the field, they said, Lincoln voted for all measures necessary to win the war; today's resisters seek to cut funding and ensure defeat.[72] They also noted that Lincoln endured harsh criticism while he led the country. As history proved him right, so it would vindicate President Lyndon Johnson's management of the Vietnam War.[73] He, too, would be seen in hindsight as a symbol "to all men who yearn for freedom everywhere."[74]

Invocations without deep reverence—such uses of Lincoln are characteristic of the post-heroic era. After the war, liberals found in Lincoln's call for "malice toward none" and "charity for all" a guiding vision for amnesty and reconciliation. He was magnanimous and forgiving to the "sincerely penitent," the *New York Times* recalled, and President Nixon should be equally generous.[75] Lincoln's policy, however, justified opposition to as well as support for amnesty. "Perhaps you know some draft evaders who are 'sincerely penitent,'" Margaret Gordon of New York wrote to the *Times* editor; "my impression of them is that they are mostly morally supercilious and sanctimonious beyond endurance, and certainly do not look upon their past actions as 'misdeeds.'"[76] Nevertheless, Nixon's second inauguration committee decided to drop a specially prepared concert based on Lincoln's second inaugural address. The committee offered no reason for its decision but was reported to have found Lincoln's comments on Union military success and forgiveness "not in spirit" with President Nixon's situation and aims.[77]

If Watergate, according to columnist Anthony Lewis, helped make Richard Nixon "as divisive a President as most of us can remember,"[78] Abraham Lincoln was a medium through which the divisions formed. Bitter feelings on both sides adhered to him. In summer 1973, senator Lowell Weicker and senate Watergate committee chairman Sam Ervin publicly compared Nixon's evasiveness to Lincoln's voluntary appearance before the House Judiciary Committee to deny charges that his family communicated with the enemy. Why did President Nixon not defend himself so openly?[79] Six months later, Franklin Gannon, staff assistant to the president, submitted to the *New York Times* a Lincoln's birthday article comparing Lincoln's troubles with Nixon's. The crux of the issue, Gannon wrote, are the rights and powers of the presidency on the one hand, and, on the other, the American people's traditional fear of presidential power. Gannon said that President Nixon, like Lincoln before him, was misunderstood. His "abuse of power" was in fact a courageous effort to protect the presidency.[80]

On the very day Gannon's article appeared, President Nixon made a surprise visit to the Lincoln Memorial, placed a wreath, and, in a variation on Gannon's theme, declared that no president was more vilified yet better poised under pressure than Lincoln. He promised to follow Lincoln's example.[81] Nixon's allusion prompted a storm of criticism. "A better comparison for Mr. Nixon to make," according to a *Times* columnist, "is with President Grant," whose two terms were marked by major scandals.[82] Richard Harris wondered in the *New Yorker* whether Nixon's use of presidential power to punish critics through "wiretapping, and bugging, physical surveillance, tax audits, campaign fraud, illegal entry, extortion, bribery . . . " were good examples of Lincoln's "poise under pressure." Harris added that Lincoln was a humanitarian who could not bear to see men suffer; Nixon was harsh and authoritarian. "The other day, for instance, he ordered his latest Attorney General to press Congress for passage of a law restoring the death penalty for a variety of crimes."[83] Commentators distorted Lincoln in order to give their criticisms of Nixon more bite.[84] Lincoln, in truth, believed in and used capital punishment. We will never know, however, whether Lincoln signed more death warrants than pardons, or whether, for that matter, he was more or less compassionate in this regard than his counterpart, Jefferson Davis.[85]

Nixon's successor, Gerald Ford, also found that Lincoln's example could get a president into trouble. When Ford entered the oval office, he found portraits of Eisenhower, Wilson, and Theodore Roosevelt. Ford kept Eisenhower's picture but replaced Wilson and Roosevelt with Lincoln and Truman—two down-to-earth men like himself. Ford, like so many Americans maturing during the Great Depression, admired Lincoln "for his humility, his devotion to hard work, his dry sense of humor, his generosity of spirit, his love of God and common men."[86] Ford spent many long hours in the Lincoln cabinet room brooding over issues and decisions, and he always felt revived upon leaving.[87]

One of Ford's decisions concerned amnesty for men who had fled the country to evade the Vietnam War draft and wished to return home. Too harsh a policy would divide the country further; too mild a policy would offend the memory of the men who had fought, sustained injury, or died. Contemplating Lincoln's example of "how to bind up the nation's wounds," he threw the weight of the presidency, as did Lincoln before him, on the side of leniency. "As I reject amnesty, so I reject revenge."[88] Middle Americans supported Ford's policy of "earned amnesty," but not pardon. As soon as he issued his pardon of former President Nixon, critics accused him of making a deal to attain the presidency. Although Ford voluntarily appeared before the House subcommittee on criminal justice to deny the accusation, his Lincoln-like gesture to "bind the nation's wounds" helped to reduce his Gallup Poll approval rating from 71 percent to 49 percent and contributed to his defeat in 1976.[89]

While consensus prevailed over division, Lincoln could represent the nation as a whole. Now there was no whole to represent. As America's political consensus shrank, so did Lincoln's role as a unifying symbol.

Post-Heroic Cinema. The crises of the late 1960s and early 1970s are captivating, even entertaining, in the sense that democratic people feel close enough to their leaders to be curious about their personal affairs. Intrusive media feed the appetite for exposé, exemplified by the taped revelations of Nixon's private conversations. To these kinds of embarrassments Lincoln was immune.

Joshua Meyerowitz declared that potentially great leaders are ruined by excessive exposure to the electronic media. "The great-leader image depends on mystification and careful management of public impressions. Through television, we see too much of our politicians, and they are losing control of their images and performances."[90] Despite the relevance of mystification and impression management, television alone cannot undermine presidential prestige. As early as the 1930s, motion pictures devastated reputations. Charlie Chaplin's spoof on *The Great Dictator,* Adolph Hitler, was a spectacular success, and if Franklin Roosevelt's physical handicap and romantic indiscretions were as much a political handicap as many today believe,[91] the film technology of the 1930s was advanced enough to reveal them. The authority of the office protected Roosevelt from the intrusions of the sort that wounded or destroyed his successors. Eroded authority permitting media intrusion is evident in the wall that protects African American civil rights leaders and other minorities. Martin Luther King Jr.'s womanizing and plagiarism, wrongdoing by rabbis as opposed to Catholic priests and Protestant ministers, are cases in point. The availability of intrusive practices and technologies does not guarantee their use; they are set aside in cases where they could harm minorities, set into motion when leaders of powerful majorities do wrong.

In the second half of the twentieth century, celebrity, itself the product of mass communications technology (the "graphic revolution," as Daniel Boorstin called it),[92] at once challenged and merged with politics. Artist Steven Shepard captured this relationship in his painting of Abraham Lincoln and Elvis Presley arm wrestling in heaven on the Sierra Club's behalf (fig. 6.2). Lincoln, Moses, Elvis Presley, and the Sierra Club are an incongruous combination, but it is precisely this incongruity—this absurdity—that makes contemporary viewers appreciate it.

The successful president, as Richard Neustadt maintained, no longer must persuade, but must entertain; must not only raise the right questions, give the right answers, and make the right decisions, but charm and enchant. John Kennedy, although a skillful statesman, was the first president to mesmerize the world through television, and since his death several entertainers have entered politics and attained offices as high as the United States Senate and presidency. This new presidential ideal, infused with cynicism, affects the way Americans feel about and judge presidents of the past and present alike. Cynicism's challenging the authority on which every president's prestige rests is nowhere more evident than in the changing content of films about the presidency. Before 1960, films mapped the abilities and character of former presidents, including Lincoln, into epic narratives. Since 1960, no such films have been produced for a mass theater audience.

New films dramatize the faults of contemporary presidents. *Advise and Consent*, appearing in 1962, depicts the president as an eminently practical man, but less able than his colleagues to distinguish between

FIGURE 6.2. *Elvis Presley and Abraham Lincoln Arm-Wrestle in Heaven,* no date, painting by Steven Shepard. Reproduced with permission of the artist.

decency and dishonor. Two years later, *The Best Man* reveals the vulgarity of presidential politics by portraying the corrupt nominating convention. The comedy *Kisses for My President* (1964) trivializes the office, while *Dr. Strangelove* (1965) mocks it. *The President's Analyst* (1967) does not depict the president himself, but the plot to kidnap his psychiatrist invites viewers to draw their own conclusions about his mental state. Not every film is deprecating. *Seven Days in May* (1964) and *Failsafe* (1964) depict a besieged but honorable president leading the nation through crisis. Positive films of the sixties, however, left no legacy, while critical films set the stage for subsequent portrayals of presidential malfeasance, highlighted by *All the President's Men* (1977), a chronicle of President Nixon's role in the Watergate scandal.

Late 1980s and early 1990s films highlighted the media's role in both the making of the president and the discovery of his vices. In *Being There* (1979), the press and television take a mentally retarded man to be a profound thinker, and after months of rave commentary the public is ready to vote him into office. A later film, *Dave* (1993), shows White House officials mistakenly recruiting a double to substitute for the disabled but corrupt president, while *The Pelican Brief* (1994) portrays a Washington reporter exposing an amoral president protecting criminal conspiracies (involving murder) orchestrated by his biggest contributor.

In *Patriot Games* (1995) the president conspires with the secretary of state against Congress to wage a secret war in Colombia and in the end betrays his own fighters. *Nixon* (1995), the drama, and semi-comedies *Secret Honor* (1984) and *Dick* (1996) emphasize the president's weakest moments while ignoring his admirable qualities and achievements.

It is no accident that Nixon, the most vilified president, should be the topic of the most movies, including *Nasty Habits* (1977), *Blind Ambition* (1979), *Concealed Enemies* (1987), *Kissinger and Nixon* (1995), and *Elvis Meets Nixon* (1997). Mark Feeney in *Nixon at the Movies* goes further to assert that a wide range of films, from *Sweet Smell of Success* (1957) to *Patton* (1970) and *Conversation* (1974), owe part of their meaning to their reflection of Richard Nixon's character at different stages of his career.[93]

Sex is central to many of the new movies. In *The American President* (1995), a liberal but pragmatic chief executive becomes idealistic after a sexual liaison with an environmental lobbyist (who disrobes and beds down with him in the White House on their second meeting). In *My Fellow Americans* (1996), two former presidents—one preoccupied with money, the other with sex—are pursued by assassins in a plot devised by an imbecilic vice president. At length, the vice president is imprisoned; the president resigns. In *Absolute Power* (1997), the president engages in rough sex with his friend's wife. When she protests being knocked about, he tries to strangle her. Defending herself with a knife, she is shot dead by the secret service. As the story proceeds, the president orders the murder of an innocent woman who might know about his tryst. In *Wag the Dog* (1999), the president comes under scrutiny for making sexual advances toward one of the Girl Scouts visiting the White House. To direct attention away from the matter, he hires consultants to fabricate news stories about a war in Albania.[94] *The Contender* (1999) concerns a female senator whose vice presidential candidacy is challenged by an adversary possessing evidence of her collegiate sexual misconduct. The protagonist admits to being sexually active to a congressional committee, but the president, a clever politician given to smelling his own shoes, affords her the necessary political protection.[95] *Head of State* (2003) is a story about a black alderman prone to sprinkle his ghettoese with *f*-words and *s*-words. Adorning himself with an earring and MTV garb, he runs for the presidency on a liberal platform promising to fight capitalism and injustice. To reduce carnal temptation on the campaign trail, the party furnishes him with a private prostitute. He wins the presidency.

In *Man of the Year* (2006), a talk show comedian runs for the presidency against two media-savvy competitors. He fails to excite the public until he brings comedy, peppered with sexual and scatological content, into his campaign. When an admirer tells him that a voting-machine programming error caused him to win the election, he immediately resigns against advice to feign ignorance of the actual vote. During his days as president elect, however, he shows himself to be a decent man who at one point feels too small for the office. The incumbent, by way of contrast, appears as ridiculous as the voters who put him into office.

So it goes: proceeding from the early 1960s to the turn of the twenty-first century, the president is transformed from cheat to mad-dog murderer to street-wise sharpster; the art of grand narrative gives way to the art of depravity, ridicule, and trivialization.[96] This transformation warrants attention because it results from the same erosion of traditional authority, the same post-heroic egalitarianism, that produces indifference toward Lincoln.[97]

ACIDS OF EQUALITY

Hollywood denigrates the president by representing him as a person no better than the rest of us. Nothing so disunifies a society and vexes authority, however, as such pursuit of equality, and no one has described its pathological edge as persuasively as Alexis de Tocqueville. Abraham Lincoln was a twenty-three-year-old living in New Salem, Illinois, when the French visitor began his nine-month tour through the United States. Tocqueville was struck by the interdependence of individualism and equality. "[N]ot only does democracy make every man forget his ancestors, but it hides his descendants and separates his contemporaries from him; it throws him back forever upon himself alone and threatens in the end to confine him entirely within the solitude of his own heart."[98] In the twenty-first century, democracy remains an irresistible force, and the most intense passion it generates continues to be equality. As long as the yearning for equality had something to feed on—tyranny, irrational hatred, suffocating bigotry, and discrimination—it was creative, fulfilling, beneficent. Once the burdens of the most serious injustices were overcome, however, equality began to eat away at itself. Equality's discontent has always been self-sustaining: the more equal people become, the more unbearable are remaining inequalities. The receding presence of great men is one aspect of this egalitarian trend.

Local narratives diminish national pantheons when they combine "diversity" and egalitarianism.[99] Mount Rushmore souvenirs now include a poster depicting ethereal images of four Native Americans—Chief Joseph, Sitting Bull, Geronimo, and Red Cloud—above the existing images of Washington, Jefferson, Roosevelt, and Lincoln respectively. What the artist had in mind is unknown, but the Indians' supernal placement in the image suggests that the chiefs are more worthy, more

FIGURE 6.3. *Peaceable Kingdom*, 1994 painting by Malacha Zeldis. Reproduced with permission of the artist.

entitled to the land, than the white presidents.[100] Malcha Zeldis's depiction of the *Peaceable Kingdom* (fig. 6.3) centers on its two largest figures: Abraham Lincoln and a contemporary black man. In front of them appear members of diverse ethnic groups: a Jew, an Arab, caricatures of Harpo Marx and Mohandas Ghandi, blond and brunette men and women in traditional and modern dress. If Zeldis means for the single figure of Lincoln to symbolize the ideal of multiculturalism, however, she is opposed by the American Association of Colleges, whose guiding premise is that heroes of the dominant community can only marginalize members of minority communities. "To endorse cultural pluralism," the Association resolved, "is to endorse the principle that there is no one model American."[101] But is the association wrong? Has Lincoln become the representative man of multiculturalism itself? If so, will his new identity restore his old renown?

Symbolizing Diversity. "Every Group Its Own Historian," declares historian Peter Novick.[102] He means that every group interprets historical events and leaders in its own way.[103] Artist Harry Wood depicts Novick's idea in his painting of *Every Man His Own Lincoln* (fig. 6.4). Five

FIGURE 6.4
Every Man His Own Lincoln, 1970 painting by Harry Wood. The Harry Wood Collection, Abraham Lincoln Library and Museum, Lincoln Memorial University. Courtesy of the Abraham Lincoln Library and Museum, Harrogate, TN.

different versions of Lincoln's face demonstrate visually how malleable is the man, how dependent on the eye of the beholder. If one man's version of Lincoln is as good as another's, however, the real Lincoln and his accomplishments become irrelevant.

Diversity—the recognition of every citizen's worthiness and his or her inclusion into the social mainstream—is the post-heroic era's greatest achievement. Diversity, however, also means nonjudgmentalism, including respect for the varying outlooks and perspectives of different groups, regardless of achievement. If Abraham Lincoln is but one American among many, for example, George Washington must be, too. No one could object, therefore, when the U.S. Mint decided to replace the one-dollar bill bearing Washington's image with a one-dollar coin bearing Susan B. Anthony's. That coin's awkward shape helped to doom it, but Sacagawea, temporary guide of Meriwether Lewis and William Clark, spearheaded the United States Mint's second try. Sacagawea's historical role is less pivotal than Susan B. Anthony's; her coin, "the Sac," no more successful, but its introduction was a product of the U.S. Mint's effort to substitute the nation's minorities for the man who did most to found and form the nation itself.[104] George Washington devoted twenty-five years of his life to the making of the new American republic, and he fired Abraham Lincoln's imagination. "Washington's is the mightiest name on earth," Lincoln declared. "To add brightness to the sun or glory to the name of Washington is alike impossible. Let no one attempt it. In solemn awe pronounce his name and in its naked, deathless splendor leave it shining on."[105] That Lincoln would have said the same of Sacagawea is inconceivable. Yet, if the politics of recognition make Sacagawea as worthy as George Washington to decorate the dollar coin, it can make another Native American as worthy as Sacagawea. When inflation makes the five-dollar bill obsolete, what tribe will supply Abraham Lincoln's replacement?[106] Diversity thus casts doubt on all political legacies, promotes the belief that all social distinctions are arbitrary, that any one viewpoint and heritage can no longer be considered more relevant than another, regardless of its historical importance.[107]

The U.S. Mint's latest project, therefore, is to produce a series of one-dollar coins that will feature the likeness of every president, regardless of his accomplishment. "This could be a renaissance for some of our lesser-known presidents," explained the mint's director, Edmund C. Moy, to a *New York Times* reporter. The reporter's failing to ask Mr. Moy why the mint would ever want to replace George Washington with a lesser president is symptomatic of the great drive toward equality.[108] Neither questioner nor respondent seemed to know that to admire all ethnic, racial, and national heroes equally is to esteem none.[109]

The incompatibility of equality and greatness is hardly a new idea. Friedrich Hegel, writing in the early nineteenth century, asserted that the desire for recognition (*Anerkennung*) is the core of institutionalized power relations. Drawing on Rousseau's observation that human beings see themselves mirrored in the opinion of others, Hegel argued that the individual is naturally self-centered, wishing to be recognized and esteemed by others but reluctant to bestow recognition in turn. History itself begins with the conquered and enslaved recognizing the superiority of their masters, but in the course of time the slaves grow resentful, regard their own recognition worth dying for, and rebel violently.[110]

In modern democracies, the need for recognition is manifest in many spheres, including curriculum and textbook selection, which, from elementary schools to universities, minimize the significance of traditional heroes and depict minority group members in visible historical roles. Doing so, as Arthur Schlesinger Jr. observed after resigning from the

New York Regents committee on history, distorts the past, minimizes authentic greatness, and weakens the values that once united the nation. Joined to multicultural coin iconography and satirical films, the new history textbook's function is to inform through the politics of recognition—in particular, to assign Abraham Lincoln a leading but narrower place in the nation's history, not by criticizing or belittling him but by deemphasizing his key accomplishment—saving the Union, the achievement that unlocked all other doors to the further perfection of democracy—and surrounding and obscuring him with figures whose accomplishments have been less pivotal than his.

Evidence of diversity's effects is not limited to the United States. In France, the grip of the past weakened between 1950 and 1980, when the framework of the nation eroded, power diffused, and economic growth displaced civic values as the basis of national cohesion. In the late 1980s and 1990s there occurred a further shift wherein a previously unitary model of commemoration was replaced by a "splintered system composed of disparate commemorative languages, which presuppose a different relationship to the past. . . . There is no longer a commemorative superego, the canon has disappeared."[111] Pierre Nora's representation of collective memory in France parallels closely Jean-Francois Lyotard's observation of petit narratives replacing grand narratives that once affirmed the solidarity of the nation.

In Great Britain, as in America, diversity attends the dawning of a post-heroic era. Celebrity role models replace great men while victims replace conquerors; guilt replaces pride; contrition follows triumphalism. With expectations lowered, Mick Hume adds, aspirations and expectations diminish; suffering and victimhood replace triumph as objects of historical attention.[112]

For many years sociologists have believed that memories change as generations replace one another, but it is precisely this linkage—successive generations seeing themselves in new conceptions of the past—that postmodern scholars explicitly deny. What is socially rooted for them, as noted, are not new or revised grand narratives but an unprecedented sense of their irrelevance; not the replacement of one great man for another, but the repudiation of all great men.[113] Equality replaces distinction as the core of post-heroic culture.

Post-Heroic Stamps And Media. The inflation of renown—commemorating too many people for too few achievements—and the miniaturization of memory—petit narratives commemorating mundane rather than epic events—are relevant to the integration of American society. The orderly circulation of goods and money is indispensable to this integration process, which is why every nation-state engraves images and symbols of its own legitimacy upon its monetary and postal currency. Post-heroic states, however, define and legitimate themselves by the ordinariness of those portrayed.

The U.S. Mint's determination to remove traditional images from its coins, paper money, and bonds reappears in the work of the U.S. Postal Service. The sheer number of people portrayed on American postage stamps, table 6.3 shows, increased gradually from twenty-eight during the first two decades of the twentieth century to 201 during the last two.[114] The abrupt increase during the century's final decades results from a series of administrative decisions. Established in 1957, the Citizens' Stamp Advisory Committee ensures representation of as wide a spectrum of American life as possible. This committee provides the postal service with a "breadth of judgment and depth of experience in various areas that influence the subject matter, character, and beauty of postage stamps." Since 1957 the membership of the committee has changed many times over. In 2005, eight of the fifteen committee members were in the fields of art and entertainment; two members were academics; two members were executive officers of public relations and retail design firms; one member was a former congressional aide; one, a prominent member of the philatelic community; one, a "patron of the arts," namely Joan Mondale, wife of former Democratic senator Walter Mondale.[115] Whether or not the background of the present committee is more devoted to diversity than previous committees is unknown, but the character of postage stamps has changed drastically and will continue to change. In 2000, the U.S. Postal Service announced that "there would be no more stamps in the Great American series, the largest definitive series in U.S. postal history. . . . It is being replaced by a similar series that the Postal Service and collectors call the Distinguished Americans."[116] Lowering the criterion from "great" to "distinguished" secures the trend of making more Americans eligible for postal commemoration. Thus, occupations and achievements commemorated at the beginning and end of the twentieth century differ drastically. As the twenty-first century progresses, this difference will probably expand.

During the twentieth century's first two decades, 75.1 percent of those represented on stamps were political figures, statesmen, and men engaged in the nation's governance, including Benjamin Franklin, George Washington, Andrew Jackson, Henry Clay, and Abraham Lincoln. Military figures and the New World's discoverers, explorers, and settlers account together for 14.2 percent of the total; the remaining 10.7 percent consist mainly of presidents' wives.

TABLE 6.3. Occupations of figures depicted on U.S. postage stamps: 1900–1999

Occupation	1900–1919 (n = 28)	1920–39 (n = 45)	1940–59 (n = 110)	1960–79 (n = 109)	1980–99 (n = 201)
Percentages					
1.	75.1	53.3	40.0	36.6	28.8
2.			20.9	16.5	9.4
3.	7.1	37.7	9.0	8.2	5.4
4.	10.7	4.4	2.7		1.0
5.	7.1	2.2	1.8	2.7	2.9
6.			10.9	14.6	9.9
7.		2.2			4.4
8.					3.4
9a.			3.6	4.5	2.4
9b.			5.4	8.2	12.4
9c.			1.0	4.5	13.9
10.			4.5	2.7	3.9
11.				1.0	1.4
Concentration index	.58	.43	.23	.20	.15

Source: Occupations codes for postage stamps: 1. Politics, government; 2. Science, discovery, education; 3. Military and related occupations; 4. Symbolic roles (women); 5. New World discovery, exploration, and settlement; 6. Author, poet; 7. Sports figure; 8. Minority leader, resister; 9a. Entertainer: high brow; 9b. Entertainer: middle brow; 9c. Entertainer: low brow; 10. Reformer, philanthropist, social worker; 11. Religious figure.

During every decade of the century, one or more issues of an Abraham Lincoln stamp appear, but Lincoln becomes smaller as the field in which he stands becomes more crowded. Not only Lincoln but all the great men and women of American history—those who have done most to establish, build, and defend their country—are now outnumbered by those who have entertained or distracted their countrymen, or claim membership in oppressed groups.[117] Moving from the first to the last two decades of the century, the number of political figures, statesmen, and military figures drops from 75.1 percent to 28.8 percent while a new category consisting of entertainers, appearing for the first time in midcentury, makes up 28.7 percent of the total. If sports figures are added to this entertainer list, the percentage rises to 33.1 percent.[118] Correspondingly, the percentage of minorities, including nonwhites, has increased from 10.3 to 30.6 percent. The table shows the greatness of the field diminishing as it becomes more diverse.[119]

Postage stamp content tracks the identity of those with whom Americans actually identify. Celebrities first appeared on stamps between 1940 and 1959, increasing from 10 percent of the total at this time to

17 percent between 1960 and 1979, then to 33 percent after 1980. Fred Greenstein's analysis of school children in five local surveys, 1901 to 1958, indicate that the most significant increase in celebrity influence occurred between 1944 and 1958, which includes the advent of the television age, when entertainers and athletes increased from 8 to 38 percent of the most admired.[120] Thus, postal iconography does more than express postal service tastes; it describes the changing moral models of the American people.

The Library of Congress's Web site, listing "Amazing Americans"—"the inventors, politicians, performers, activists and other everyday people who made this country what it is today" is another "official," i.e., governmental, definition of distinguished Americans. Twenty-four percent of the twenty-five figures named in the list made their mark by political achievement; 20 percent as minority reformers, resisters, and activists; 16 percent as entertainers.[121] *Time* magazine's special issue on "American Legends" (2001) covers the more than 500 years passing since the New World's discovery, selecting eighty-three individuals, 50.6 percent of whom are entertainers and sports figures. Abraham Lincoln is prominent on *Time*'s list, but the number of political, and military figures—the objects of traditional commemoration—make up only 12.2 percent of the total.[122] *Life* magazine also devoted a special issue to the American hero, but its format and content, which includes not only ordinary Americans facing challenges but also *animal* heroes, differed from *Time*'s. Men and women of state, including Lincoln, comprise 22.3 percent of this list; entertainers are not considered and only a small number (3.2 percent) of athletes is included. The largest of the remaining categories, 31.1 percent of the total, are minority leaders, activists, reformers, and victims.

The academic version of the Library of Congress, *Time*, and *Life* Web sites is the *Dictionary of American Biography*, whose original twenty volumes (1928–36) contained almost 14,000 articles on subjects distinguished by "some significant contribution, achievement, or activity, whether or not this may have been long obscured." The first editor indicated that "The Dictionary cannot find space for average or merely typical figures."[123] The successor series, *American National Biography* (1999), containing more than 18,000 entries, draws upon a "wealth of research that has immeasurably deepened our knowledge of the American past." The latter includes "men and women from all walks of American life, from the well-known to the infamous and obscure," including athletes, singers, dancers, and journalists. The move from the *Dictionary of American Biography* to the *American National Biography* parallels the changing content of American postage stamps, the Amazing Americans list, and popular magazines.[124]

In a June 2005 project sponsored by America Online and shown on the Discovery Television Channel, a self-selected sample of Americans nominated and voted for "The Greatest American." Of the most frequently mentioned individuals, 24 percent fell into the category of traditional heroes (presidents, statesmen, and military figures); 14 percent were scientists, inventors, explorers, discoverers, and pioneers; 26 percent of the votes were scattered among reformers, business people, presidents' wives, and others. The most popular category, 36 percent, consisted of entertainers and athletes.[125]

The *USA Today Weekend* magazine celebrates diversity by endorsing ten destinations in its Annual Travel Report to summer vacationers. The recommended sites express the same values embodied in stamps, Library of Congress commemorative choices, magazines, biography, and television contents. The "ten defining moments and places" in American democracy, in order of mention, are monuments to ethnic diversity (Ellis Island, New York); the framing of the Declaration of Independence and Constitution (Independence Hall, Philadelphia); equality and peace [not Union] (Lincoln Memorial, Washington DC); representative government, slavery, and violence against the American Indian (Jamestown, Virginia); racial injustice (Edmund Pettus Bridge, Selma, Alabama); women's rights (Esther Morris Statue, Cheyenne, Wyoming); oppression of workers (the Haymarket Riot Statue, Forest Park, Illinois); survival of America's first people despite "land grabs, gold rushes, and oil booms" (Saxman Native Totem Park, Saxman, Alaska); American technology (Kennedy Space Center, Cape Canaveral, Florida); and appreciation of the environment (Walden Pond, Concord, Massachusetts). Contributing editors' listing includes September 11 Ground Zero; the statue of FDR in a wheelchair; Valley Forge; Lincoln's home, office, and tomb; the First AME Church, Los Angeles; and the Manzanar monument to Japanese Americans interned in camps during World War II.

"Can it be that in its desire to make room for everyone, for every particularism," Edward Tiryakian asks, "the postwelfare national state has set aside the idea of the nation?"[126] Tiryakian's question admits of no simple answer. If the nation were irrelevant, it would make no difference who is recognized on its war memorials and stamps. However, when particularisms eat away at the idea of the nation, they destroy the very entity that defines their meaning. Massive deterioration has yet to happen, but its progress is unmistakable. (For a demonstration of American civics textbooks setting aside the idea of the nation, see appendix K.)

Deteriorating authority, depthlessness, ridicule, lust for recognition and rights, mockery of duty—if this "psychohistorical dislocation" is the cultural context of Lincoln's fall, then its effect must extend to all presidents. On no point does the evidence converge more precisely. While Lincoln's presidential greatness rating, as noted in the previous chapter (table 5.1), fell from 62 to 40 percent from 1956 to 1999, Roosevelt's rating fell from 64 to 24 percent, Washington's from 47 to 24 percent, and Eisenhower's from 38 to 8 percent. Truman's post-presidential reputation peaked in 1975 at 37 percent, then fell to 10 percent. From 1975 to 1999 Kennedy's rating dropped from 52 to 35 percent. The decline of Roosevelt, Truman, Eisenhower, and Kennedy is partly due to what Tom W. Smith calls a "presentism bias"—the tendency to forget presidents of the remote past and to admire current and recent presidents.[127] In the past, however, incumbent presidents gained prestige without older ones losing it. Gallup ratings for Roosevelt, Lincoln, and Washington were highest when Eisenhower was in office and deemed great by one third of the respondents—a greater percentage than for any subsequent incumbent president. Thus, if recent presidents gained the nominations that past presidents lost, no one of the former gained very much or kept what he had gained for very long.

History books reflect the same tendency. In the 1940s, 61 percent of all references to presidents were positive or neutral; in the 1980s this figure had declined to 29 percent. The consequence for the future, according to Peggy Noonan, is grim:

> Who is at fault? Those of us who let the myth die, or let it change, or refused to let it be told? The politically correct nitwit teaching the seventh-grade history class who decides the impressionable young minds before him need to be informed, and their first serious history lesson, that the Founders were hypocrites, the Bill of Rights nothing new and imperfect in any case, that the Indians were victims of genocide, that Lincoln was a clinically depressed homosexual who compensated for the storms within by creating storms without.[128]

Article counts, independently of the matter Noonan describes, also show reputations diminishing together. During the 1940s and 1950s, the *New York Times* published 29 articles per year about George Washington. During the 1960s, this number dropped to 17, then to 12 by the 1980s. *Readers' Guide* and *Congressional Record* entries for George Washington display the same pattern: frequent citations during the decades prior to 1960, then permanent post-1960 decline. The trend for Franklin

Roosevelt is similar. For five-year periods from 1950 to 1964, the number of *New York Times* articles on Roosevelt clustered around an annual average of 35, fell to 16 between 1965 and 1969, and has fallen further since.[129] The details of Lincoln's particular case thus highlight a general process.[130]

Monument visitation, like opinion polls, article counts, and textbooks, follow a downward trend for all presidents. During every decade since the Civil War, visits to Mount Vernon had increased, reaching a peak of over 1.2 million per year from 1960 to 1969, then declining for the very first time during the 1970s. Washington Monument visits also peaked at 1.8 million per year during the 1960s and have since fallen. George Washington's birthplace (remotely located in Wakefield, Virginia) visits reached 151,586 annually in the 1970s and have fallen every subsequent decade. Even the home of the presidents, the White House, has never regained its 1960s peak of 1.5 million visits. Wilbur Zelinsky's representative sample of other "nationally significant historical parks and sites" also drew steadily growing numbers of visitors until the late sixties, then declined through the seventies and eighties.[131]

UNWELCOME DISTINCTIONS

Growing indifference to Abraham Lincoln and other members of America's pantheon is evident in national surveys, media citation counts, monument visitation, holiday practices, and commemorative symbolism. These sources of evidence, in addition to the growing number of representations of Lincoln for playful, even ludic, purposes, indicate the blurring of the line between matters of import and passing consequence, gravity and lightness, existential crises and sporadic troubles, greatness and celebrity.

The United States has faced successive conflicts in the late twentieth century, but none has produced a sense of mission comparable to that felt during the Depression and World War II. A lessened sense of mission is not to be confused with the total diffusion of national sentiment. Nationalistic displays accompanying the 1991 Gulf War, 9/11, and the beginning of the Iraq War, for example, were intense and sincere. Such manifestations of nationalism, however, possessed no time frame, included no effort seriously to relate present events to the events of the past. True, there was mention of Pearl Harbor after 9/11 and the analogizing of Hitler and Saddam Hussein during the Gulf and Iraq Wars, but there is no evidence that the public took them literally or even believed the parallels were very close. Nationalism and patriotic displays are nowadays present-oriented; they draw no sustainable connection to the great events of American history.

Diminishing of national mission and lessening relevance of national heroes, according to Ori Soltes, "is a warning sign that our culture is adrift.... There is a sense of being at a loss, of being ungrounded."[132] Soltes expresses a popular view that is only partly correct. Equality and distrust of authority, the conditions leading to the rupturing of the tissue connecting present and past, are benign conditions to be maintained, not pathologies to be deplored and abolished. Alienation, the sense that one belongs to no special community, or to a community not particularly special, is a correlate of racial, ethnic, and religious groups' achieving equal dignity. The same conditions that strip us of a precious and necessary heritage also save us from the bigotry, hatred, and inequalities to which that heritage is related.

Present conceptions of equality are part of this multivalent complex. Post-industrial communicative technologies, including air travel, television, and computer communication, extend the range of human contact and create new forms of social attachments that abolish belief in the idea of truth as monolithic; identity, stable; commitment, focused and permanent. To embrace any singular conception of the self let alone any singular model *for* the self, whether that model be Abraham Lincoln or Elton John, is difficult in a time that neither awaits nor seeks such models. As the twentieth century ended, Abraham Lincoln began to represent a form of equality that resisted the acknowledgment of human distinction, including his own. Such is Lincoln's paradox. Every scholar and commentator who has ever written about historical reputation asserts that the hero inspires because he embodies his society's ideals. But what if the function of the representative hero is to symbolize the equality of all men? What if the American people see in Lincoln the tendency toward the elimination rather than cultivation of distinction? In that case, Abraham Lincoln's prestige is undermined rather than reinforced by the very ideal he represents. Such is the fate of all great men in the post-heroic era.

* 7 *

Inertia

THE ENDURING LINCOLN

February 12, 2001, passed with few if any mentions of Abraham Lincoln in America's newspapers, but there were exceptions. The *Arkansas Democrat-Gazette*'s editorial, "The Power of Myth: Lincoln's Birthday, 2001," lamented the nation's loss of its great men. Columnist Paul Greenberg attributed Lincoln's diminished stature to the people's inability to see him as the extraordinary man he was and to understand the powerful enemies and great difficulties he faced. "No wonder Abraham Lincoln seems quite beyond our mittened grasp now. For we demand a man for one season—our blank own." As if to underscore Greenberg's point, the *Democrat-Gazette's* cartoonist depicted Lincoln on his memorial chair saying to himself "These 'crises' aren't what they used to be. . . ." In the lower right corner of the editorial page, the smallness of the age is reflected in the bigness of the man: from Lincoln's second inaugural address appears a biting indictment of slavery and final words of forgiveness and reconciliation. The *Arkansas Democrat-Gazette* reacts not only to the diminishing of Lincoln's stature but also to the spirit of the age, a hand-wringing one in which past accomplishments are denied lest they obscure present grievances.[1] Is this commentary idiosyncratic or an expression of something deeply rooted in contemporary American culture?

Heartfelt admiration of Lincoln is now at a low point, but there is a floor below which it cannot fall, a limit inherent in the character of nationhood itself. French historian Ernest Renan believed that a nation is "a soul, a spiritual principle. Only two things, actually, constitute this soul, this spiritual principle. . . . One is the possession in common of a rich legacy of remembrances; the other is the actual consent, the desire to live together, the will to continue to value the heritage which all hold in common."[2] Nations consist of more than memories; they consist of interdependent citizens, common goals and actions, boundaries distinguishing natives and foreigners, and patriotic attachment. Yet common memories, although insufficient to sustain nationhood, are necessary to its constitution. To forget the national story is only possible in a nation that has ceased to cherish its own existence. But how much has America forgotten, and what is Lincoln's place in what it remembers?

Inertia

Throughout the Depression, World War II, Cold War, civil rights movement, and post-heroic era, discontinuities in Lincoln's prestige and reputation have been relatively easy to track.[3] Continuities in Lincoln's prestige and reputation—that which constitutes his memory's inertia—are more opaque.

In the physical world, inertia refers to "a property of matter by which it remains at rest or in uniform motion in the same straight line unless acted upon by some external force."[4] The greater the mass of an object, the greater the force required to alter its motion. In the social world, inertia is a metaphor portraying objects maintaining their structures in a changing environment. The more solid a historical figure's prestige and reputation, the greater the social force necessary to modify them. The prominence of the Great Emancipator, for example, resulted not from the discovery of new data or methodological precision but from greater attention to Lincoln's beliefs about slavery, an aspect of Lincoln's life made more relevant by the civil rights movement. From this viewpoint, Lincoln's earlier virtues remain recognizable but appear less relevant. Once we know why relevance declines, we will be in a better position to understand how cultural inertia works.

Institutionalized in the school curriculum, examinations, and public rituals, Lincoln's memory, in Michael Schudson's words, "accumulates a self-perpetuating rhetorical power. It gathers partisans, partisans beget schools, schools beget cultural authority, cultural authority begets an established tradition."[5] Michael Frisch is more concrete. When students in his college history courses were asked to write ten names that come to mind in connection with American history from its beginning to the Civil War, the ranking, led by George Washington, Abraham Lincoln, and Thomas Jefferson, was almost constant over a decade despite the fact that earlier and later cohorts rarely discussed the matter with one another. This pattern reflects lessons learned and internalized at an early stage of life, Frisch believes, and they "stick" because they are based on highly stable symbolic structures consisting of flags and other objects marking the nation's beginning.[6]

Representations of Lincoln are "autocatalytic" or "path dependent"—shaped not only by their social contexts but also by their history.[7] The process that Schudson and Frisch describe is familiar, but we have precious little knowledge of what makes it so. Now is the time to bring the least mutable aspect of collective memory into the open, where it can be understood. Now is the time to see how inertia preserves perceptions of Lincoln.

Lincoln's inertia is maintained by three forms of commemoration. History and English teachers exemplify *routine commemoration* by devoting time to Lincoln's words and achievements and, in the many schools where "value education" is part of the curriculum, to what Lincoln stands for. Memorials and shrines, statues and paintings, spectacular ritual events such as centennials and sesquicentennials, exemplify *grand commemoration,* which reinforces the information and historical consciousness instilled in childhood. *Mundane commemoration* refers to the display of mnemonic objects that are part of the everyday landscape, taken for granted, unnoticed until someone makes explicit reference to them. Such objects make up in quantity what they lack in dramatic appeal. In the United States geological survey, for example, are listed more than ten thousand places named after Lincoln, including townships, villages, districts, counties, subdivisions of counties, cities, schools, hospitals, airports, commercial and public buildings, commercial centers, churches, cemeteries, parks, forests, cliffs, rivers, streams, bridges, tunnels, bays, and channels. The number of businesses naming themselves after Lincoln approaches ten thousand. Hundreds of thousands of individuals carry Lincoln as a first, middle, or family name. Language, too, sustains inertia. Few phrases occupy more pages of *Bartlett's Familiar Quotations,* are as widely cited, or reach more people, than Abraham Lincoln's.[8]

Lincoln's inertia is countered by revisionist attacks defining his presidency as an epitome of racism, tyranny, and military brutality. But these representations, available in specialized sources, including magazines and Web sites, are not so widely communicated as to negate the traditional Savior of the Union, Great Emancipator, and Man of the People.[9] This is because, in the words of Roy LeGoff, "[i]nertia is a crucially important historical force" and "[m]entalities change slower than anything else. . . ."[10]

NATIONAL TRAGEDY: ANCHOR OF TRADITION

Abraham Lincoln's memory is preserved chiefly through texts and symbols whose primary function is not only to teach us about the past, but also to enable us to live within it. The mere exposure to things reminding us of Lincoln cannot, in this regard, affect us; we must first place ourselves within their range of influence: "in a word, it is necessary that we act, and that we repeat the acts thus necessary every time we feel the need of renewing their effects."[11] Texts and commemorative symbols are thus more than means by which knowledge of the past is transmitted; they are the means by which the past becomes part of life, learned and relearned in the mind of the living. The framing of sudden death constitutes an example.

By late November 1963, Abraham Lincoln's stature had fallen from its Depression-World War II zenith. The keying of President John F. Kennedy's assassination to Lincoln's, however, helped to solve the universal problems of contemplating sudden death[12] and transforming shock into meaning. Invoking Lincoln on this occasion, in turn, sustained his prestige as it enlarged Kennedy's.

In one of her last acts as first lady, Jacqueline Kennedy conceived a memorial inscription for the White House: "In this room lived John Fitzgerald Kennedy with his wife Jacqueline during the two years, ten months and two days he was President of the United States." She then ordered her message carved beneath the existing inscription, "In this room Abraham Lincoln slept during his occupancy of the White House, March 4, 1861–April 13, 1865."[13]

Jacqueline Kennedy could not help thinking of Lincoln. He was in the air. Outside the frame of Lincoln's death, Kennedy's would have felt differently. Richard Cardinal Cushing, concluding his nationally televised message from Boston, could think of no comfort to extend the president's mother and father "beyond the knowledge that they have given history a youthful Lincoln. . . ."[14] On the same day, television cameras showed a succession of dignitaries converging on the White House as actor Van Heflin, off-camera, read "O Captain! My Captain!" which Walt Whitman composed on the occasion of Lincoln's assassination:

> Oh the bleeding drops of red,
> Where on the deck my Captain lies,
> Fallen cold and dead.[15]

Next day, President Kennedy's coffin was carried by the same horse-drawn caisson and placed on the same catafalque that had borne Abraham Lincoln's remains. As Mrs. Kennedy looked upon the rotunda scene, her thoughts must have drifted back to the night she stepped off the plane from Dallas and instructed Angier Biddle Duke, state department chief of protocol, to find out about Lincoln's funeral. Seven aides went to work and by morning they had found a key.[16] Common ritual paraphernalia revealed continuity and common fate: two presidents, two martyrs. Ritual symbols transformed external parallels involving bullets, fleeing assailants, and hurried oath-takings into emotional bonds uniting generations.

Throughout the late night and early morning hours, 200,000 people passed the president's flag-draped coffin. Then came the late-morning rotunda ceremony, the Saint Matthew's Cathedral service, and the final cortege to Arlington Cemetery: banners and drums, spirited horses dressed in black, officers parading with glistening swords, distant trumpets, relentless, scraping sounds of the march, soldiers everywhere—before, behind, alongside the flag-draped coffin. Millions of television viewers saw the great pageant approach the Lincoln Memorial, wind around its southern side, move across Memorial Bridge into the cemetery, arrive at graveside. They heard the last words, the roar of fifty fighter jets, the twenty-one-cannon salute. They saw the coffin's flag folded and transferred to the new widow. They would never forget what they had seen.

Remembrances of the graveside drama were reinforced by their connection to the past. Maurice Halbwachs noticed how events occurring over time are fixed in collective memory by the arrangement of objects in space.[17] So it was on the day of the great funeral. Television cameras scanning downhill, past the cemetery and across the Potomac River, revealed the direct line from Kennedy's grave through the Memorial Bridge to the Lincoln Memorial.

Martyrdom as Tradition. John Kennedy's funeral pageant revitalized Lincoln's as it reaffirmed the permanence of the nation and made the American people realize who they were: one people with one past and one destiny. State funerals, as Murray Edelman might have described them, are "meaning machines"[18] answering ultimate questions about national purpose and identity, transmitting the people's sense of themselves to posterity. Coupled images of Kennedy and Lincoln were plausible because they were part of a cultural pattern everyone recognized and found relevant. When James Garfield was assassinated in 1881, printmakers marked the occasion's significance by placing Garfield's likeness next to Lincoln's. If two assassinations, Lincoln's and Garfield's, seemed like separate events, three assassinations might seem more like interconnected episodes of a single narrative. Thus, as soon as William McKinley died, a new song appeared—"History Has Given Us Another Lincoln": "Sent to his death on the altar of fame; / And on liberty's scroll, with Garfield and Lincoln, / In letters of gold we'll write his grand name."[19] Simultaneously, *Harper's Weekly* showed the North and South as two robed females, escorting McKinley to the Hall of Martyrs, its entrance adorned by elevated busts of Lincoln and Garfield. Sixty-three years later, another mourning song, "America, America"[20] added a new chapter to the great narrative, symbolized by "these AMERICANS martyred for liberty, / Lincoln, James Garfield, McKinley / and John F. Kennedy."

Cartoon images of Lincoln, the war president, outnumbered Garfield's and McKinley's in representations of Kennedy's death.[21] Uncle Sam seated between Kennedy's and Lincoln's coffins, resting his elbows on each and bending forward in grief, or Lincoln sitting on his chair of state, assuming the same mournful pose as Uncle Sam,[22] evoke a mood and sense of historical connection that neither a Garfield nor McKinley symbol could duplicate.[23] The Lincoln pictures indeed redefined the significance of Kennedy's presidency. Alive, the young Kennedy seemed anything but a great president; dead, he became Lincoln's equal. Here, an etherealized Lincoln, hat in hand and clutching *Profiles in Courage*, gazes on his successor's rocking chair (fig. 7.1); elsewhere, Kennedy's profile foregrounds Lincoln's. Just as nineteenth-century mourning prints showed George Washington welcoming Lincoln to Glory, twentieth-century cartoons depicted Lincoln welcoming Kennedy (fig. 7.2).[24] "Four Sad Days" (1964), by Corlus Walker and Andrew Spalding, set the images to music: "He was greeted at the gate / By a great host of heaven / And there's a gallant Mr. Lincoln by his side."[25]

To dismiss Lincoln-Kennedy couplings as polite fictions, hypocritical hindsights, or admirers' excesses, is to miss their symbolic accomplishment. In the early 1960s Abraham Lincoln was hard to imagine in the company of a living president. That form had gone out of style with Franklin Roosevelt, but the murder of a president brings the past to life and makes obsolete forms of homage seem natural. Thus, on December 22, 1963, a month of national mourning ended with a candlelight ceremony at the Lincoln Memorial. From a torch ignited at Kennedy's grave, President Johnson lit his candle, then turned and spoke to a shivering audience of 17,000 people. No one so much as lifted an eyebrow as Johnson wrapped Kennedy's memory in the Gettysburg Address: "Thirty days and a few hours ago, John Fitzgerald Kennedy, 35th President of the United States, died a martyr's death. The world will not forget what he did here."[26] No one missed the intended effect: the representation of John Kennedy as Abraham Lincoln's successor.

As Johnson spoke, a document listing extraordinary parallels and proving the presence of supernatural forces suffused the country. "Lincoln-Kennedy: Coincidence?" described a miracle that could not fail to impress the most hardened cynic:

> Both President Lincoln and President Kennedy were concerned with the issue of civil rights. Lincoln was elected in 1860 . . . Kennedy was

FIGURE 7.1
Lincoln, hat in hand, mourning Kennedy, 1964, Lloyd Ostendorf.

FIGURE 7.2
"Somebody will finish the job . . . ," November 25, 1963, Jim Berryman, *Washington Star.*

elected in 1960, one hundred years apart. Both were shot from behind in the head. Their successors, both named Johnson, were Southern Democrats with seats in the Senate. Andrew Johnson was born in 1808 . . . Lyndon Johnson was born in 1908, one hundred years apart. John Wilkes Booth, the man who shot Lincoln, was born in 1839 . . . Lee Harvey Oswald, the man who shot Kennedy, was born in 1939, one hundred years apart. Booth and Oswald were Southerners favoring unpopular ideas. Booth and Oswald were both assassinated before going to trial. Both Presidents' wives lost children through death while in the White House. Both Presidents were killed on Friday . . . and in the presence of their wives. President Lincoln's secretary, whose name was Kennedy, advised him not to go to the theater . . . President Kennedy's secretary, whose name was Lincoln, advised him not to go to Dallas. John Wilkes Booth shot Lincoln in a theater and ran to a warehouse. Lee Harvey Oswald shot Kennedy from a warehouse and ran to a theater. The names Lincoln and Kennedy each contain seven letters. The names Andrew Johnson and Lyndon Johnson each contain thirteen letters. The names John Wilkes Booth and Lee Harvey Oswald each contain fifteen letters.[27]

Rational men and women "knew" these parallels were coincidences; yet genuine chance, as Roland Barthes observed, "is always distributive, never repetitive: chance is supposed to vary events; if it repeats them, it does so in order to signify something through them; to repeat is to signify."[28] Who but God could give such a signal? To the many Americans who saw history as a divine plan,[29] possibility meant plausibility. True, the parallels stretched the facts. Asserting that Booth and Oswald were "Southerners favoring unpopular ideas" confounds Oswald's attraction to a cause which most Americans opposed (communism) and Booth's attraction to a cause (slavery and the right to secede) in which many Northern as well as Southern contemporaries believed.[30] The sheer number of coincidences, however, overwhelmed rational explanation. In Lincoln's and Kennedy's deaths, believers saw more than two links in a historical chain—they saw an identity: Lincoln's foreshadowing Kennedy's death and Kennedy's postshadowing Lincoln's. The frame, as it were, sanctified the picture; the picture enlarged the frame.

In 1965, Nashville artist Buddy Starcher set the Lincoln-Kennedy coincidences to music. "[F]riends, it is true that history does repeat itself," he said as his chorus responded with words from the *Battle Hymn of the Republic*'s "His truth is marching on!"[31] Ten years later, an educational film, *Parallels in History: Kennedy and Lincoln* (1974), visualized the "uncanny similarities" between the two presidents' lives.[32] The coincidence of Lincoln's and Kennedy's fate remained profound and mystical, to be reinforced by the deaths of other men, ordinary men who identified more with Lincoln than with any other president. Such are the forces that keep his renown intact.

President Kennedy died in the midst of the Civil War centennial and the civil rights struggle, for which Lincoln was a relevant symbol for both segregationists and their opponents. Thirty years later the situation differed—no major crises, but there transpired minor events proving the enduring significance of Lincoln's memory. James Hudson, a National Park Service employee responsible for cleaning the Lincoln Memorial, had worked a double shift, sixteen hours in withering heat, on July 4, 1993. Next day he was back on the job after five hours rest, sweeping and mopping the memorial's floors and steps. He became sick and was taken to the air-conditioned central office, where he collapsed and died. The *Washington Post* carried Hudson's story under the front-page headline "Lincoln Memorial Loses Its Keeper," and continued it under a second headline: "Park Service Foreman Loved Lincoln Memorial." Unlike hundreds of the laborers on the Park Service's temporary payroll, Hudson was not just putting in time. He "was proud to work on the Lincoln statue" and on the wall of his living room, the *Post* revealed, hangs a picture of his cleaning it.[33]

James Hudson's untimely death, local in its significance, infused Lincoln's local memory with more affect than it would otherwise possess. Youngsters called Hudson "Daddy," and a neighbor described him as a "daddy figure" who treated all children "as though they were his own." As Lincoln was "Father Abraham" to the Northern people, Hudson was a "daddy" to the city. Amid official corruption and incompetence, ordinary people like James Hudson kept Washington intact, one letter-writer observed. Printed beneath a picture of Hudson and Lincoln, the letter concluded: "Goodbye, Mr. Hudson, and thanks for taking such good care of us."[34]

Before he began to take care of the Great Emancipator, Hudson, a black man, had received a Purple Heart while trying to defend Vietnam against communism. A father and defender of the oppressed in his own right, Hudson's memory became coupled with Lincoln's. Even more, Hudson had helped to maintain the immortality of Daniel Chester French, the man who had enshrined Lincoln in marble. Larry Chapman, a descendant of French, was moved by James Hudson's death, attended his funeral, and later gave Mrs. Hudson a cash gift to help cover expenses. Chapman explained that he felt indebted to James Hudson because he had cared so well for his ancestor's statue and had so much affection for Lincoln.[35]

The story of a forty-three-year-old man working himself to death out of affection for the memory of Abraham Lincoln is a moving story. That this man was African American made the story even more poignant. Lincoln had died for the slaves; now a slave's descendant died for him. Public interest would have ended with Hudson's burial, however, if certain officials had not enlarged it, drawn out details, secured old points of contact with Lincoln, and developed new points of contemporary relevance.

Hudson had worked eight years for the National Park Service, but since he was registered a "temporary employee" ineligible for pension and life-insurance benefits, his death left his family financially devastated. Outraged, District of Columbia delegate Eleanor Holmes introduced a "private bill" (all 435 House members concurring) to provide the Hudson family compensation equal to the basic life insurance benefit permanent workers received. The *Washington Post* applauded the measure as representative Frank McClosky invoked a familiar connection: slavery as metaphor of labor exploitation. "The federal government," he said, "should not be the plantation of last resort." Soon the James Hudson Temporary Employee Act of 1993, as its authors named it, remedied the "disgrace."[36]

James Hudson's story is worth remembering because it reflects so well its cultural setting and Lincoln's place in it. A poor but dedicated black worker dying on Abraham Lincoln's behalf, yet exploited by his government, solidified Lincoln's reputation as champion of labor and minority rights. If the man who died at the Lincoln Memorial on July 5th were anyone but James Hudson, or if James Hudson had died tending any monument but Lincoln's, he would have received less sympathy. The combination of modern problems (race relations and labor policy) and modern sentiments (toward previously ignored Vietnam War veterans) framed by the traditional symbol of human equality, Abraham Lincoln, made Hudson's story engaging and resonant. Hudson's story kept Lincoln's poignant.

Inertia and Racial Equality

Reaction to James Hudson's death reinforced Abraham Lincoln's reputation as a champion of racial justice. However, if Lincoln appeared to some as John Brown's successor and Jim Crow's enemy, he appeared to others as the reluctant emancipator, the eager colonizer, the president whose highest aspiration was to keep whites safe from the presence of blacks. Many years of surveys show blacks trailing whites in rating Lincoln's presidential greatness; but these data alone capture the level, not the quality, of black sentiment. African Americans who love the Great Emancipator seem to love him more intensely than do those who disdain him as an Indifferent Colonizer.

In 1949, a foreign student named Andres Berger-Kiss wrote about his nighttime visit to the Lincoln Memorial and conversation with the African American guard—a predecessor of James Hudson—earning money for law school. "Lincoln here, he freed my grandfather, who was a slave." Speaking at a time of rapidly rising black incomes and standard of living,[37] the admiring guard recognized persisting racial prejudice but insisted "there's no single minority group in the whole world that has made as much progress as we have. The people of this country have made that progress possible."[38]

He meant white people, and he could have cited plenty of evidence to support his claim. In June 1947, President Harry Truman climbed the Lincoln Memorial steps and became the first American president to deliver a speech to the NAACP.[39] Two years later, sculptor Charles Keck reaffirmed belief in Lincoln's championing racial justice in his statue, "Lincoln and Child" (fig. 7.3). Dedicated in 1948 and placed at the center of the Abraham Lincoln Houses, a low-rent housing project in New York's Harlem, the statue portrays Lincoln seated, his arm around a young black child who looks up to him reverently. Scores of children line up to take their place beside their liberator and friend. Keck's Lincoln looks more like a grandfather than a paternal savior; he embraces the child he emancipates, symbolizing the child's equality and foreshadowing the onset of a great civil rights revolution.

From the end of Dwight Eisenhower's administration through the 1960s, Lincoln is securely associated with liberal politics. From the steps of the Lincoln Memorial, President Lyndon Johnson declares: "Let the World Abandon Racism."[40] A cartooned Lincoln covers his face in despair as Republican Barry Goldwater makes known his sympathy for the John Birch Society;[41] Coretta King recites the words of Aaron Copland's "Lincoln Portrait"[42] in the presence of Martin Luther King's brother and the governor of Kentucky, seated beneath Lincoln's statue. The occasion: Kentucky's passage of the first Southern civil rights bill.[43]

As ceremonies featuring Lincoln increased, the meanings of his presidential decisions, including the Emancipation Proclamation, changed. Lincoln had military necessity in mind when he drafted the Proclamation, but when Martin Luther King asked President Kennedy to issue a second Emancipation Proclamation condemning segregation,[44] he was exploiting the fact that legal emancipation was the first step (however unintended) toward a racially integrated society. King privately doubted Lincoln's benevolence,[45] but he publicly defined racial integration as the *motive* rather than *consequence* of Lincoln's actions. President Lyndon Johnson confirmed King's interpretation when he signed the

FIGURE 7.3. *Abraham Lincoln and Child,* 1949 statue by Charles Keck. The LaGuardia and Wagner Archives, La Guardia Community College / The City University of New York.

historic 1965 Voting Rights Act in the room where Lincoln had signed the Emancipation Proclamation.[46]

While black moderates praised Lincoln as a civil rights leader, black radicals condemned him as a bigot. Many radical sympathizers, however, had changed their minds. Two years after the *Chicago Defender* denounced Lincoln as a racist, it dredged up and endorsed an old Adlai Stevenson speech, delivered eight years earlier, portraying the Civil War as a complicated event involving good and bad motives on both sides. By 1975, Lincoln the white supremacist was "Honest Abe" again, and the

FIGURE 7.4. "Two Martyrs," 1971 announcement, *Ebony Magazine*. Courtesy Viad Corporation.

Defender's editor refuted evidence to the contrary. "The Emancipation Proclamation meant more than it said." It was really a declaration of support for the civil rights revolution of the 1960s and the equal opportunity and affirmative action programs of the 1970s. As to Lincoln's real feelings about black people: that "remains in the realm of speculation."[47] Likewise, in 1971, three years after publishing Lerone Bennett's attack, *Ebony* magazine produced a full-page portrait of Abraham Lincoln and Martin Luther King as dual symbols of social equality and civil rights (fig. 7.4).

Lincoln's interpreters on the left made him a symbol of their pro-minority causes by attributing to him opinions he never held and ideals to which he was never committed. Throughout the 1960s, the anniversary of his birth was the date chosen for initiating Chicago's Great Society programs, including a job training program for young women and the opening of Urban Opportunity Centers throughout the city. Chicago's annual Youth Service Conference was also held with its speakers being photographed and featured on Lincoln's birthday. Scheduled to overlap "Brotherhood Week" as well as Lincoln's birthday, the observance of Negro History Week (now Black History Month) connected Lincoln to Frederick Douglass and W. E. B. Du Bois (who had replaced Booker T. Washington as the leading symbol of black aspiration).[48] The History Channel documentary, *Lincoln*, which focused on the president's inner life, was aired on the 2006 anniversary of Martin Luther King's birth. Directly or by implication, each event contemporized Lincoln by attributing to him mid-twentieth century social and political sympathies.

The militant and impatient have always opposed these efforts by invoking the evidence of history, but commemorative images, not historical evidence, reach the most people, make Lincoln retrievable, give his memory rhetorical force, and make it resonate with the life and interests of the black community. Even as Lincoln's friendliness to black people came under hostile scrutiny, his image continued to express their interests. He may have been the "white supremacist" that Lerone Bennett believed him to be; he may have done "more to trick Negroes than any other man in history," as Malcolm X believed;[49] but his stature remained secure, if not preeminent, in the African American mind.

Abraham Lincoln, in truth, stands in a field occupied by others whose sympathy for black people exceeded his own. Whenever we perceive a historical figure, we "appresent" or "pair" it by adding to our mental image aspects which are not actually within the range of perception but without which we are unable to think about him.[50] To see Lincoln in this way is to associate his image with invisible predecessors, contemporaries, and successors. Travis Somerville's mysterious painting of *Smokey Joe* is a case in point. The Sambo caricature engraved on Lincoln's forehead is either a mark of Cain, indicating Lincoln's disdain for black people, or an indicator of obsessions not included in the picture—obsessions about slavery, emancipation, and racial equality. Rituals and symbols also shape the perception of Lincoln by an explicit coupling process that incorporates him into a commemorative network, a family of past heroes and events that black communities value. Activating Lincoln's memory through a newspaper article, statue, painting, cartoon, or ceremonial observance stirs memories that include but extend beyond him. Hence the constant coupling of Lincoln and representative black leaders. Lincoln's significance changes as each new

FIGURE 7.5
Lincoln 89, 1998 painting by Wendy Allen. Reproduced with permission of the artist.

FIGURE 7.6
"Abraham Lincoln Mourns Roy Wilkins," 1981, Paul Conrad. Courtesy *Los Angeles Times.*

generation places him in a commemorative network composed of new members not present in previous networks. These include Lincoln standing between Rosa Parks and witnesses to King's assassination (fig. 7.5) and Lincoln wearing a black armband to mark the death of civil rights leader Roy Wilkins (fig. 7.6). Lincoln's place in each composition is less important than the progressive racial attitudes his appearance implies. At any given time, the coupling processes fan out broadly not only within a network of people whose prestige enhances Lincoln's, but also to networks of events (Supreme Court decisions, job programs, Negro

History Week activities). In such memory structures, existing beliefs about Lincoln are organized, their institutional roots deepened, and a new and autonomous collection of beliefs accumulates. As common features of people and events with which Lincoln is ritually connected are generalized to Lincoln himself, Lincoln changes through the twentieth century from a symbol of Union and equality to a symbol of race relations reform. In the process, his relevance is preserved.

Employing Lincoln to legitimate race relations reform involves what James M. Fields and Howard Schuman[51] call "looking glass perceptions"—the tendency to see our own thoughts and values in others. Americans find it hard to imagine Abraham Lincoln referring to the slaves he emancipated as "niggers" or deliberately planning to ship them to other continents. They imagine his thinking of slaves as men and women who have been wronged and must now be brought into society as full citizens. To think of Lincoln in this way is easier because our sense of who we are as a nation presupposes a sense of who he was as a person. In short, commemoration is a structuring process that partially overrides the real Lincoln and imposes upon him its own pattern. The key to this process is not the mere act of coupling Lincoln with another; it is the attribution to Lincoln of qualities of other individuals located in the same network of memory. Commemoration fills in what was lacking in Lincoln by generalizing to him the qualities of African American leaders.

The remaking of Abraham Lincoln, although based on some invention and much exaggeration, is nonetheless constrained by the historical record. With the exception of a small number of abolitionists, Lincoln and his supporters saw no connection between freeing slaves and assimilating them socially as equals; yet, dedication to equality is logically inferable from Lincoln's loathing of slavery. Also, if Lincoln's historical role had been less decisive, his place in the black community's memory would now be smaller than it is. Americans made Lincoln a symbol of racial equality by starting with the real man and improving him, in Charles Horton Cooley's view, by "omitting the inessential and adding whatever was necessary to round out the ideal."[52] Their commemorative networks fabricated a racial equality champion out of a "colonizationist" because that colonizationist *did* something to make the transformation plausible. The materials of the "constructed" past, after all, include the inertia of facts as well as biases and interests.[53] Despite Barack Obama's conviction that Lincoln's motives for emancipation were pragmatic, therefore, he chose Springfield's Old Capitol Building to announce his presidential candidacy. No one seemed surprised. Nor does it seem strange to see Obama's being interviewed on a Senate stairway in front of Francis Bicknell Carpenter's painting of Lincoln announcing to his cabinet the Emancipation Proclamation.[54]

The "good Lincoln" never replaced the "bad," but was superimposed upon him. To be simultaneously interrogated and commemorated, condemned and canonized, has been the fate of the Great Emancipator. The same kind of ambivalence sustains Lincoln's stature among Southerners.

Inertia and Reconciliation

In 1908, architect Charles Rollinson Lamb, designer of New York's Dewey Arch, asked Lyon G. Tyler, son of President John Tyler and president of William and Mary College, whether he would join him in establishing a statue of Abraham Lincoln in the South. Tyler responded: "To ask the South to put up a monument of Lincoln, who represents Northern invasion of their homes and firesides of the South would be as absurd as if I were to ask the North to put up a monument to Jefferson Davis." Both men, Tyler insisted, were "champions of sections" still embittered with one another.[55]

In fact, images of Lincoln had already been established in the South. In 1899, Congress acted to create a Vicksburg National Military Park, inviting each of the twenty-eight states sending soldiers to the battle of Vicksburg to erect a monument of their own choosing. In 1906, Illinois sent a monument containing a bas-relief bust of Abraham Lincoln. In 1917, Vicksburg's National Peace Jubilee drew 8,000 Union and Confederate veterans and transported them in a great cortege celebrating "Our Heroes: Lincoln, Grant, Lee, and Jackson."

Rituals might lose relevance and be eventually abandoned, but hostile force rarely contributes to their demise. Once a major ritual is enacted, it tends to be repeated, following paths laid down in earlier commemorative acts. In October 2001, Kentucky was the last of the twenty-eight states to place a monument in Vicksburg. Two statues, sculpted by Gary Casteel, depict Abraham Lincoln and Jefferson Davis holding their hats by their sides. Lincoln's free hand grasps his lapel; Davis's rests on his ceremonial sword. The images are set before the Kentucky state seal, which itself shows two men, one in buckskin, the other in formal dress, shaking hands; the motto, "United We Stand; Divided We Fall." Engraved on the nearby walls are the names of the Kentucky units that fought at Vicksburg. The original statue design portrayed Lincoln and Davis also shaking hands, but one of the Kentucky representatives, despite the affinity with Kentucky's own official seal, believed such a representation would be unrealistic. And so the two figures are shown merely looking

FIGURE 7.7
Abraham Lincoln and Jefferson Davis, 2001 statue by Gary Casteel. Kentucky State Memorial at Vicksburg National Military Park. Photo courtesy of J. Williams.

upon one another (fig. 7.7). The unveiling of the two adversaries provoked some neo-Confederate resentment, but its expression was mild, limited, and short lived.

RICHMOND'S LINCOLN: BEHIND THE SOUND AND FURY

On April 5, 2003, less than two years after the state of Kentucky dedicated Abraham Lincoln's image in Vicksburg, Richmond, Virginia, marked the 138th anniversary of Lincoln's visit to the city by dedicating David Frech's statue. Unveiled, the victorious war president sits on a simple bench, eye level with the viewer, head lowered, beside his son Tad, who looks up to him. At the left hand of the president lays the April 5, 1865, issue of the Richmond Whig and, in the fashion of Gutzon Borglum's famous 1911 statue of Newark's seated Lincoln, there is room on both sides of the bench for visitors to sit. Behind the sculptural group is engraved a line from Lincoln's second inaugural address, delivered a month earlier: "To Bind Up The Nation's Wounds" (fig. 7.8).

Great passion motivated Lincoln's admirers to establish a monument for him in the Confederate capital. Directors and friends of the United States Historical Society believed that Lincoln's yearning for reconciliation remained unfulfilled, that regional animosities continued to poison the South's civil atmosphere. They wanted a statue to mark the achievement of union and emancipation, a statue including father and son to symbolize the peace and union that had endured across generations.[56]

FIGURE 7.8. *Abraham Lincoln and Son*, 2003 statue by David Frech. Richmond, VA. Courtesy of United States Historical Society, Richmond, VA.

Robert Kline, fifty-year resident of Richmond and chairman of the Historical Society, a nonprofit organization that consults with museums and educational institutions, conceived the idea of the Lincoln image, and Martin J. Moran, president of the society, executed Kline's plan. After years of deliberation and work, the statue was placed and dedicated by a former governor, one of the Lincoln Bicentennial Commission's directors, and other notable figures.

As the dedication date approached, opposition to the statue mounted, aided by media hyperbole. The *New York Times* published an editorial statement titled "Lincoln Returns to the Old South"—the adjective "old" allowing, if not inviting, the implication that not much had changed since 1865. The *New Jersey Sunday Herald* left less to the imagination: "Great Emancipator regarded as 'bad guy' in the South." The project's supporters insisted that Lincoln visited Richmond in a spirit of reconciliation, not triumph, but protesters overwhelmed the positive voices. A great monument to the Confederate soldiers is one thing in Arlington Cemetery; it is quite another on the Washington Mall. Just so, Lincoln and Davis in Vicksburg's Memorial Park has an impact that differs from what it would be if placed downtown. The Lincoln statue, although located on U.S. Park Service property, is centrally located, just outside the central business and legislative district and near the Tredeger Iron Works, which supplied heavy armament to Confederate forces.

For the Sons of Confederate Veterans (SCV), the whole affair was an affront to the gallant men killed defending Southern soil. Bragdon Bowling, commander of the Virginia Division of the SCV, declared "There hasn't been any clamoring for a Lincoln statue here." On the contrary, the SCV saw Lincoln as a war criminal. Other organizations, including the Heritage Preservation Association, an organization opposing anti-Southern bigotry and attacks on Confederate symbols, and the Virginia League of the South, a neo-Confederate organization with separatist aspirations, opposed vehemently the planned Lincoln statue. Thousands of letters poured into the *Richmond Times-Dispatch*, almost all negative. How would a statue of Hitler look in Jerusalem? John Wilkes Booth in Springfield, Illinois? Osama Bin Laden in New York? Why commemorate "this country's most notorious war criminal"? On another level, U.S. representative Virgil Goode questioned and investigated the U.S. Historical Society's nonprofit status. That both Robert Kline, the project founder, and David Frech, the sculptor, were both born in Illinois sustained the belief that strangers were shoving the Lincoln monument down the throats of Richmond's people.

A week before dedication day, a new front opened. The Library of Virginia and The Museum of the Confederacy sponsored a "Lincoln Reconsidered" conference of scholars and writers critical of Lincoln and his policies. For their part, the Virginia Historical Society and U.S. Park Service organized a conference on Lincoln's virtues and how a monument to his Richmond visit would make for a richer understanding of the war.

On the day of the statue dedication, the SCV marched from the grave of Confederate president Jefferson Davis to the dedication site. At the dedication ceremony, 150 protesters, some dressed in Civil War uniforms, waved Confederate flags and chanted "Dixie, Dixie." Overhead, for the duration of the ceremony, an airplane circled, displaying the banner "Sic Semper Tyrannus" ("Thus Always to Tyrants")—the words John Wilkes Booth shouted after murdering Lincoln.

The dissenters hardly represented Richmond's general population, a large percentage of which was black. Most of the estimated 850 people who turned out for the event, however, were white, and almost all approved it. Many parents brought their children; many self-described "Lincoln fans" came alone to watch and lend their support to the ceremony. That the resistance itself died down so quickly after the monument's dedication raises serious questions about its depth and breadth of support.[57] The quality of any sentiment must be questioned when its intensity diminishes abruptly. True, many people fiercely resisted the erection of the statue; many would have resorted to violence if circumstances permitted.[58] For the typical resister, however, the relation between outward conduct, which typically involved letter writing or, at most, participation in a parade, and inner sentiment, is problematic. The more we think about the protest's orchestration and aftermath, the more it seems that individuals were working up consciously the indignation they were supposedly venting. Their resistance, then, was meaningful but ineffective: by assembling in reaction to the threat against their culture and beliefs, they expressed ideas that would have been otherwise lost or less clearly understood. Denunciations of Lincoln's image stopped suddenly because they were generated in part by the ritual itself. When the ritual ended, the participants dispersed, not to be heard from again. The statue has been standing for many years without having been seriously threatened, let alone damaged.

However deep the passions of Richmond's dissenters, one must ask whether their hostility toward Lincoln can be generalized to most Southerners. During the early twentieth century, as noted, Southern writers and artists sought to perpetuate the memory of Lincoln as a man with whom all the South could identify. During the late twentieth century, this tradition continued. In 1965, Emory University historian Bell Irvin Wiley marked the end of the Civil War centennial with a public address titled "Lincoln and Lee." Professor Wiley did not present a historical statement but an allegory of national unity. The two men, he told his Atlanta audience, "were the finest products of the Civil War." That they had never met was unfortunate. "They would have gotten along well."[59] Seven years later, in 1972, the University of Tennessee Press published *The Image of Lincoln in the South.* Author Michael Davis emphasized (although not to the satisfaction of all reviewers) that Lincoln's assassination converted the South's hatred for him into sincere affection.[60] Wiley's and Davis's writings, whatever their factual merit, were symptomatic of a trend toward regional reconciliation. The benign current shows in surveys demonstrating narrowed regional differences in attitudes toward a wide range of race relations issues, from school and neighborhood life to job opportunities, voting rights, and participation in the political process. Because Southern attitudes have become strongly pro-integration,[61] Southerners no longer need a segregationist Lincoln to embrace. Lincoln now appears in a light that makes Southerners receptive to race-neutral Lincoln portrayals. In 1991, the American

Broadcasting Company rewrote and telecast *The Perfect Tribute,* Mary Richman Shipman Andrews's 1908 story about Lincoln's comforting a dying Confederate soldier.[62] *With Malice Towards None*, a 1991 educational video, includes reenactment of Lincoln's second inaugural address, without his words about God's vengeance for two hundred years of Southern slavery.[63] Plays written for middle-school children are equally conciliatory. Juvenile author Graham DuBois writes about a Northern girl caring for a sick Southern boy, Billy, at Gettysburg; the two soon fall in love. When a staunch Southerner tells Abraham Lincoln that Billy should marry his own kind, the president replies that we must all disregard regional differences and think of ourselves as Americans.[64]

Only a small portion of contemporary affection for Lincoln can be attributed to contemporary writers and artists. They reflect and sustain, rather than create, affection for him. Former Alabama governor and presidential candidate George Wallace was no avid reader of Lincoln biography, but when Joseph Garrera, president of the Lincoln Group of New York, asked for his opinion of Abraham Lincoln, the dying governor replied: "President Lincoln would have been very kind toward the South had he lived. Military occupation and Reconstruction would not have been imposed on the South. His being killed made it a very sad and tragic time for the people of the South."[65] Three years later, General William Westmoreland, retired general in North Carolina, responded to Garrera's question by stressing the South's solidarity with the nation, rather than its suffering under Reconstruction:

> During the American Civil War, my grandfather fought for the South. In spite of the political diversity of our nation during that difficult time in history, one can not help but admire the strength of Lincoln. Since it was him, in effect, who saved our nation by being a major factor in the ultimate unification of the nation. Therefore I think it is prudent to appreciate what he did (perhaps our greatest president).[66]

"I think it is prudent to appreciate what he did." Westmoreland's compliment is more obligatory than passionate. In neither his nor Wallace's comment does one detect deep affection for Lincoln, but they both acknowledge what he accomplished or would have accomplished had he completed his second term. Yet, others not only have kind things to say about Lincoln but feel a personal stake in preserving his memory and endeavoring to convince other people to agree with them. Among these "reputational entrepreneurs"[67] is the founder of the Lincoln Society of Virginia, Philip Stone, who stands prominently in a century-long list of Lincoln's Southern admirers.

The Virginia Lincolns. In 1986, Philip Stone lunched with friend and fellow attorney, John Paul, and discussed the matter of commemorating Abraham Lincoln's ties to Virginia. Stone was thinking about the old Rockingham County cemetery, which contained the remains of John Lincoln, the sixteenth president's great-grandfather, John's brother Jacob, and two of their slaves, Ned and Queen. Five generations of Lincolns had lived on the land, including descendants of a Lincoln-Pennebaker marriage. The land containing the cemetery, Jacob Lincoln's house, and the Pennebaker house had long been in the family of Stone's wife. Abraham Lincoln's grandfather, also named Abraham, was born and reared in Rockingham County, saw service at Yorktown under George Washington, and moved his family to the Kentucky region of the Commonwealth of Virginia, where he acquired more than 5,000 acres before Indians killed him.

The Virginia Lincolns and their cemetery have always been known among Abraham Lincoln admirers. Robert Todd Lincoln, Carl Sandburg, and historian Louis Warren visited it. John Wayland, in 1946, published a book about the Virginia Lincolns. Lincoln himself knew about his great-grandfather and the place where his father had been born; he wanted to know more about his forebears and corresponded with David Lincoln, a cousin, in 1842, while serving in Congress. To this day, local dislike of President Lincoln, inhibits, in some degree, commemoration of his family. The family land, after all, is located near Harrisonburg in the Shenandoah, which General Philip Sheridan ravaged and burned toward the end of the war. Lincoln's Virginia relatives fought for the Confederacy, and one of them declared that he would kill his cousin if he ever met him. Neighbors joked with Stone about Abraham Lincoln but appreciated his interest in the Lincoln family's local roots.

In 1986, Phillip Stone and John Paul Hall decided to conduct their own gravesite ceremony, reading to one another about aspects of Lincoln's life and presidency. Since then, Stone has held an annual ceremony, almost always in terrible weather, and the number attending has grown from a handful (on one particularly snowy day, he conducted the service alone with his dog) to more than 100. Not only local newspapers, but also the Washington DC and Richmond papers report the event. Over the years, Stone's thirty-minute eulogies and accounts of Lincoln's activities have included Thomas Lincoln's character and its effect on how Abraham saw and managed the issues of slavery, conscription, habeus corpus, and other wartime dilemmas. Stone regularly challenges Lincoln's critics, including those opposed to the Lincoln statue in Richmond. At length, he formed the Lincoln Society of Virginia, an official body chartered by the State Corporation Commission, which held its first annual meeting in 2005.[68]

Stone's success in establishing the commemoration of the Virginia Lincolns raises questions of timing and reception. If he had begun his commemorative project twenty-five or thirty years earlier, during the first phase of the civil rights movement (1955–65) and the Civil War centennial (1961–1965), his efforts would have been received less enthusiastically. Is there an elective affinity, therefore, between the present generation's ideological openness and Philip Stone's effort to recognize Abraham Lincoln and connect him to his ancestral roots? The latter seems plausible, but the question cannot be answered for certain before other facets of Lincoln in the present-day South are explored.

SURVEYS

Beliefs and feelings about Lincoln have changed significantly throughout the South, but the developments narrowing differences in regional conceptions of presidential greatness have occurred largely outside the South. In 1999, table 5.6 (chapter 5) shows, 44 percent of non-Southerners and 36 percent of Southerners included Lincoln among the three greatest presidents—an eight-point difference. In 1956, as noted, the comparable difference was 25 percent.[69] The small regional gap in admiration for Lincoln persists mainly among the college educated and, to a somewhat lesser extent, high school graduates; however, the *level* of beliefs about Lincoln have always been most positive among these better educated. The percentage of least educated *non-Southerners* naming Lincoln has fallen so far since 1956 that it now equals the least educated Southern percentage[70] (table 5.6).

Statistics must be read in the generational context that produces them. Among non-Southern whites, the decline in Lincoln's being named a great president occurred entirely between 1956 and 1975, a period that includes the coming of age of the Rebellious Generation. Since 1975, however, the downward trend has leveled. The diminished frequency with which Southerners named Lincoln a great president was less steep and required an additional ten years, until 1985, to reach a plateau, after which no further decline took place. The stabilizing of Lincoln's prestige in the South, thus, occurred during the sway of an Uncommitted Generation of indifference.

That no generation gives to its successor the same Lincoln it receives from its predecessor is axiomatic because each generation sees him differently—not so differently as to make him unrecognizable, but different enough to make a difference in Lincoln's legacy and meaning. Not only has the Southern/non-Southern gap in admiration of Lincoln greatly narrowed; traditional contrasts in his historical meaning are well on their way to disappearing—if they have not already disappeared. No longer is Lincoln invoked in legitimation of a caste system or as a special friend of the South. When Southerners are asked to indicate why Lincoln was a great president, what they would tell their young relatives about him, or why they considered him a greater man than George Washington, the answer they typically give is emancipation. This finding, discussed in chapter 4, provides another measure of the extent to which Southern and non-Southern mentalities have merged.

The broader significance of the Southern case is what it tells us about the inertia of memory. In the South as elsewhere, Lincoln maintains his historical identity by changing. New crises sustain his renown because participants in that crisis see him in light of their own realities. But they are not "recreating" or "reinventing" him; they are adapting a heretofore deemphasized part of his persona to a new situation.

African Americans coupled Lincoln with images of Frederick Douglass, Sojourner Truth, Booker T. Washington, Martin Luther King Jr., as well as ordinary black people. When, in this connection, Bell Wiley told his Atlanta, Georgia, audience that Abraham Lincoln and Robert E. Lee would have liked one another had they met, he was performing a coupling very rare in the South. Nowhere outside memorial parks is Lincoln portrayed in the presence of, let alone shaking the hands of, Confederate leaders. In this sense, the South's Lincoln is viewed in a field devoid of symbolism. He is not part of a network of traditional Southern memory—as that tradition is defined in museums and public monuments of the Confederacy. In the South, there is considerable admiration of Lincoln, but no widespread commemoration.

Carriers of Tradition

In one respect, Lincoln has been unaffected by the contemporary mood. Given the substance of best-selling biographies and history textbooks, Americans probably believe the same things about him as did their forebears. Assumed truths about Lincoln, on the other hand, are now empirical truths, not "commanding truths." Commanding truths refer to much more than factual evidence; they refer to "the 'shoulds' and 'should nots' of our experience and, accordingly, the good and the evil, the right and the wrong, the honorable and the shameful."[71] Thus, Lincoln's story, although still told, is less relevant and less authoritative.

It makes a difference, however, whether Lincoln is treated with uniform apathy or whether a compact minority continues to admire him —its sentiment perhaps to someday revitalize and spread. The social distribution of admiration for Lincoln (table 5.2), in this regard, is remarkable. Although a symbol of the common man, Abraham Lincoln remains a hero of middle-class and upper-middle-class America. He is most admired by whites, college educated, and the affluent; he is least admired by blacks, the least educated, and the poor. Thus, one learns about Lincoln not as a student in the abstract, but as a wealthy or poor person, graduate or dropout, white or black. These intricate relationships are difficult to decompose, but their effects are powerful. College and university faculties presently embrace an anti-heroic ethos and promote "critical thinking," even cynicism, toward American history;[72] yet, their students provide the market for Lincoln biographies, the audience for television documentaries, the organizers of commemorative observances on different phases of Lincoln's life.

The present data do not reveal whether the positive attitudes of the university educated result from their knowledge of Lincoln's achievements or from class-related interests inclining them to embrace society's leading narratives. Nor can these data tell whether the least educated devalue Lincoln because of their ignorance of his life or because dissatisfaction with society induces them to disdain heroes that the privileged embrace. A separate analysis, however, suggests a partial answer: because the least educated rate certain contemporary presidents (especially Kennedy) more highly than others, they must be admiring leaders whom they know, rather than simply rejecting their society's traditional values.

Postmodern explanations fail to explain why the privileged strata admiring Lincoln the most include a "postmodern class" whose appreciation of great men is supposedly precarious. The professionals, managers, and administrators who comprise this class are believed to be the "consumers par excellence of post-modern cultural products" and the "hegemonizing missionaries" of postmodern values. They are the new cosmopolitans whose "habitus" (cognitive structures and classifying schemes) inclines them to live for the moment, "untrammeled by constraints and brakes imposed by collective memories and expectations." Anne-Marie Rosenau tries to argue that postmodern people remain fascinated with the traditional and the sacred, but since they have no need for "universal claims or ideological consistency," their appreciation is superficial.[73] Rosenau might be right, but because, like most postmodern scholars, she asserts what must be demonstrated, she finds no need to pose, let alone address, key questions. How are we to distinguish superficial from profound admiration for Lincoln? What is at stake in the distinction itself?

Inertia Enshrined

Abraham Lincoln's significance is to be found not only in surveys and the writings of political commentators but also in shrine visitation. Forty years ago, Lloyd Warner discovered that shrines and monuments are "non-rational symbols whose source and power are beyond the individual and express for him a feeling of belonging to a vital eternal world."[74] What about Lincoln shrines and monuments? Visitation rates for these have dropped, but the absolute number of visitors remains high. What about the visitors themselves? Are they pilgrims seeking contact with a transcendent order or tourists seeking amusement? Postmodern theorists assert that erosion of tradition and authority manifests itself in their shrines, which is why the "heritage industry" figures prominently in postmodern society. Creating a "shallow screen that intervenes between our present lives [and] our history," the shrines and monuments maintained by the heritage industry are deemed superficial, "hyperreal," "self-referential," unrelated to any mundane let alone transcendent concern. People who visit these sites arrive as tourists rather than pilgrims. Tourists seek novel experience, not spiritual renewal; they feel neither commitment to the sites they visit nor an obligation to visit them, and they judge them according to whether or not they are interesting or aesthetically pleasing. Tourists, as personifications of postmodernity ("creatures of surfaces"), make no distinction between revelation and entertainment. Indeed, massive commodification of celebrities and men of state makes their sites of birth, accomplishment, and death equivalent. The postmodernists from whom these observations are drawn (Robert Hewison, Jean Baudrillard, Zygmunt Baumann, George Allan, and Chris Rojek) are not alone in believing that shrines have become distractions rather than sacred destinations. For David Lowenthal, "mass visitation and market forces cater to vulgarity, turning historic sites into plastic Disneylands." For Pierre Nora, shrines are *lieux de memoire*, and, unlike historical objects, "*lieux de memoire* have no referents in reality; or, rather, they are their own referents—pure signs."[75]

To assess a theory defining shrines and monuments as remnants of a meaningless past, one must study their visitors. The Lincoln shrines in Springfield, Illinois, are good places to start. Are visitors making contact with a sacred past or distracting themselves? Are they transcending time or passing it? We will never know how our national survey respondents would have answered these questions, but local surveys, including the National Park Service[76] and Springfield Visitor Bureau[77] surveys, tell us something about the people's feeling. Self-selected respondents in the

Park Service and Visitors Bureau samples are not perfectly comparable to Lincoln admirers in randomly selected national samples,[78] but the vast majority are white, middle class, well educated, and their reactions tell us more about this class of Americans' feelings than would speculation alone.[79]

The Springfield Visitors Bureau drew its sample of visitors over two summers. The 1991 results—585 responses from an unknown number of people questioned—indicate what visitors liked most and least about Springfield's sites and include a brief statement explaining what prompted their reactions. The 1992 results consist of responses from 929 visitors. These response rates are probably similar to the unknown 1991 response rates. The third sample consists of 1,033 National Park Service (1989) respondents. That only 30 percent of these respondents completed the comments section of the questionnaire brings to mind a similar finding reported by Edward Shils and Michael Young. When they surveyed East London street parties celebrating the coronation of Elizabeth II, "nothing was more remarkable than the complete inability of people to say why they thought important the occasion they were honoring. . . ."[80] In Springfield, too, the people expressed themselves hesitantly and incompletely; yet in doing so they revealed much about what they wanted to see and what the shrines meant to them.

Describing their visit to Springfield, respondents often referred to the "historical" and "educational" merit of its Lincoln sites. They used the word "history" often. To be in Lincoln's home makes one "feel history," as one visitor put it. It was like "stepping back in time" to see "how they [Lincoln and his family] lived." To feel and see more, visitors wanted more information. They wanted a more leisurely and informative tour of Lincoln's home. It should be kept open longer, they said, so more of the place could be seen. Many complained about being unable to get into the home after coming expressly to visit it. Those who had time to endure the long wait resented being rushed through. They also complained that different park rangers—their own and the one they overheard in another room—gave different information, which meant that everyone received incomplete information. Some visitors asked that tour guides be replaced by audio cassettes and headphones.

Respondents raised the authenticity issue often. They wanted to know which pieces of furniture actually belonged to Lincoln and which did not. If security prevents Park Service rangers from identifying the authentic Lincoln pieces, then "put them in a secure museum so we can be sure we're looking at the *real* thing." And what happened to the old wax statue that showed what Lincoln looked like when he lived in the house? It "made a lasting impression on me," said one visitor, and it ought to be restored. A copy of the Gettysburg Address in Lincoln's own writing had been on display in previous years. Where is it now? Others wanted to see in the Springfield depot a replica of the train car that took Lincoln to Washington. This would help everyone envision Lincoln speaking from the rear platform. He made a touching speech that the present exhibit and slide show fail adequately to capture. People commented on mundane things, too. Some complained that the house seemed artificial because it was "too neat," but they were pleased to see a replica of the family outhouse in the back yard—an observation confirming the public image of Lincoln as prototype of the common man.[81]

Visitors' desire for facts did not stem from an irrational fascination with "authenticity" as an end in itself. Their concern was to know what kind of entity they were gazing upon and touching, with what relics they were making contact. Many visitors also wanted a list of the events of Lincoln's life in Springfield. They wanted to see markers on built-over sites at which those events occurred. They wanted to know what became of his family after he died. They wanted to know about his religious beliefs. They wanted some examples of Lincoln's humor in order to "bring out the people-caring man he was."

If Lincoln's Springfield home were part of a "heritage industry" built on ignorance, if it were a place of recreation or embodied a contrived past rather than a real past, then its visitors' comments would bear on matters of beauty, convenience, and pleasantness rather than authenticity. Springfield visitors' concern for authenticity of information and artifact was prefigured forty years earlier in "Yankee City" (Newburyport, Massachusetts), where Lloyd Warner noted the vast amount of time and energy local organizers spent on the tricentennial displays. Careful assembling of historical evidence was a necessary "secular rite of legitimation." Since people had to "believe in the intrinsic authority of historic fact" if commemorative symbols were to be meaningful, historical evidence performed a ritual as well as an intellectual function.[82]

In Springfield, however, the rite of legitimation was performed as an end in itself. In 1987, the National Park Service sought to restore Lincoln's house to its condition in 1860, the year he was elected president. The firm commissioned by the Park Service agreed to work on the house with tools and techniques available at this time. Workers moved from brick to brick, replacing new ones for old only when the latter could not be repaired. They preserved existing materials, like the original plaster behind the walls, and used replacement wood as close to the original as possible, even though it would be painted over and no visitor would ever know the difference. It was as if restorationists and preservationists believed, no less than visitors, that authentic artifacts facilitated communion with the past and that contact with Lincoln would be incomplete if the contents of his home were not as they were when he and his family lived there.

Authentic artifacts are vehicles of sacred contact: to be in the presence of an object that Lincoln touched is to be in Lincoln's presence. "It was like Lincoln himself still lived there," said one man. "It's hard for me to believe I actually walked in his house," said another. "A special feeling of nostalgia hits you," yet another remarked. The awkwardness of the language reflects the uncanniness of the experience. People were attracted to Lincoln's tomb for the same reason: "You really get the feel of Lincoln there." It is the man himself that makes it so: "The fact that Lincoln is buried in there" is what makes the place "very moving and meaningful." This is why "sight-markers"—photographs and souvenirs to capture the moment of contact with a great presence—are so necessary.[83] "We feel we have to come again," said one distraught visitor, "because we have no pictures of us there."

That the Lincoln sites are much more than interesting places to visit is evident in what people said about Lincoln himself. Designating what he liked least about his experience, one visitor said: "The thought of no more Abraham Lincolns." Other visitors resented tour guides referring to Mr. Lincoln as "Abraham" in a casual, informal fashion. "The tour would have been enhanced," as one put it, "without the attempt at familiarity."

The context in which such words were spoken differentiates Lincoln's Springfield home from celebrity sites, like Elvis Presley's Graceland mansion. The number of people visiting Graceland vastly exceeds the number visiting Lincoln's home, but all know that Lincoln's home is different. As part of a network of shrines affirming the sanctity of the nation and presidency, a network whose visitors are oriented to the larger scheme of things, Lincoln's home distinguishes itself from other celebrity sites unconnected to the political center of society.[84] In the words of one visitor: "We felt pretty humble to be in the midst of our historic roots." This greater "seriousness" of Abraham Lincoln's shrines is evident in their characterization as "assets to the United States." As medieval pilgrims found God's presence in the relics of the saints,[85] so twentieth-century Americans found the dignity of the state embodied in the objects Lincoln had touched and used.

The obligation felt by so many parents to bring their children to Lincoln sites underscores the moral separateness of the zone where they are located. Typical is the father who "felt I *had* [italics added] to come through before dropping my son off at the University of Illinois." Standing on the front steps of Lincoln's house or near his tomb, the first thing one notices is that visitors rarely come alone. In late spring, schools and churches bring students and congregants. Throughout the summer, parents bring children, and three-generational clusters consisting of children, parents, and grandparents are common. Nine out of ten summer visitors to Lincoln's Springfield home arrive in the company of family members.[86] Shrine-visiting is a time for family activity and for recognizing the family's solidarity with the state. The school, church, or family, not the individual, is the basic unit for entering into communion with the nation's past. This is why Lincoln's Springfield home is remembered and mentioned by visitors so much more often than any other Lincoln shrine, including his tomb. It is the home, symbol of Lincoln's relation to his family, that proves his essential kinship with the ordinary American.

Lincoln's Springfield home, like his Kentucky log cabin, is a *lieu de mémoire* (site of memory) in two *non*-postmodern senses: first, it symbolizes enduring values uniting the mundane and the exalted; second, it sanctifies memory by tying it to place.[87] *Hic locus est*: "Here is the place," inscribed on the martyrs' shrines of North Africa,[88] is applicable to the shrine of the great martyr of America.

The appeal of Lincoln museums is based on the same force that draws individuals to Lincoln shrines. People come to visit the Lincoln home or tomb to be in the presence of something connecting them to Lincoln. In museums they come to stand in the presence of clothing he wore, objects he used, documents he wrote. Katharine W. Hannaford, commenting on Huntington Library's "Now He Belongs to the Ages" exhibit, observes that the written documents anchoring the exhibit were overwhelmed by the physical objects originally meant to supplement them. The latter connected visitors to Lincoln "in a way similar to that by which bones and scraps of wood enabled the medieval pilgrim to venerate, commemorate and commune with a long dead saint around whom interwoven layers of history and legend had accreted."[89] When Jacqueline Kennedy carved her and her murdered husband's name into the Lincoln bedpost, she explained her feelings in comparable terms: "I love the Lincoln Room the most, even though it isn't really Lincoln's bedroom. But it has his things in it. . . . To touch something I knew he had touched was a real link with him. . . . I used to feel his strength. I'd sort of be talking with him."[90]

Objects displayed by shrines and museums presuppose the positive sentiment they concretize, but it is the concretization that sustains memory's inertia. What Sigmund Freud said about the Acropolis might have been said for Lincoln's log cabin, Springfield home, executive mansion bedroom, and tomb:

> When, finally, on the afternoon after our arrival, I stood upon the Acropolis and cast my eyes around upon the landscape, a remarkable thought suddenly entered my mind: 'So all this really *does* exist, just as we learnt at school!' Or it would be possible to maintain that when I was a schoolboy I had *thought* I was convinced of the historic reality of the city of Athens and its history, but that the occurrence of this idea on the Acropolis had precisely shown that . . . I had *not* believed in it . . . !

In fact, the two sentiments, belief and disbelief, are interconnected. To see something with one's own eyes promotes a conviction that is deeper and more durable than merely reading or talking about it. And this first fact makes the second more meaningful. Relics not only maintain belief but also stunt the growth of doubt.

Given the seriousness with which visitors view Abraham Lincoln's shrines, postmodernist claims about the disappearance of grand narratives, the separation of past from present, and the replacement of real history by nostalgia must be modified. This does not imply that today's Lincoln is the same as the Lincoln of the first half of the twentieth century. On the contrary: every generation has handed down to the next an image of Lincoln different from the one it received. Every new Lincoln, however, is distinguished by the same "essential elements" that distinguished the old ones.[91] These "essential elements," sources of inertia and markers of Lincoln's participation in the drama of America's national existence, explain why Springfield's sites make commemorative sense across generations, why they belong more to *la vie serieuse* of history and moral example than to *la vie legere* of "hyperreality, whose objects represent nothing but themselves."[92]

Unforgettability

One way to appreciate memory's inertia is to imagine what it would take to wipe away the memory of Lincoln from the culture and the minds of the American people. Where would one begin? Imagine the destruction of all history texts and analytic monographs, magazine and newspaper articles, television documentaries, monuments, shrines, statues, paintings, illustrations, place names, ritual observances. How would such a task be accomplished? Abraham Lincoln's prestige has declined over the past half century, but he remains part of America's political culture, preserved in its vast system of texts and commemorative structures. Remembering great figures, then, is much more than adapting the past to present tastes and moods. Memory, indeed, forms tastes, regulates moods, and so enables us to act meaningfully.[93]

Abraham Lincoln's prestige may decline even further. The monumental, after all, is no longer conventional, and this is partly because so few events (September 11 notwithstanding, because it was no threat to America's survival) are worthy of epic monuments.[94] True, Lincoln occasionally frames domestic issues in editorial-page cartoons, but he now appears more a convenient symbol of victimhood than a transcendent compass for moral direction. The *Los Angeles Times* (1976) depicts Lincoln choking on the smoke and debris of industrial pollution. In the same newspaper (1982), Ronald Reagan in Lincoln's body completes his second inaugural address "... with malice toward the poor; with charity toward the rich." When the full extent of the 1990 savings-and-loan scandal became known, Lincoln appeared on one editorial page in his underwear—stripped by the con artists and embezzlers. As the 1994 Congress debated a phase-in provision for universal health care, another cartoon showed representatives of the 1863 Congress advising Lincoln that they had worked out a compromise freeing 95 percent of the slaves by 1899.[95] Lincoln is more than ever a critical symbol standing for America's faults rather than its virtues. But is he more than that?

If America's *existence* were threatened or its president assassinated at the turn of the twenty-first century, would Lincoln be invoked again to articulate the national mood and purpose? Would that event be framed by images of the more recent war president, Franklin Roosevelt, or the more recently assassinated president, John Kennedy? Or would such an event be keyed to the past at all? Catastrophic events like the Kennedy assassination or even World War II may recur, yet some historians, like John G. Gillis, believe that we live in a "post-national" age wherein patriotic memories lack the capacity to mobilize and heal.[96] Postmodernists have gone even further, declaring that all grand narratives and their heroes, whether political or religious, have lost credibility.[97] Gillis and the postmodernists are raising fundamental questions. How long the American people will remain conscious of themselves as a nation, and what symbols might signify and frame that consciousness, are open questions that time alone will answer.

For now, Lincoln representations are not only tools for preserving the past, they are also frames for assessing the meaning of the life that surrounds and, at times, overwhelms us. The living of this life is what makes Lincoln worth thinking about. Abraham Lincoln's prestige has eroded, but its valence remains positive, and its capacity to connect current events to America's past is still strong. Lincoln's place in American memory is an ambiguous place defined by a "residual" pattern of reverence, a "dominant" pattern of affectively neutral admiration, and an "emergent" pattern of indifference. The relationship among these patterns is complex. The residual pattern, in Raymond Williams's words, "has been effectively formed in the past, but it is still active in the cultural process, not only and often not at all as an element of the past, but as an effective element of the present."[98]

Williams's concept of the "residual" is manifest in Ron DiCianni's painting *Praying for Peace*. DiCianni, an artist adept at placing current events in the frame of religious symbolism, shows Abraham Lincoln with hat in hand, head lowered, with left hand on the shoulder of President George W. Bush, whom he joins in prayer. On Bush's left stands George Washington, also uncovered in prayer, his right hand on the president's shoulder. The background consists of five interconnected images: a cross whose beams intersect behind the head of the president, an ethereal seal of the presidency which adjoins the American flag, and, in the bottom left and right, images of the Statue of Liberty and the Iwo Jima Marine Monument. The president, seemingly at a time of crisis, defined by the cross and Lincoln's and Washington's presence, prepares to address the American people. Although common during and prior to World War II, this genre is for many today corny and out of place. Rarely would such an image appear in a major newspaper or magazine. The reason is not the identity of the president (Albert Gore or John Kerry would not change the image's meaning); it is the spectacle of the president of the United States impassioned by faith rather than secular reason and compassion. DiCianni's placement of history and political authority under a sacred canopy is alien to American culture's dominant strain, but it dramatizes the continuing vitality of earlier perspectives and, under their shadow, defines an adamantine boundary below which the erosion of tradition cannot descend. Commissioned by Christian business leaders to show support for President Bush following the September 11 attacks, the painting has become popular. The original is in President Bush's private collection, but copies of it appear on the walls of thousands of homes, in two of Cianni's books, on postcards, mugs, t-shirts, and bumper stickers.[99] Residual mentalities, then, are not necessarily fading mentalities; they are vital remnants of ideas, values, and sentiments once dominant. Why residual patterns are always active in the cultural process is a question that takes us into deep water, defining the limit between what our data permit us to say and what we must say in order to make sense of our data.

Presiding over a "new birth of freedom," in the broad sense of preserving democratic government rather than the narrower sense of ending slavery (which would have been impossible without the preservation of that government), Lincoln incarnates America's transition from a republic to a modern democracy. For religion scholar Mircea Eliade, the "founding moment," sacred and resistant to revision, incarnates a "golden age" because it is "the first manifestation of a thing that is significant and valid." For sociologist Edward Shils, too, founding moments arouse a *tremendum numinosum* because they consist of decisive events—"great moments"—that shape what comes later. There are many variations on this theme,[100] and its invocation lends power to the work of DiCianni and his Depression and World War II–era predecessors. Some great moments are concealed in myth; others, like the role of Lincoln's presidency in the unification of American society, are supported by historical evidence. Information and commemorative symbols, however, do not cause people to admire Lincoln's achievement; rather, facts and symbols articulate the people's existing conception of it—a vague conception, on average, of wartime leadership and liberation of an oppressed people. To see Lincoln in this way is to acknowledge that the character of events and their men limits what can be remembered and forgotten about them, that images of great men change from one generation to the next, but such changes involve emphases and deemphases, not fundamentals. The essential achievements, not the marginalia, of Lincoln's life and presidency render him unforgettable, and as we observe his memory imposing itself, consistently if not profoundly, upon the present generation, we see that his role in American culture is no mere contrivance of reputational enterprise. Abraham Lincoln is a cultural power in his own right.

Conclusion

> *Tradition is the living faith of the dead;*
> *Traditionalism is the dead faith of the living.*
>
> Jaroslav Pelikan
> *The Vindication of Tradition*

Abraham Lincoln, a light sleeper, did a lot of dreaming, and when he asked a friend about the meaning of a dream in which he finds himself dead in the White House, the friend replied:

> What matters most is that in your dream you will walk in the halls of the White House. And that for generations to come, children and presidents, citizens and legislators, average Americans, and world leaders will walk these same halls and listen for the echo of your footsteps, hoping to hear one distant reassuring sound of honesty and goodness and genuine sacrifice. For the people of this country and the century to come will not simply honor your memory, sir; they will need it; they will cling to it in the days when the real heroes are hard to find, when the little boys and little girls wonder whether principles mattered more than politics, when parents need an example of courage to point to. They will need you, men and women of every religion who will continue the struggle that you began, who will fight for freedom and fairness, who will even sacrifice their own lives—the fighters and the dreamers who will follow you to the mountaintop.

These words are spoken to Abraham Lincoln on the last day of his life in a once popular television drama, *Touched by an Angel.* These same words would have been significant during the Progressive Era, World War I, the Depression, and World War II, but their meaning would have differed. In this twenty-first-century monologue, the condition requiring an example to cling to is African American poverty and inner-city street life.

The episode in which Lincoln appears concerns an African American boy, Calvin, who tells his teacher that he wishes to be a "hit man" when he grows up. In response, Calvin's teacher tells him the story of America's greatest president, Abraham Lincoln, and its best-known hit man, John Wilkes Booth. She then takes Calvin to the Lincoln Memorial, where he confesses his real hope: to be president of the United States. The youngster's transformation from potential murderer to potential president is sealed by his entering the memorial and gazing at his new idol.

Inside the Lincoln Memorial, conceived and approved during the Progressive Era and dedicated in 1922, the following inscription appears on the wall directly behind Daniel Chester French's seated Lincoln:

IN THIS TEMPLE
AS IN THE HEARTS OF THE PEOPLE
FOR WHOM HE SAVED THE UNION
THE MEMORY OF ABRAHAM LINCOLN
IS ENSHRINED FOREVER

This inscription summarizes the sentiment of the early 1900s, but it also captures the sentiment of Lincoln's time. Many currents conveyed the Union's sacredness to Lincoln's contemporaries: the invocation of George Washington and the Founding Fathers, belief in God's role in the formation of the Union, the conservative force of romanticism and sentimentalism, the popularity of "family" and "home" as metaphors of nation and state. The passing of these conventions and beliefs, which Lincoln embraced and expressed repeatedly throughout his political life,[1] render the meaning of Union almost incomprehensible to us.

By the time Lincoln's admirers succeeded in establishing his national memorial, "the founders," of whom Lincoln and his generation spoke so warmly, existed in a more distant relation, but the paternal heritage endured because the Union remained sacrosanct. At the turn of the twenty-first century, people think about Lincoln differently. If his army had put down the rebellion directly and he had not been compelled to attack the institution of slavery, his story would have possessed less emotional resonance and moral salience. Indeed, some historians, notably David Blight, are now admired for portraying the most touching demonstrations of regional unity, including the 1913 (and 1938) Gettysburg reunions of Federal and Confederate veterans, as ritual displays of racism. Such arguments confound cause and consequence. Civil War reunions, like other ritual activities of the period, including religious and civic ceremonies, were held in segregated settings, but this does not mean that race relations were on the participants' minds. Racial segregation was the taken-for-granted condition of ritual exclusion; the rituals themselves had a reconciliationist, not a racist, cast.

In the early twentieth century, national unity required the reconciliation of regions, not races, and as America became a global actor, contemplating and engaging in foreign wars, regional grudges could only weaken the nation. Whether America's remaining a weak, insignificant nation would have strengthened "emancipationist" rather than "reconciliationist" memories of the Civil War, on the other hand, is doubtful; American racism has never been contingent on American global power. Resentment over displays of regional unity, however, remains palpable in certain academic circles.[2] The prospect of this resentment entering into the 2011 sesquicentennial of the Civil War, which follows the Lincoln bicentennial by only two years, is a matter of interest and practical concern.

Epic heroes show the ideals of a people through their deeds. The ideals that Lincoln's deeds defined, according to many scholars, include the Union's permanence, but he eventually made emancipation the Civil War's primary goal, even while embracing the rebellious states that had brought so much grief to the nation. This is a fair summary of what historian Edward Ayers calls the "generous interpretation" now organizing beliefs about the Civil War and healing the wounds of decades of regional and racial conflict. What is wrong with such an interpretation?

> After all, it puts the ideals of democracy and nationhood at the center of the story, offering a counterweight to those who have appealed to the less expansive interpretation of the nation's ideals. It holds up heroes worth emulating. It reconciles the North and South to each other, giving respect where it has not always been found. It places the struggle for black freedom and equality at the heart of American history. It connects Americans with their past. All these worthy purposes have been won only after great effort, and a person of goodwill might think twice before questioning them.[3]

Ayers's tongue-in-cheek statement raises questions about history's truth claims and societal role. Minimizing Lincoln's devotion to the Union and asserting his emancipation plans to be unconditional contributes to a generous interpretation of the Civil War. One must neither praise nor condemn this interpretation but try to understand how the conditions making it plausible also transformed Lincoln's reputation and diminished his prestige. The path is twisted but inexorable.

Lincoln and the New History

Three major questions about Abraham Lincoln's image are posed in this book's introduction: (1) Why did Lincoln's prestige fall so abruptly and so far during the last third of the twentieth century? (2) Why did Lincoln's reputation change so suddenly and focus so sharply on emancipation? and (3) Did Lincoln's fallen prestige and new reputation affect one another, or did both result from a third and more fundamental condition? Answers to these questions are important not only for what they tell us about the way we think of Lincoln, but also for how they clarify the way we think of all great men of national history.

The late twentieth-century's civil rights movement strongly affects Lincoln's place in American memory. The initial 1955–65 phase of this movement[4] was like a giant planet with a gravitational pull so powerful as to acutely bend light beams launched from the past. Those observing the past in the earlier part of the twentieth century saw it differently from those witnessing it today. How the civil rights movement induced historians to reinterpret Lincoln's Civil War and Reconstruction goals is the question. The answer is embodied, at least partially, in the New History.

The New History's roots go back to the early twentieth century, when progressive historians made social reform their priority. They believed history must be useful and enable reform to occur more readily. History cannot be too far from life; analytic models must bridge the gap between past and present; history concerned only with the content of past events without regard for present significance is lifeless and irrelevant. Beginning in the 1970s, several intellectual currents—literary theory, women's history, and ideological analysis by New Left historians—contributed to historians' effort to make history itself a form of moral reflection. To this end, the historian had to overcome "contextualism"—the effort to know the past from the viewpoint of those living in the past—in order to judge, correct, and redeem the present. History had to be universally life-encompassing, had to describe current life from below, respond to the present needs and interests of all the people.

The new, present-oriented, history is grounded methodologically in narrative analysis. Narratives are said to be filters between the mind and the world not because their plot structures are similar to real-world events, but because authors must create this similarity in order to interpret events. To what extent readers of these narratives are affected by, let alone convinced by, the connections they assert is a separate matter. New historians, like many social scientists, believe that the past comes down to us in the form of texts; that because we have access only to texts, the practice of historiography boils down to different ways of producing them. Inspired by William James, John Dewey, Hayden White, and Richard Rorty, historian David Harlan defends historians' right to select and ignore evidence according to their view of what will be meaningful to contemporary readers:

> What is at issue in American history . . . is not our ability to know the past but our ability to find the predecessors we need—to think with their thoughts, to work through our own beliefs by working through their beliefs. Only thus does history become a mode of moral reflection.[5]

But what is to be said of the predecessors we do not need and of the historical realities irrelevant to present beliefs and sentiments?

The story of Abraham Lincoln has always been a source of moral reflection, but before Lincoln studies became professionalized in the late 1920s and 1930s under the tutelage of academic historians like James G. Randall, those responsible for conceiving and telling it, those who selected details from the record of Lincoln's life for the light they throw on the present, had always been orators, editorial writers, columnists, biographers, ideologists—never historians. No historian lacks moral conviction, but we have just begun to see historians elevate such conviction to a research principle. Those who write history in terms of moral reflection confound memory and history, and when this happens, we can never know what conditions stretch the real Lincoln in one direction or another. Reputation and prestige, after all, are determined partly by accomplishment and partly by timeliness, publicity, and luck. If we cannot tell these things apart, there is no way to tell how far we distort Lincoln as we adapt him to our times, or how Lincoln's accomplishments limit what our imaginations can make of him.

To assert that Lincoln shifted his war goal from saving the Union to emancipating slaves simplifies his motivation and reduces his presidency's significance, but it bears on the racial issues and historical exaggerations of our day. Before the 1960s, textbook writers literally ignored African Americans; since the 1980s, they have distorted by overstatement. Crispus Attucks, a totally unknown dark-skinned man shot during a demonstration against British troops in Boston is now defined as a black man, America's first martyr, and occupies more space in the average textbook than Paul Revere, whose role in the making of the Revolution vastly exceeded his horse ride. Harriet Tubman, organizer of the Underground Railroad, now occupies as much space as Harriet Beecher Stowe, whose *Uncle Tom's Cabin* altered the opinion of millions of Northerners about slavery and had a far greater effect on the course of events.[6] Although overstatement balancing understatement makes for a certain moral logic, it disables our intellect by preventing us from attributing influence to Lincoln accurately and, above all, from discerning the meaning of his conduct for ordinary men and women of his own time.

Lack of a sense of irony is one of the deficits affecting America's memory of Lincoln and the Civil War. "Our current understanding of the war," Edward Ayers observes, "makes us impatient with those in the North—the great majority, at the beginning—who argued that they were fighting only for the Union, not for the end of bondage. . . . We are disappointed with those many white men who died for the Union who would not willingly have risked their lives for the end of slavery."[7] Why does Ayers insert the phrase "The great majority, at the beginning," which insinuates a fundamental change at the end of the war in Northern opinion toward slavery? In August 1864, after all, Lincoln expected election defeat—devastating defeat—because the war, not emancipation, had been going so badly. Also, why should anyone today be disappointed with the motives of white soldiers? Through their deaths, slaves and free blacks gained hope for the future. It is as if Jews were impatient with Allies who argued they were fighting only to defend themselves, and who gave no thought to war victims, Jewish or otherwise. American Jews visiting American military cemeteries throughout Europe, from Normandy to Rome, know that many of the young men who lost their lives defending them were anti-Semites, but they are fully aware of the difference between the men's motives and their achievement, and they can, and do, ignore the first while expressing gratitude for the second. Allied victory saved the Jewish people from annihilation, but World War II was not "about" the Jews' survival any more than the Civil War was "about" emancipation. Without this capacity to distinguish personal motive, social cause, and historical consequence, or to grasp the mid-nineteenth-century meanings of slavery and secession, there can be no rational understanding of history, let alone its meaningful commemoration.

Memory and the Unfolding of Democracy

Long before Lincoln became their symbol, white Americans treated one another as "equals," but their idea of equality differed from that of the present day. Although one man might be wealthier or better educated than another, that did not make him a better man. Equality afforded people equal dignity, but did not necessarily make them good neighbors. Irishmen and Yankees, laborers and merchants, immigrants and native born saw themselves alike in God's eyes but did not allow their children to marry one another. Throughout the nineteenth and early twentieth centuries, the ideal of equality prevailed in the context of rigid social boundaries. In both its industrial and pre-industrial ages, America was a "high-grid"[8] society, one in which ethnic, racial, and religious distinctions were deemed essential to communal order and dignity. By the end of the 1960s, however, a great cultural revolution had begun to break down America's gridwork.

The first stage of this revolution began fifty years earlier, when a Progressive government intervened in the free market to ensure fair competition and abolish exploitation. The second stage was reached when a New Deal government provided relief after the free market collapsed. The third stage emerged after World War II, when a new welfare state imposed itself on social as well as economic institutions, regulating racial, ethnic, and gender relations once governed by local authority and personal discretion. This third phase of the egalitarian revolution involved a weakening of local power centers. The Supreme Court's overruling discrimination ordinances; the great suburban movement and increased intermetropolitan mobility (which scattered the city's once compact ethnic communities); the expansion of national communication networks, largely, although not exclusively, through low-cost travel, telephone connection, and television—these developments increased the integration of once separated communities.

Now more than sixty years old, this revolution has shattered the fantasies by which the old order enchanted itself. Enchantment works through stereotyped representations magnifying social distance as it deifies heroes and demonizes aliens and outcasts.[9] The logic that convinces people George Washington told no lie and Abraham Lincoln raised himself by hard work alone also leads them to believe blacks are shiftless, Jews crafty, Irish unruly. Stemming from the same stereotyping process, hero worship and ethnic prejudice grow and diminish together.

The enchanted world that made Lincoln godlike was a Victorian world of clear moral distinctions and hierarchical boundaries, one whose great men were utterly different from the average run of men. Out of the disenchantment of that world—its "rationalization,"[10] as Max Weber described it—arose more complicated perceptions of the hero. Good and evil, strength and weakness, achievement and failure were seen in men once deemed flawless. Attributes that once distinguished the great man from the ordinary could now be recognized in all men, and the line between them blurred. Simultaneously, late twentieth-century reform movements promoted not only racial equality but also equal job opportunity, Native American rights, women's rights, gay rights, animal rights, ethnic antidefamation, humane treatment of the criminal and mentally ill, and abolition of invidious religious distinction. Simultaneously, new sociological formulations, including "labeling theory," revealed that traditional distinctions between the deviant and the conventional resulted from artificial boundaries sustained by old fashioned moralists and interest-driven "silent majorities" rather than natural variations of moral character and personality.[11] Men and women, whites and blacks, ethnics and WASPs, Christians and Jews, gays and straights, rich and poor, parents and children, teachers and students, criminals and victims, sinners and saints—all seemed less distinguishable than before.[12]

Such is the temper of our time: the same conditions blurring lines between majority and minority communities blur distinctions between great and ordinary people. Even the legitimacy of their historical renown has diminished. America's "inequality anxiety,"[13] however, is symptomatic of a benign and just society. "What is more newsworthy," asks postmodernism scholar Kenneth Gergen, "than information contradicting the public image, or demonstrating at last that the 'hero' is, after all, 'just like us,' or worse?"[14] Critics of this postmodern argument assert that its proponents speak "on behalf of a humanity whose gods they alone have declared dead."[15] These critics are wrong. The decline of grand narratives and their heroes, of which the story of Abraham Lincoln is but one instance, has been amply demonstrated.

However, the decline of reverence is to be distinguished from its disappearance. If America's grand narrative has deteriorated as fully as postmodern theorizing suggests, the minority of Americans still revering Lincoln would not be as large as it is. In his study of Lincoln's New Salem, Edward Bruner noted how

> "in postmodern writings, contemporary American tourist attractions tend to be described in ways that replicate elements of the theory of postmodernism, emphasizing the inauthentic constructed nature of the sites, their appeal to the masses, their imitation of the past. . . . This is a narrow and distorted view that fails to account for the popularity and frequency of such sites on the American landscape, that begs the question of the meaning of the sites to the participants. . . ."[16]

Because the nation is constituted by its memories, postmodern claims about their disappearance must be exaggerated. Pierre Nora's formulation, "If we still dwelled among our memories, there would be no need to consecrate the sites [*lieux de memoire*] embodying them,"[17] exaggerates because it assumes, without proof, that the very commemorative activities affirming commitment to the past are nostalgic symptoms of its receding presence. The opposite claim, that commemorative sites symbolize authentic memories and transmit society's values, shows in local survey data, notably Springfield, Illinois, visitors professing attachment to what the city's Lincoln sites symbolize, and national survey data showing Lincoln's prestige receding, not plunging, after 1975. The numbers of newspaper, magazine, and congressional citations concerning Lincoln have also stabilized since their late 1960s and early 1970s decline, suggesting that the past is an enduring, if not constantly powerful, source of orientation and meaning. Contemporary society's condition is as steady as it is transitional, for its traditional beliefs and practices have not vanished.

As traditional beliefs motivate efforts to renew ties to a past that new beliefs challenge, hundreds of thousands of Americans presently undertake genealogical inquiries to identify their forebears, and thousands of amateur oral historians seek to recover the ethnic communities of their parents and grandparents. Americans also admire archetypal presidents—from real men managing the Cuban Missile Crisis (*Thirteen Days* [2000]) to fictional ones, such as the warrior-presidents appearing in *Independence Day* (1996) and *Air Force One* (1997). Beginning in the 1980s, moreover, the decade in which revisionist history matured, a great surge of monument- and museum-building began, and has lasted to the present. The millions who continue to revere Lincoln, seek information about him, and visit his shrines also include those driven by reaction against recent deconstructions of history and tradition.

Might Lincoln's heroic reputation and its encompassing narrative be someday restored? Two theoretical models say no. Jean-Francois Lyotard, the postmodern theorist, envisions a social order in which grand narratives lack all necessary foundational supports. As national narratives are replaced by incoherent swarms of local and even private ones, "consensus has become an outmoded and suspect value."[18] A second theory, constructed by political scientist Alan Wolfe, depicts a "decentered" social order moving away from core values and seeking a new cultural center to replace the old.[19] In Wolfe's model, too, present and past are discontinuous.

This project on Abraham Lincoln suggests a third theory: stability persists in the midst of change; collective memory, like the collective consciousness of which it is a part, is "independent of the particular conditions in which individuals are placed; they pass on and it remains. . . . It does not change with each but, on the contrary, it connects successive generations with one another."[20] Emile Durkheim's generalization, Stjepan Mestrovic explains, must apply today, for even a postmodern society needs national stories "to communicate its invisible transcendence to its members."[21] The abrupt decline of Lincoln's stature (along with

Washington's, Roosevelt's, Truman's, Eisenhower's, and Kennedy's) results from the emergence of a post-heroic culture, with its attendant alienation and moral vacancy; but the invocation of Lincoln in the context of crisis and the sentiments evoked in the midst of Lincoln's shrines exemplify the limit of that diminution, the continued, albeit attenuated, transcendence of his memory. As each generation modifies beliefs held by its forebears, an assemblage of old beliefs remains and coexists with the new, including old beliefs about the past itself. Lincoln therefore remains the man of the people and the man above the people, the Savior of the Union and emancipator of its slaves, the embodiment of rugged individualism and the welfare state, the personification of humor and sorrow, iron will and compassion. That is the man we knew yesterday; that is the man we know today.

However, these continuities do not restore the Lincoln of the 1930s and 1940s, the man Americans looked up to and emulated. He is now less the Savior of the Union, less the rugged individualist, less the man of sorrow and humor, less the man of steel and velvet. He is now a smaller man, known by more, adored by fewer, emulated by fewer still. The people's identification with Lincoln has diminished, but thanks to the efforts of the Lincoln historical community, we possess more information about him than any other historical figure of his time, and the public's future access to such information has become easier and fuller. Why, then, is the situation so paradoxical? Why do people who know about Lincoln fail to see themselves in him?

Identification, according to Sigmund Freud, is the first expression of an emotional tie with another person.[22] In other words, identification induces change within the personality so that the admirer of Lincoln becomes like Lincoln and immortalizes Lincoln in his own moral conscience and conduct. The generation that asked "What would Lincoln do?" betrays his presence in their inner lives. Given so many influential establishments seeking to enhance Lincoln's relevance and stature, there is every reason to expect this sentiment to be sustained, if not restored to earlier levels.

Bicentennial

"There can be no society that does not feel the need of upholding and reaffirming at regular intervals the collective sentiments and the collective ideas which make its unity and personality." This often quoted statement by Emile Durkheim is especially appropriate today. Organizers of the 2009 anniversary of Abraham Lincoln's 1809 birth intend it to be the kind of observance Durkheim describes, one in which American society will find and symbolically reaffirm itself.

The Lincoln Bicentennial Commission established by President Clinton in 1999 consists of noted Lincoln scholars, Congressional representatives from states where Lincoln was born and lived, and members of the House of Representatives and Senate. Before this Commission could be officially formed, the bill establishing it, dated April 15, 1999, the 134th anniversary of Lincoln's death, had to be discussed and voted on. The discussion betrayed a view of Lincoln at once reflecting and shaping the Bicentennial Commission's work. In the words of a member of Illinois's congressional delegation, "On November 19, 1863, in the midst of the war on a battlefield near Gettysburg, Pennsylvania, President Lincoln presented to the people his vision for our Nation, conceived in liberty where everyone is created equal. This speech known as the Gettysburg Address shaped the destiny of the United States of America." America's government would be a "government of the people regardless of race, or color, or gender."[23] Emphasizing equality more than unity, this statement, among others printed in the bill, reiterates the emancipationist/multicultural version of Lincoln's legacy. That the Gettysburg Address, a eulogy to fallen Union soldiers, was actually a speech about racial justice that shaped America's destiny the way a constitution would, or an industrial or cultural revolution would, is a small tail wagging a very big dog, but the view is widely held.[24] A subcommittee consolidated this and similar beliefs into a curious *Statement of Findings of the Bill to Establish the Abraham Lincoln Bicentennial Commission*:

Congress makes the following findings:

(1) Abraham Lincoln, the 16th President, was one of the Nation's most prominent leaders, demonstrating true courage during the Civil War, one of the greatest crises in the Nation's history.
(2) Born of humble roots in Hardin County, Kentucky, on February 12, 1809, Abraham Lincoln rose to the Presidency through a legacy of honesty, integrity, intelligence, and commitment to the United States.
(3) With a belief that all men were created equal, Abraham Lincoln led the effort to free all slaves in the United States.
(4) Abraham Lincoln had a generous heart, with malice toward none and with charity for all.
(5) Abraham Lincoln gave the ultimate sacrifice for the country Lincoln loved, dying from an assassin's bullet on April 15, 1865.
(6) All Americans could benefit from studying the life of Abraham Lincoln, for Lincoln's life is a model for accomplishing the "American Dream" through honesty, integrity, loyalty, and a lifetime of education.
(7) The year 2009 will be the bicentennial anniversary of the birth of Abraham Lincoln, and a commission should be established to study

> and recommend to Congress activities that are fitting and proper to celebrate that anniversary in a manner that appropriately honors Abraham Lincoln.[25]

This *Statement of Findings* could not have been written by earlier generations of congressmen, for it includes reference to Lincoln's emancipating the slaves but is silent on his saving the Union. On the other hand, the findings include traditional images of the Man of the People, the First American growing up on the frontier, and the Self-Made Man. The sixth finding, that Lincoln is a model for Americans to emulate, is perhaps the most traditional, and its content, "accomplishing the 'American Dream' through honesty, integrity, loyalty, and a lifetime of education," touches on a theme, "Self-Made Man," that appears low on the list of virtues Americans now attribute to Lincoln. This theme was high on the list of virtues their forebears ascribed to him—although the latter would have mentioned "hard work and perseverance" instead of "a lifetime of education"—which would have made little sense to them.

We stand at the beginning of the twenty-first century. The 2009 bicentennial activities will probably maintain the content of Lincoln's reputation, for they are expressly designed to emphasize the Civil War as an instrument of emancipation and to explain its significance for contemporary race relations. The 2003 appointment of Jesse Jackson Jr. to the Bicentennial Commission by Speaker of the House Nancy Pelosi will help guarantee that this design will be followed. Likewise, the 2007 Bicentennial Commission Advisory Committee and State Liaison Meeting was opened by John Hope Franklin's lecture on Abraham Lincoln and African American history. Franklin spoke at the New York Avenue Presbyterian Church, where, according to the commission's executive director Eileen Mackevich, "the Lincoln family worshiped during their time in the White House and it also played an active role in the Civil Rights movement." Franklin's talk, she said, "continues our commitment to exploring the evolving views of the African American community toward Lincoln."[26]

There is no more interest in the commission today in Lincoln as Savior of the Union than in 1999, when Congress established it. In the words of a Public Awareness Committee member: "[O]f the themes that Executive Director Michael Bishop elaborated on in the opening at the beginning of the session, none of them addressed the idea of the Union or 'one nation indivisible' which was one of Lincoln's accomplishments."[27] But will the deemphasizing of Union help to recover the aura surrounding Lincoln in 1909, or at any time prior to the end of World War II? On the other hand, would American society be willing to turn back the clock to the prewar bigotry and stereotyping of which this aura was a part?

Prospects

Friedrich Nietzsche grasped the essence and function of great men when he asserted that no person can live purposefully without a horizon of unquestioned beliefs. "No artist will paint his picture, no general win his victory" without commitment to what he does and without loving what he does "infinitely more than it deserves to be loved."[28] Nothing illustrates the point better than what early twentieth-century Americans thought of Lincoln. They imagined him more perfect than he was, and they revered him more than he deserved to be revered. This power of mind, the power to admire, did more than elevate Abraham Lincoln—it attached the generation of the 1930s and 1940s to traditions giving it endurance and drove it to history-turning achievement.

From every single representation of Abraham Lincoln—every statue and bust; every cartoon, print, painting, magazine and calendar illustration; every film, video, television commentary and drama—one drops a plumb line deep into the mentality of the generation from which it arose, gauging its ultimate meanings, styles of thinking, feeling, and moralizing. Given the mood of the present generation, the sacred pictures of yesterday, like Lincoln's, are pressed to the service of mockery: Leonardo's Virgin is now represented with cow dung; Jesus now appears with an erection or as a naked black woman; the Cross of Calvary now attains fuller meaning when set in a jar of urine. The moral mediocrity, shallowness, and triviality of the day is radiated in the symbols of the day.

Today, so many alternative frameworks exist that one can no longer believe in the absolute truth of any one of them. Late twentieth-century man, "The Last Man," as political scholar Francis Fukuyama calls him, "knows better than to risk his life for a cause, because he recognizes that history was full of pointless battles in which men fought over whether they should be Christian or Muslim, Protestant or Catholic, German or French. The loyalties that drove men to desperate acts of courage and self-sacrifice were proven by subsequent history to be silly prejudices."[29] World War II was not fought over silly prejudices, but victory rendered the loyalties needed to annihilate fascism superfluous. These loyalties seem, indeed, irrelevant if not harmful today.

Our loss is twofold. Not only do the categories defining heroes and gods lose credibility; heroes lose the eminence arising from being compared with gods. Americans who think about Lincoln feel that he cannot be forgotten, that their privileges and comforts are somehow built upon his gains and sufferings; yet they feel even more keenly that Lincoln's achievements, however memorable, are not quite heroic enough. They therefore split the difference. Amid new biographies and television documentaries, they have made Lincoln an object of quiet reverence and temperate admiration—in line with America's quieter religious faith and more mature patriotism. The new Lincoln serves a new generation of American people—nonideological, nonjudgmental, present-oriented, fairminded, at peace with itself, good humored, in need of neither great heroes nor great villains.[30]

More exact historiography or more attractively packaged artifacts cannot reawaken the ancient need for heroism and villainy. History contributes to Lincoln's changing reputation as emancipator and friend of the oppressed, but it cannot capture the affective elements of Lincoln's image—his prestige. Diminishing of that prestige is part of the fraying fabric of American nationhood and self-esteem. The contemporaneity of the past has been lost, and historians and commemorative artists are the last persons we expect to restore it. Abraham Lincoln's depictions remain part of the present and will be even more present during his 2009 bicentennial, but they will not forge the mentality of our generation. Here, precisely, the new mentality distinguishes itself from the old: as Americans cease to believe in the sanctifying fullness of the past, they lose sight of the link between their present life and the transformations wrought by their forebears; they lose sight of themselves as historical beings, forget that they have inherited, not created, the most valuable of their possessions.

Peter H. Gibbon, an authority on the status of great men, believes that America's vision of greatness can be restored by teaching about greatness more effectively. "Our society is uneasy with greatness," he says, yet greatness is indispensable to maintaining morality. "With heroes, we experience the extraordinary and expand our notion of what it means to be human." To this end, a "moderate triumphalism" recognizing both great achievement and moral failure must replace the dogmatic cynicism of the day.[31] Gibbon believes America's indifference to its great moments and men result from admirers' inflated claims—as if more moderate claims would be more inspiring. The new history has more than realized such moderation but without the result Gibbon expects. Gibbon also assumes that average people are inclined to perform a calculus of merits and demerits, arrive at a net evaluation, and compare one case against another on which similar operations are performed. Thus, Washington the slave owner, military commander, and Founding Father, could be compared to Woodrow Wilson the segregationist, war president, and political reformer by assigning weights to their separate qualities. This is not the way people commonly think about great men; indeed, the very process of assessing them so rationally diminishes their heroic potential.

That the American people might soon identify with the past and its heroes as closely as they did before the post-heroic era is doubtful. Culture, after all, does not come a la carte. If Lincoln is to be revered today as deeply as he was six or seven decades ago, then we must restore a social order of more authoritative institutions, less negotiable loyalties, and sharper social discriminations. Such a restoration is not on the horizon, and few would look forward to the racial, religious, and ethnic tribalism accompanying it. The equal dignity of the individual, the real equality of political and economic opportunity, the absorption of minorities into a mainstream, the disappearance of invidious group distinctions and individual stereotypes—Lincoln's fallen renown is part of the price we pay for these precious gains. The other part of this price includes a disbelief in the sacred, weakening commitment to the nation and its institutions, and, outside the world of entertainment and sport, diminished relevance and recognition of human distinction (see table 6.1). Accordingly, even if some great crisis befalls the nation, it would be faced by a generation taught that America is no better than most countries and worse than some, that its great men are admirable but imperfect, that its great events are as much episodes of oppression as salvation, that the elevation of any man diminishes everyone else by implication or, even worse, by design. In that great crisis, American history's greatest men would continue to be used and admired; they would rarely be embraced and emulated.

What, then, is to be said of Abraham Lincoln? He is no longer America's singular model. Yet, how can the man who contributed so much to the realization of its democracy be no better than other men? Why should he not be adored? It is because the egalitarianism that made American society more just and decent also eroded his prestige. America has never been freer of religious, ethnic, and racial hatred, never more worthy of the love of *all* its citizens. The moral flowering of America affirms Lincoln's ironic place in the memory of its people.

APPENDIX A

The Populist Strain in Depression-Era Lincoln Representation

Populism, strictly speaking, refers to late nineteenth-century political movements for the restoration of rural and small-town values and for restraints on corporations, monopolies, political machines, immigrants, and religious minorities. Historian Richard Hofstadter characterized populism as a kind of cranky conservatism opposing change and diversity,[1] but he ignored its positive aspect, namely, recognition of the common man's contribution to the nation. Abraham Lincoln epitomized the extraordinariness of the ordinary American, but no facet of his persona has lost more resonance during the late twentieth century. Every national survey of his reputation converges on the public's diminishing interest in the Man of the People, First American, and Self-Made Man. Why these lineaments of Lincoln's image were once so relevant and how they were represented to the people must be known if we are to grasp the full extent of his transformation.

Whites and blacks, Southerners and Northerners, liberals and conservatives, spoke of Lincoln in their own way, but their accents, well captured by John Steinbeck, expressed a generation's sense of injustice and resentment:

> I been thinkin' a hell of a lot, thinkin' about our people livin' like pigs, an' the good rich lan' layin' fallow, or maybe one fella with a million acres, while a hundred thousand' good farmers is starvin'. An' I been wonderin' if all our folks got together an' yelled, like them fellas yelled, only a few of em—"
>
> Ma said, "Tom, they'll drive you, an' cut you down like they done to young Floyd."
>
> "They gonna drive me anyways. They drivin' all our people."

The dialogue had a new ring. Progressive Era ideals, although infused with populist elements, were nonetheless abstract: democracy, equal opportunity, equal rights. In contrast, Depression culture was earthy and made of the common people a veritable cult:

> People is goin' on—changin' a little, maybe, but goin' right on.
> "How can you tell?" Uncle John demanded. "What's to keep ever'-thing from stoppin'; all the folks from jus' gittin' tired an' layin' down?"
> Ma considered. . . . "Hard to say, she said. Ever'thing we do—seems to me is aimed right at goin' on."[2]

John Steinbeck's words are Lincolnesque; but there is a dramatic connection, too. The actor who played Tom Joad in the film version of *Grapes of Wrath* was Henry Fonda, the same actor who played *Young Mr. Lincoln* a few years earlier. Fonda brought out the similarities between young Abe of the 1830s and the young Toms of the 1930s.

From *Citizen Kane* and John Dos Passos's *U.S.A.* to Billie Holiday's "Strange Fruit," the culture of the left, with its emphasis on class and racial struggle, gained prominence.[3] Lincoln films were part of, if not central to, this genre. Depression-era magazines, no less than films, published hundreds of stories and poems about Lincoln's affinity with America's ordinary people.

Pictures: Moving and Still

Biographies published during the late 1920s and early 1930s, notably Carl Sandburg's folklore Lincoln, influenced the Depression generation's historical perception. Visual images, however, take us beyond what we can know verbally. Visual art, like literature, "is social evidence and testimony. It is a continuous commentary on manners and morals."[4] Visual art distinguishes generations from one another by representing their worldviews and helping us to penetrate their moral and affective habits of the heart. The feelings a people have for the past appear in many places other than art, but nowhere more vividly. Charles Horton Cooley declared: "We think of America as the land of freedom, simplicity, cordiality, equality, and so on, in antithesis to other countries which we suppose to be otherwise—and we think of these traits by imagining the people that embody them."[5] Sensible appearances, whether moving or still, articulate the traits that lie beneath all surfaces.

The Dramatic Life of Abraham Lincoln (1925), the first full-length motion picture biography distributed nationally, was viewed widely but forgotten as soon as the first Lincoln "talkie" appeared in 1930.[6] Written by Stephen Vincent Benét and performed by an outstanding cast led by Walter Huston, *Abraham Lincoln* gained great acclaim. Critics voted it second best picture of the year—behind *All Quiet on the Western Front.* Young Lincoln is good at heavy work and fighting—a semiliterate who rarely utters a grammatically correct sentence. By the end of the story, the cretinous backwoods lad has become a stately gentleman intoning noble thoughts about democracy and Union. The film's theme, the transition from commonness to greatness, is summarized in its last scene: the log cabin dissolves into the new marble temple enclosing it, which dissolves further into the Lincoln Memorial, then, at last, into Daniel Chester French's Lincoln Memorial statue shimmering in an aura of light.

If the purpose of *Abraham Lincoln,* like the Lincoln films of the 1920s, was to show how an indisputably ordinary man became godlike, the films of the late 1930s showed what kind of man that god had been. People whose fortunes have suddenly fallen are troubled and disoriented; they want to make sense of their circumstance; they need help to realize who they are and what they are worth; they need to know that their lives possess a dignity transcending jobs and money.[7] Film narratives, thus, confined themselves to Lincoln's youth and pre-presidential years—the part of his life that a Depression audience found most relevant to theirs.

The millions of people who bought tickets for *Young Man Lincoln* in 1937 saw a variation on this theme. Attorney Lincoln (played by Henry Fonda) defends two young men wrongly accused of murder. He wins the case because he knows about mundane things, like farmers' almanacs, and because he is of the same stock as the people he is defending. He goes to the same local fairs, takes part (and mischievously cheats) at the same tug-of-war. Since his clients' mother and sisters remind him of his own family and childhood, he chops wood for them as if their land were his, and defends the two boys as if they were his own brothers. Lincoln sees himself as both his clients' lawyer and kinsman, but when the mother pays him the small sum she can afford, he takes it, understanding his place and the family's pride. With this troubled and impoverished family, and with this Lincoln, most Americans could identify. As one reviewer put it:

> Lincoln is not the Great Emancipator here. He's not a great anything. His beard hasn't started to sprout and he's just a gangling, gawking, grinning young man who doesn't much know what it's all about but who is determined to do his best while finding out. He splits rails, judges pie-baking contests and wins tugs-of-war and, thanks to Henry Fonda's restrained and sane interpretation, remains a real, lovable human being without any stuffy man-of-destiny nonsense about him.[8]

Abe Lincoln in Illinois (1940), like *Young Mr. Lincoln,* is a "young man who doesn't much know what it's all about." He maneuvers a flatboat of pigs down the Sangamon River until it hits a rock and breaks up. The pigs escape and run free, but Abe chases them through the mud. He slips and slides and sprawls as he tries to hang on to the slippery creatures. This is no presumptuous gentleman but a simple fellow. *Abe Lincoln in Illinois,* however, is a complex story. Based on Robert Sherwood's (1938) Pulitzer Prize–winning drama of the same name, the film deals with Lincoln's inner life, his desire for advancement and security, his ambivalence toward his wife and resistance to her overweening ambition, his disdain for the sordid politics that brought him to the presidency. Drawing on Carl Sandburg's *Prairie Years,* Sherwood sets before his Depression audience a simple, unheroic youth. Lincoln is physically lazy and unambitious; he walks with a slow, shuffling gait, fights town bullies, grows into politics despite himself, becomes politically committed, debates Stephen Douglas, and eventually wins the presidency. Despite its dramatic sophistication, positive reaction to Sherwood's film, in the opinion of the *North American Review,* resulted from its depiction of Lincoln's early years, reflecting the public's "growing desire . . . for simple stories about great and good people."[9] The narrative itself, as the *Review*'s editor believed, is dubious, a popularized newsreel of a great man's life. But the "continuing [Depression] crisis, which has put a damper on sophistication in the arts, has revived the feeling for the immemorial beatitudes wholesomely presented."[10]

Besides being simple, Sherwood's story was an indigenous product, inspired as well as produced by an American. The last great play about Abraham Lincoln had been written during World War I by a Briton, John Drinkwater, who based his characterization on his countryman Lord Charnwood's biography.[11] In Carl Sandburg's *The Prairie Years* and Robert Sherwood's *Abe Lincoln in Illinois,* America had for the first time its own biography and drama.[12] Now its people could see themselves in a mirror of their own making. Moving pictures of Lincoln, then, did more than express Depression-era sentiment; they organized it, made it conceivable, intelligible, communicable, and public. The primary power of art, according to Susanne Langer, is the power of "formulating experience, and presenting it objectively for contemplation."[13] Just so, the function of film was to represent Lincoln not so much as a historical entity as a historical symbol through which the calamities of the present could be made meaningful.

In film, impressions are determined pictorially and sequentially. In the still picture, meaning derives from composition, which allows viewers to place Lincoln into a narrative they themselves supply. This is why

FIGURE A1. *Indiana Boy,* 1934 charcoal drawing by M. Leone Bracker. Courtesy of the Lincoln Museum, Fort Wayne, IN (reference number 5860).

the Lincoln National Life Insurance Company made extensive use of Abraham Lincoln's image. If the right kind of Lincoln helps to sell insurance policies, then we gain insight into the customer's mind by analyzing the compositions to which he or she is attracted. One such image, M. Leone Bracker's *Lincoln—Indiana Boy*, a Lincoln National Life Insurance Company project, depicts a young man cutting down a tree (fig. A1); in the background, an etherealized head of the president. Transcending visions of commonness growing into self-made greatness, Bracker gives Lincoln a look of dreamy benevolence rather than strength, moral rather than individual superiority. Lincoln's is no mere Horatio Alger story. His success consists in doing other people's work: preserving the Union and ending slavery. He presides over a suffering nation, and no generation

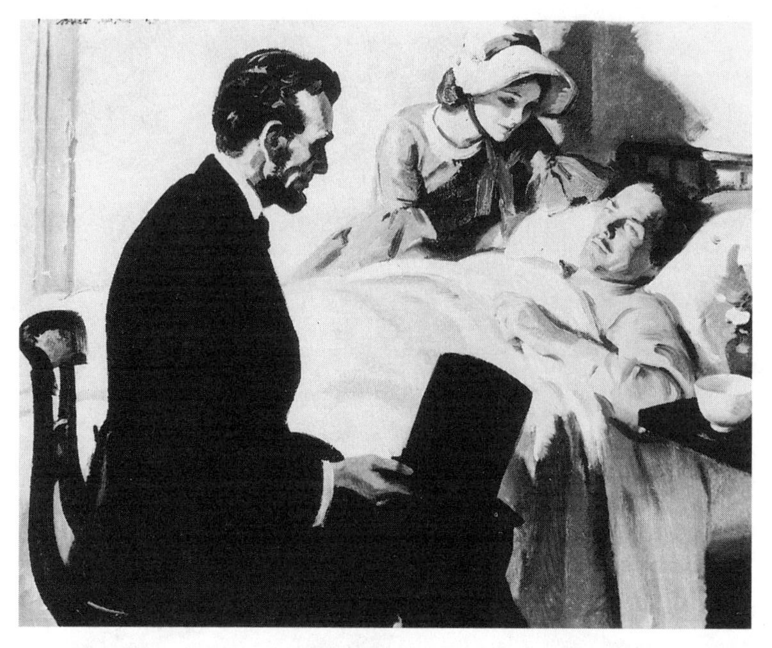

FIGURE A2. *Lincoln Visiting the Wounded,* 1937 painting by Pruett Carter. Courtesy of the Lincoln Museum, Fort Wayne, IN (reference number 1616).

seems to know that better or appreciate it more than the people of the Depression.

Pruett Carter's *Lincoln Visiting the Wounded* (fig. A2) is equally resonant with Depression taste. Carter places Lincoln closest to the viewer, a stovepipe hat on his lap, talking with a wounded soldier. The young man's expression is matter-of-fact, despite his being in the company of the president of the United States. His wife ignores Lincoln, as if he were a member of the family, as she fixes her husband's pillow. In a way, Carter's painting is the most representative of Depression realism: the wounded soldier is a plausible symbol of a wounded people; the solicitous president, a plausible symbol of a compassionate state.

Since children, like the injured, symbolize vulnerability, kindness shown them by the politically strong affirms symbolically the merit of the newly compassionate state. In L. C. Leyendecker's *A Good Friend to Little Children* (fig. A3), President Lincoln stoops over to accept a gift of flowers from a young admirer, just as his successor, President Franklin Roosevelt, accepts his admirers' plaudits. Lincoln's shawl hanging from his shoulders accentuates his physical awkwardness while common solicitation for the child's feelings bond Lincoln and her nursemaid. The

FIGURE A3. A *Great Friend to Little Children*, 1937 painting by J. C. Leydendecker. Courtesy of the Lincoln Museum, Fort Wayne, IN (reference number 1615).

black servant and white head of state playing identical roles makes democracy tangible.

Statue and Shrine

A picture's meaning cannot be inferred directly from its content, but good artists know what moves their viewers.[14] Neoclassical statues bring out Lincoln's magisterial side by depicting him in formal attire and cloak, body and head erect, one leg slightly bent, one hand resting upon a pillar or fasces, or upon an ornate table or chair, or holding a scrolled public document, or pointing in some direction; if seated, his back and arms are fully supported by a symbolic chair of state.[15] In contrast, realist statues, common after 1910, portray Lincoln as a common man. One such statue shows him standing as a frontier lawyer in seedy, ill-fitting attire; another, seated, slightly stooped, on a simple bench rather than an ornate chair of state; others portray him with head lowered and body hunched forward in despondency or grief.[16]

The nine Depression-era statues dedicated in the 1930s embody the "shirtsleeve" or "slouch democracy" condemned by an earlier generation of critics.[17] Five statues show Lincoln as a boy and identify him

FIGURE A4. *First American*, 1932 statue by Paul Manship. Courtesy of the Lincoln Museum, Fort Wayne, IN (reference number 2021).

with the frontier. Paul Manship's statue, commissioned by the Lincoln National Life Insurance Company and erected outside its Fort Wayne, Indiana, headquarters in 1932, shows an adolescent Lincoln with ax leaning on a felled tree stump, his right hand secures the book lying upon it; his left rests upon the head of a dog (fig. A4). Leonardo Crunelle also presses a heroic medium to the service of simplicity. His statue of Lincoln as a Black Hawk War officer hardly reminds us of George Washington, Andrew Jackson, and the other warrior presidents. Lincoln stands in ordinary garb, no epaulettes or military headgear; the only item suggesting his military role is the sword buckled to his waist. "This

FIGURE A5. *Blackhawk Captain,* 1930 statue by Leonardo Cruette. Courtesy of the Lincoln Museum, Fort Wayne, IN (reference number 850).

Lincoln wins your sympathy, perhaps your smiles,"[18] observed Lorado Taft at the statue's 1930 dedication (fig. A5).[19]

In each case, we are trying to determine what comes to the mind of people when they think about Abraham Lincoln, and we have done so by sampling the symbolic forms—movies, pictures, statues—with which these people represented Lincoln to themselves and to one another. The New Salem restoration project is another such form. New Salem, the museum town, shows Americans what Lincoln saw when, as a young man, he opened his eyes to the world. Begun in 1932, the year before the New Deal, Lincoln's New Salem became an "Altar of Memory." Contemporary scholars complained that the project's directors, Joseph Booton and Jerome Ray, failed to make it as authentic as they claimed, that they produced a caricature rather than an authentic replica of the village. In the 1930s, however, New Salem seemed like anything but a caricature. Booton and Ray's report,[20] published in 1934, was applauded because it demonstrated how much archeological and historical evidence they had gathered and how effectively they had used it to recreate that part of Lincoln's life in which the public was most interested. Few cared about the site's imperfections: the place's cleanliness, the exaggeration of features that gave it the look of an agricultural village rather than a commercial center. Few cared about the paved roads and public restrooms. Everything stood on the ground where Abraham Lincoln had once walked—that was the crucial thing. This "wholly American Town"—Lincoln's alma mater, as Carl Sandburg called it, was the miraculous place that transformed a prairie boy into the greatest American who ever lived.

To undertake a sampling of the populist Lincoln—the Man of the People, Frontier Youth, and Self-Made Man—would take us through representations of Lincoln's religiosity and family life, his early days as legislator and lawyer. Prominent among such portrayals would be the story of young Abe's romance with Ann Rutledge, perhaps the most appealing love story of the early twentieth century, and of his love for his mother and stepmother.[21] Many authors have written on these topics; many artists have portrayed them in marble, canvas, and paper. Perhaps the most important thing to say about them, from the standpoint of Depression-era readers and viewers, is that they have nothing literally to do with the environment in which they appear, nothing to do with joblessness, breadlines and soup kitchens, hunger and sickness. Yet, when people distract themselves, as they do when they contemplate the life of any historical figure, they do not do so randomly; they escape into what makes sense to them and that with which they can identify. Populist images of Abraham Lincoln depicted the economic stability, self-reliance, interpersonal ties, and family unity that Americans felt they had lost and wanted back.

APPENDIX B

*Percentage of Respondents Designating Abraham Lincoln as One of the Two or Three Greatest Men Who Ever Lived in this Country, 1945**

	White (n=2,346)	Black (n=225)	South (n=733)	Non-South (n=1,839)
Region				
South	44	51		
Non-South	61	56		
Race				
White			44	61
Black			51	56
Education				
0–11 grade	50	50	44	54
H.S. grad	65	56	52	69
Any college	68	83	52	77
Sex				
Male	59	53	50	62
Female	55	52	43	60
Age				
< 19	50	0		50
20–29	57	59	47	61
30–39	61	50	48	65
40–49	54	49	43	58
50–59	55	56	47	58
60–69	52	50	41	57
70+	68	58	63	69
Religion				
Protestant	59	53	45	65
Catholic	48	29	36	49
Jewish	73	0	92	70
Other	58	0	50	58
None	50	0		40
Residence				
Big metro	57	53	81	56
Small metro	55	54	43	62
Rural non-farm	60	44	47	66
Farm	55	59	43	64

*National Opinion Research Center.

APPENDIX C

Survey Information

This project is based on four national surveys administered by different organizations using different methods of data collection yielding different cooperation and response rates.

The Maryland Survey reports an overall response rate of 57 percent. This rate is fairly typical of good academic surveys at present, and recent studies by Curtin, Presser, Singer, and Keeter et al. have indicated almost no effects of variations in response rates near this level.[1]

Twelve percent (122) of the total Maryland sample declined to answer or were not able to name a single great president. These respondents were necessarily omitted from our later analyses, leaving 879 cases. Each question (original and follow-up) allowed but did not require two codeable responses, and the number of possible code categories was large. Using 110 random responses, we obtained 90 percent agreement, which breaks down into complete agreement on two codes in 66 percent of the cases and partial agreement in 10 percent of the cases. In 14 percent of the cases there was agreement on one of two codes, but disagreement on the other (sometimes one coder provided two codes and the other included only one). After discussion of coding differences, final decisions were made by one coder after taking full account of the two responses. Agreement was almost perfect for the major codes, including Savior of the Union and Great Emancipator, and very high for the codes involving Lincoln's character.

Knowledge Networks uses an Internet survey based on respondents enlisted from a national telephone sample and then given an easy-to-use hardware device and free Internet access through which surveys are administered. Because both the Maryland and Knowledge Network survey organizations provide a weight variable based on Current Population Survey data, we use those weights throughout our analysis. Once weights are applied to each data set, there are no significant differences between them in terms of the four social background variables on which we drew for our analysis: race, region, gender, and education. In terms of age/cohort, the Maryland sample averages two years older than the Knowledge Networks sample panel, which is appropriate given the dates for the two surveys. Prior to applying weights, there were small differences in race and region (more blacks and more Southerners in the Maryland data) and somewhat larger differences in gender and education (more women and a higher educational level in the Maryland data); the same age/cohort difference occurs without weights as with weights. Using STATA we determined that no serious problem occurs in our statistical analysis by employing weight variables.

The Knowledge Networks response rate is reported to be 58 percent, but if one takes account of nonresponse to the original Random Digit Dial (RDD) telephone sample, the final response rate is 28 percent. Post-stratification is used to match the general population and Knowledge Networks provides evidence that their final samples produces results comparable to those from a standard RDD telephone sample. The main issue about nonresponse is whether it is correlated with the key substantive variables in a study, and there is little reason to expect that to be the case for our questions about Lincoln once demographic variables are adjusted to fit the general population.

To assess coding reliability, two judges compared 142 responses and assessed agreement according to the same rules used in the Maryland survey. The agreement rate was 84.5 percent. On Savior of the Union and Great Emancipator the agreement rate was nearly perfect.

Gallup Poll and National Employee Survey. Cohort effects within a single sample can constitute evidence of generation differences in collective memory,[2] but they constitute an imperfect measure. Not only are such effects difficult to distinguish from those of aging; there are many instances in which period changes are not reflected in age/cohort correlations. After 1950, Lincoln's rating falls over time, but at any given time the youngest, not the oldest, rank him most positively. Blacks' admiration for Lincoln seemed to fall more rapidly than whites' admiration during 1930s (chapter 1), but no age/cohort effects exist among blacks or whites in the 1945 NORC or Gallup samples.

Many events intervene between the birthdate defining one's cohort and the date on which one is questioned. The majority of 60- and 65-year-olds questioned in 1985, for example, looked back on the war years, when they were children and adolescents, as a period of shortages and deprivation for their families.[3] Because these same people were Depression-era children, however, they and their parents probably experienced the war era years as a time of full employment and economic wellbeing. Immersed in the inclusive culture of the late twentieth century, these same 60- and 65-year-olds may have lost the appreciation for Union that they had acquired during the war. Aggregated responses of older members of 1999 and 2001 samples are uncertain indicators of what their aggregated responses would have been as younger members of an earlier sample or of the prevailing climate of belief in the environment of their early years. Comparable surveys taken at two or more points in time mitigates this problem.

Original open responses obtained by Gallup (Poll No. 340, January 31, 1945; Roper Center, Storrs, CT) are no longer available, but we applied to the 2001 National Employee Survey (NES) the Gallup code categories reported in appendix B. Because the NES survey covered only the employed population, all housewives, students, unemployed, disabled, and retired persons were removed from the original Gallup sample. The NES response rate was 60.5 percent. Agreement on open response coding, based on 71 random cases and following the Maryland and Knowledge Network procedure, was 85.6 percent. Again, agreement rates were almost perfect for Savior of the Union and Great Emancipator. Approximately half the disagreements in this sample, as in the previous ones, were about whether to code an ambiguous response as "vague positive," "uninterpretable," or too ambiguous to code as a response.

To further increase the comparability of the Gallup and NES samples, we compared the Gallup results, based on one response per respondent, with both NES first responses and all NES responses. In the process, we took note of sample differences in first mentions. Maryland interviews explicitly asked respondents to expand on their first response. Knowledge Network respondents answered questions at their leisure on an Internet apparatus, providing much longer responses than the Maryland respondents. Since NES interviewers did not probe respondents deeply for additional comments on Lincoln, the latter's responses were shortest of all and yielded the smallest proportion of second responses. For Maryland and Knowledge Network samples, the number of first responses as a percentage of all response is 61.6 percent and 65 percent respectively; for the NES sample, the comparable percentage is 80.7 percent.

So far, the appendix has shown how all the surveys used to gauge Lincoln's prestige and reputation differ. The 1999 University of Maryland replication of the Gallup surveys (1956, 1975, 1985, 1991) on presidential greatness warrants separate comment. In table 5.2, all Gallup nonresponses are included in the computations, and the number of observations equals the sample sizes. However, in table 5.5, focused expressly on white-black differences in attributions of greatness to six presidents, the University of Maryland sample differs from the Gallup samples. This difference involves the codings of race, which account for 70 of the 103 cases excluded from the table. Weighting accounts for most of the remaining difference.

The 1956 Gallup survey contained two response categories, White and Black, as was the case in the 1945 Gallup and NORC surveys (table 4.3 and appendix B). In the 1975 and 1985 surveys, the response categories included White, Black, and Other; in 1991, White, Black, Other, Don't Know, and Refused. The latter two codes measure heightened racial sensitivity and the growing number of mixed-race respondents. The University of Maryland survey consists of similar categories: White, Black, Asian, Other, and Refused.

Exclusion of Asian, Other, Refused, and Don't Know responses, all of which were included in 1975 and 1985 to make them comparable with the earlier (1945, 1956) surveys, explain most of the reduction in table 5.5 cases. All 1999 subsamples, including African American, were weighted to match the actual population. Because the Asian and mixed-race (Other and Don't Know) populations grew significantly by 1999, it had to be excluded from cross-tabulation it diluted the number of African Americans, who once monopolized the nonwhite category.

Responses to identical questions posed to another sample show coding differences across time have only a minor effect on the white-black comparisons. Contracted in 2001 for a survey eventually conducted by Knowledge Networks, the University of Maryland mistakenly replicated the 1999 questions, collecting 849 cases before realizing the mistake. The author and Howard Schuman purchased these data (Project #1408) and the author weighted and analyzed them. Although the sample is 151 cases short of completion, with the number of blacks reduced to 89, it perfectly replicates, within sampling error, the 1999 results. Race differences remain robust in this sample, with 46 percent of whites and 27 of blacks naming Lincoln. The 1999 percentages in table 5.3 were 42 and 28 respectively.

Although no statistically significant differences appear in the 1999 and 2001 samples, three findings are important. The percentage naming Lincoln a great president rises from 40 to 44, which suggests a bottoming out of Lincoln's declining prestige. Also the 8-point spread in South and non-South percentages naming Lincoln drops to 4 points. The political preference difference (Repupblican-Democrat) was 6 percentage points in 1999; 3 percent in 2001. As always, the affluent and better educated are most likely to recognize Lincoln.

In short, changes in sample size have a minimal impact on presidential greatness and on attributions of reasons for greatness. When the truncated 2001 findings are compared to table 5.5, which breaks down these (1999) reasons by race, region, and political-party preference, we find an almost identical pattern.

APPENDIX D

Codes for 1945 Gallup Poll (Roman Font) and 2001 NES (Italic Font)

1. More of a humanitarian, more humane, the people's president, did more for the people and the country, demonstrated the principals of true democracy, more down to earth, a real Christian spirit, more foresight in necessities.

DEMOCRATIC CREED. *Faith in democracy, faith in the people, promoted freedom for all. (No implication about race, though possibly included implicitly as part of more general democratic concern.)*

THE COMMON MAN. *One of the people, poor, humble, down to earth, common sense (soundness as opposed to brilliance of mind); salt of the earth, plain fellow, joke-teller, stays in touch with the people.*

COMPASSIONATE. *Kindness, humanitarian. He sympathized with the underdog, regretted personally the deaths and injuries occurring under his command, commuted death sentences whenever he could.*

RELIGIOUS MAN. *Trusted in God, religious devotion and/or convictions.*

2. Freed the negroes, eliminated slavery, kept the country united.

SAVIOR OF THE UNION. *Kept the states together, healed the nation, preserved Union, kept Americans as one people, prevented secession.*

GREAT EMANCIPATOR. *Slavery, freed slaves, Emancipation Proclamation, gave freedom to all people, freedom.*

RACIAL EQUALITY. *Favored equal rights, with race either explicit (e.g., racial equality, racial integration, racial justice, or against racism) or assumed to be implicit (e.g., equal rights, equality).*

3. Great orator, more eloquent, Gettysburg Address, Emancipation Proclamation.

EXCEPTIONAL ABILITIES OR CHARACTERISTICS. *Oratorical and writing skills, eloquence; great communicator.*

GETTYSBURG ADDRESS. *(Mentioned without reference to other aspect of his policy, his eloquence, or the war.)*

4. Came up the hard way, rose from a mere nobody, overcame poverty, self-made, from log cabin to White House.

SELF-MADE MAN. *Rose from poverty with very little education, log cabin to White House, became successful lawyer despite hardship of early youth, rags to riches.*

WORK ETHIC. *Persistence. Perseverance. Hard Worker. Kept trying despite personal limitations.*

5. Washington too much of an aristocrat, Washington great American myth.

WASHINGTON'S SHORTCOMINGS. *Explicit comparison to Lincoln based on deficit in Washington's personal quality, moral character, or actions.*

6. Lived at a time when need was greater, had more complicated problems to deal with, more trials and tribulations, only a handful in Washington's day.

OVERCOMING OBSTACLES. *Faced and/or overcame political crises and challenges. The times in which he served, the problems he faced, were the most difficult.*

7. Greater statesman.

LEADERSHIP. *Accomplished a lot during war; changed the course of the country; managed the country well; was president during Civil War. (Political leadership is explicit or implied.)*

8. Honest.

HONEST. *Honesty, Honest Abe, truthful.*
INTEGRITY. *Reliability, trustworthy, sincere.*

9. Miscellaneous.

Bravery, Commitment, Moral Characteristics, Physical Appearance, Assassination Victim, Negative Traits, Visual Images, Monuments, School Exposure, Civil War Mention, Greater Knowledge of Lincoln, Direct or Indirect Relation with Lincoln, Vague Positive belief, Wrong but Positive or Neutral belief, Wrong but Negative belief, True but Rarely Mentioned belief.

10. No reason given.

APPENDIX E

Reasons for Designating Abraham Lincoln Greater than George Washington: National Employee Survey 2001: Any Mention

	Any mention[1] N = 1378
1. Emancipation, saving the Union[2]	50.4
2. Humane people's president	6.3
3. Self-made man	3.5
4. Honesty	2.6
5. Greater statesman	14.0
6. Greater problems	9.7
7. Great communicator	1.3
8. Washington's shortcomings	2.2
9. Other	33.8

[1] The percentages are based on an N of 1378, with 104 nonresponses and 45 uninterpretable responses excluded. The percentages do not add to 100 percent because the survey allowed respondents to give more than one response. See appendix D for the codes included under "other." Eighty-one percent of the respondents gave one answer only; 19 percent gave two answers.

[2] This category consists of three separately coded components: saving the Union = 6.8 percent; emancipation = 35.8 percent; equal rights = 7.8 percent.

APPENDIX F

History Textbook List

Adams, James Truslow, and Charles G. Vannest. *The Record of America*. New York: Charles Scribner's Sons, 1935.

Augspurger, Everett, and Richard A. McLemore. *Our Nation's Story*. Chicago: Laidlaw Brothers, 1954.

Barker, Eugene C., William E. Dodd, and Henry Steele Commager. *Our Nation's Development*. Evanston, IL: Row, Peterson and Company, 1934.

Beard, Charles A., and Mary R. Beard. *History of the United States*. New York: Macmillan Company, 1921.

Berkin, Carol, Alan Brinkley, Clayborne Carson, Robert W. Cherry, Robert A. Divine, Eric Foner, Jeffrey B. Morris, Rev. Arthur Wheeler, C. S. C., and Leonard Wood. *A History of The United States: American Voices*. Glenview, IL: Scott. Foresman and Company, 1992.

Boller, Paul F., and E. Jean Tilford. *This Is Our Nation*. St. Louis: Webster Publishing Company, 1961.

Boorstin, D. J., and B. M. Kelly. *A History of The United States*. Upper Saddle River, NJ: Prentice Hall, 1992.

Boyer, Paul, Lewis P. Todd, and Merle Curti. *The American Nation*. Austin: Holt, Rinehart, and Winston, 1995.

Bragdow, Henry W., Samuel P. McCuthen, and Donald R. Ritchie. *History of a Free Nation*. Lake Forest, IL: Glencoe Division of MacMillan/McGraw-Hill School Publishing Company, 1992.

Branson, Margaret Stimmann. *Land of Challenge*. New York: Ginn and Company, 1975.

Buggey, L. Joanne, *America! America!* 2nd ed. Glenview, IL: Scott, Foresman and Company, 1987.

Caughey, John W., John Hope Franklin, and Ernest R. May. *Land of the Free: A History of the United States*. New York: Benziger Brothers, Inc., 1966.

Cayton, Andrew, Elisabeth Perry, Linda Reed, and Allan Winkler. *America: Pathways to the Present.* Saddle River, NJ: Prentice-Hall, 2000.

Danzer, Gerald A., J. Jorge Klor de Alva, Louis E. Wilson, and Nancy Woloch. *The Americans.* Evanston, IL: McDougal Littell, 1998.

Davidson, James W., and Mark H. Lytle. *The United States: A History of the Republic.* Englewood Cliffs, NJ: Prentice-Hall, Inc., 1984.

Downey, M. T., J. R. Giese, and F. D. Metcalf. *United States History: In the Course of Human Events.* St. Paul: West Publishing Co., 1997.

Drewry, H. N., and T. H. O'Connor. *America Is.* New York: Glencoe Division of MacMillan/McGraw-Hill School Publishing Company, 1995.

Faulkner, Harold Underwood, Tyler Kepner, and Hall Bartlett. *The American Way of Life: A History.* New York: Harper & Brothers Publishers, 1941.

Freeland, George E., and James T. Adams. *America's Progress in Civilization.* New York: Charles Scribner's Sons, 1936.

Freeman, Melville. *The Story of Our Republic.* Philadelphia: F. A. Davis Company, 1938.

Garraty, John A. *The Story of America.* Austin: Holt, Rinehart, and Winston, Inc., 1991.

Graff, Henry F., and John A. Krout. *The Adventure of the American People: A History of the United States.* Chicago: Rand McNally & Company, 1966.

Guitteau, William B. *Our United States: A History.* New York: Silver, Burdett and Company, 1920.

Halleck, Reuben P. *History of Our Country: For Higher Grades.* New York: American Book Company, 1923.

Harlow, Ralph V. *Story of America.* New York: Henry Holt and Company, 1943.

Jordan, Winthrop D., Miriam Greenblatt, and John S. Bowes. *The Americans: The History of a People and a Nation.* Evanston, IL: McDougal, Littell & Company, 1985.

King, David C., and Charlotte C. Anderson. *Windows on Our World: The United States.* Boston: Houghton Mifflin Company, 1976.

Moon, Glenn W., and John H. MacGowan. *Story of Our Land and People.* New York: Henry Holt and Company, 1955.

Platt, Nathaniel, and Muriel Jean Drummond. *Our Nation from Its Creation.* Englewood Cliffs, NJ: Prentice-Hall, Inc., 1966.

Reich, Jerome R., and Edward L. Biller. *The Building of the American Nation.* New York: Harcourt, Brace & World, Inc., 1968.

Reigel, Robert E., and Helen Haugh. *United States of America: A History.* New York: Charles Scribner's Sons, 1948.

Schwartz, Melvin, and John R. O'Connor. *Exploring American History*. New York: Globe Book Company, Inc., 1986.

Sellers, Charles G., Henry Mayer, Edward L. Paynter, Alexander Saxton, Neil L. Shumsky, and Kent Smith. *As It Happened: A History of the United States*. New York: Webster Division of McGraw-Hill Book Company, 1975.

Stuckey, Sterling, and Linda Kerrigan Salvucci. *Call to Freedom: Beginnings to 1914*. Austin: Holt, Rinehart and Winston, Inc., 2000.

Todd, Lewis Paul, and Merle Curti. *America's History*. New York: Harcourt, Brace and Company, 1950.

Todd, Lewis Paul, and Merle Curti. *Rise of the American Nation*. 3rd ed. New York: Harcourt and Brace Jovanovich Inc., 1972.

Todd, Lewis Paul, and Merle Curti. *The American Nation*. New York: Holt, Rinehart and Winston, 1972.

Tryon, Rolla M., and Charles R. Lingley. *The American People and Nation*. Boston: Ginn and Company, 1927.

Vannest, Charles G., and Henry L. Smith. *Socialized History of The United States*. New York: Charles Scribner's Sons, 1946.

Weinstein, Allen, and R. Jackson Wilson. *Freedom and Crisis: An American History*. New York: Random House, 1974.

Wilder, Howard B., Robert P. Ludlum, and Harriett McCune Brown. *This Is America's Story*. 3rd ed. Boston: Houghton Mifflin Company, 1966.

APPENDIX G

Religious pilgrimage refers to a journey to sacred places possessing relics of divine significance; secular pilgrimage, to places symbolizing or containing relics of events and men of social and political significance. The capital city of Washington, the Mount Vernon mansion, home of the first president, Independence Hall, where the Constitution was framed, Boston's North Church from whose steeple flashed the signals leading to revolution—these exemplify the immense body of sites attracting annually millions of Americans (for discussion, see chapter 7).

Secular and religious sites perform similar functions: (1) visitation unites citizens by bringing them together at a single place, reaffirming their membership in a single national community and making explicit the values they share; (2) shrines and monuments make tangible the events that frame present problems, struggles, achievements, and failures; and (3) the meanings concretized in historical sites bolster individual patriotism as they legitimate the authority of the state by reinforcing national mores and values.

Shrine visitation has not always been a popular activity. Not until the National Park Service took shape in the 1920s and expanded during the 1930s did the nation's historical sites become democratized. Not until then did the Department of the Interior, in which the Park Service was situated, encourage Americans to visit its 160 sites—including national monuments, military parks, and battlefields—by supplying food, restrooms, maps, and convenient access. Michael Kammen includes this development, an aspect of "ideological populism," shared by both officials and the public to which they appealed, among the main reasons for the Park Service's successful growth.[1]

Given the functions of secular pilgrimage and ideological populism, site visitation trends assume importance. The graphs displaying these trends, which are almost uniformly downward, are limited to sites relevant to the life of Abraham Lincoln, but an identical pattern of decline can be found in most historical sites.[2]

Lincoln sites appearing in the following graphs, with the exception of New Salem and Lincoln's tomb, are under the National Park Service's jurisdiction.

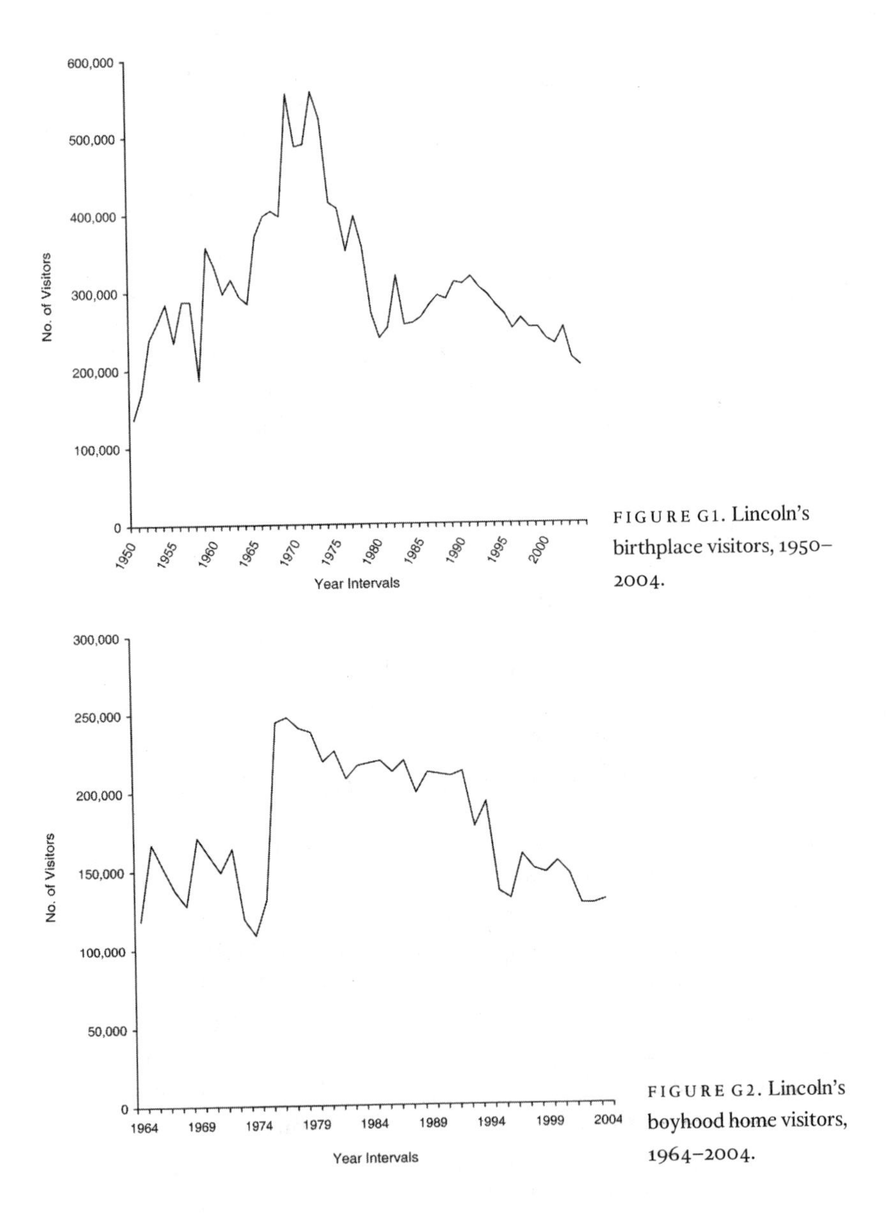

FIGURE G1. Lincoln's birthplace visitors, 1950–2004.

FIGURE G2. Lincoln's boyhood home visitors, 1964–2004.

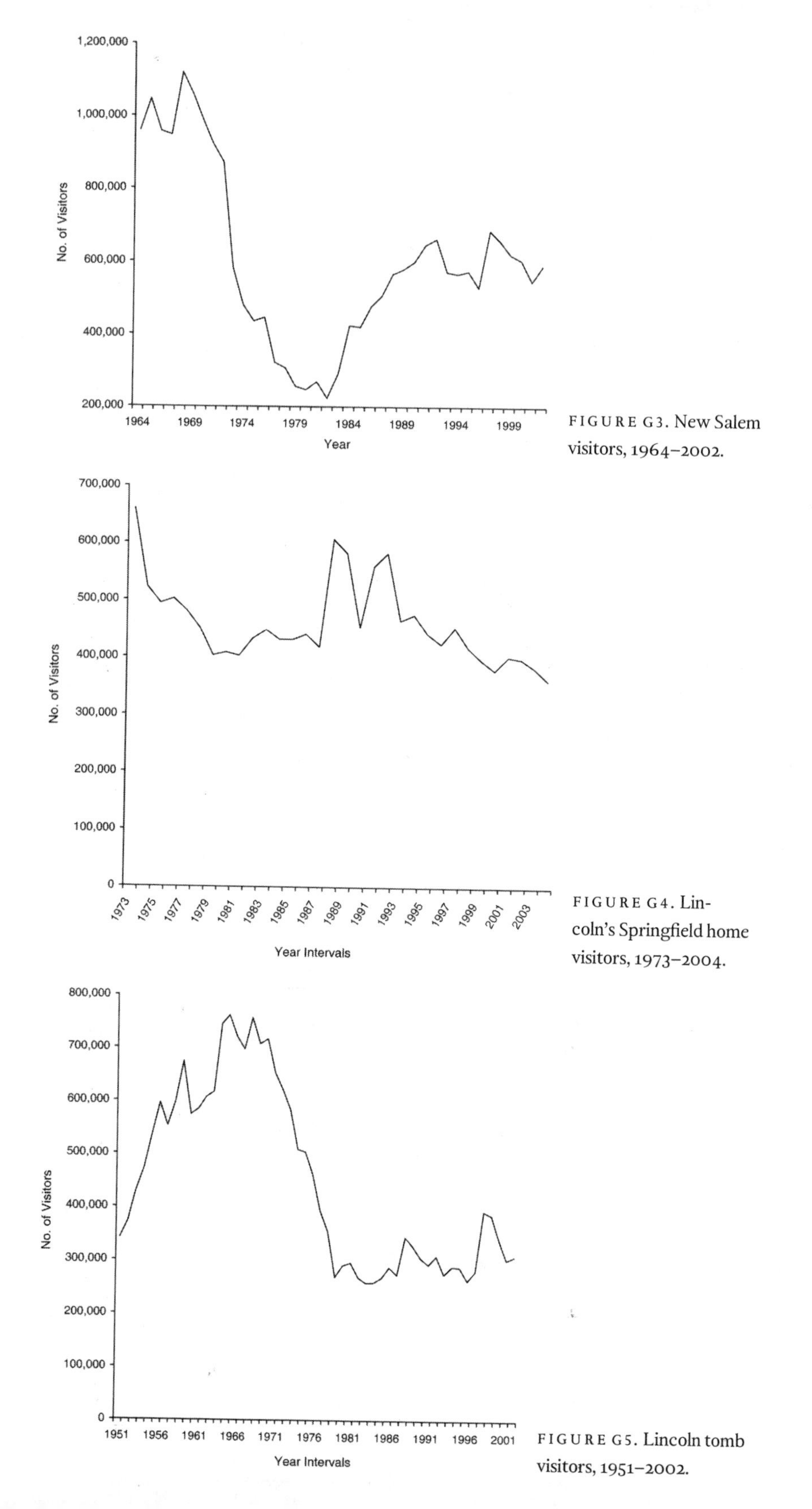

FIGURE G3. New Salem visitors, 1964–2002.

FIGURE G4. Lincoln's Springfield home visitors, 1973–2004.

FIGURE G5. Lincoln tomb visitors, 1951–2002.

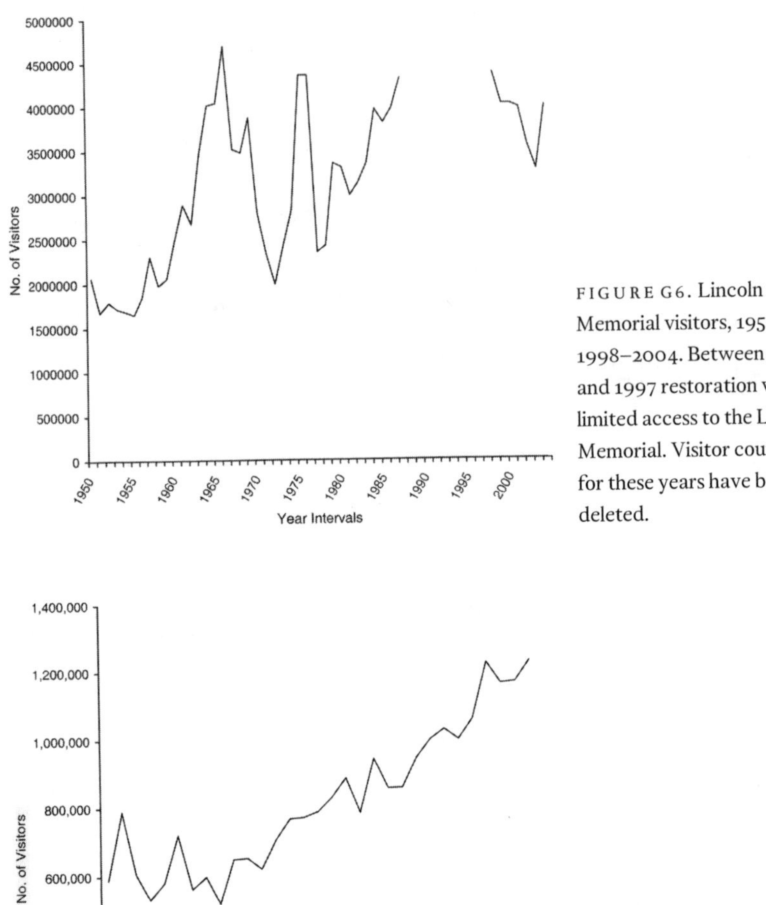

FIGURE G6. Lincoln Memorial visitors, 1950–87, 1998–2004. Between 1988 and 1997 restoration work limited access to the Lincoln Memorial. Visitor counts for these years have been deleted.

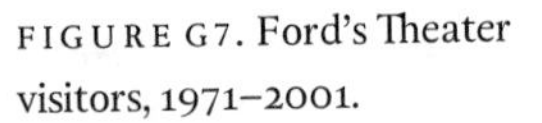

FIGURE G7. Ford's Theater visitors, 1971–2001.

APPENDIX H

*Percentage of Respondents Designating Abraham Lincoln as One of America's Three Greatest Presidents, by Race**

	1956		1975		1985		1991		1999	
	White (n=1,218)	Black (n=151)	White (n=1,362)	Black (n=145)	White (n=1,359)	Black (n=181)	White (n=857)	Black (n=147)	White (n=779)	Black (n=119)
Region										
South	47	34	42	39	34	49	37	31	39	28
Non-South	70	61	52	35	50	44	51	38	46	31
Party										
Republican	73	52	58	20	53	56	54	47	44	36
Independent	69	55	54	30	50	42	49	32	44	48
Democrat	56	49	40	41	41	42	38	32	42	25
Education										
0-11 grade	54	44	33	37	30	40	20	14	23	40
H.S. grad	70	55	49	41	43	46	36	32	35	21
Any college	80	71	64	28	61	49	59	45	52	34
Sex										
Male	63	49	48	43	46	45	49	38	45	44
Female	65	48	51	31	49	46	44	31	43	22
Age										
<20			56	30	51	67	43	23	60	50
20-29	70	60	61	47	56	62	52	44	62	40
30-39	70	55	51	48	57	48	55	41	53	42
40-49	66	49	45	32	51	50	52	30	53	20
50-59	54	45	45	33	45	18	36	42	50	36
60-69	54	38	40	22	41	21	41	0	37	25
70+	56	31	43	29	27	50	30	14	38	33
Residence										
<2,500	62	35	49	42	41	41				
2,500–99,999	72	45	48	43	49	40				
100,000–499,999	59	62	49	30	48	31				
500,000+	66	52	52	35	51	48				

	1956		1975		1985		1991		1999	
	White (n=1,218)	Black (n=151)	White (n=1,362)	Black (n=145)	White (n=1,359)	Black (n=181)	White (n=857)	Black (n=147)	White (n=779)	Black (n=119)
Income										
<10,000			42	36	34	32	42	32		
10,000–14,999[1]			50	41	37	53	36	47	44	26
15,000–19,999			54	9	42	72	47	21		
20,000+[2]			59	71	47	44	50	39	51	37
Religion										
Protestant			50	35	50	44	47	27		
Catholic			44	33	43	40	46	43		
Jewish			57		38		57			
Other			57	60	54	62	52	43		
None			64	44	51	56	45	38		

* Differences in data collection methods and coding for race in Gallup and University of Maryland surveys are discussed in appendix C.

[1] 1999: < 14,999

[2] 1999: > 15,000

APPENDIX I

Percentage of Respondents Designating Abraham Lincoln as One of America's Three Greatest Presidents, by Region

	1956		1975		1985		1991		1999	
	Non-South (n=1,004)	South (n=381)	Non-South (n=1,192)	South (n=335)	Non-South (n=1,285)	South (n=275)	Non-South (n=711)	South (n=302)	Non-South (n=622)	South (n=354)
Race										
White	70	47	52	42	50	34	51	37	46	39
Black	61	34	35	39	44	49	38	31	31	28
Party										
Republican	73	64	61	42	55	42	58	44	45	40
Independent	73	50	54	46	53	33	48	39	47	40
Democrat	64	37	41	38	43	35	41	29	40	32
Education										
0–11 grade	58	39	35	31	33	32	20	17	25	24
H.S. grade	73	53	50	40	44	37	38	30	36	25
Any college	88	51	63	58	63	41	62	45	52	45
Sex										
Male	68	43	50	40	48	35	50	40	43	46
Female	71	46	51	44	51	39	47	31	46	29
Age										
<20			56	38	57	42	39	24	60	40
20–29	75	51	61	58	58	51	52	42	57	56
30–39	75	47	54	38	58	47	57	44	56	46
40–49	71	41	46	33	53	41	53	40	54	37
50–59	60	43	42	49	43	38	43	21	53	38
60–69	56	42	41	29	42	26	43	28	37	33
70+	60	40	46	29	31	18	31	21	36	39
Residence										
<2,500	76	36	54	35	45	29				
2,500–99,999	69	59	49	42	49	45				

	1956		1975		1985		1991		1999	
	Non-South (n=1,004)	South (n=381)	Non-South (n=1,192)	South (n=335)	Non-South (n=1,285)	South (n=275)	Non-South (n=711)	South (n=302)	Non-South (n=622)	South (n=354)
100,000–499,999	70	43	46	49	51	34				
500,000+	64	30	51	47	52	44				
Income										
<10,000			42	39	33	36	50	21		
10,000–14,999[1]			52	38	42	27	35	44	40	40
15,000–19,999[2]			55	43	50	36	46	34		
20,000+			59	59	55	43	54	37	52	42
Religion										
Protestant			52	39	53	36	49	35		
Catholic			44	50	43	36	50	24		
Jewish			59	50	42	29	47	100		
Other			66	0	56	0	50	44		
None			59	89	52	50	45	42		

[1] 1999: < 14,999

[2] 1999: > 15,000

APPENDIX J

Percentage of Respondents Designating Lincoln as One of America's Three Greatest Presidents by Party Identification and Ideology, 1991

Non-South				
Party identification	Conservative (n=291)	Moderate (n=94)	Liberal (n=242)	Total (n=647)
Republican	56	71	64	59
Independent	43	48	53	48
Democrat	38	42	43	41
Total	49	62	52	55

South				
Party identification	Conservative (n=169)	Moderate (n=26)	Liberal (n=75)	Total (n=270)
Republican	45	38	35	43
Independent	47	20	38	40
Democrat	23	25	43	30
Total	37	27	40	38

APPENDIX K

Diversity and the Ideal of Citizenship

America's post-heroic culture, a culture distinguished by the simultaneous expansion of rights and vulgarity, a greening and coarsening of values and demeanor, emerged after World War II. Deepening respect for the dignity of all people is rooted in a disconnection between the individual and his or her nation's history. Opposites comfortably exist. A cultural revolution wherein non-judgmentalism accompanies blind assertion of minority virtues and mainstream vices, rage against establishments, popular films demeaning the presidency and its incumbents, a drive toward diversity marked by new coins, stamps, more inclusive historiography and national biography, the leveling of all authority, marked by the replacement of Washington's birthday with an ambiguous Presidents' Day—none of these items bears directly on the image of Abraham Lincoln, but each constitutes part of the environment within which Lincoln is now perceived and appraised.

Civics texts assigned to secondary school students are crucial parts of this new environment. During the first half of the twentieth century, civics writers followed an "indoctrination" or "citizen transmission" model emphasizing obligation to local, state, and federal governments. Carrying traces of Noah Webster and William McGuffey's readers, these civics texts conveyed their messages through stories of great men and by stressing the privilege of citizenship. "In our time, " wrote William Backus Guitteau, "the greatest thing that any man can say is that he is a citizen of the United States."[1]

Early texts gave highly detailed information about choosing a political party, studying party platforms, voting on taxes, grasping international issues, and organizing holiday celebrations. Authors condemned as "unworthy citizens" those who ignore "Our National Ideals" and fail to learn self-reliance, self-control, kindness, sportsmanship, and the spirit of democracy.[2] Civics instruction, then, conveyed what James Hunter calls an "orthodox" vision of moral authority, secular as well as religious, that arises from a "reality that is independent of, prior to, and more powerful than human experience."[3] One of these realities, the nation-state, transcends the individual as it dignifies him and promotes within him a sense of purpose and wholeness. Embracing absolute definitions of right and wrong, civics education conceives of no multiple truths or "alternate lifestyles." Immigrants are to be treated kindly, their foreign ways tolerated until they assimilate into and appreciate their new world. "The government of the United States and the spirit of American democracy," declared the U.S. Bureau of Education, "know no groups. They know only individuals. . . ."[4] There is one lifestyle, the American Way, for which there is a limited number of heroic models. In this world, proportional ethnic, racial, religious, and gender representation makes no sense; diversity is not found in America's pantheon and is not expected to be found there.

To understand the mentality of early civics education, one must recognize that matters of minority rights, including racial justice, were not merely underemphasized; they were ignored. *The American Citizens Handbook*, produced during the late 1930s by the National Education Association, was organized according to patriotic theme. One section contained patriotic music designed to reinforce post–Civil War reconciliation: "Battle Hymn of the Republic," "Dixie," "Kentucky Home," "God Bless America." Other sections of the book offered patriotic poetry, including Julia Ward Howe's eulogy to Robert E. Lee, Vachal Lindsay's "Abraham Lincoln Walks at Midnight," and pictures of New York University's Hall of Fame residents, which include George Washington, Robert E. Lee, and Abraham Lincoln. The National Education Association urged students to visit the Hall of Fame and provides a list of other historical sites commemorating American achievement and victory. To even imagine such topics occupying a prominent place in contemporary civics textbooks is difficult.[5]

In an effort to characterize this mentality, Rogers M. Smith's *Civic Ideals: Conflicting Visions of Citizenship and American History* (1997) defines the decades up to and, by implication, immediately following, the Progressive Era as an era of "ascriptive Americanism," which implicitly denies full rights to racial, ethnic, religious, and other minorities.[6] However, as the cultural revolution of the 1960s made America more egalitarian and schools urged their students to scrutinize rather than embrace their nation's history, national heroes, the symbols of ascriptive Americanism, seemed out of place.[7] The meaning of citizenship changed. Civics texts urged students to identify with their provincial roots, and taught a new "street law" that ensured the rights of singles living together, gay rights, legal protections in matters of divorce, custody, child and spouse abuse, and abortion. Great achievements and great men are not required to solve these kinds of problems. Tolerance and open-mindedness, not self-control and self-reliance, constitute the core of the post-heroic era's moral character. Accordingly, new texts, like the old, see voting as the major form of citizen participation, but they emphasize advocacy and reform through letter writing, petitioning, lawsuits, protest demonstrations, and, as a last resort, civil disobedience.[8]

The superfluousness of great men in such an environment cannot be exaggerated. Great men are the definers or defenders of national institutions and values; but today's students must make America a place where communities cultivate their own values, a multicultural nation composed of the great arc of human experience. The breadth of that arc can be defined with almost mathematical accuracy in civics textbook illustrations, which display minorities far out of proportion to their presence in the general population, and a disproportionately large part of the book is devoted to their place in American history.

> As you explore what it means to be a citizen of this nation called the United States, it will be useful to look more closely at the diversity of our backgrounds and learn how that diversity contributes to who we are as a people. Our cultural differences make it clear that Americans have not melted together to form one identity. Instead of giving up our separate cultures, we have retained parts of them and, in the process, have enriched American culture as a whole.[9]

In the post-heroic environment, concepts of historical greatness recede in the context of minority rights and minority recognition. Such is the meaning of the "American Mosaic."

To live in a world of growing productivity, expanding markets, and dramatic demographic change, American citizens must cultivate a cosmopolitan rather than national outlook. Not all states have gone as far as Florida in requiring public schools expressly to teach that no "culture is intrinsically superior or inferior to another," but many if not most imply as much. Not all textbooks promote the "cosmopolitan vision," which, according to Ulrich Beck, embraces the globalization of everything, but in most textbooks the link between contemporaneity and nationalism has never been weaker. Because America is but "one land among many," students must know how to participate in international political and economic systems. National boundaries, patriotism, and assertions of national superiority perform no function in a shrinking world.[10] To ask, in a world devoid of exceptionalism and greatness, "What would

Lincoln do?" or what any great man would do in any situation, is to ask an irrelevant question.

American civics reform translates into contemporary language Max Weber's concept of the legal-rational state wherein tradition and charismatic leadership are minimized. State administrative structures are opposed to "heroic leadership" of any kind,[11] but this is not to say that gifted officials, like presidents and military figures, do not arise and are not respected in times of crisis; rather, citizens express gratitude through respect for station, not person. Not President *Lincoln,* but *President* Lincoln, defender of diversity, not unity, is to be recognized in a post-heroic America—especially on its annual Presidents' Day.

Notes

PREFACE

1. Scott Sandage, "A Marble House Divided: The Lincoln Memorial, the Civil Rights Movement, and the Politics of Memory, 1939–1963," *Journal of American History* 80 (June 1993): 135–67.

2. Barry Schwartz, *Abraham Lincoln and the Forge of National Memory* (Chicago: University of Chicago Press, 2000).

3. Clifford Geertz, *Interpretation of Cultures* (New York: Basic Books, 1973), 89.

INTRODUCTION

1. "Epilogue," in U.S. *Report of the Joint Committee on Arrangements on the Commemoration Ceremony in Observance of the 150th Anniversary of the Birth of Abraham Lincoln, 1809–1959*. House Document No. 211 (Washington DC: United States Government Printing Office, 1959), 13–14. House members, in a sequence of speeches, thanked Iowa Representative Fred Schwengel for organizing both the sesquicentennial dinner at which President Eisenhower spoke and the congressional Lincoln Day ceremony (*Congressional Record*, March 9, 1959, 3656–59).

2. Ibid., xii.

3. U.S. *Final Report of the Abraham Lincoln Sesquicentennial Commission* (Washington DC: Government Printing Office, 1959), 69–99.

4. U.S. *Report of the United States George Washington Bicentennial Commission*, 5 vols. (Washington DC: United States Government Printing Office, 1932).

5. Merrill Peterson, *Abraham Lincoln in American Memory* (New York: Oxford University Press, 1994).

6. Gladys E. Lang and Kurt Lang, *Etched in Memory: The Building and Survival of Artistic Reputation* (Chapel Hill: University of North Carolina Press, 1990); Gary A. Fine, "Reputational Entrepreneurs and the Memory of Incompetence: Melting Supporters, Partisan Warriors, and Images of President Harding," *American Journal of Sociology* 101 (1996): 1159–93.

7. Wulf Kansteiner, "Finding Meaning in Memory: A Methodological Critique of Collective Memory Studies," *History and Theory* 41 (2002): 190.

8. For detail on the concept of "structural memory," see Kerwin Lee Klein, "On the Emergence of *Memory* in Historical Discourse," *Representations* 69 (2000): 127–50. For the pioneering exposition of the individual as unit of analysis of collective memory, see Maurice Halbwachs, *The Collective Memory*, ed. Mary Douglas (New York: Harper and Row, [1950] 1980).

9. Pierre Nora, *Realms of Memory*, 3 vols. (New York: Columbia University Press, 1996).

10. Richard Terdiman, *Present Past: Modernity and the Memory Crisis* (Ithaca: Cornell University Press, 1993), 34.

11. Although Michael Schudson's version of the "new structural memory," *Watergate in American Memory* (New York: Basic Books, 1994), is clear and influential, he recognizes that these "rules, laws, standardized procedures, and records . . . books, holidays, statues, souvenirs" (51) derive cultural power from their subjective meaning. See also his exemplary essays on the subjective dynamics of memory and its distortion: "Dynamics of Distortion in Collective Memory," in *Memory Distortion: How Minds, Brains, and Society Reconstruct the Past*, ed. Daniel Schacter (Cambridge, MA: Harvard University Press, 1996), 346–64, and "How Culture Works: Perspectives from the Media on the Efficacy of Symbols," *Theory and Society* 18 (1989): 153–80. Schudson, however, never explored the relation among texts, symbols, observances, and individual beliefs.

12. Mary Douglas, *How Institutions Think* (London: Routledge and Kegan Paul, 1987). Jeffrey Olick dissociates himself from a radically structural approach to memory, but he defines the past represented through sites and symbolic structures as "genuinely collective memory"; the past represented by surveys of individuals constitutes something less: "collected memory" ("Collective Memory: The Two Cultures," *Sociological Theory* 17 [1999]: 345). Taking "collective representations" and other "social facts" as their ultimate units of analysis, many sociologists share Olick's conception. Robert Wuthnow (1987) asserts that we can never know what objects (including history texts and memory sites) mean to individuals; we can only know how these objects relate to one another and to institutional structures. See Emile Durkheim, *The Rules of Sociological Method* (New York: Free Press, [1895] 1964), 1–13; "Individual and Collective Representations," in *Sociology and Philosophy by Emile Durkheim*, ed. Talcott Parsons (New York: Free Press, [1911] 1974), 1–34; Robert Wuthnow, *Meaning and Moral Order: Explorations in Cultural Analysis* (Berkeley: University of California Press, 1987).

13. Klein, "On the Emergence of *Memory* in Historical Discourse," 136. Amos Funkenstein provides the New Structural Memory's most precise formulation:

> Collective memory . . . , like 'language,' can be characterized as a system of signs, symbols, and practices: memorial dates, names of places, monuments and victory arches, museums and texts, customs and manners, stereotyped images (incorporated, for instance, in manners of expression), and even language itself (*Perceptions of Jewish History* [Berkeley: University of California Press, 1993], 6).

Funkenstein, like Merrill Peterson, excludes the individual as an essential unit in collective memory research.

14. James V. Wertsch, *Voices of Collective Remembering* (Cambridge: Cambridge University Press, 2002).

15. Many investigators have insisted on the significance of subjectivity, but since they fail to state positively what subjectivity and its exclusion mean, their comments produce more confusion than clarity. Alon Confino asserts that models excluding the individual have been used "either perfunctorily or as a hollow metaphor defining memory as a monolith" in expressions like "the collective memory of the state." For Susan Crane, in contrast, "all narratives, all sites, all texts remain objects until they are 'read' or referred to by individuals thinking historically." Disconnected from the "actual thought processes of any particular person," James Fentress and Chris Wickham say, collective memory theory renders the individual an automaton and therefore reifies the psychological in the social. The welter of criticism, plainly, contains no concrete alternatives. Jeffrey Prager is more specific than most, but no more concrete: "[c]ollective memory is a sociological concept, though shot through with psychological presumptions" about cognitive frames, identity, and trauma. To recognize that collective memory is permeated with psychological presumptions, however, is not necessarily to know how to bring individuals into collective memory scholarship. Noa Gedi and Yigal Elam, in this regard, throw up their hands. "Since only individuals, not groups, can remember," they declare, the only proper use of collective memory is a metaphorical one.... 'Collective memory' is but a misleading new name for the old familiar 'myth.'" On the other hand, Barbie Zelizer, reviewing the state of collective memory research in 1995, observed: "The collective nature of memory has become so broad that it now seems to include all thoughts, sentiments, and actions about the past that are not recognized as traditional history." All these analytic writings identify a basic problem but they define the problem differently, fail to explain how to solve it, and confuse by taking us in different directions. The relationship between history and perceptions of history is clearly problematic, and the interdisciplinary nature of the field only aggravates the problem by making social memory studies "a nonparadigmatic, transdisciplinary, centerless enterprise." The confusion, however, refers to the analysis, not the reality, of collective memory (or "mnemonic practices," as Jeffrey Olick and Joyce Robbins prefer to call it). See Alon Confino, "Collective Memory and Cultural History: Problems of Method," *American Historical Review* 102 (1997): 1386; Susan A. Crane, "Writing the Individual Back Into Collective Memory," *American Historical Review* 102 (1997): 1381; James Fentress and Chris Wickham, *Social Memory* (Oxford.: Blackwell, 1992); Jeffrey Prager, "Psychology of Collective Memory," in *International Encyclopedia of the Social and Behavioral Sciences*, ed. Neil J. Smelser and Paul L. Baltes (Oxford: Elsevier, 2001), 2223; Noa Gedi and Yigal Elam, "Collective Memory—What is It?" *History and Memory* 8 (1996): 47; Barbie Zelizer, "Reading the Past against the Grain: The Shape of Memory Studies," *Critical Studies in Mass Communications* 12 (1995): 234; Jeffrey K. Olick and Joyce Robbins, "Social Memory Studies: From 'Collective Memory' to the Historical Sociology of Mnemonic Practices," *Annual Review of Sociology* 24 (1998): 105–40.

16. For detail, see citation analysis in Barry Schwartz, *Abraham Lincoln and the Forge of National Memory* (Chicago: University of Chicago Press, 2000), 108–13.

17. Peter H. Gibbon, *A Call to Heroism: Renewing America's Vision of Greatness* (New York: Atlantic Monthly Press, 2002), 125.

18. W. H. Auden, "For the Time Being: A Christmas Oratorio," in *For the Time Being* (London: Faber and Faber, 1945), 61–124.

19. In the Anglo-American Whig tradition, as opposed to the romantic traditions of Western and Central Europe, great men may display ordinary rather than extraordinary talents, must endeavor to maintain, not transform, existing social structures, and, above all, must be anti-authoritarian, transcending ambition and lust for power. The Whig conception of heroic leadership is the opposite of Max Weber's conception of charisma. For discussion of the relationship between eighteenth-century republicanism, historical greatness, and charisma, see Barry Schwartz, "George Washington and the Whig Conception of Heroic Leadership," *American Sociological Review* 48 (1983): 18–33. See also Philip Rieff, *Charisma: The Gift of Grace, and How It Has Been Taken Away from Us* (New York: Pantheon Books, 2007).

20. Octavio Paz, *In Search of the Present*, 1990 Nobel Lecture (New York: Harcourt Brace Jovanovich, 1990), 29.

21. Jean-Francois Lyotard, *The Postmodern Condition* (Minneapolis: University of Minnesota Press [1979] 1984), xxiv, 14, 37–41.

22. Grand narratives are positive narratives that certify themselves "in the pragmatic of [their] own transmission," but this discourse has lost its persuasiveness. Ibid., 27.

23. Clinton Rossiter, *The American Presidency* (New York: New American Library, 1960), 108; Rogers M. Smith, *Stories of Peoplehood: The Politics and Morals of Political Membership* (Cambridge: Cambridge University Press, 2003).

24. Seymour Martin Lipset, *American Exceptionalism: A Double-Edged Sword* (New York: W. W. Norton, 1996), 19–23; *Continental Divide: The Values and Institutions of the United States and Canada* (Washington DC: Canadian-American Committee, 1990).

25. Robert Penn Warren, *The Legacy of the Civil War* (New York: Vintage, 1964), 4.

26. Jim Cullen, *The Civil War in Popular Culture* (Washington DC: Smithsonian Institution Press, 1995).

27. Robert N. Bellah, "Civil Religion in America," in *Beyond Belief: Essays on Religion in a Post-Traditional World* (New York: Harper and Row, 1976), 177–78.

28. Garry Wills, *Lincoln at Gettysburg: The Words That Remade America* (New York: Simon and Schuster, 1992).

29. Christopher Lasch, *The Culture of Narcissism* (New York: W. W. Norton, 1979), 5. Lasch is describing the essence of a cultural pattern which, in David Ashley's (1994) view, is the "inevitable reflection of a logic of disintegration." To be disconnected from the past is inevitably to live without place, orientation, or purpose. Postmodernists on opposite sides of the ideological spectrum bear witness to this condition. Whether resulting from late capitalism, as Frederic Jameson argues on the left, or from the breakdown of traditional institutions, as Daniel Bell claims on the right, the loss of historical continuity is a key aspect of contemporary alienation. Alienation is manifest in the experience of the individual because he or she needs categories, rules, standards of judgment, and behavioral programs that are acquired from moral communities of the past. Temporally fractured communities cannot provide these anchor points. Alienation is also manifest in the society. Societies are not constituted by their existence at a single point in time; they exist through time. Because societies are temporally constituted, collective amnesia weakens their structures, confounds their members' self-conceptions, and intensifies their alienation from the traditions in which they once located themselves. "To be cut off from the past of one's society is as disordering

to the individual and to the society as being cut off in the present" (Edward A. Shils, *Tradition* [Chicago: University of Illinois Press, 1981], 326–27). See also David Ashley, "Postmodernism and Antifoundationalism," in *Postmodernism and Social Inquiry*, ed. David R. Dickens and Andrea Fontana (New York: Guilford Press, 1994), 57; Frederic Jameson, "Postmodernism, or, The Cultural Logic of Late Capitalism," *New Left Review* 146 (1984): 53–92; Daniel Bell, *The Contradictions of Capitalism* (New York: Basic Books, 1976).

30. Karl Mannheim, "The Problem of Generations," in *Essays in the Sociology of Knowledge*, ed. Paul Keckemeti (London: Routledge and Kegan Paul, [1928] 1952), 290.

31. William Straus and Neil Howe refer to the "Rights and Justice Generation" as "the Silent Generation" in *Generations: The History of America's Future, 1584 to 2069* (New York: William Morrow and Company, 1991), 279–94.

32. Ibid., 299–316.

33. Ibid., 317–34. Straus and Howe designate "The Uncommitted Generation" (popularly known as Generation X) as the "The 13ers," which refers to its place in a complex generational cycle beginning with the Puritans.

34. This typology of generations draws on William Strauss and Neil Howe's *Generations*. The moral life of the Uncommitted Generation is epitomized in *One Nation, After All* by Alan Wolfe, who is struck by his respondents' extraordinary nonjudgmentalism, which is in turn an aspect of the new "Morality Writ Small" (New York: Viking, 1998), 275–322.

35. For detailed analysis of the concept of collective memory, including the relationship among history, commemoration, and belief, see Barry Schwartz, "Collective Memory," in *Blackwell Encyclopedia of Sociology*, ed. George Ritzer (Oxford: Blackwell, 2006); Barry Schwartz, "Commemorative Objects," in *International Encyclopedia of the Social and Behavioral Sciences*, ed. Neil J. Smelser and Paul L. Baltes (Oxford: Elsevier, 2001), 2267–72. For formulations that place less emphasis on the relations among history, commemoration, and belief, see Olick and Robbins, "Social Memory Studies."

36. Katherine W. Hannaford, "'Now He Belongs to the Ages': The Legacy of Abraham Lincoln, Abstract and Concrete," *American Quarterly* 51 (1999): 877.

37. Jay F. Gubrium, "For a Cautious Naturalism" in *Reconsidering Social Constructionism: Debates in Social Problems Theory*, ed. Gale Miller and James A. Holstein (New York: Aldine de Gruyter, 1993), 89–101. See also Gary A. Fine, *Constructing Difficult Reputations* (Chicago: University of Chicago Press, 2001), 13–17. The radical claims of "strict constructionism," which parenthesizes reality and minimizes its relevance as a determinant of perception, must be distinguished from the moderate claims of "cautious naturalism" and "contextual constructionism," which requires an objective baseline for analysis of perception and belief. See Joel Best, "But Seriously, Folks: The Limitations of the Strict Constructionist Interpretations of Social Problems," in *Reconsidering Social Constructionism*. Nachman Ben-Yehuda applies this conception to collective memory in *The Masada Myth: Collective Memory and Mythmaking in Israel* (Madison: University of Wisconsin Press, 1995), 20–22.

38. Gabor S. Boritt, *Lincoln and the Economics of the American Dream* (Urbana: University of Illinois Press, [1978] 1994).

39. Max Lerner, "Lincoln in the Civil War," in *Ideas for the Ice Age: Studies in a Revolutionary Era* (New York: Viking Press, 1941), 395.

40. David Donald, *Lincoln* (Cambridge, MA: Harvard University Press, 1995), 464.

41. Abraham Lincoln to Edward Everett, November 20, 1863, *Collected Works of Abraham Lincoln*, 9 vols., ed. Roy A. Basler (New Brunswick: Rutgers University Press, 1953), 7:24.

42. Edward Everett, *Address of Hon. Edward Everett at the Consecration of the National Cemetery at Gettysburg, 19th November, 1863* (Boston: Little, Brown and Company, 1864), 69–70. This document, published for the benefit of the Cemetery Monument Fund, contains all religious and musical exercises of the occasion, including President Lincoln's address.

43. Ibid., 70.

44. For detail on the impact of secession in the Mississippi Valley, see E. Merton Coulter, "Effects of Secession upon the Commerce of the Mississippi Valley," *Mississippi Valley Historical Review* 3 (December 1916): 275–300.

45. Michael Lind, *What Lincoln Believed: The Values and Convictions of America's Greatest President* (New York: Doubleday, 2004). The most commonly mentioned weakness of this book is invariably Lind's conclusion that Lincoln's passion for emancipation did not include a passion for racial integration in the twenty-first century's understanding of the word. James M. McPherson's review of the book deals with nothing but Lind's treatment of Lincoln on race ("Twist and Shout," *The Nation*, June 13, 2005). Allen Guelzo presents a far more comprehensive and informative review, but he too finds Lind's characterization of Lincoln on race to be his "most egregious failure" ("Two Cheers for Lincoln," *Christianity Today*, January 1, 2006). On the other hand, Scott Malcomson, a *Times* magazine editor, delivers a review of Lind focusing on what is unique in his book: Lincoln's understanding of the fate of democracy (*New York Times*, May 22, 2005). Wayne A. Holts, too, is willing to bracket if not accept Lind's argument about race and appreciate his fresh insights into Lincoln's concerns about democracy (*National Catholic Reporter*, October 7, 2005).

46. Robert Darnton, *George Washington's False Teeth: An Unconventional Guide to the Eighteenth Century* (New York: W. W. Norton, 2003), 89–106. See esp. 96–101.

47. Eric Foner, *Free Soil, Free Men: The Ideology of the Republican Party before the Civil War* (New York: Oxford University Press, 1970). James G. Randall, *Lincoln and the South* (Louisiana State University Press, 1946), 108–9. To mark the official day of emancipation, January 1, 1863, Secretary of War Stanton suggested a medal inscribed with the words *omne ignotum pro mirifico* (*All things unknown are thought to be wonderful*), 102–3.

48. Schwartz, *Abraham Lincoln and the Forge of National Memory*.

49. Foner, *Free Soil, Free Men*; Donald, *Lincoln*; John Patrick Diggens, *On Hallowed Ground: Abraham Lincoln and the Foundations of American History* (New Haven: Yale University Press, 2000); Edward L. Ayres, *What Caused the Civil War: Reflections on the South and Southern History* (New York: W. W. Norton, 2005), esp. "Worrying about the Civil War," 103–30; Ayres, *In the Presence of Mine Enemies: The Civil War in the Heart of America, 1859–1863* (New York: W. W. Norton, 2003); Lind, *What Lincoln Believed: The Values and Convictions of America's Greatest President*. See also Herman Belz, *Reconstructing the Union: Theory and Policy during the Civil War* (Ithaca: Cornell University Press, 1969); Barrington

Moore, "The American Civil War: The Last Capitalist Revolution," in *Social Origins of Dictatorship and Democracy* (Boston: Beacon Press, 1966), 111–58.

50. As one example, Richard Norton Smith, first director of the Abraham Lincoln Museum, declared that the museum must be judged in terms of its effect on race relations. *High Tech Lincoln*, DVD documentary, A&E Television Networks, 2005.

51. Tom Brokaw, *The Greatest Generation* (New York: Random House, 1998).

52. Daniel Bell, *The Coming of Postindustrial Society* (New York: Basic Books, 1973).

53. Jameson, "Postmodernism, or, The Cultural Logic of Late Capitalism"; Bell, *The Cultural Contradictions of Capitalism.*

54. The matter transcends academic circles. Studs Terkel observes that memory was "throbbingly present" throughout the 1940s and 1950s; ever since, "amnesia has been easier to come by." The fragmenting of past and present leads to another aspect of postmodern consciousness—"nostalgia," which operates "through stylistic conventions, conveying pastness through the glossy qualities of the image." Nostalgia replaces the succession of events that once defined "real history" with a succession of aesthetic styles and embellished facsimiles. Not the grief of the Civil War, but its fashions, musical sounds, and etiquette; not the pain of the Great Depression, but the shape of its automobiles, style of men's hats and women's dresses—this is what nostalgia is about. Incorporating the waning of affect and depthlessness of the postmodern age, nostalgia explains how massive interest in the past is sustained in a present-oriented culture. In the nostalgic mode, the present is colonized by images valued solely for their capacity to distract and entertain. Frederic Jameson, "Postmodernism, or, The Cultural Logic of Late Capitalism," 60–62, 64, 66–68; Michael Kammen, *The Mystic Chords of Memory* (New York: Knopf, 1991), 656–57; Donald N. Levine, *Visions of the Sociological Tradition* (Chicago: University of Chicago Press, 1995), 10; Alasdair MacIntyre, *After Virtue: A Study in Moral Theory* (London: Duckworth, 1981), 201; Robert J. Lifton, "Protean Man," *Partisan Review* 35 (1968): 14–17; Scott Lash and John Urry, *The End of Organized Capitalism* (Madison: University of Wisconsin Press, 1987), 299; David Harvey, *The Condition of Postmodernity,* (London: Blackwell, 1990), 54; Zygmund Bauman, "From Pilgrim to Tourist—or a Short History of Identity," in *Questions of Cultural Identity*, ed. Stuart Hall and Paul du Gay (London: Sage, 1996), 24–25; Studs Terkel, *The Great Divide* (New York: Pantheon, 1988), 3. See also Steven Best, *The Politics of Historical Vision* (New York: Guilford Press, 1995), xii.

55. Arthur M. Schlesinger Jr., *The Disuniting of America: Reflections on a Multicultural Society* (New York: W. W. Norton, 1991); John Bodnar, *Remaking America: Public Memory, Commemoration, and Patriotism in the Twentieth Century* (Princeton: Princeton University Press, 1992); Charles Taylor, *Multicultualism: Examining the Politics of Recognition,* ed. and introduced by Amy Gutman (Princeton: Princeton University Press, 1994).

CHAPTER ONE

1. Edmund Stillman, "The Great Euphoria," in *American Heritage: 1920s & 1930s* (New York: American Heritage, 1987), 80, 82, 96.

2. Nathaniel W. Stephenson, *Lincoln: An Account of His Personal Life, Especially of Its Springs of Action as Revealed and Deepened by the Ordeal of War* (Indianapolis: Bobbs-Merrill, 1922); "Lincoln and the Progress of Nationality in the North," *Annual Report*

of the American Historical Association 1 (1919): 351–63 (reprinted by the Government Printing Office in 1923); Mark E. Neely Jr., *The Abraham Lincoln Encyclopedia* (New York: Da Capo Press, 1982), 291.

3. Ida M. Tarbell, "Abraham Lincoln's Money Sense," *The American Magazine* 99 (September 1923): 13–15.

4. Frederick Dallinger, *Congressional Record*, February 21, 1925, 4444. Not all biographers portrayed Lincoln positively. During the 1920s, the heyday of muckraking, many biographers made a name for themselves by ridiculing American heroes. Lincoln's policies, even his moral character, were criticized during this decade, but not a single debunking biography appeared outside the South. When Edgar Lee Masters's genuinely hostile biography of Lincoln appeared in 1930, most reviewers attributed it to Masters's personality, not the culture of the previous decade (*Lincoln: The Man* [New York: Dodd, Mead, 1931]).

5. Carl Sandburg, *Abraham Lincoln: The Prairie Years*, 2 vols. (New York: Harcourt Brace, 1926).

6. Michael Kammen, *Mystic Chords of Memory: The Transformation of Tradition in American Culture* (New York: Alfred Knopf, 1991), 417–43.

7. John Steinbeck's *Grapes of Wrath* (New York: Vintage Press, 1939) depicts vividly the grief of leaving the land. Return to the land, one of the most appealing themes of Depression populism, is played out in King Vidor's *Our Daily Bread* (1934). Vidor's film makes no mention of Lincoln but captures the essential pattern of his myth. It begins with a city couple moving to the countryside and establishing a commune with desperate people looking for work. It ends with an irrigation project engaging the strength of the whole community. Rhythmic sounds of the people's picks and shovels echo those of Lincoln's ax. The people save the commune, just as he saved the Union.

8. Alfred Kazin cited in Alfred Haworth Jones, *Roosevelt's Image Brokers: The Use of the Lincoln Symbol* (Port Washington, NY: Kennikut Press, 1974), 24.

9. Bernard DeVoto, cited in ibid., 49.

10. Max Lerner, "Men Who Would Be President," *Nation*, July 22, 1940, 752.

11. Emile Durkheim, *Suicide* (New York: The Free Press, 1951), 208.

12. Harvey Swados, ed., *The American Writer and the Great Depression* (Indianapolis: Bobbs-Merrill, 1966), xv.

13. Ibid., xiv. See also Frank Freidel, *America in the Twentieth Century* (New York: Knopf, 1960), 352–58.

14. Cited in Michael Kammen, *Mystic Chords of Memory*, 479; see also 443, 504–5. Walker Evans and James Agee are the representative men, producing stories and pictures that America had come to associate with the youth of Abraham Lincoln (*Let Us Now Praise Famous Men* [Boston: Houghton Mifflin, 1941]).

15. See Alan Dawley, *Struggles for Justice: Social Responsibility and the Liberal State* (Cambridge, MA: Harvard University Press, 1991).

16. In the introduction to *Our Nation's Development* ([Evanston, IL: Row, Peterson and Company, 1934], iv), Eugene Barker, William Dodd, and Henry Steele Commager explained: "Since civilized man is largely controlled by his real or supposed economic wants, it follows that . . . their interpretation of American history [must be] wholly social and largely economic." James T. Adams and Charles G. Vannest's *The Record of America* ([New York: Charles Scribner's Sons, 1935], 2) took a similar approach: "The

political life of a country is only a small part of its history. That is a part and a very important part, but the development socially, economically, and culturally is equally and sometimes more important." George Freeland's *America's Progress in Civilization* ([New York: Charles Scribner's Sons, 1936], iv) attempted "to make citizens better equipped to face realities" and to know that historical reality consists of a complex set of impersonal forces. To know history well, "geography, civics, economics, sociology, and anthropology [must be] brought together."

17. Eric C. Bellquist, *National Republic* (December 1936): 18.

18. Abraham Lincoln to Albert G. Hodges, April 4, 1864, in Roy P. Basler, ed., *Collected Works of Abraham Lincoln* (New Brunswick: Rutgers University Press, 1953), 7:281.

19. Henry F. May, *The End of American Innocence* (New York: Quadrangle, [1959] 1964), 200.

20. Claude Levi-Strauss, *Totemism* (Boston: Beacon Press, 1962).

21. J. G. A. Pocock, "The Classical Theory of Deference," *American Historical Review* 81 (1976): 516; David Spring, "Walter Bagehot and Deference," ibid.: 524–31; Richard W. Davis, "Deference and Aristocracy in the Time of the Great Reform Act," ibid.: 532–39; Edward A. Shils, "Deference," in *Center and Periphery: Studies in Macrosociology* (Chicago: University of Chicago Press, 1975), 276–303.

22. Robert Emmet Sherwood, cited in Richard J. S. Gutman, "Three Outstanding Abes: Lincoln's Image in the Cinema, Part II, 1931–1977," *Lincoln Herald* 80 (1978): 123.

23. Michael Deming, *The Cultural Front: The Laboring of American Culture in the Twentieth Century* (New York: Verso, 1997). Deming excluded the *Grapes of Wrath* from this Popular Front literature because it focused too much on weather and not enough on oppression as the cause of the Oakies' problems.

24. Lerner, "Men Who Would Be President," 753.

25. Jones, *Roosevelt's Image Brokers*, 29. That Lincoln needed "reputational entrepreneurs"—professional scholars, artists, and commentators who found some reason to represent him to the public and keep his image alive—is certain, but there were more general influences. Lincoln Day banquets became more numerous and elaborate as Roosevelt and his fellow Democrats challenged Republican dominance. In large non-Southern cities, hundreds of churches observed Lincoln Day with sermons devoted to his virtues (see, for one example, *Los Angeles Times*, February 11, 1935, pt.2, 3, 5). Boy Scout troops, GAR posts, business clubs, municipal bodies, schools, and scores of other civil organizations recognized Lincoln in their own ways.

26. The great men of the 1930s included George Washington as well as Abraham Lincoln. In 1932, the federal government marked the bicentennial of Washington's birth with a major celebration. The Bicentennial Commission spent nine months coordinating four million separate ceremonies by local, state, and federal organizations; it distributed millions of monographs, brochures, and pictures, and funded scholarly research. The 1937 bicentennial of the Constitution sustained, if not enlarged, Washington's great stature. In 1939 another sesquicentennial marked Washington's first inauguration—the beginning of constitutional government. New York City marked the occasion with its most conspicuous emblem: a sixty-five-foot plaster statue of the first president at the entrance to the world's fair. However, the values that Washington embodied—liberty, strength, justice, duty, and patriotism (as opposed to equality,

justice, and compassion)—resonated with the culture of the 1920s, when the bicentennial and sesquicentennial events were conceived. Because the Depression had drastically changed the public mood, the 1932 bicentennial failed to do for Washington what the 1909 centennial did for Lincoln. Public interest in Washington was relatively strong during the late 1920s and early 1930s, but it could not sustain itself throughout the Depression. The Depression years belonged to Lincoln.

27. Jan Assman, "Collective Memory and Cultural Identity," *New German Critique* 65 (1995): 125–33.

28. See, for example, *Philadelphia Record,* February 2, 1937,1, 9, 12.

29. Charles Horton Cooley, *Human Nature and the Social Order* (New York: Schocken [1902] 1964), 386.

30. George S. Viereck, "Our Appalling Crisis—What Would Lincoln Do?" *Liberty Magazine* (February 1935): 11.

31. *Los Angeles Times,* February, 12, 1931, pt. 2, 4.

32. *Chicago Tribune,* February 12, 1930, 1.

33. For a discussion of the political and moral functions of "bringing to presence" or "manifesting" the past iconographically, see Eugene Miller and Barry Schwartz, "The Icon of the New Republic," *Review of Politics* 47 (1985): 516–43.

34. *Boston Daily Globe,* February 12–13, 1933, 18. Lincoln's providing a "guiding pattern" rather than concrete motive is illustrated in the day's editorial cartoons. "Ideals of Lincoln," for example, appear at the summit of a hill toward which an automobile carrying "Young Republicans" is headed. The caption: "It Is Still the Right Road" (*Chicago Tribune,* February 12, 1936, 16). No specifics, but the general point is clear for all who can see.

35. *New York Times,* "The Leadership of Lincoln Has Potent Meaning Today," February 12, 1933, sec. 8, 7.

36. Alan Wolfe, *Return to Greatness: How America Lost Its Sense of Purpose and What It Needs to Do to Recover It* (Princeton: Princeton University Press, 2005), 6. Wolfe asserts that national greatness is built upon the foundation of large states in which power is centralized. The conservative paradigm, from Emile Durkheim to de Tocqueville, structures power in such a way that intermediary, local units buffer the individual from the irresistible power of the state. Wolfe believes this conservative paradigm is conducive to national weakness.

37. *Mansfield (Ohio) News-Journal,* editorial cartoon, February 12, 1935, 4.

38. A Bell Telephone Company advertisement, too, shows a young boy standing in front of a portrait of Lincoln as he listens to a story told by his uncle, for whom "the memory of the Great Emancipator was a kind of religion" (and his likeness, accordingly, a sacred icon).

39. Plutarch's lives are *paradigmata* because they are intended to provide the reader with models for living. Paradigmata take the form of pictorial images as well as narrative. No great war can be fought, no great man or woman can survive or die, without being framed and made into a paradigm. Pictorial paradigmata are sustained by a psychological warrant. To gaze upon another, psychoanalyst Otto Fenichel observed, is to establish a relationship with him and what he represents. Through "ocular introjection" the object of the gaze can become an object of identification. "We derive moral strength by looking at someone whom we desire to copy—the very word copy

implies looking" (Otto Fenichel, "The Scoptophilic Instinct and Identification," in *Collected Papers* [New York: W. W. Norton, 1953], 1:393).

40. Images of people looking at images of Lincoln and Lincoln looking down on his people appeared not only on canvas and print but also in film. In *Mr. Smith Goes to Washington,* the protagonist, Jefferson Smith, is entranced by the statue of Lincoln and gazes upon it intently to the strains of "Red River Valley," "Battle Hymn of the Republic," and "Star Spangled Banner." The music defines what Mr. Smith sees in the Memorial: America itself. The scene's climax is reached when a young boy reads the Gettysburg Address, inscribed on the granite wall, while his grandfather gazes at Lincoln. Such visual rhetoric seemed perfectly natural on the screen of the 1939 movie theater.

41. *Chicago Tribune,* February 12, 1930, 1.

42. Sculpture, too, portrayed the epic man. In South Dakota appeared a new monumental form, chiseled into the side of Mount Rushmore. The first image, Lincoln's head, was unveiled and dedicated in 1937. Neoclassical statues made a similar, if less massive, impression. Although dedicated in smaller number during the 1930s than in any previous decade, neoclassical forms sustained a heroic conception of Lincoln that almost everyone shared. (For detail, see Barry Schwartz, "Iconography and Collective Memory: Lincoln's Image in the American Mind," *Sociological Quarterly* 32 (1991): 301–20, esp. 313).

43. Max Lerner, "I Thought of Lincoln," *New Republic* 104 (February 10, 1941): 177.

44. Clarence C. Dill, *Congressional Record* (Senate), February 12, 1930, 3499.

45. Ibid., February 14, 1932, 3806. Senator Dill appears to have been the poem's author.

46. Pennsylvania governor Gifford Pinchot, assuming the public's receptiveness to such analogy, announced that "Our greatest task is to rid our people of the shackles of concentrated wealth and power." Liberty, in Lincoln's view, means that no man, "black or white," should ever have to bow "in personal or economic submission" to any other man: "As Lincoln understood liberty, this Nation is not free to-day. How can men be free and equal when multimillionaires grow fat and multiply while millions go hungry and cold? How can the Nation be free when the policies of its Government are dictated by a handful of the overrich? How can its people be free when its God-given wealth is taken from the many and so concentrated in few hands that the 1930 incomes of 504 men could have bought the entire wheat crop of this country and the entire cotton crop besides? How can its business be free when 200 out of 300,000 corporations control half of its corporate wealth?" How can the nation's people be free, the governor concluded, when America's president (Hoover) is the corporations' rather than the people's servant? Democratic representative James Major of Illinois inserted Governor Pinchot's Springfield, Illinois, address into the *Congressional Record,* February 22, 1932, 4471.

47. Carl Sandburg, "Lincoln-Roosevelt," *Today* (February 10, 1934): 5. For another comparison of Lincoln and Roosevelt, see *New York Times,* February 13, 1940, 25.

48. Cited in Jones, *Roosevelt's Image Brokers,* 69.

49. Lerner, "I Thought of Lincoln," 177.

50. Many metaphors conveyed the Democratic position. When Republicans claimed that the New Deal endangered American liberties by interfering in the free

market, Roosevelt responded with Lincoln's words: "The shepherd drives the wolf from the sheep's throat, for which the sheep thanks the shepherd as his liberator, while the wolf denounces him for the same act, as the destroyer of liberty... Plainly, the sheep and the wolf are not agreed upon a definition of the word liberty; and precisely the same difference prevails today among us human creatures... and all professing to love liberty. Hence we behold the process by which thousands are daily passing from under the yoke of bondage hailed by some as the advance of liberty, and bewailed by others as the destruction of all liberty." Roosevelt concluded: "My friends, in 1936, the people have again been doing something to define liberty. And the wolf's dictionary has again been repudiated." Roosevelt did not need to explain which political party was the wolf's. "Remarks on Liberty," October 23, 1940, *The Public Papers and Addresses of Franklin D. Roosevelt* (New York: Macmillan Company, [1941] 1950), 9:484.

51. Victor Turner, *Dramas, Fields, and Metaphors* (Ithaca: Cornell University Press, 1974), 26–27.

52. Inserted into the record by Edward H. Rees, "We Are Coming, Father Abraham!" *Congressional Record* (House of Representatives; hereafter HR), February 13, 1940, 735–36.

53. Inserted into the record by John Joseph O'Connor, *Congressional Record* (HR), February 29, 1932, 4978.

54. Roosevelt, January 7, 1939, *Public Papers and Addresses*, 8:65.

55. As the Grand Old Party elephant points to a cartooned bust of Lincoln, he asks Roosevelt and his "communist" supporters: "Which of you borrowed my Lincoln last?"

56. Alexis de Tocqueville, *Democracy in America* (New York: Alfred Knopf, 1945), 2:336–37.

57. *Chicago Daily Tribune*, February 12, 1938, 1.

58. *Los Angeles Times*, February 13, 1931, 2.

59. *Nebraska State Journal*, February 14, 1939, 5.

60. Inserted into the record by Arthur H. Vandenberg, *Congressional Record* (Senate), June 16, 1930, 10868, 10869–71. See also John Wesley Hill, "Abraham Lincoln of Today," *National Republic* 20 (August 1932): 24–25.

61. Senator Daniel Hastings, inserted into the record by George P. Darrow, "Lincoln and the Republican Party," *Congressional Record* (HR), February 14, 1935, 1985.

62. A few ultrasuspicious men, including Representative Jacob Thorkelson of Montana, believed that "an intensely organized and financially powerful international anti-Christian horde, seeking world conquest" had gained control of the government. Thorkelson was referring to a Jewish conspiracy. Most Americans, however, thought about domestic matters in the context of a world struggle among democracy, communism, and fascism. In 1932, New Deal tickets gained the most votes, but more than a million people voted for socialist and communist candidates. Less visible, but equally significant, was the appeal of fascism. This influence was less evident in the claims of fascist organizations, like the German-American Bund, and fascist agitators, like Father Charles Coughlin, than in the insinuations of the popular media. *Gabriel Over the White House* (1933), a film produced by Randolph Hearst in his own image, is about a president who proclaims himself dictator. He puts the unemployed to work in camps, treats criminals to summary trial and execution, and uses force to compel other nations

to pay their war debts and to disarm. The story seemed to many a good model for dealing with the difficult problems of the day, but to others it represented fascism. Ann Morrow Lindbergh's book, which had gone through seven printings by 1940, took a subtler approach. Wife of the famous aviator, Charles, who admired Nazism and opposed American aid to Great Britain, Mrs. Lindbergh criticized both Hitler and Stalin but declared that "the wave of the future is coming and there is no fighting it." It was the wave that put Hitler and Stalin into power, and which America had to understand, in her view, sooner or later. Anne Morrow Lindbergh, *The Wave of the Future: A Confession of Faith* (New York: Harcourt, Brace and Company, 1940), 37.

63. *New York Times,* March 31, 1935, sec. 4, 8.

64. *Congressional Record* (HR), February 21, 1935, 2405.

65. *Papers of Letitia B. Martin,* U.S. Library of Congress, Manuscript Division, Box 3316.

66. Poster copyright by Arthur L. Brownell, 1932. The text is printed as a column on rectangular cardboard with a hole punched in the top for the purpose of mounting it with a string to a wall hook or other object.

67. Ralph E. Church, "Abraham Lincoln Warned Us," *Congressional Record* (HR), October 14, 1940, 6501.

68. *Papers of Letitia B. Martin,* Box 3316.

69. In the conservative worldview, tyranny and taxation were aspects of one another. Staunch conservatives therefore put the slavery metaphor to their service of reducing taxation rather than protecting the interests of labor. "If / Abe Lincoln / Were to return / To earth on this / His birthday," according to one of the *Chicago Tribune*'s poetic columnists, he would reduce the size of government and get rid of the bureaucrats, "Who swarm the streets / Like clouds of grasshoppers." Above all, Abe would say to himself: "When I was on earth / I freed / The slaves. / I wish I might return / That I could free / The taxpayers"(February 12, 1932), 12.

70. Charles A. Plumley, "Lincoln's birthday." Inserted into the record by James T. Davis, *Congressional Record* (Senate), February 14, 1935, 1908.

71. Andrew J. Polsky, *The Rise of the Therapeutic State* (Princeton: Princeton University Press, 1991), 139–45.

72. Max Lerner, "The Lincoln Image," *New Republic* 98 (March 8, 1939): 135–36.

73. Hamilton Fish, "Constitutional Government." Inserted into the record by Dewey Jackson Short, *Congressional Record* (HR), February 14, 1935, 1988.

74. *Atlanta Daily World,* February 12, 1932, 8.

75. Ibid.

76. *Atlanta Daily World,* February 12, 1935, 12.

77. *New York Amsterdam News,* February 8, 1933, 6.

78. Ibid., February 8, 1936, 8. Newspaper editors and columnists were for the most part as ambivalent about Lincoln in the 1930s as they had always been. He was at once the Great Emancipator and "That Slave Hound from Illinois" who committed grave crimes against the black people (see, for example, *Chicago Defender,* February 10, 1934, 12). His condescending air toward Frederick Douglass, the most educated black he had known, proved him to be, when all was said and done, an alien rather than friend to blacks. Lincoln's letter to Horace Greeley indicating that "If I could save the Union without freeing any slave I would do it," appeared regularly in Lincoln-Douglass

Day editions. (See, for one of many examples, *Chicago Defender*, February 14, 1931, 2.) African Americans' growing awareness of their own history, evidenced in Negro History Week, devised and sustained by Carter G. Woodson, induced black intellectuals to recognize and write about Lincoln's ambivalences more openly and lessened the naive adoration of earlier decades.

79. *New York Age*, February 12, 1944, 6.

80. *Afro-American (Washington DC)*, February 18, 1933, 2.

81. Ibid., February 16, 1935, 9.

82. Nancy J. Weiss, *Farewell to the Party of Lincoln: Black Politics in the Age of FDR* (Princeton: Princeton University Press, 1983), 218.

83. Ibid., 209–35.

84. Ibid.

85. *New York Age*, February 23, 1935, 6.

86. *Chicago Defender*, February 13, 1932, 12.

87. For detail, see Richard Weiss, "Ethnicity and Reform: Minorities and the Ambience of the Depression Years," *Journal of American History* 66 (1979): 566–85.

88. *Boston Daily Globe*, February 13, 1933, 18; *Philadelphia Record*, February 13, 1939, 1, 2.

89. Gary Gerstle, *American Crucible: Race and Nation in the Twentieth Century* (Princeton: Princeton University Press, 2001).

90. Gunnar Myrdal, *American Dilemma* (New York: Harper, [1944)] 1962), 74. See also John Hope Franklin, *From Slavery to Freedom* (New York: Vintage, 1969), 523–45; Raymond Wolters, *Negroes and the Great Depression* (Westport, CT: Greenwood Press, 1970); Joseph P. Lash, *Eleanor and Franklin: The Story of the Relationship Based on Eleanor Roosevelt's Private Papers* (New York: New American Library, 1971).

91. Alfred Hayes and Earl Robinson (lyrics), Earl Robinson (music), *Abe Lincoln* (New York: Bob Miller, Inc., 1938).

92. Robert S. McElvaine, *The Great Depression* (New York: Times Books, 1961), 206–23.

93. *New York Times*, February 13, 1935, pt. 2, 6.

94. George H. Gallup, *The Gallup Poll* (New York: Random House, 1971), 2:142.

95. Scott Sandage, "A Marble House Divided: The Lincoln Memorial, the Civil Rights Movement, and the Politics of Memory, 1939–1963," *Journal of American History* 80 (1993): 135–67.

96. Karen Cerulo, *Identity Designs: The Sights and Sounds of a Nation* (New Brunswick: Rutgers University Press, 1995), 145–66.

97. *Atlanta Daily World*, February 13, 1940, 1; *New York Times*, February 13, 1941, 12. District of Columbia's African Americans contemplating the most effective time and place to demonstrate against municipal segregation ordinances chose the (1940) opening of the film *Abe Lincoln in Illinois* at RKO Keith's Theatre, from which they were banned. At the same time, a *Chicago Defender* columnist linked the film to the debate over the Anti-Lynching Bill and reminded his readers of their moral duty to see it: "ABE LINCOLN IN ILLINOIS is certainly a timely FILM. With the NATIONAL ASSOCIATION for THE ADVANCEMENT OF COLORED PEOPLE fighting in CONGRESS for the ANTI-LYNCHING BILL it is timely that the hopes and dreams of a real AMERICAN are being told to the NATION in this great SYMBOL OF DEMOCRACY. It is the DUTY of every

real AMERICAN, black or WHITE to find TIME to see this great EPIC" (*Chicago Defender*, February 3, 1940, 21).

98. "Coupling," as opposed to "pairing," occurs when an two objects appear together in the same verbal phrase or picture. "Pairing" occurs when an object is "appresented," that is, its appearance is associated with another that does not appear but without which one is unable to understand the first object's significance. Examples of pairing will be shown in a later chapter. Alfred Schutz, *On Phenomenology and Social Relations*, ed. Helmut R. Wagner (Chicago: University of Chicago Press, 1970), 321.

99. *Chicago Defender*, December 3, 1940, 1.

100. Senator Schwellenbach added another non-sequitur: "Respect for law must be maintained. To maintain respect for law, we must be sure that laws do not reflect the interests of only one class or group. These simple conditions may be summed up with one word: Tolerance." *Philadelphia Inquirer*, February 12, 1939, 1–2.

101. Berlin's original lyrics made no mention of slavery or emancipation, but these themes are central to the revised lyrics for the movie.

102. Sandburg, *The Prairie Years*, 1926, and *The War Years*, 4 vols. (New York: Harcourt Brace, 1939). Lincoln scholarship during the 1930s was dominated by James G. Randall and other "revisionist" Civil War historians.

103. For the history of American nationalism, see Ernest Gellner, *Nations and Nationalism* (Ithaca: Cornell University Press, 1983); Wilbur Zelinsky, *Nation Into State: The Shifting Symbolic Foundations of American Nationalism* (Chapel Hill: University of North Carolina Press, 1988); Stuart McConnell, "Reading the Flag: A Reconsideration of the Patriotic Cults of the 1890s," in *Bonds of Affection: Americans Define Their Patriotism* (Princeton: Princeton University Press, 1996), 102–19; Robert J. Goldstein, *Saving Old Glory: The History of the American Flag Desecration Controversy* (Boulder, CO: Westview Press, 1995); Anthony D. Smith, *Nationalism and Modernism: A Critical Survey of Recent Theories of Nations and Nationalism* (New York: Routledge, 1998); Cecilia O'Leary, *To Die For: The Paradox of American Patriotism* (Princeton: Princeton University Press, 1999).

104. David W. Blight, "Historians and 'Memory,'" *Common-Place* 2 (April 2002): 3.

105. Ibid.

106. Michael Davis, *The Lincoln Image in the South* (Knoxville: University of Tennessee Press, 1971), 166–69; Barry Schwartz, *Abraham Lincoln and the Forge of National Memory* (Chicago: University of Chicago Press, 2000), 217–22.

107. Mary Raymond Shipman Andrews, *The Perfect Tribute* (New York: Charles Scribner's Sons, 1907). At the academic level, *The South in the Building of the Nation* (1909–13), a multivolume encyclopedia of the Southern role in American nation-building, devoted an equal amount of space to Lincoln and Lee, and reached a wide readership during the Lincoln centennial.

108. Schwartz, *Abraham Lincoln and the Forge of National Memory*, 217–22. A separate analysis of New Orleans, Charleston, and Savannah newspapers shows increases in the number of Lincoln articles after the 1909 centennial.

109. *Richmond News Leader*, February 17, 1928, 8.

110. Lyon G. Tyler and Giles B. Cook et al., *Confederate Leaders and Other Citizens Request the House of Delegates to Rescind the Resolution of Respect to Abraham Lincoln, the Barbarian*, 1928.

111. *Richmond News Leader*, February 14, 1928, 1, 8; February 17, 1928, 8; March 7, 1928, 1.

112. W. J. Cash, *The Mind of the South* (New York: Vintage [1941] 1961), 377.

113. Gavin Wright, *Old South, New South: Revolutions in the Southern Economy since the Civil War* (New York: Basic Books, 1986).

114. Linda Reed, *Simple Decency and Common Sense: The Southern Conference for Human Welfare* (Bloomington: Indiana University Press, 1991).

115. The South's love affair with Roosevelt is relevant to the NORC finding because it meant the beginning of the end of a way of life. "Looking at the South in those days," W. J. Cash wrote, "one might readily have concluded that at last the old pattern was on its way to conclusive breakup, that new ideas and a new tolerance were sweeping the field, and that the region as a whole [was] growing genuinely social-minded and realistic. . . ." How far the change had actually gone by World War II is hard to say, but change itself was unmistakable. W. J. Cash, *The Mind of the South*, 377.

116. Cited by Tony Horowitz, *Confederates in the Attic: Dispatches from the Unfinished Civil War* (New York: Parthenon, 1998), 147–48.

117. Foote was hardly alone. As late as the 1930s, July 4th passed in Mississippi without observance because it was also the date of the fall of Vicksburg.

118. Archibald Rutledge, "A Southerner Views Lincoln," *Scribner's Magazine* 83 (1928): 209.

119. All media furthered the nationalization of Lincoln's image. Southern commentators were silent while Southern views of Lincoln changed. Schoolchildren still enjoyed watching Lincoln visit the dying Confederate soldier in the film version of Andrews's *The Perfect Tribute* while adults watched Abe Lincoln bounce Shirley Temple, "the littlest rebel," on his knee. Lincoln as Friend of the Old South was a variation on an old reconciliation theme, but most of the Depression-era writers and filmmakers—almost all Northerners—developed this theme along liberal lines.

120. Quoted and discussed in *The (Danville, Virginia) Bee*, February 12, 1930, 1

121. Rixford J. Lincoln, "Abraham Lincoln," *Cullman Democrat*, February 13, 1936.

122. Raymond Pitcairn, "Washington and Lincoln," *Cullman Democrat*, May 4, 1939.

123. William Harris, "Abraham Lincoln" and "Robert E. Lee," *Congressional Record* (Senate), February 17, 1930, 3740.

124. David Spence Hill, "Personification of Ideals by Urban Children," *Journal of Social Psychology* 1 (August 1930): 379–392.

125. Ibid.

126. National Opinion Research Center Survey 235-B, University of Denver, July 1945.

127. Marcus Anderson, "Father Abraham: Analysis of a Myth," *Tyler's Quarterly Magazine* 20 (1937): 77–78. *Tyler's Quarterly* sustained its anti-Lincoln diatribe. See Paul S. Whitcomb, "Lincoln's 'Gettysburg Address,'" *Tyler's Quarterly Magazine* 12 (1930): 221–35; Landon C. Bell, *The Lincoln Myths are Passing—But Slowly* (Columbus, OH: reprinted from *Tyler's Quarterly*, January 1930); Lyon G. Tyler, "How Lincoln Got Rich," *Tyler's Quarterly* 17 (1935–36): 3–9.

128. Roosevelt, "Address at the Dedication of the Memorial on the Gettysburg Battlefield, Gettysburg, Pennsylvania," July 3, 1938, *Public Papers and Addresses* 7:420.

129. Wilbur Zelinsky, *Nation into State: The Shifting Symbolic Foundations of American Nationalism* (Chapel Hill: University of North Carolina Press, 1988), 8.

130. The term "the greatest generation" was popularized by Tom Brokaw's book of that title: *The Greatest Generation* (New York: Random House, 1998).

CHAPTER TWO

1. Franklin D. Roosevelt, "Message to the Special Convocation at the University of Oxford," June 19, 1941, *The Public Papers and Addresses of Franklin D. Roosevelt* (New York: Macmillan Company, [1941]1950), 10:226.

2. Ralph G. Lindstrom, *Papers of Letitia B. Martin*, U.S. Library of Congress, Manuscript Division, Box 5.

3. Roosevelt, "Radio Address to the New York 'Herald Tribune' Forum," October 24, 1940, *Public Papers and Addresses* 9:495–96.

4. Carl Sandburg, *Remembrance Rock* (New York: Harcourt Brace, 1948), 18–19.

5. Erving Goffman, *Frame Analysis: An Essay on the Organization of Experience* (New York: Harper and Row, 1974), 21. Goffman's analysis can be related to collective action frames. As William Gamson defines them, action frames are beliefs that promote reform and stimulate participation in social movements. Action frames define present injustices, induce victims or indignant observers to see themselves as remedial agents and to construe their conduct as self-defining. Analysis of the keying of problematic presents to the past shows contemporary action frames to be deeply embedded in collective memory. See William A. Gamson, *Talking Politics* (Cambridge: Cambridge University Press, 1992); William A. Gamson, "Hiroshima, the Holocaust, and the Politics of Exclusion," *American Sociological Review* 60 (1995): 5–20.

6. For a general discussion of this "extrinsic theory" of thought, see Clifford Geertz, "Ideology as a Cultural System," in *The Interpretation of Cultures* (New York: Basic Books, 1973), 214. For recent comparative perspectives on the Civil War and World War II, see Gabor Boritt, ed., *War Comes Again: Comparative Vistas on the Civil War and World War II* (New York: Oxford University Press, 1995), a book of scholarly essays to mark the fiftieth anniversary of the end of World War II. Fort Sumpter is here compared with Pearl Harbor; Eisenhower with Grant; Roosevelt with Lincoln.

7. Alphonse de Lamartine, cited in Geertz, *Interpretation of Cultures*, 221.

8. Between 1915 and 1919 the *New York Times* published an annual mean of 33 articles about Lincoln. The *Readers Guide* listed 18 articles; the *Congressional Record*, 12 entries. Thus, the number of items published during World War II was considerably greater than the number published during World War I. The complex reasons for this difference include the elevation of Lincoln's prestige during the Great Depression.

9. Karen Linn, compiler, "Politics and Political Movements, ca. 1817–1982," *Register of the Sam DeVincent Collection of Illustrated American Sheet Music, ca. 1790–1982*, series 5 (Washington DC: National Museum of American History, Smithsonian Institution Archives Center, 1991). Between 1900 and 1989, thirty-eight songs featuring Lincoln appear. Four of these songs appear during World War I; seven during World War II. Four songs appeared during the years leading up to the 1909 Lincoln centennial; four during the Depression.

10. Charles R. Brown, "A Parallel," *Journal of the National Education Association* 30 (February 1941): 52.

11. *New York Times*, March 19, 1943, 22; Stewart W. McClelland, "Lincoln Prescribes for Today," *Vital Speeches of the Day* 10 (March 1, 1944): 304–6. In *Saturday Review* (27 [February 12, 1944]: 14), a series of direct quotes answer the urgently headlined question: "What Would Lincoln Do?"

12. *New York Times*, February 12, 1941, 20.

13. The sheet music of the period, while appropriating Abraham Lincoln, rarely made George Washington central to its lyrics. Where Lincoln's sheet music titles peak in the World War II era, Washington's titles peak during the century's first decade and his 1932 centennial observance.

14. George H. Gallup, *The Gallup Poll, Public Opinion 1935–1971* (New York: Random House, 1972), 1:54; National Opinion Research Center, 1945.

15. Philip Smith, "Codes and Conflict: Toward a Theory of War as Ritual," *Theory and Society* 20 (1991): 191.

16. Robert Bellah, "Civil Religion in America," in *Beyond Belief* (New York: Harper and Row, 1970), 177–78.

17. Talcott Parsons and Neil Smelser, *Economy and Society* (London: Routledge and Kegan Paul, 1956). See also Richard Munch, "Commentary" in *Neofunctionalism*, ed. Jeffrey C. Alexander (Beverly Hills: Sage, 1985), 225–37; Jeffrey C. Alexander, *Theoretical Logic in Sociology* (Berkeley: University of California Press, 1982).

18. The Athens, Alabama, *Limestone Democrat* recalled Lincoln's comments to a committee of black leaders: "You and we are different races," he told them, "and even when you cease to be slaves you are far from being placed on an equality with the white race." But since the African American has in many places "risen from savagery to voter and property-owner in many parts of the nation, he should be grateful and adjust himself to injustice during this national emergency." *Limestone Democrat*, April 9, 1942, 2. The *Limestone Democrat*'s open admission of injustice is prophetic of the postwar explosion of civil-rights demands.

19. Max Weber, "Traditional Society," in *The Theory of Social and Economic Organization*, ed. Talcott Parsons (New York: Oxford University Press, 1947), 341.

20. *New York Times*, June 28, 1941, 11.

21. *New York Times Magazine*, March 2, 1941, sec. 7, 23.

22. George Herbert Mead, "The Nature of the Past," in *Essays in Honor of John Dewey*, ed. John Coss (New York: Henry Holt, 1929), 353. As one of Mead's interpreters puts it, "there could be no awareness of any past or the history of anything, if it were not for the sake of understanding how to account for some present experienced phenomenon that obstructs effective action." David L. Miller, *George Herbert Mead: Self, Language, and the World* (Austin: University of Texas Press, 1973), 76.

23. Americans chronically and grossly underestimated the war's duration. Three weeks after Pearl Harbor, exactly 50 percent of Gallup's respondents believed the war would be over in two years or less. Six months later, perhaps due to military successes in the Pacific, 61 percent anticipated the war's lasting two years or less (Gallup, *Gallup Poll*, 318, 336).

24. Roosevelt, 761st press conference, August 16, 1941, *Public Papers and Addresses*, 10:328–29.

25. *New York Times*, August 20, 1941, 16.

26. *New York Times*, March 10, 1943, 4.

27. George MacGregor Burns, cited by William E. Leuchtenburg, *In the Shadow of FDR* (Ithaca: Cornell University Press, 1993), 171.

28. Michael Schudson, "How Culture Works: Perspectives from Media Studies on the Efficacy of Symbols," *Theory and Society* 18 (1989): 171–72.

29. *Limestone Democrat*, March 11, 1943, 2.

30. See, for one example, "Ideals of Lincoln Hailed in Sermons," *New York Times*, February 14, 1943, 13.

31. Rosemary Benet (Words) and Katherine K. Davis (Music), *Nancy Hanks: Abraham Lincoln's Mother* (New York: Galaxy Music Corporation, 1941).

32. Alfred Kreymborg, "Ballad of the Lincoln Penny," in *Collier's Weekly* 109 (February 14, 1942): 12.

33. Jay Mechling, "Dress Right, Dress: The Boy Scout Uniform as a Folk Costume," *Semiotica* 64 3/4 (1987): 322.

34. Similarly, Rockwell's *Spirit of America* includes the profile of a Scout, looking to the left, backgrounded by identically oriented profiles of Lincoln, Washington, Theodore Roosevelt, and Charles Lindbergh.

35. Gallup, *The Gallup Poll*, 1:359.

36. The Office of War Information (OWI) was established in April 1942. Directed by journalist Elmer Davis, the OWI commented on Hollywood movie production, produced its own radio programs, films, still photographs, and posters to explain the purpose of the war and to sustain the motivation to fight it. The OWI was terminated in September 1945. All war posters described in this chapter were obtained from the National Archives and Records Administration, Still Picture Branch (NSSP), Washington DC; Library of Congress, Prints and Photographs (Yankel Collection, 6-U.S. 1119), Washington DC; Abraham Lincoln Museum, Harrogate, Tennessee.

37. *Alabama Courier*, March 20, 1944, 4. Speech delivered in Washington DC on August 22, 1864, to 166th Ohio Regiment. See *Collected Works of Abraham Lincoln*, 8 vols., ed. Roy P. Basler (New Brunswick: Rutgers University Press, 1953), 7:512.

38. Variations on this theme include depictions of Franklin Roosevelt as the new Lincoln fighting a new form of slavery. Solidarity, marked by Lincoln's and Kosciusko's hands on Roosevelt's shoulders, is joined to militancy, marked in one Polish-American cartoon by the harshest words of Lincoln's second inaugural address: "until every drop of blood drawn by the lash shall be paid by another drawn with the sword. . . ." A symbolic reproduction of this sword appears in Roosevelt's right hand (c.1943, personal scrapbook, the Abraham Lincoln Museum, Harrogate, Tennessee).

39. Understanding how "adoration portraits" and "guiding spirit portraits"—pictures of people looking at Lincoln and being looked at by him—were exploited throughout the war extends Otto Fenichel's observation on ocular introjection. Identifying with Lincoln, viewers embrace the moral standard he represents. Identifying with Lincoln's own admirers, contemporary viewers take their place: it is now they who look up to Lincoln and are looked at by him; it is now their shoulder on which Lincoln places a guiding hand. Ocular introjection refers to a first order of identification where Lincoln appears as an "ego ideal," itself intensified by a second order of identification—viewers take the place of people admiring Lincoln in pictures. During World War II, these levels of identification multiplied the reasons for looking at Abraham Lincoln in the first place, which included the need to make the suffering

of war intelligible and manageable (Otto Fenichel, "The Scoptophilic Instinct and Identification," in *Collected Papers*, 2 vols. (New York: W. W. Norton, 1953), I:373–76, 378–81.

40. *New York Times*, February 12, 1942, 14. E. F. L. Wood, Earl of Halifax, was regarded as one of the architects of appeasement prior to World War II. He was foreign secretary at the time of the Munich Agreement. Newly elected Winston Churchill allowed him to retain this post for a short while, failed to gain confidence in him, and sent him to the United States as ambassador. In later years of the war, foreign dignitaries regularly paid their respects to the United States at the tomb of Lincoln.

41. Ibid., May 5, 1940, sec. 10, 1; February 13, 1943, 7, 14; 15; March 19, 1943, 22; March 17, 1943, 18. Victor Bulwer-Lytton, Earl of Lytton, held many key diplomatic posts. He was best known for his directorship of the League of Nation's Lytton Commission, which established Japan's responsibility for the hostilities in China. Shortly after the issuance of the report, Japan withdrew from the league. In England, too, Lincoln's symbolic role was reinforced by John Drinkwater's drama *Abraham Lincoln*. Drinkwater's play, enormously popular during World War I, reopened in 1940 to a London audience that included the king and queen.

42. Aaron Copland and Vivian Perlis, *Copland: 1900 through 1942* (New York: Saint Martin's Press, 1984), 342, 344.

43. Ibid., 344.

44. *New York Times*, February 13, 1942, 14.

45. Bernard de Voto, cited by Richard M. Simpson, "Abraham Lincoln," *Congressional Record* (HR), February 1, 1945, A409.

46. Not many people knew these soldiers, let alone what they were thinking. When Hollywood visited the Memorial, however, millions knew. In 1943, Betty Grable, in the film *Pin Up Girl*, donned a WAC uniform and, with solemn expression, led a close-order drill on the patio of the Lincoln Memorial. Buxom Betty, her gleaming blond hair flouncing about beneath a military cap in front of Lincoln's statue, presents an undignified scene to late twentieth-century viewers. But in 1943 it was a serious and understandable scene, one that connected the war to what Lincoln symbolized, and many who witnessed it knew more about the war's meaning than they had known before.

47. By 1943, adoration symbolism had become conventional in calendar and poster art: father and son gazing at Lincoln; husband and wife gazing at Lincoln; the president and his aides gazing at Lincoln. Lincoln's appearance on any official announcement implicitly connected the current war to the Civil War, but in most instances the connection was explicit. "Today's a Day for Memory—But It's Also a Day for Action!" headlines one Lincoln Day announcement. Below the headline a war bond appeal exploits existing family ties to the Civil War generation: "Translate your reverence for [Civil War] heroes . . . into full support to their grandsons and great-grandsons who are now fighting another war on battlefronts that are farther flung and still more deadly!" Above the appeal on the viewer's left, Lincoln's face is backgrounded by the current (forty-eight-star) flag and, on the right, a fatigued but determined soldier engaging the enemy (Abraham Lincoln Museum, Harrogate, Tennessee).

48. Edward A. Shils, *Center and Periphery: Essays in Macrosociology* (Chicago: University of Chicago Press, 1975), 158.

49. The stores invoked Revolutionary War themes as well. One of Philadelphia's Strawbridge and Clothier's department store's advertisements recalled the Declaration of Independence and Constitution before declaring: "Our flag . . . still flies / Where evil forces scourge the world. . . . We'll crush the foe and wars shall cease / With victimless and lasting peace." A Snellenburg's department store advertisement bears an image of the Liberty Bell, whose rings "intonate the earth where they have died to keep the faith."

50. *Congressional Record* (Senate), February 5, 1942, A390.

51. *New York Times,* June 28, 1942, sec. 7, 5.

52. Sociologist Talcott Parsons, a consistent and ardent war hawk, probably never read Stoddard's article, but the imperative to which it refers—continued effort despite defeat and loss—was central to his postwar formulation of *The Social System,* whose functional prerequisites included the capacity to "motivate actors adequately to performances which may be necessary if the social system in question is to persist" ([New York: Free Press, 1951], 29). In the early 1940s, a good way to inspire "adequate motivation" for the struggle was to connect it to the legacy of the early 1860s.

53. Clifford Geertz, "Religion as a Cultural System," in *Interpretation of Cultures,* 92.

54. Bellah, *Beyond Belief,* 177–78.

55. *New York Times,* April 14, 1943, 92.

56. Louis. L. Ludlow, *Congressional Record* (HR), June 29, 1942, 5757.

57. Frederick L. Bullard, *Lincoln in Marble and Bronze* (New Brunswick: Rutgers University Press, 1942), 325.

58. *New York Times,* February 12, 1940, 16.

59. *Saturday Review of Literature* 27 (February 12, 1944): 5. See also Arthur M. Schlesinger, *New Republic* (February 14, 1944), 207. For a forethought, see "Lincoln Today," *New York Times,* February 12, 1940, 16.

60. As Norman Rockwell worked on his own depiction of the war's end, he contemplated the same lines of the second inaugural as appear above. Rockwell's *Saturday Evening Post* painting, appearing on page 12 of the February 10, 1945, issue, centers on the theme of permanent injury, symbolized by a wounded veteran. Around him a builder goes about his job of reconstructing the world. The artist puts himself (or finds himself) in his own picture, chin in hand, surveying the vastness of the scene. In the lower left stands a teacher and her students—the new generation; above them a hand of brotherhood is extended to the downtrodden; in the background are third-world peoples moving toward Lincoln; on the right, women at prayer, humbled by the massiveness of the destruction and the task of re-creation. In the lower right of this image (as of the preceding one) appear widow and orphaned sons. Lincoln appears at the upper left corner, dark in color and placed among shadows—almost invisible at first and even second and third glances; however, the composition's central character, the injured soldier, gazes upon him. The *Post*'s editors placed Rockwell's painting beside Carl Sandburg's poem "The Long Shadow of Lincoln," inspired by Lincoln's December 1862 message to Congress: "As our case is new, so we must think anew and act anew. We must disenthrall ourselves." Rockwell's painting and Sandburg's poem are united by their aspiration for a new world, a world healed and transformed: "There is dust alive / With dreams of the Republic, / With dreams of the family of man / Flung wide

on a shrinking globe; / With old timetables, / Old maps, old guideposts / Torn into shreds, / Shot into tatters, / Burnt in a fire wind . . ."

61. *Statesville Daily Record*, February 23, 1945, 5.

62. Alexis de Tocqueville, *Democracy in America*, ed. Phillips Bradley (New York: Vintage, 1945), 2:173.

63. Ibid., 191.

64. Sandburg, "Long Shadow."

65. According to a new patriot song, "Every time of strife in America's life has produced a leader of men / Like Washington and Lincoln . . . And this time it happened again" (Clarence Kelley, Frank H. Stanton, Bob Mathews (Words and Music) *There's an F.D.R. in Freedom*. New York. Nationwide Songs, Inc., 1942).

66. Archibald MacLeish, "April Elegy, April 15–April 12," *Atlantic Monthly* 43 (June 1945): 43. In late 1944, Decca records released a new version of "The Lonesome Train," a song about Lincoln's funeral journey, sung by Burl Ives. It was a popular song, once performed in the Hollywood Bowl.

67. See, for example, *New York Times*, April 20, 1945, 18.

68. M. L. Wilson, "Lincoln and Roosevelt," entered into the record by George A. Dondero, *Congressional Record* (HR), April 17, 1945, A1767.

69. *The (Alabama) Cullman Banner*, September 20, 1945, 9.

70. This is why popular symbols of the public's regard for Roosevelt are so well represented by the popular "Steersmen" clocks, which consist of a statuette of him at the wheel of the Ship of State, accompanied by Lincoln and Washington.

71. Edward Hart, *Congressional Record* (HR), February 23, 1942, A659.

72. Gallup Poll, February 3–8, 1945. Respondents asked to compare Lincoln to Washington depend on their *recognition* of both men and their achievement; respondents asked to name the greatest men in American history (appendix B) depend on *recall* in order to answer the question. In the latter question, no one is named; respondents must recall and rank past heroes in their own minds before they can respond.

73. DeVincent Collection, Smithsonian Museum of National History, Washington DC; Still Pictures Division, National Archives, Washington DC.

74. Barry Schwartz, "Social Change and Collective Memory: The Democratization of George Washington," *American Sociological Review* 56 (1991): 221–36.

75. Sigmund G. Hecht and Monte Carlo (words) and Alma Sanders (music), "God Bless Our President" (New York: Mills Music Inc., 1942).

76. Lt. D. W. Dorsey (words) and Johnny Allegro (music), "The Good Old U.S.A." (San Jose: Jay [JD] Dee Publishing Co., 1943).

77. Emile Durkheim, cited in Steven Lukes, *Emile Durkheim: His Life and Work* (New York: Penguin Books, 1973), 550.

78. Roosevelt, *Public Papers and Addresses* 9:495.

79. Emile Durkheim, *Suicide* (New York: The Free Press, [1897] 1966), 208.

CHAPTER THREE

1. Roger Callois, *L'Homme et Le Sacré* (Paris: Gallimard, [1939] 1950), 228.

2. Lloyd Warner, *The Living and the Dead*, vol. 6 (New Haven: Yale University Press, 1959).

3. *Redlands (CA) Daily Facts*, May 18, 1954, 2; *Kannapolis (IL) Daily Independent*, May 18, 1954, 1.

4. *Hammond Times*, March 13, 1957. The student's name was Stephan Cohen.

5. *Odessa (TX) American*, December 31, 1960, 15.

6. For these same two periods, the annual number of George Washington articles dropped from 11 to 9—considerably below Lincoln in both periods, but considerably above Benjamin Franklin, Alexander Hamilton, John Adams, Thomas Jefferson, James Madison, Andrew Jackson, and Ulysses Grant. Comparable *New York Times* counts of George Washington articles are 30 and 32, about 10 articles below Lincoln in both periods. *Congressional Record* counts for George Washington show a postwar decrease from 18 to 14 entries per year.

7. Gallup Poll, February 6–11, 1948, question GK08A. Roper Center for Opinion Research, *Public Attitudes toward American Presidents, 1935–1993*. Prepared for Barry Schwartz (Storrs, CT: University of Connecticut, 1993).

8. Gallup Poll, March 9–24, 1949, question GK06.

9. George H. Gallup, *The Gallup Poll: Public Opinion 1935–1971* (New York: Random House, 1972), 2:986.

10. Ibid., January 6–11, 1956, question G009.

11. Ibid., May 7–12, 1958, question 29.

12. Jay Monaghan, "The Growth of Abraham Lincoln's Influence in Literature since His Death," in *The Many Faces of Lincoln: Selected Articles from the Lincoln Herald* (Mahomet, IL: Mayhaven Publishing, 1997), 110–22. The WorldCat collection is available at http://www.worldcat.org. The "Named Person" criterion was used to select Lincoln material, although the "Keyword" selection criterion (e.g., title, title phrase) produce almost identical trend lines. Monaghan's data ends in 1950; the New York Public Library Collection data ends in 1960.

13. Thomas Carlyle, *On Heroes, Hero Worship, and the Heroic in History* (Lincoln: University of Nebraska Press, 1966), 13.

14. D. T. Miller and M. Nowack, *The Fifties* (Garden City, N.J.: Doubleday, 1977), 50.

15. Gallup, *The Gallup Poll: Public Opinion, 1935–1971* 2:1309, 1365.

16. Ibid., 843, 933, 1306.

17. Frances Fitzgerald, *America Revised* (Boston: Little, Brown, 1979), 56–57, 121.

18. William Graebner used the term "culture of contingency" to understand the interaction between nuclear power and the continuing personal anxieties produced by World War II. William S. Graebner, *The Age of Doubt: American Thought and Culture in the 1940s* (Boston: Twayne Publishers, 1991).

19. Michael Kammen, *Mystic Chords of Memory* (New York: Basic Books, 1992), 546.

20. James T. Patterson, *Grand Expectations: The United States, 1945–1974* (New York: Oxford University Press, 1996); William L. O'Neil, *American High: The Years of Confidence, 1945–1960* (New York: The Free Press, 1986).

21. Henry Luce cited in Alan Brinkley, "World War II and American Liberalism," in *The War in American Culture: Society and Consciousness during World War II*, ed. Lewis A. Erenberg and Susan E. Hirsch (Chicago: University of Chicago Press, 1996), 324.

22. Economic expansion was accompanied by increased family size, per capita income growth, rapid suburban development, and a youth culture with significant buying power.

23. Cultural differences in perception and comprehension made the global propagation of Lincoln's philosophy difficult. Richard N. Current, for example, explains how India understood Lincoln's words in terms of its own vocabulary and meanings, and assimilated him to its own history. Richard N. Current, "Through India with Abraham Lincoln," in *The Many Faces of Lincoln: Selected Articles from the Lincoln Herald*, ed. Charles M. Hubbard, Thomas R. Turner, and Steven Rogstad (Mahomet, IL: Mayhaven Publishing, 1997), 165–70.

24. *Abraham Lincoln Sesquicentennial 1959–1960*, final report (Washington DC: U.S. Government Printing Office, 1960), ix, 101. The exporting of Lincoln was in no way devious. "There was a time," explained American Legion Commander Preston Moore, when "American ideals and principles were the light of the world. . . . They can be again if we consciously and persistently make them so. With long range planning, with massive use of all the techniques of building opinion, the United States can again become a dynamic force to win the hearts and minds of men everywhere" (*Chicago Daily Tribune*, February13, 1959, pt.1, 6).

25. Clyde Doyle, "Presentation of Bust of Abraham Lincoln by Eloy Alfaro International Foundation," *Congressional Record* (HR), February 20, 1950, A1238.

26. For a brief panorama emphasizing England and Scotland, see Harold F. Humbert, "Abe Lincoln Walks Abroad," *Rotarian* 50 (1951): 50.

27. Herbert Mitgang, *New York Times Magazine*, March 31, 1957.

28. Dwight Eisenhower, "Remarks by the President," *Report of the Joint Committee on Arrangements on the Commemoration Ceremony in Observance of the 150th Anniversary of the Birth of Abraham Lincoln, 1809–1859*. House document no. 211 (Washington DC: U. S. Government Printing Office, 1959), 13–14.

29. Carl Sandburg, "Address to Joint Session of Congress," ibid., 3–4, 6.

30. Willy Brandt, *Chicago Tribune*, February 13, 1959, 1.

31. Dean Rusk, *Congressional Record* (HR), November 26, 1963, 22833.

32. Usher L. Burdick, "Lincoln: A Great American," *Congressional Record* (HR), February 7, 1955, 1237.

33. Herbert Blum, *Congressional Record* (HR), 1963, A5743. Before Rhee was forced to leave office, however, William Frank Zornow, a Rhee supporter, compared his situation to Abraham Lincoln's. "Lincoln and Rhee: An Historical Analogy," unnamed and undated Chicago Historical Society document.

34. Sancomb to Grant, November 19, 1960, United States Civil War Centennial Commission, U.S. National Archives, Box 76. Mrs. Sancomb is referring to Lincoln's 1847 travels throughout New York and New England prior to assuming his U.S. House of Representatives seat, which he occupied from 1848 to 1850.

35. In domestic matters, Wisconsin representative Lawrence H. Smith asked seriously: "What would Lincoln say about the infiltration of subversive elements in high government positions?" *Congressional Record* (HR), February,13, 1950, 1773.

36. Alexander Wiley, "Birthday Anniversaries of Tackusz Kosciusko, Abraham Lincoln, Frederic Chopin, and George Washington," *Congressional Record* (Senate), February 8, 1950, 1627–28; Clement J. Zablocki, "Lincoln and Kosciusko," *Congressional*

Record (HR), February 14, 1955, 1522–23; James G. Fulton, "Statement on Poland," *Congressional Record* (HR), February 7, 1955, 1240.

37. The image appeared in the *New York Times*, February 15, 1951. "You can fool all of the people some of the time; some of the people all of the time; but you cannot fool all of the people all of the time" is an expression incorrectly attributed to Lincoln.

38. Image appeared in the *Newark News*, 1954 (specific date unavailable). U.S. Library of Congress, Photoduplication Service, image #USZ62-98239.

39. Alexander Wiley, "Can Mankind Endure Half Slave and Half Free?" *Congressional Record* (Senate), June 6, 1955, 7683–85. Under the threat of advanced nuclear weapons and global annihilation, Americans drew upon the Civil War to assert their ideals and moral unity. There was something urgent about the parallel: "Dark hung the clouds o'er the nation during that fateful year [1860]. Our country was fatalistically headed for a long and bitter and exhausting war among ourselves. The issue began with whether the United States could endure half-slave and half-free. . . . This is not like the bitter struggle of 100 years ago within our own family. This is a global showdown whether the WORLD can endure half slave and half free." (*Milwaukee Sentinel*, February 12, 1960, pt. 1, 8).

40. Daniel A. Reed, "Shades of George Washington and Abraham Lincoln," *Congressional Record* (HR), March 20, 1946, A1537; "The Shades of Washington, Lincoln, and Jackson Gather at the Hermitage," *Congressional Record* (HR), July 15, 1946, A4140. See also Reeds's remarks in the House on April 2, 1946, A1856; April 12, 1946, A2114; April 30, 1946, A2376; June 12, 1946, A3418.

41. Cited in Robert Rich, "Was Lincoln a Reactionary?" *Congressional Record* (HR), February 13, 1950, A996.

42. For evidence, see representative Andrew Jacobs's statement in *Congressional Record* (HR), February 2, 1950, 2017. On a related issue, see "Abraham Lincoln on the Tariff," *Congressional Record*, May 3, 1955, 5439–42.

43. Rich, "Was Lincoln a Reactionary?" A996–97.

44. Anthony Summers, *The Arrogance of Power: The Secret World of Richard Nixon* (New York: Viking, 2000), 13. Nixon also quoted Lincoln in his Checkers speech ("God must have loved the common people—he made so many of them"). Many responded to that highly successful statement by proclaiming Nixon "a Modern Day Lincoln" (120–21).

45. Richard M. Nixon, "Address before 70th Annual Lincoln Day Dinner," *Congressional Record* (Senate), February 14, 1956, 2549.

46. David McCullough, *Truman* (New York: Simon and Schuster, 1992), 838.

47. In *Variety Reviews* (vol. 11, February 19, 1975), "Carl Sandburg's Lincoln" played by Hal Holbrook is compared to former president Harry Truman (unpaginated).

48. *New Republic*, January 15, 1951, 3; see also June 14, 1948, 12.

49. *New York Times*, February 13, 1956, 25.

50. *Reader's Digest*, August, 1944, 112–18.

51. *New York Times*, April 2, 1969, 1.

52. *Time*, October 29, 1956, 22–23.

53. *New York Times*, March 30, 1969, 12; April 1, 1969, 46; *Time*, April 11, 1969, 26–27; *Newsweek*, April 14, 1969, 38–39.

54. *Chicago Tribune*, February11, 1959, pt.2, 3; February 12, 1959, pt.1, l4.

55. Robert Penn Warren, *All the King's Men* (New York: Harcourt Brace, 1946).

56. Erich Fromm, *Escape from Freedom* (New York: Holt, Rinehart, and Winston, 1941).

57. Theodor Adorno, "Freudian Theory and the Pattern of Fascist Propaganda" in *The Essential Frankfurt School Reader*, ed. A. Arrato and E. Gebhardt (Oxford: Blackwell, [1951] 1978), 118–37; Theodor Adorno, E. Frenkel-Brunswik, D. J. Levinson, and R. N. Sanford, *The Authoritarian Personality* (New York: W. W. Norton, 1950).

58. Dwight D. Eisenhower, "An Open Letter to America's Students," *Reader's Digest* 53 (1948): 1–5.

59. Dwight D. Eisenhower, "Lincoln Had the Proper Attitude toward Power," *Vital Speeches* 15 (1949): 335.

60. Karl Stefan, "Abraham Lincoln," *Congressional Record*, House of Representatives, February 13, 1950, A986.

61. Frank Carlson, "Lincoln and New Slaves," *Congressional Record* (HR), February 15, 1946, A811.

62. Karl E. Mundt, "Modern Republicanism as I See It," *Congressional Record* (Senate), February 14, 1957, 2079.

63. Eisenhower, "Remarks by the President," *Report of the Joint Committee on Arrangements on the Commemoration Ceremony in Observance of the 150th Anniversary of the Birth of Abraham Lincoln, 1809–1859*, 14.

64. Numan V. Bartley, *The New South, 1945–1980* (Baton Rouge: Louisiana State University Press, 1995), 124.

65. Pete Daniels, *Lost Revolutions: The South in the 1950s* (Chapel Hill: University of North Carolina Press, 2000).

66. Stephan Thernstrom and Abigail Thernstrom, *America in Black and White: One Nation Indivisible* (New York: Simon and Schuster, 1997), 34, 152, 185–87.

67. Howard Schuman, Charlotte Steeh, Lawrence Bobo, and Maria Krysan, *Racial Attitudes in America: Trends and Interpretations* (Cambridge, MA: Harvard University Press, 1997), 104–5, 141, 221, 222.

68. Melvin Price, "Lincoln, Friend of Labor," *Congressional Record* (HR), February 12, 1946, A679. In the same document, see also A683.

69. *Congressional Record*, February 6, 1950, A1027. For a religious perspective, see *New York Times*, February 13, 1955, 9.

70. *Milwaukee Sentinel*, November 20, 1958.

71. The socialist press, however, designated the Republicans who remained for dinner as the party's true representatives (*Daily Worker*, February 15, 1955, 5).

72. Nixon, "Address before 70th Annual Lincoln Day Dinner," 2549. Vice President Nixon's address followed a "Thanksgiving Pilgrimage" to the Lincoln Memorial to celebrate the Supreme Court's *Brown* decision. In this same year, 1957, Martin Luther King Jr. appeared at the Memorial to speak on the voting rights issue (personal communication Philip Kunhardt III).

73. Summers, *Arrogance of Power*, 13. In early May 1970, President Nixon, unable to sleep, invited his personal assistant Monola Sanchez to accompany him on a 3:30 AM visit to the Lincoln Memorial. There, amid a crowd forming to protest his decision to invade Cambodia for the purpose of depriving the enemy of supply and staging points, the president gazed at the statue of Lincoln.

74. *Congressional Record*, February 20, 1956, 2972.

75. *New York Times*, February 13, 1956, 25.

76. The moderate view was legitimated by America's moderate clergy. Thus, Billy Graham, raising money for a new high school to replace the one bombed by white supremacists, declared: "We must recognize that love of mankind cannot be enforced by bayonets alone. The law in itself is powerless to change the human heart. Only love can do that and only Christ can bring that love" (*Milwaukee Sentinel*, date unknown).

77. *New Republic*, September 15, 1958, 3–4.

78. Overall, Republican and Democratic conservatives appealed to Lincoln more often in opposition to than in avoidance of civil rights issues. In a debate titled "Integration of Schools," Democratic senator Absalom Robertson of Virginia tried to summarize the conservative position by inserting into the *Congressional Record* a *U.S. News and World Report* (July 6, 1956) article on "Conformity and Coercion" by David Lawrence. Lawrence declared that "equality is a theoretical goal," but so is discrimination. "One need not agree at all with the reasons given for such discriminations—indeed, one may be offended by their practice. But if we are to rely on theory, there is as much right to discrimination as there is to non-discrimination" (*Congressional Record* [Senate], February 12, 1959, 2231).

79. Elijah L. Forrester, "Civil Rights," *Congressional Record* (HR), 1956, 3209. See also Mississippi Democrat John Bell Williams, "Where is the Reign of Terror?" March 27, 1956, 5690.

80. *Kannapolis (NC) Daily Independent*, June 6, 1954, 1.

81. *Panama City Herald*, September 3, 1957, 2.

82. James Byrnes, "Address . . . before Illinois State Bar Association," *Congressional Record* (Senate), February 14, 1957, 2020.

83. *Richmond News Leader*, February 7, 1959, 8. The quote can be found in Thomas Dixon, *The Clansman* (New York: Grosset and Dunlap, 1905), 46. In this same editorial, Thomas Jefferson's name is invoked: "Nothing is more certainly written in the book of fate than that these people are to be free; nor is it less certain that the two races, equally free, cannot live in the same government."

84. August E. Johansen and Noah M. Mason, *Congressional Record* (HR), January 27, 1959, 1221.

85. John E. Rankin, "Lincoln, Jackson, and Jefferson Would Turn Over in Their Graves," *Congressional Record* (HR), February 13, 1950, A1010.

86. Benjamin Thomas, *Abraham Lincoln: A Biography* (New York: Knopf, 1952); Donald W. Riddle, *Congressman Abraham Lincoln* (Urbana: University of Illinois Press, 1957); Reinhard H. Luthin, *The Real Abraham Lincoln* (Englewood Cliffs, NJ: Prentice-Hall, 1960); James G. Randall, *Lincoln and the South* (Baton Rouge: Louisiana State University Press, 1946); *Lincoln the Liberal Statesman* (New York: Dodd, Mead, 1947).

87. Criticism of Lincoln from the Left, including Richard Hofstadter's "Abraham Lincoln and the Self-Made Myth," in *The American Political Tradition* (New York: Knopf, [1948] 1974), 118–74, had the same effect.

88. William Hughes, *James Agee, Omnibus, and Mr. Lincoln: The Culture of Liberalism and the Challenge of Television, 1952–1953* (Lanham, MD: The Scarecrow Press, 2004), 85; see also 1–40.

89. Sandburg, "Address to Joint Session of Congress," 5.

90. *New York Times*, February 12, 1959, 1.

91. Emile Durkheim, *The Elementary Forms of the Religious Life* (New York: The Free Press, [1915] 1965), 475.

92. William Boddy, *Fifties Television: The Industry and Its Critics* (Urbana: University of Illinois Press, 1990).

93. A new technology, television, helped maintain Lincoln's stature. Supplementing magazine and newspaper articles, television brought dramatic depictions of Lincoln's life to unprecedented numbers of people. Almost one televised Lincoln drama appeared annually during the fifteen years following World War II. "How Chance Made Lincoln President," "Sandburg's Lincoln," "Lincoln's Doctor's Dog," and "Abe Lincoln in Illinois" presented character portraits on *Omnibus* and *Kraft Theater*. See also "The Gettysburg Address" and "The Nomination of Abraham Lincoln," shown as part of the CBS *You Are There* series. Among the first popular Lincoln television dramas was CBS's "The Day Lincoln Was Shot." Other programs wrote Lincoln into their scripts. Perry Como reserved part of one of his musical shows for Raymond Massey to read the Gettysburg Address, and he followed the great words on paper for his daughter as the actor spoke them.

94. Orrin Klapp, *Heroes, Villains, and Fools: The Changing American Character* (Englewood Cliffs, NJ: Prentice-Hall, 1962), 144.

95. Ibid., 165.

CHAPTER FOUR

1. Phil L. Snyder, ed., *Detachment and the Writing of History: Essays and Letters of Carl L. Becker* (Westport, CT: Greenwood, 1958), 61.

2. Charles Horton Cooley, *Human Nature and the Social Order* (New York: Schocken, [1902] 1964), 121.

3. Wulf Kansteiner, "Finding Meaning in Memory: A Methodological Critique of Collective Memory Studies," *History and Theory* 41 (2002): 129.

4. Peterson incorporates typologies formed earlier and independently by Roy P. Basler *The Lincoln Legend* (New York: Octagon, 1935); Dixon Wector (*The Hero in America: A Chronicle of Hero Worship* (New York: Charles Scribner's Sons, 1941); David Donald, "The Folklore Lincoln," in *Lincoln Reconsidered* (New York: Vintage, [1974] 1989), 144–66; David M. Potter, *The Lincoln Theme and American National Historiography* (Oxford: Clarendon Press, 1948). For updates on Peterson's compendium, see Richard Morris, *Sinners, Lovers, and Heroes: An Essay on Memorializing in Three American Cultures* (Albany: State University of New York Press, 1997); Cullom Davis's presidential address to the Association of Documentary Editing: "Now He Belongs to the Sages: Lincoln and the Academy," *Documentary Editing* (March 1999), 1–8.

5. Kerwin L. Klein, "On the Emergence of *Memory* in Historical Discourse," *Representations* 69 (2000): 127–50.

6. The principle of reading open-ended discourse in the context of prevailing symbolic forms can be central to survey analysis in ways similar to its role in ethnography and depth interviews (Howard Schuman, "Clifford Geertz and the Interpretive Attitude Survey," *Newsletter of the Culture Section of the American Sociological Association* 17 (2003): 1, 7–8.

7. Nonresponses are included in order to make the procedure comparable to the one used in analyzing the Gallup data.

8. Maryland responses of those who had and had not named Lincoln a great president have been merged. There were few differences between the two distributions, though those not naming Lincoln great were more apt to say "don't know" when asked to speak further about him (11 percent vs. 3 percent of those calling him great), and all negative responses reported below come from such respondents. Those not naming Lincoln great are also less likely to give a Union response, though equally likely to mention emancipation.

9. Alfred Schutz, *On Phenomenology and Social Relations,* ed. Helmut R. Wagner (Chicago: University of Chicago Press, 1970), 116–22. See also Orrin E. Klapp, *Heroes, Villains, and Fools: The Changing American Character* (Englewood Cliffs, NJ: Prentice-Hall, 1962); Peter L. Berger and Thomas Luckmann, *The Social Construction of Reality: A Treatise in the Sociology of Knowledge* (Garden City, NY: Doubleday, 1967), 33–34.

10. Benjamin I. Page and Robert Y. Shapiro, *The Rational Public* (Chicago: University of Chicago Press, 1992).

11. George Sinkler, *The Racial Attitudes of American Presidents* (Garden City, NY: Doubleday, 1971); George Fredrickson, "A Man but Not a Brother: Abraham Lincoln and Racial Equality," *Journal of Southern History* 61 (1975): 39–48.

12. Leadership and Savior of the Union are positively correlated ($r = 0.12$ and 0.10, each with $p < 0.001$) in the Maryland and Knowledge surveys respectively; leadership and Great Emancipator are negatively correlated in the Maryland survey (−0.13, with $p < 0.001$).

13. Edwin Markham, "Lincoln, the Man of the People," in *The Praise of Lincoln,* ed. A. Dallas Williams (Freeport, NY: Book for Libraries, [1911] 1970), 13–15.

14. Because we intended to discuss none of the "other positive responses," we collapsed them into a single category. To assign an essentially "other" or "miscellaneous" category an "any mention" code would be meaningless because this category involves disparate items, like "decent man," "face on penny," or "Gettysburg Address."

15. The National Employee Survey, conducted by Paul Roman, University of Georgia, is the third in a series of surveys dealing with workplace experiences and problems.

16. The significance of the three comparisons, estimated by Chi- square, $df = 3$) is < 0.01.

17. Peter Karsten, *Patriot Heroes in England and America: Political Symbolism and Changing Values over Three Centuries* (Madison: University of Wisconsin Press, 1978); Marcus Cunliffe, *The Doubled Images of Lincoln and Washington,* 26th Annual Robert Fortenbaugh Memorial Lecture (Gettysburg: Gettysburg College, 1988); Wilbur Zelensky, *Nation into State: The Shifting Symbolic Foundations of American Nationalism* (Chapel Hill: University of North Carolina Press, 1988).

18. The greater percentage of Lincoln mentions in 2001 compared to 1945 appears in all demographic categories, but mostly in the South and West, and among whites generally. In the South, the percentage choosing Lincoln over Washington increased from 30 percent in 1945 to 47 percent in 2001. In the West, the comparable figures are 47 percent and 62 percent. Thus, the South is just below the national average of 51 percent; the West, far above that average. In both 1945 and 2001, 51 percent of African Americans chose Lincoln over Washington. In 1945, 41 percent of whites chose Lincoln; in 2001, 50 percent.

19. Appendix D shows close correspondence between the coding instructions for the 1945 and 2001 categories, but there is one exception: we cannot be certain that the content of our National Employee Survey 2001 "leadership" category corresponds to Gallup's undefined 1945 "greater statesman" category. The first, second, third, and fifth row differences reported in table 4.2, assessed by difference of proportions tests, are significant beyond the 0.01 level.

20. U.S. Bureau of the Census, *Historical Statistics of the United States: Colonial Times to 1970* (Washington DC: U.S. Government Printing Office, 1975), 11; U.S. Bureau of the Census, *Statistical Abstracts of the United States* (Washington DC: U.S. Government Printing Office, 1990), 17.

21. George Frederickson, *Racism: A Short History* (Princeton: Princeton University Press, 2002); Howard Schuman, Charlotte Steeh, Lawrence Bobo, and Maria Krysan, *Racial Attitudes in America: Trends and Interpretations* (Cambridge, MA: Harvard University Press, 1997).

22. John D. Skrentny, *The Minority Rights Revolution* (Cambridge, MA: Harvard University Press, 2002); Joseph T. Rhea, *Race Pride and the American Identity* (Cambridge, MA: Harvard University Press, 1997).

23. Present-minded historians projecting their sympathy for civil rights reform onto Lincoln's reconstruction aims is described in Herman Belz, *Abraham Lincoln, Constitutionalism, and Equal Rights in the Civil War Era* (New York: Fordham University Press, 1998), 246.

24. Cooley, *Human Nature and the Social Order*, 319.

25. Roman Pucinski, "February 12: Birthday of Lincoln and Kosciusko," *Congressional Record* (HR), February 9, 1960, 2369.

26. For detail and theoretical analysis, see Barry Schwartz, "The New Gettysburg Address: Fusing History and Memory," *Poetics* 33 (2005): 63–79.

27. Lyrics make the connection explicit: "Has anybody here seen my old friend Abraham? He freed a lotta people, but it seems the good die young." Bobby's name is not in the title, but "I thought I saw him walkin' up over the hill with Abraham and Martin and John."

28. Illinois State Historical Library, Lincoln Collection.

29. Mario Cuomo, "Abraham Lincoln and Our Unfinished Business," in *Building the Myth: Selected Speeches Memorializing Abraham Lincoln*, ed. Waldo H. Braden (Urbana, IL: University of Illinois Press, [1986] 1990), 238. See also Barbara Field quoted in Steven Hayward, "The Children of Abraham," *Reason* 23 (1991): 26.

30. Director Smith's statement appears on *High Tech Lincoln*, DVD documentary, A&E Television Networks, 2005. His canceling of the Lind book order is described by his friend Richard Brookhiser on "The Corner" (http://nationalreview.com/), June 7, 2005. On this same site, Lind explains that Smith blacklisted his book: "because like many historians I do not follow the new (and unsubstantiated) view that Lincoln became a modern color-blind liberal shortly before his death."

31. Because racial-equality advocates are intent on maintaining Lincoln as a symbol of racial justice, they concentrate their hostility on those who base his greatness on nonracial achievements. James G. Randall, the unquestioned pioneer of professional Lincoln scholarship, is the primary example, but Carl Sandburg and David Donald are also prominent. Randall's explicit refusal to acknowledge that emancipation justified

the war's suffering causes many contemporary scholars to believe that he and his students' works are built on the foundation of insensitivity at best, racism at worst. For a useful survey, see Kevin Fields, "Historiographical Trends and Interpretations of President Abraham Lincoln's Reputation and the Morality of the Slavery Question, Part 1," *Lincoln Herald* 106 (Winter 2004): 150–67. For a case study associating Randall and his colleagues' revisionism with racism, see C. Wyatt Evans, *The Legend of John Wilkes Booth: Myth, Memory, and Mummy* (Lawrence: University Press of Kansas, 2004).

32. Cooley, *Human Nature and the Social Order*, 341.

33. The number of slavery entries per year during the 1930s, 1940s, and 1950s were 60, 36, and 42 respectively. The phase of the late twentieth-century increase, however, is difficult to determine. During the 1960s and 1970s, the annual volumes rose to 201 and 316. For the suddenness and volume of the latter peak there is no present explanation, except that it consisted of 600 and 674 entries concentrated in two years—1969 and 1970. When these highly anomalous years are excluded, the annual means for the 1960s and 1970s are 156 and 276. During the 1980s and 1990s the annual averages were 192 and 228, then 310 for the first six years of the twenty-first century.

34. In the *Readers' Guide to Periodical Literature*, the average annual number of articles on American slavery, sampled at ten-year intervals, ranges from 1.7 to 13, with a mean of 7 between 1900 and 1990. After 1990, the ranges extend from 7 to 65, with a mean of 24.8. The trend's spike of 65 articles occurs in 1998. The *American Book Publishing Record*'s trend, sampled at two-year intervals, is less distinctive but in the same direction: 15 to 41 books on slavery were published in the 1980s with a mean of 32.2; in the 1990s, 21 to 55 with a mean of 35.2. From 1998 to 2001, however, an average of 51.3 books were published. In each source, slavery publications increase abruptly during the late 1990s and early 2000s. None of these collections is confined to American slavery. Prior to 1960, almost all references to slavery and emancipation concerned foreign cases. The important point, however, is the trend rather than the national makeup of its subject matter. Even if one assumes the percentage of American slavery articles in the entries to be constant, the shape of the trend—low numbers from 1930 to 1960, highest numbers from 1990 to present—remains the same.

35. The survey was based on responses of 1,109 University of Georgia undergraduate students surveyed between 1998 and 2000. Forty-one percent of these students named slavery the most negative phenomenon of American history. The ranking includes Vietnam War, 36 percent; treatment of Indians, 32 percent; segregation, 17 percent; internment of Japanese, 10 percent. The most ambiguous category is the Vietnam War. Some deemed it shameful because it was unnecessary; others, because it ended in defeat. For detail, see Barry Schwartz and MiKyoung Kim, "Honor, Dignity, and Collective Memory: Judging the Past in Korea and the United States," in *Culture in Mind: Toward a Sociology of Culture and Cognition*, ed. Karen Cerulo (New York: Routledge, 2002), 209–26.

36. Ira Berlin, "Coming to Terms with Slavery in Twenty-First-Century America," in *Slavery and Public History: The Tough Stuff of American Memory*, ed. James Oliver Horton and Lois E. Horton (New York: The New Press, 2006), 3.

37. In a *Chicago Defender* editorial, Joseph Phillips explains: "The civil rights movement of the of the 50's and 60's was victorious because the demands of the movement

were based on the theory of natural rights and the duty of the government to defend those rights regardless of race. Following those victories, the movement was infected by Marxist thought, which moved from demanding the protection of equal rights for individuals to the extension of community rights; away from the celebration of individual initiative and character to the politics of group identity and the deconstruction of American institutions. . . ." *Chicagodefender.com*, February 22, 2007.

38. In 1955, for example, attorney Charles Langford, assisting Fred Gray, represented Rosa Parks after her December, 1955, arrest. Nine years later, in 1964, he successfully sued to integrate Montgomery's schools. In 1993, his mission changed: representing the state's black legislators, he sued successfully for a change in the state flag. During the 1950s and 1960s, then, Mr. Langford engaged in struggles against the most fundamental forms of racial injustice; in the 1990s, he struggled against offensive symbols. As a civil rights protester, Langford was a member of what Richard Rorty called the "reform left"; afterward, during the last third of the twentieth century, he was a member of the "cultural left" (*Achieving Our Country* [Cambridge, MA: Harvard University Press, 1998], 73–107).

39. Committee on Conference, *Congressional Record* (HR), 1999, H10543.

40. Roy P. Basler, ed., *Collected Works of Abraham Lincoln* (New Brunswick: Rutgers University Press, 1953), 8:24.

41. *Chicago Tribune*, May 9, 2000. Inserted by Jackson as an amendment to the Department of Interior appropriation bill, the congressional directive seems ironic. If the Committee of Conference required the National Park Service to condemn the Confederate soldier defending slavery as well as slavery itself, Congress would have rejected its bill. The separation of cause and participant is common in commemorative projects, allowing recognition of soldiers fighting unpopular wars (Robin Wagner-Pacifici and Barry Schwartz, "Vietnam Veterans Memorial: Commemorating a Difficult Past," *American Journal of Sociology* 97 [1991]: 376–420). Thus, slavery can be recognized as a national sin while the selfless motives and gallantry of its defenders, less than 25 percent of whom owned slaves, are commemorated.

42. Reflecting their generation's disillusionment with World War I and reacting against the "national" tradition of Civil War history, James G. Randall, Wesley Craven, Reinhard Luthin, Benjamin Thomas, and T. Harry Edwards, among other historians, formed the Revisionist school of Civil War history.

43. For each generation of textbooks considered, i.e., texts published between 1920–44; 1945–64; 1964 to present, the author and second reader agreed on the relative emphasis of Union and emancipation. Emancipation bore a utilitarian, subordinated, relation to Union until 1965; after 1965, emancipation assumed a significance equal to or greater than Union.

44. Frances Fitzgerald, *America Revised: History Textbooks in the Twentieth Century* (Boston: Little, Brown, 1979), 227–34.

45. See, for example, Nathaniel Platt and Muriel Jean Drummond, *Our Nation from Its Creation* (Englewood Cliffs, NJ: Prentice-Hall, 1966); Howard B. Wilder, Robert P. Ludlum, and Harriet McCune Brown, *This Is America's Story* (Boston: Houghton Mifflin, 1966); Lewis Paul Todd and Merle Curti, *Rise of the American Nation*, 3rd ed. (New York: Harcourt Brace Jovanovich, 1972).

46. Melvin Schwartz and John R. O'Connor, *Exploring American History* (New York: Globe Book Co., 1986), 320. In 1983, Pulitzer Prize winner William S. McFeely, without mentioning Union, extended the war's significance to poverty as well as freedom: "The existence in the United States of an uneasy relationship between black and white people, rich and poor people, is what the Civil War was all about." William S. McFeely, "The Civil War's Lure," *New York Times*, July 4, 1983, 19.

47. Winthrop D. Jordan, Miriam Greenblatt, and John S. Bowes, *The Americans: The History of a People and a Nation* (Evanston, IL: McDougal, Littel, and Company, 1985), 348. Changing emphasis from saving the Union to freeing the slaves resonates with ideological interests. According to the conservative American Textbook Council (Gilbert T. Sewall, *History Textbooks at the New Century: A Report of the American Textbook Council* [New York: American Textbook Council, 2001]), "high-school history textbooks started to turn sharply to the historiographic left" during the 1990s (23, 26). The change was in fact gradual and close to realizing itself in the 1980s. The few new juvenile books randomly coming to our attention leaned in the same direction. Cheryl Harness's *Ghosts of the Civil War* presents an informative story of the war, but from the very first page she tells that story in an abolitionist accent: "Americans of the 19th century were haunted by the memory of their 18th-century ancestors, who fought a revolution and founded a democratic republic 'conceived in liberty,' yet which allowed human beings to be held in bondage. There had to be bloody justice. This had to be settled, even if it meant tearing the Union of states apart, so we could be one free nation where we, the people, governed ourselves" (New York: Simon and Schuster, 2007), 1.

48. Henry W. Bragdon, Samuel P. McCutchen, and Donald R. Richie, *History of a Free Nation* (Lake Forest, IL: Glencoe, 1992).

49. M. T. G. Downey Jr. and E. D. Metcalf, *United States History: In the Course of Human Events* (St. Paul, MN: West Publishing, 1997), 375, 461–62.

50. Joanne L. Buggey, Gerald A. Danzer, Charles L. Mitsakos, *America! America!* 2nd ed. (Glenview, IL: Scott Foresman and Company, 1987), 391.

51. Quoted by Paul Boyer, Lewis P. Todd, and Merle Curti, *The American Nation* (Austin: Holt, Rinehart, and Winston, 1995), 379–80.

52. Fitzgerald, *America Revisited*, 83.

53. Although we place aggregated survey responses in the context of aggregated texts and symbols, we cannot know which particular texts and symbols specific individuals are apprehending. This shortcoming distinguishes our method from that of reader-reaction studies. (See, for example, Wendy Griswold, "The Fabrication of Literary Meaning: Literary Interpretation in the United States, Great Britain, and the West Indies," *American Journal of Sociology* 92 [1987]: 1077–117; Janice Radway, *Reading the Romance: Women, Patriarchy, and Popular Literature* [Chapel Hill: University of North Carolina Press, 1984]; Janice Radway, *A Feeling for Books: The Book-of-the-Month Club, Literary Taste, and Middle Class Desire* [Chapel Hill: University of North Carolina Press, 1997]). We only know that texts and symbols (cultural objects) contextualize individual beliefs (reception), and it is from this relation that we draw inferences about causation.

54. Wendy Griswold, "A Methodological Framework for the Sociology of Culture," in *Sociological Methodology*, ed. Clifford Clogg (Washington DC: American Soci-

ological Association, 1987), 17:1–35; James V. Wertsch, *Voices of Collective Remembering* (Cambridge: Cambridge University Press, 2002).

55. Hans Robert Jauss, *Toward an Aesthetic of Reception* (Minneapolis: University of Minnesota Press, 1982), 3–45.

56. Eviatar Zerubavel, *Time Maps: Collective Memory and the Social Shape of the Past* (Chicago: University of Chicago Press, 2003).

57. U.S. Abraham Lincoln Bicentennial Commission, *Interim Report, June 2004* (Washington DC: U.S. Government Printing Office, 2004), 7, 48.

58. U.S. Abraham Lincoln Bicentennial Commission. *U.S. Abraham Lincoln Bicentennial Commission Strategic Plan and Preliminary Fundraising and Communication/Marketing Recommendations,* prepared by Metropolitan Group, February 12, 2005, 5, 9

59. U.S. National Park Service, "Interpretation of the Civil War," *Interpretation at Civil War Sites: A Report to Congress,* March 2000; "U.S. Urged to Discuss Slavery at War Sites," *Chicago Tribune,* May 9, 2000.

60. In drawing conclusions about differences in belief, distinctiveness of pattern is considered along with statistical significance.

61. A separate analysis shows three additional background factors in play, but the effects in each case are mediocre. Among age, education, and gender groupings, the clearest and most consistent relations are for Savior of the Union: educated and older respondents are more likely than those less educated and younger to mention Union. The association with education probably reflects greater knowledge of American history. Older Americans were probably exposed to Lincoln when more Americans considered saving the Union to be his key achievement. The one other clearly significant relation for Savior of the Union involves gender. In the Maryland survey, men mention Union more than women. Lincoln's leadership abilities are most likely to be mentioned by highly educated respondents in both surveys, and by males in the Maryland survey.

62. Howard Schuman, Barry Schwartz, and Hannah D'Arcy, "Elite Revisionist and Popular Beliefs: Christopher Columbus, Hero or Villain?" *Public Opinion Quarterly* 69 (2005): 2–29.

63. Washington's slaveholder reputation endures despite Henry Wiencek's sympathetic treatment. *An Imperfect God: George Washington, His Slaves, and the Creation of America* (New York: Farrar, Strauss, and Giroux, 2003).

64. Jeffrey K. Olick, *In the House of the Hangman: The Agonies of German Defeat, 1943–1949* (Chicago: University of Chicago Press, 2005); "The Value of Regret: Lessons from and for Germany, *Religion and Public Life* 33 (Spring 2003): 21–32; Jeffrey K. Olick and Brenda Coughlin, "The Politics of Regret," in *The Politics of the Past: On Repairing Historical Injustices,* ed. John B. Torpey (Rowman and Littlefield, 2003), 37–62; Bernhard Giesen, *Triumph and Trauma* (Boulder, CO: Paradigm Publishers, 2004); Avishai Margalit, *The Ethics of Memory* (Cambridge, MA: Harvard University Press, 2002); W. James Booth, "Communities of Memory: On Identity, Memory, and Debt," *American Political Science Review* 93 (1999): 249–63.

65. For a discussion of the relative salience of hierarchical, fatalistic, egalitarian, and individualist values as they bear on presidential reputation, see Richard Ellis and Aaron Wildavsky, *Dilemmas of Presidential Leadership: From Washington through Lincoln* (New Brunswick: Transaction, 1989). See also Michael Thompson, Richard Ellis, and Aaron Wildavsky, *Cultural Theory* (Boulder, CO: Westview, 1990).

66. For sociological perspective on Hans Robert Jauss's concept of "horizon of expectations" and the reception of cultural objects, see Wendy Griswold, "A Methodological Framework for the Sociology of Culture," 10–16.

CHAPTER FIVE

1. *Chicago Tribune,* February 12, 1931, 16; *Los Angeles Times,* February 13, 1931, pt.1, 2; "Defending Honest Abe against Debunkers," *The Literary Digest* (February 28, 1931): 34.

2. In contrast, when a 1946 Gallup Poll asked respondents to choose the best of four particular presidents—Washington, Lincoln, Wilson, and Franklin Roosevelt—the top choices, Roosevelt (39 percent) and Lincoln (37 percent) exceeded Washington (15 percent) by a wider margin. The preferences for Wilson and "don't knows" were 5 percent and 4 percent respectively (Hadley Cantril, *Public Opinion, 1935–1946* [Princeton: Princeton University Press, 1951]), 590.

3. For detail, see Barry Schwartz, *Abraham Lincoln and the Forge of National Memory* (Chicago: University of Chicago Press, 2000), 107–17.

4. The WorldCat database was accessed with Abraham Lincoln as "Named Person" (327n12). Other search criteria, including "Keyword," yielded larger numbers of books but an identical pattern. Each search criterion yielded many superfluous items, the percentage of which can be assumed to be constant from one year to the next. Figure 5.4 contains two peaks, not one, both at the beginning of the twentieth century. The year 1900, celebrated in churches as well as national, state, and municipal organizations, occasioned a dramatic increase in publications about national heroes, including George Washington, whose 1900 peak far exceeded Lincoln's. The 1909 peak is the Lincoln centennial year. The effervescence of the new century observances was rooted, at least in part, in the role of public spectacle at a time when mass entertainment did not exist. Great men were often the objects of such celebrations, which in turn stimulated interest in biographical and related historical information.

5. The U.S. Park Service provides annual statistics on visitation to Lincoln's Springfield home. The Springfield Convention and Visitors Bureau reports on local sites. In September 2004, the Lincoln-Herndon Law Office and New Salem reduced their days of operation from seven to five per week. This would have no effect on the 2005–6 comparison, which is a measure of the new Lincoln Museum and Library's effect on visitation to other sites. Moreover, in 2005 the New Salem park hosted fifteen festivals, and in 2006, seventeen, which are both unusually high numbers—twice the usual eight festivals in other years. This peak, which corresponds to the year of and the year after the Lincoln Museum's opening, has no influence on other sites. For 2005–6, the changes in visitation to Lincoln's Kentucky birthplace is +4.8 percent; for his (Indiana) boyhood home: −16 percent; Lincoln Memorial: +4.7 percent; Ford's Theater: + 0.002 percent.

6. Simulated sites, too, are losing appeal. One of the few attractions for which there is only a short waiting line in Florida's Disneyworld is the Hall of Presidents, where robotic former chief executives speak to one another and to the audience.

7. U.S. Department of the Interior, National Park Service, *Public Use Data Collecting and Reporting Reference Manual,* Director S Order 82: Public Use Data Collecting and Reporting Program (Washington DC, 2000). For detail, see http://www2.nature.nps.gov/stats/methpolicy.htm.

8. Lincoln statue production has not altogether ceased. In addition to the Richmond and Vicksburg statues (to be discussed in chapter 7, this volume), see Gabor Boritt, *The Lincoln Enigma: The Changing Faces of an American Icon* (New York: Oxford University Press, 2001), 237–78.

9. Most of the twenty-nine films featuring Lincoln and appearing between 1910 and 1919 were 20–30 minute reels shown in neighborhood store nickelodeons. In contrast, nine of the sixteen films produced between 1920 and 1939 were feature length (an hour and a half or more) and shown in movie theaters.

10. Charlie Brown spoof on the 1939 film, *Mr. Smith Goes to Washington.*

11. The origin of this concept, part of the inventory of derogatory terms applied to seemingly backward rural people, is unclear. It was used as early as the 1890s and probably spread with the growth of the city.

12. "Abraham, Martin, and John are Back!" *Weekly World News,* May 14, 2000.

13. Corniness is possible only for pictorial depictions with which viewers identify. Jefferson Smith, the Boy Scout leader in *Mr Smith Goes to Washington,* seems corny to many if not most contemporary Americans, but comparable pictures of the Hitler Youth do not; pictures of American young men gazing at Lincoln's image epitomize corn; pictures of German young men gazing at Hitler's picture seem anything but corny. Corniness is a characteristic of familiar, not alien, representations; its opposite is not the hostile cynicism of the alienated but the cynicism of one who considers oneself part of the community that once embraced the corny representation.

14. Three years later, the Uniform Holiday Bill unintentionally prompted states, public, and private organizations to create a Presidents' Day. The official holiday, Washington's Birthday, is now a source of public confusion. Some believe Presidents' Day commemorates Washington and Lincoln; others, all presidents. See "Ritual in the Post Heroic Era," chapter 6, this volume.

15. Cartoons are taken from disks 1 and 2 accompanying *The Complete Cartoons of The New Yorker*, ed. Robert Mankoff (New York: Black Dog & Levanthal, 2004). In order of mention in the text, the cartoon dates are February 6, 1965; March 15, 1976; June 7, 1976; February 14, 1983.

16. Charles E. Morris III, "My Old Kentucky Homo: Lincoln and the Politics of Queer Public Memory," in *Framing Public Memory,* ed. Kendall Phillips (Tuscaloosa: University of Alabama Press, 2003), 89–114; Gabor Boritt affirms the relevance of the issue in his editorial introduction to *The Lincoln Enigma: The Changing Face of an American Icon*, xiv–vi.

17. *Weekly World News,* June 3, 2002. (See also "Abraham Lincoln was a Woman!" *Weekly World News,* January 22, 2002; Letter to the editor: "Was Babe Lincoln more than a Cross-Dresser?" *Weekly World News,* February 13, 2002). Such is Lincoln's status during the sexual revolution. Commenting on a second, moral, revolution, which has made lying and dishonesty more common, *Weekly World News* reveals that the past was less perfect than we might think. "Dis-Honest Abe Lincoln did not write the Gettysburg Address. . . . His brother-in-law [Ernest "Ernie" Todd] did, says historian!" (December 9, 2002). Regarding the third, scientific, revolution, the *Weekly World News* reported on December 5, 1993, that Lincoln had been the subject of an experiment on Revivitol, a compound designed to bring the dead back to life. Scientists secretly removed Lincoln's body from his tomb to Walter Reed Army Hospital, where they

injected him with the wonder drug, watched his heartbeat and pulse quicken and his body squirm on the table. The former president's eyes opened and, after looking about and asking, "Gentlemen, where am I?" he lost consciousness and died a second time.

18. *Desmond Pfeiffer* was funny because it satirized the Clinton White House from a historical distance. Abe and Mary Lincoln were both depicted as sexual perverts, with Abe staining his intern's dress and making cigar jokes. There is no evidence of anyone complaining about this portrayal of the sixteenth president and his wife. In the scene that helped to kill the show, Pfeiffer, a black British butler, relaxes in the kitchen when Kilbourne, Lincoln's chief of staff, tells him: "The slaves haven't been emancipated yet, Pfeiffer. Get your feet off that table." Pfeiffer stands and in his British accent asserts that we are both men and equal as human beings. Kilbourne laughs: "Both equals? *Hello!* You're in Americaaaa!" The scene is clearly a criticism of slavery, but sensitivities can undermine logic. California assembly member Rod Wright was "outraged at the promotion and airing of UPN's (United Paramount Network's) so-called comedy" because he saw no humor in the mocking of slavery. The Los Angeles City Council condemned the show and called for a special commission to review its appropriateness for broadcast. UPN, the comedy's producer, boasted more black viewers than any other network, and its hiring of minorities for key positions was unmatched. The vice president of comedy development and executive director of programming were both African American, as were other members of the program staff. Desmond Pfeiffer was by far the cast's most intelligent character.

19. See also *The Hideous Jabbering Head of Abraham Lincoln*, located on another Web site of the same name. The headline: "I was the President of the United States of America, back when it was cool to be President, instead of now, which is just lame."

20. Max Weber, "Science as a Vocation," in *From Max Weber: Essays in Sociology*, ed. Hans Gerth and C. Wright Mills (New York: Oxford University Press, 1958), 155.

21. Julius Lester, *Look Out Whitey! Black Power's Gon' Get Your Mama!* (New York: Dial Press, 1968).

22. Richard C. Gregory, "The Myth of Emancipation," in *No More Lies: The Myth and the Reality of American History* (New York: Harper and Row, 1971), 178–97.

23. Lerone Bennett, "Was Abe Lincoln a White Supremicist?" *Ebony* 23 (February 1968): 36–37.

24. *Chicago Defender*, February 12, 1968, 13.

25. Vincent Harding, *There Is a River: The Black Struggle for Freedom in America* (New York: Harcourt Brace Jovanovich, 1981), 236.

26. Personal communication from Bernice McNair Barnett, Department of Sociology, University of Illinois.

27. *Atlanta Daily World*, February 13, 1975, 1, 4.

28. Senator Obama made his statement at the Abraham Lincoln Museum, Springfield, Illinois, May 11, 2006 (http://blacknews.com). See also "Jackson [Jesse Jackson Jr.] Appointed to Abraham Lincoln Bicentennial Commission," May 9, 2003 (http://www.house.gov); "Transcript from Minister Louis Farrakhan's Remarks to the Million Man March," October 17, 1995 (http://www.cnn.com).

29. In 1975, too, ordinary African Americans seemed to hold a low opinion of Lincoln. Yvette Fulcher, a Washington University student, assessed Lincoln's status by sending mail questionnaires to 120 black adults in the St. Louis area. Her six questions

covered three areas: What does the respondent know about Lincoln's Emancipation Proclamation and colonization policy? Does he believe Lincoln was good or bad for blacks in the 1860s and the 1970s? What does he think of Lincoln overall? Combined, 66 percent or about two-thirds of the respondents expressed negative feelings about Lincoln. Among students, professional, and white-collar respondents, the percentage holding negative opinions was even higher: 74 percent. Yvette Fulcher's findings appear in "Emancipation: 113 Years Later," *Lincoln Lore* (November 1975), 1–3.

30. In 1990, fifteen years after Fulcher's results were published, Barry Schwartz and Bernice Barnett designed a survey to place blacks' negative feelings about Lincoln into better perspective. They asked a small sample of students at a large, Southern state university to rank eight historical figures in terms of their greatness. White and black students gave Martin Luther King Jr. and John F. Kennedy equally high ratings. On Lincoln, however, the consensus broke down. Ninety-five percent of white students rated Lincoln positively, placing him alongside King and Kennedy, compared to only 77 percent of their black classmates. Student comments about Lincoln's achievement make the reasons for this difference evident. Most whites were impressed with Lincoln's preserving the Union and freeing the slaves, while 60 percent of the black students believed that his primary accomplishment, emancipation, was either inconsequential or reflected political rather than idealistic motives. On the other hand, black students rated Lincoln higher than George Washington, Andrew Jackson, and Dwight Eisenhower, and equal to their grandparents' idol, Franklin Roosevelt.

31. In the smaller, less representative, local sample described in note 29, attitudes toward Lincoln are the most negative.

32. Joseph R. Bryson, "Lincoln and the South," *Congressional Record* (HR), February 12, 1946, A683.

33. Richard Harwell, in *Lincoln for the Ages*, ed. Ralph G. Newman (Garden City, N.Y.: Doubleday, 1960), 203.

34. *Atlanta Journal*, February 12, 1955, 4.

35. John E. Huss, *Senator for the South* (Garden City, NY: Doubleday, 1961).

36. *Congressional Record* (Senate), February 29, 1960, 3750.

37. U.S., *Final Report of the Abraham Lincoln Sesquicentennial Commission* (Washington DC: Government Printing Office, 1959).

38. In 1959, the Lincoln sesquicentennial year, Walter Washington Williams, the last of four million Americans who participated in the Civil War, passed away at the age of 117. He was buried in a grey Confederate uniform. President Eisenhower declared a day of national mourning and ordered all flags to fly at half staff. Representatives of the president, the Texas governor, along with scores of representatives from other states, attended Mr. Williams's funeral. His death, they knew, ended an era. It lent significance not only to the Lincoln sesquicentennial but also the Civil War centennial, which was already in the process of organization. Designed to clarify Lincoln's reputation and enhance his stature, the Civil War centennial beclouded both as it played itself out.

39. Lincoln was conducting tension rather than consensus, as was evident in the *Richmond News Leader*'s February 1959 editorial, "Postscript on Tom and Abe." Peeved at patronizing Northern comments on the beginning of integration in Virginia, including the *New York Times*'s "sanctimonious claim" that immediate equality might move the nation nearer the ideals of Thomas Jefferson and Abraham Lincoln, the

Richmond editor explained that Jefferson "regretfully" regarded the black race as naturally inferior to the white race, while Lincoln "doubted whether ideal union could ever be attained 'with millions of an alien, inferior race among us. . . .'" (February 7, 1959, 8). Since the view of the *News Leader*'s editor was shared by many if not most Southerners, it reinforced beliefs that a Civil War centennial would divide the country. Harry Golden's 1962 *Saturday Evening Post* article "Let's End the Civil War" explained why a Civil War centennial in the midst of a civil rights movement could stir up nothing but antagonism. In a private letter, the Florida Commission chairman disagreed with Golden, citing the cultural value of national commemorations. Golden responded: "The Civil War Centennial is no Passover and it is no July 4. It was fought to maintain slavery and to Balkanize the United States of America." Its commemoration, Golden believed, would complete the job. Trouble peaked at the very first meeting of the state commissions, scheduled for Charleston, South Carolina. Learning that segregated hotels would deny black state commission members lodging and meals, President Kennedy instructed National Commission chairman Ulysses Grant III to accept nothing less than equal treatment for all commission members. Moving the affair to the Charleston air force base would inconvenience everyone, but it was the only way to hold a racially integrated meeting. The Southern state committees, meanwhile, organized their own informal association and met separately in Charleston—which is precisely what the centennial's opponents feared would happen. The subsequent dismissal of centennial executive director Karl Betts and national director Ulysses S. Grant III had no effect on existing regional activities. Northern events were conducted and attended by white and black participants, stressed the unity of the nation, and honored Abraham Lincoln; Southern events were segregated, celebrated states rights, reenacted battles, and honored the heroes of the Confederacy. (See Colehow to Betts, September 23, 1958, *Civil War Centennial Collection,* National Archives, Box 112; Mrs. Dallas Scarborough to Carl S. Betts, July 18, 1959, Box 126; Betts to Colehow, October 1, 1958; Adam G. Adams to Harry Golden, August 17, 1962; Harry Golden to Adam G. Adams, August 22, 1962, Box 126; Kennedy to Grant, March 14, 1961; Golden to Florida Civil War Centennial Commissioner Adams," August 22, 1862. See also Adams to Golden, August 17, 1862; Golden, "Let's End the Civil War," *Saturday Evening Post,* 1962, Box 111).

40. Ralph McGill, "The Meaning of Lincoln Today," *Vital Speeches* (February 12, 1960): 330. For more on the myth of state sovereignty, see Dwight L. Dumond, "Emancipation: History's Fantastic Reverie," placed in *Congressional Record* by Michigan Democrat Charles Diggs, June 17, 1964, House of Representatives, pp.14105–14107. On the other hand, Northern representatives were eager to retain the good feeling of the South. Everett Dirksen, a supporter of racial integration, inserted into the *Congressional Record* a speech made in the U.S. House or Representatives in 1913 by James M. Graham of Illinois, explaining that Lincoln "never lost his love and sympathy for his native Southland, and that had he lived he would have never permitted the reign of robbery and ruin which that fair land experienced in reconstruction days" (April 22, 1965, Senate, p.8241.) In another effort to pacify the South, Hubert Humphrey, speaking in Durham, North Carolina, called the Reconstruction period "a distressing chapter in American history." Even more, "the radicalism that dominated the Reconstruction era is a vivid example of the mindless, vengeful kind of extremism that even

today, if left unchecked, could bring our great democracy to its knees" (*Civil War Centennial Collection,* April 25, 1965, National Archives Box 121).

41. Ross Barnett, "Centennial Address," November 5, 1961, Civil War Centennial Collection, National Archives, Box 117. Texas state officials were "opposed to taking part in the celebration, as 'they do not care to celebrate the South's defeat in a celebration in which the South was not adequately represented in the national organization'" (Box 117).

42. *Ibid.,* "News Release from the Office of Senator Strom Thurmond," August 19, 1962, *Ibid.,* Box 117. The Centennial's first director shared Thurmond's views. Before retired Major General Ulysses S. Grant III was appointed Chairman of the United States Civil War Centennial Commission, he had designed successful strategies to keep blacks out of certain Washington, D.C. real estate markets. Ms. Virginia Doris of Clearwater Beach, Florida did not know this when she dedicated her Centennial poem to him. Chairman Grant's attention must have peaked at the last stanza: "Young warriors up on war, chanted / an ode to eager destiny, moving / From green farm to battle soil, being / nourished by their deathless / Dream, of civil liberty." Ms. Doris's poem crossing General Grant's desk was a historic coincidence, for Grant's June 15, 1958 redlining activities were precisely the kinds of discrimination that civil rights advocates had recently begun seriously to oppose (Doris to Grant, January 8, 1961, *Civil War Centennial Collection,* National Archive Box 76).

43. Ibid., Pedley to Betts, May 28, 1958, Box 83.

44. Ibid., State of New York, Executive Chamber, December 31, 1962, National Archive, Box 121.

45. Avery Craven, "Southern Attitudes toward Abraham Lincoln," in *Papers in Illinois History* (Springfield: Illinois State Historical Society, 1944), 10.

46. The Richmond statue reverses an event that had taken place in Washington DC almost fifty years earlier. In February 1954, the Sons of the Confederacy resolved for the first time to accept an invitation from the Sons of Union Veterans to participate in ceremonies at the Lincoln Memorial. Colonel John Virden, grandson of a Confederate cavalry officer, spoke for his association. He said nothing about Lincoln, but conceded that "ninety years was long enough to hold a grudge." After he set down his wreath at the base of Lincoln's statue, President Dwight Eisenhower appeared. The president, delivering his wreath in the name of the American people, lowered his head and stood silently for about two minutes, then turned around and slowly left. As soon as the ceremony ended, the thousand people who had braved the bitter cold entered the memorial chamber. Everyone noticed the president's wreath of red, white, and blue carnations, but the Sons of the Confederacy's drew the most attention. It was a magnolia wreath containing two miniature Confederate flags. *Richmond Times Dispatch,* February 14, 1954, sec. B, 2; *Richmond News Leader,* February 12, 1954, 2.

47. See http://www.TimesDispatch.com, http://www.DixieDailyNews.com, http://www.Chblue.com, http://Pilotonline.com, http://www.Fortwayne.com, March 2003, for a sample of articles about the dispute.

48. Willmoore Kendall, "The Declaration of Independence: A Derailment?" in Willmoore Kendall and George W. Carey, *The Basic Symbols of the American Political Tradition* (Baton Rouge: Louisiana State University Press, 1970), 75–95.

49. Comparing Lincoln to Adolph Hitler, Bradford's intemperate comments, some say, eliminated him as candidate for the National Endowment for the Humanities directorship; however, the principal target of his venom was equality, not Lincoln (M. E. Bradford, "The Heresy of Equality:Bradford Replies to Jaffa," *Modern Age* [Winter, 1976]: 74).

50. Thomas Fleming, "Lincoln's Tragic Heroism," *National Review* 41 (December 8, 1989): 40. For critical reaction, see Harry V. Jaffa, "Lincoln's Character Assassins," *National Review* 42 (January 22, 1990): 34–38.

51. Thomas J. DiLorenzo, *The Real Lincoln: A New Look at Abraham Lincoln, His Agenda, and an Unnecessary War* (New York: Three Rivers Press, 2003).

52. *U.S. News and World Report* 58 (February 15, 1965): 74–76.

53. Ralph McGinnis, "What Did Lincoln Stand For?" *Vital Speeches* 45 (May 1, 1979): 439–43.

54. Frank Carlson, "Lincoln versus Lenin—A Contrast," *Congressional Record* (Senate), February 11, 1965, 2626.

55. "If Lincoln Lived Today—A Profile in Poverty," *U.S. News and World Report* 58 (February 15, 1965): 74–76.

56. Steven Hayward, "The Children of Abraham," *Reason* (May 1991): 30.

57. The eight-minute video viewed by millions of visitors since 1994 defines the Lincoln Memorial as the site of King's "I Have a Dream" speech, demonstrations for gay rights, abortion rights, women's rights, opposition to war, and a host of other liberal interests. It gives the distinct impression that Lincoln would have more readily supported these interests than conservative ones. In 2005, the National Park Service revised the video.

58. Since 1956, the year in which Gallup asked his question about presidential greatness, neither Jefferson nor Adams was named by more than 10 percent of the respondents. No corresponding data exists for Hamilton, but the number of citations listed under his name in the *Reader's Guide to Periodic Literature*, 1880 to present, peaked at 3.25 annually between 1961 and 1965. In that same interval, Jefferson articles numbered 4.5; Adams, 3. Lincoln articles numbered 16.25.

59. See, for example, Pierre Nora, *Realms of Memory*, vol. 1 (New York: Columbia University Press, 1996).

60. Hans Meyerhoff, *Time in Literature* (Berkeley: University of California Press, 1955), 109.

CHAPTER SIX

1. Harold Holzer assembles short statements by selected admirers indicating how each became interested in Lincoln. The writers include Gabor Boritt, Mario Cuomo, Richard N. Current, David Herbert Donald, John Hope Franklin, Jim Getty, Doris Kearns Goodwin, Jack Kemp, Philip B. Kunhardt III, Brian Lamb, Lewis Lehrman, James M. McPherson, Lloyd Ostendorf, Weldon Petz, Gerald Prokopowicz, Arthur Schlesinger Jr., Paul Simon, Louise Taper, Sam Waterston, Frank J. Williams, Garry Wills, and David Wolper. Each member of this group—nine biographers, historians, filmmakers, and writers; three politicians; one impersonator; six collectors; three television figures; one museum director—found something in Lincoln to connect to himself or herself. Each is at once a defender and interpreter of Lincoln's life and presidency.

2. Merrill Peterson, *Abraham Lincoln in the American Mind* (New York: Oxford University Press, 1994), 375.

3. Unfortunately, Andrew Ferguson's *Land of Lincoln: Adventures in Abe's America* (New York: Atlantic Monthly Press, 2007) appeared after this book's completion. It is the best analysis of the Lincoln community ever written.

4. U.S. Census Bureau, *Statistical Abstract of the United States*, 2003, no. HS-10. "Native and Foreign-Born Population by Place of Birth: 1900 to 2000." The percentage of non-European immigrants by decade, beginning 1960, is as follows: 1960, 0.8 percent; 1970, 1.3 percent; 1980, 3 percent; 1990, 5.4 percent; 2000, 8.6 percent (http://www.census.gov/population).

5. Knowledge Network findings on Lincoln's reputation, based on 91 Hispanic and 38 "other" non–African American respondents (analyzed separately and jointly), are consistent with those reported by Roy Rosenzweig and David Thelen in *The Presence of the Past: Popular History in American Life* (New York: Columbia University Press, 1998): just as assimilated Mexican Americans perceive American history as do white non-Hispanic Americans, their perceptions of Lincoln's greatness are similar. In contrast, Rosenzweig and Thelen's finding African Americans and native Americans expressing the most alienation from America's past (237; see also 138–49) conforms to race differences in perception of Lincoln's greatness (discussed in chapter 5, this volume).

6. David Harvey, *The Condition of Postmodernity* (Oxford: Blackwell, 1989), 60–62.

7. Gary A. Fine, "Reputational Entrepreneurs and the Memory of Incompetence: Melting Supporters, Partisan Warriors, and Images of President Harding," *American Journal of Sociology* 101 (1996): 1159–93. See also Gladys Lang and Kurt Lang, *Etched in Memory: The Building and Survival of Artistic Reputation* (Chapel Hill: University of North Carolina Press, 1990).

8. By the 1970s, the "Southernization" of the United States was under way, evident in increased legislation for lower taxes, fewer public services, increased military preparedness, and reliance on state rather than federal solutions to social problems. Through the 1980s, increased political polarization was evident in the dissipation of white support for the civil rights movement resulting from busing, affirmative action, and black militancy. See Bruce J. Schulman, *The Seventies: The Great Shift in American Culture, Society, and Politics* (New York: The Free Press, 2001); Thomas B. Edsall and Mary D. Edsall, *Chain Reaction: The Impact of Race, Rights, and Taxes on American Politics* (New York: Norton, 1991); William C. Berman, *America's Right Turn: From Nixon to Bush* (Baltimore: Johns Hopkins University Press, 1994); Howard Schuman and Maria Krysan, "A Historical Note on Whites' Beliefs about Racial Equality," *American Sociological Review* 64 (1999): 847–55.

9. Marc Landy and Sidney M. Milkis, *Presidential Greatness* (Lawrence: University Press of Kansas, 2000).

10. For a summary see Don Fehrenbacher, *Lincoln in Text and Context* (Stanford: Stanford University Press, 1987), 207–8; Lerone Bennett, *Forced into Glory: Abraham Lincoln's White Dream* (Chicago: Johnson Publishing Co., 2000); "Was Abe Lincoln a White Supremacist?" *Ebony* 23 (1968): 36–37; Kevin Fields, "Historiographical Trends and Interpretations of President Abraham Lincoln's Reputation and the Morality on the Slavery Question: Part I" *Lincoln Herald* 106 (2004): 150–67; Kevin Fields, "Histo-

riographical Trends and Interpretations of President Abraham Lincoln's Reputation and the Morality on the Slavery Question: Part II" *Lincoln Herald* 107 (2005): 11–30.

11. Mark E. Neely Jr.'s Pulitzer Prize–winning *The Fate of Liberty: Abraham Lincoln and Civil Liberties* (New York: Oxford University Press, 1991) documents Lincoln's wartime regard for civil liberties. Gore Vidal's *Lincoln* (New York: Ballantine, 1984) is one of the most prominent examples of historical fiction. Donald P. Philips, *Lincoln on Leadership* (New York: Time-Warner, 1994) takes Lincoln as the model CEO.

12. Harry V. Jaffa, *Crisis and the House Divided* (New York: Doubleday, 1959); Don Fehrenbacher, *Prelude to Greatness* (Stanford: Stanford University Press, 1962); Lawanda Cox, *Lincoln and Black Freedom* (Columbia, SC: University of South Carolina Press, 1981); Peyton McCrary, *Abraham Lincoln and Reconstruction* (Princeton: Princeton University Press, 1978); Stephen Oates, *With Malice Toward None: The Life of Abraham Lincoln* (New York: Harper and Row, 1977); Stephen Oates, *Abraham Lincoln: The Man Behind the Myths* (New York: Harper and Row, 1984).

13. Mark E. Neely, Jr., *The Last Best Hope of Earth* (Cambridge, MA: Harvard University Press, 1993); David Donald, *Lincoln* (New York: Simon and Schuster, 1995); Alan Guelzo, *Abraham Lincoln: Redeemer President* (Grand Rapids, MI: William B. Eerdmans Publishing Company, 1999; *Lincoln's Emancipation Proclamation: The End of Slavery in America* (New York: Simon and Schuster, 2004); John Patrick Diggins, *On Hallowed Ground: Abraham Lincoln and the Foundations of American History* (New Haven, CT: Yale University Press, 2000); William Lee Miller, *Lincoln's Virtues: An Ethical Biography* (New York: Alfred A. Knopf, 2002); Richard Carwardine, *Lincoln: A Life of Purpose and Power* (London, England: Pearson-Longman, 2003), and Dorothy Kearns Goodwin, *Team of Rivals: The Political Genius of Abraham Lincoln* (New York: Simon and Schuster, 2005). Michael Lind's *What Lincoln Believed: The Values and Convictions of America's Greatest President* (New York: Doubleday, 2004) is a highly flattering analysis, but many scholars reject its portrayal of Lincoln's indifference to black interests. In Lind's view, however, critics underestimate Lincoln's greatness when they fail to emphasize his role in the preservation of democracy.

14. Edmund Wilson, *Patriotic Gore: Studies in the Literature of the Civil War* (New York: Oxford University Press, 1962), pp. 99–130; George Forgie, *Patricide in the House Divided* (New York: W. W. Norton, 1979); Dwight Anderson, *Abraham Lincoln: The Quest for Immortality* (New York: Knopf, 1982); Charles Strozier; *Lincoln's Quest for Union: Public and Private Meanings* (New York: Basic Books, 1982). See also Michael Burlingame, *The Inner World of Abraham Lincoln* (Urbana, IL: University of Illinois Press, 1994); Joshua W. Shenk, *Lincoln's Melancholy* (Boston, MA: Houghton Mifflin, 2005).

15. In chapter 4 these texts were compared in terms of their treatment of Lincoln's reunion and emancipation policies.

16. As one generation succeeds the next, the media of collective memory change in relative importance. At the beginning of the Industrial Revolution, people were reminded of Lincoln by their ministers' holiday sermons, political parties and veterans groups honoring him during their meetings, schools teaching about him in regular class and special programs, affluent citizens commissioning painters and sculptors to beautify cities and towns with lifelike images of him, and municipal authorities organizing Lincoln Day speeches, parades, and banquets. As the Industrial Revolution

matured, educational institutions assumed an increasingly important role. By the 1890s, American history textbooks were parts of many school curricula; by the end of World War I they were required in almost all. Ritual and icon, monument and place name, continued to embellish and inspire, but the volume and authority of written history has grown fastest in relative influence. During the last half of the twentieth century, commemorative forms lost their original power and textbooks became the key vehicle for conveying information about Lincoln.

17. George Earle Freeland and James Truslow Adams, *America's Progress in Civilization* (New York: Charles Scribner's Sons, 1936), iii.

18. Lewis Paul Todd and Merle Curti, *America's History* (New York: Harcourt, Brace, 1950), v.

19. E. Augsperger and R. A. McLemare, *Our Nation's Story* (Chicago: Laidlaw Brothers, 1954), 5.

20. William Backus Guitteau, *Our United States* (New York: Silver, Burdett and Company, 1920), 297–98; Harold Underwood Faulkner, Tyler Kepner, and Itall Bartlett, *American Way of Life: A History* (New York: Harper and Brothers, 1941), 92; Lewis Paul Todd and Merle Curti, *America's History* (New York: Harcourt, Brace, 1950), 398; Augsperger and McLemore, *Our Nation's Story*, 323.

21. Margaret Stimmann Branson, *Land of Challenge* (New York: Ginn and Company, 1975), v; Charles Sellers et al., *As It Happened: A History of the United States* (New York: McGraw-Hill, 1975), xi.

22. Charles Garrett Vannest and Henry Lester Smith, *Socialized History of the United States* (New York: Charles Scribner's Sons, 1946), 370; Ralph V. Harlow, *The Story of America* (New York: Henry Holt and Company, 1957), 221.

23. John W. Caughey, John Hope Franklin, Ernest R. May, *Land of the Free* (New York: Benziger Brothers, 1966), 346.

24. Robert K. Murray and Tim H. Blessing, *Greatness in the White House: Rating the Presidents* (University Park, PA: Pennsylvania State University Press, 1988); Arthur Schlesinger Jr., "Rating the Presidents: Washington to Clinton," *Political Science Quarterly* 112 (1997): 179–90; James Lindgren and Steven Calabresi, "Rating the Presidents of the United States, 1789–2000: A Survey of Scholars in Political Science, History, and Law," *Constitutional Commentary* 18 (2001): 583–605.

25. Forgie, *Patricide in the House Divided.*

26. Daniel Webster, *The Writings and Speeches of Daniel Webster* (Boston: Little, Brown), 253–54 (see also 262).

27. Ralph Waldo Emerson, *The Letters of Ralph Waldo Emerson*, ed. Ralph Rusk (New York: Columbia University Press, 1939), 120.

28. James Russell Lowell, "Self-Possession vs. Prepossession," *Atlantic Monthly* 8 (1861): 763.

29. Anonymous, "The Perilous Condition of the Republic," *New England Magazine* 1 (1831): 283.

30. American civic engagement, measured by a series of indexes, from voter turnouts to voluntary associations, increased between 1900 and 1965, then fell off rapidly and far (Robert D. Putnam, *Bowling Alone: The Collapse and Revival of American Community* [New York: Simon and Schuster, 2000]). Weakening of human connected-

ness, and fraying of the bond attaching the individual to the institutions of his society coincides with the decline in deference afforded great men of the past.

31. Marvin Karlins, Thomas L. Coffman, and Gary Walters, "On the Fading of Stereotypes: Studies in Three Generations of College Students," *Journal of Personality and Social Psychology* 13 (1969): 1–16.

32. The reasons for increase in the percentage of African Americans deemed "musical," from 26 to 47 percent, and whether this change reflects a change in the positive or negative direction, are unknown.

33. Emile Durkheim, *The Rules of Sociological Method* (New York: The Free Press, [1895] 1964), 71.

34. Octavio Paz, *In the Search of the Present,* 1990 Nobel Lecture (New York: Harcourt, Brace, Jovanovitch, 1990), 29.

35. Abraham Lincoln, "The Perpetuation of Our Political Institutions" (address before the Young Men's Lyceum of Springfield, Illinois), January 27, 1838, in *The Collected Works of Abraham Lincoln,* ed. Roy P. Basler (New Brunswick: Rutgers University Press, 1953) 1: 109.

36. Alexis de Tocqueville, *Democracy in America,* ed. Phillips Bradley (New York: Knopf, 1945), 2:4.

37. Seymour Martin Lipset and William Schneider, "The Decline of Confidence in American Institutions," *Political Science Quarterly* 98 (Fall 1983): 379–402; "The Confidence Gap during the Reagan Years, 1981–1987," *Political Science Quarterly* 102 (Spring 1987): 23.

38. Peter Karsten, *Patriot-Heroes of England and America: Political Symbolism and Changing Values over Three Centuries* (Madison: University of Wisconsin Press, 1978); Wilbur Zelinsky, *Nation into State: The Shifting Foundations of American Nationalism* (Chapel Hill: University of North Carolina Press, 1988).

39. John B. Thompson, *Political Scandal: Power and Visibility in the Media Age* (Malden, MA: Blackwell, 2000), 245.

40. Nine hundred and seventeen respondents (91.6 percent) answered this question; 7.3 percent indicated they did not know; 1.1 percent gave no response. Table 5.1, however, is limited to respondents naming the president listed on the first row (Lincoln, Kennedy, Roosevelt, Washington, Truman, and Eisenhower). Among Southerners naming Lincoln, for example, 39 and 50 percent believed he would be "equally great" or "not so great" if exposed to contemporary media; 11 percent could not answer.

41. Jacque Barzun, *Classic, Romantic, Modern* (Garden City, NY: Doubleday, [1943] 1961), 123. Barzun's essay is prophetic of the declining appreciation of great men in the post–World War II period. Alan Edelstein's narrower work, *Everybody Is Sitting on the Curb: How and Why America's Heroes Disappeared* (Westport, CT: Praeger, 1996), properly locates the beginning of the hero's disappearance at the end of World War II, but fails to document that argument.

42. Peter Collier and David Horowitz, *Destructive Generation: Second Thoughts About the 1960s* (New York: Summit, 1990).

43. Paul Goodman, *Growing up Absurd* (New York: Random House, 1969), 97.

44. Reverend Henry N. Couden, *Congressional Record* (HR), February 12, 1919, 3195.

45. Ibid.

46. Robert Nisbet, *Twilight of Authority* (New York: Oxford University Press, 1975), 109.

47. The 1.6 million member United Church of Christ, inspired by the civil rights and feminist movements, removed the word "Lord" from its new hymnals because "it is loaded with a lot of those patriarchical and hierarchical images." "Comforter" proved more appropriate. So did "Christ and Friend," but not "Christ" alone (*Washington Post*, August 22, 1993, 1A). The phrase "What would Jesus do?" appeared as an evangelical Christian slogan, but it was once a slogan for authority of any kind, especially political authority, as in the expression, "What would Lincoln do?" This religious variant has became entangled in the sale of toys, teddy bears, and knickknacks (Adelle Banks, "What Would Jesus Do?" *Atlanta Journal-Constitution*, August 29, 1998, C4).

48. Jean-Francois Lyotard, *The Postmodern Condition* (Minneapolis: University of Minnesota Press, 1988), xv.

49. Hans Koning, *Nineteen Sixty-Eight: A Personal Report* (New York: W. W. Norton, 1987), 13.

50. Tom W. Smith, "The Polls: The Most Admired Man and Woman," *Public Opinion Quarterly* 50 (1986): 575.

51. Eric Hobsbawm, *The Age of Extremes: A History of the World 1914–1991* (New York: Pantheon, 1994); Michael J. Sandel, *Democracy's Discontent* (Cambridge, MA: Belknap Press, 1996).

52. Robert J. Lifton, "Protean Man," *Partisan Review* 35 (1968): 22. For detail, see Robert J. Lifton, *The Protean Self* (New York: Basic Books, 1993).

53. Nisbet, *The Twilight of Authority*, 109–10.

54. Cited by Richard Rorty, *Achieving Our Country: Leftist Thought in Twentieth-Century America* (Cambridge, MA: Harvard University Press, 1998), 4. Cynicism helps define the late-century mood. Arthur M. Schlesinger Jr. observed that Kennedy's death had greater pathos than Lincoln's because it came early rather than late in his political career, because Kennedy "had so much to do, so much to give to his family, his nation, his world" ("Eulogy: JFK," *Saturday Evening Post* 236 [December 14, 1963]: 32). Twenty-five years later, Daniel Boorstin saw Lincoln's and Kennedy's unfulfilled potential in a different light ("JFK: His Vision: Then and Now," *U.S. News and World Report* [October 24, 1988]: 30–31). Presidents who die before they complete their work, he said, are judged more by their rhetoric than their record. Kennedy's death saved him from the testing of his policies in Vietnam and Cuba, and on civil rights, just as Lincoln's death saved him from the trials of Reconstruction. "It is their good fortune to be judged less by their fulfillment than by their promise. Would we not all like to be so judged."

55. Amitai Etzioni, "Holidays: The Neglected Seedbeds of Virtue," in *The Monochrome Society* (Princeton: Princeton University Press, 2001), 113–40.

56. The following sample of statements in the House of Representatives (*Congressional Record*) summarizes the issues: January 26, 1967, 1752–53; March 8, 1967, 5841–42; March 21, 1967, 7410–12; April 20, 1967, 10416; May 25, 1967, 14195; August 9, 1967, 22018–19; September 21, 1967, 26450; March 13, 1968, 6297; May 6, 1968, 11827–30; May 7, 1968, 12077–80.

57. *Congressional Record* (HR), April 3, 1968, 8923.

58. As racial equality and inclusion become critical issues, Abraham Lincoln occupies a more central place in the American pantheon; George Washington, an increas-

ingly marginal place. Lincoln's presidency may or may not have been directly relevant to affirmative action and school and residential integration, but it is thought to be. During the 1960s a series of events—civil rights struggle in the South, a divisive Civil War centennial observance, a new history defining the founding era as the source of racial oppression rather than national greatness—made George Washington less relevant and made Presidents' Day more appealing.

59. Presidents' Day is recognized by 11 of 13 (84.6 percent) Mountain and Pacific states, but only 3 of the 17 (17.6 percent) East Coast states, most of which were part of the original 13 colonies and wartime Union and Confederate states. Of the 9 South Central states, only 3 (33.3 percent) recognize Presidents' Day. Whether those states observing Presidents' Day are recognizing all presidents or only Lincoln and Washington is uncertain.

60. *New York Times*, February 24, 1976.

61. Sean O'Gara, reprinted in *Congressional Record* (HR), March 30, 1976, 8715.

62. *New York Times*, October 26, 1971. Cited in *Congressional Record* (HR), February 24, 1976, 4245.

63. In 1976, represtantive William Ketchum proposed a restoration of all holiday dates; in 1980, senator Jennings Randolph tried to restore Washington's birthday; in 1973 and 1999 representative Edward Derwinski and senator Daniel Inouye respectively introduced bills to restore Memorial Day to May 30. In 2003, representatives Roscoe Bartlett and Tom Tancredo tried to abolish Presidents' Day and restore February 22 as Washington's birthday. See *Congressional Record* (HR), February 24, 1976, 4244; October 23, 1973, 34899; Matthew Spalding, "By George: It's Not Presidents' Day. It's Washington's Birthday," *National Review Online*, February 16, 2004 (in "Flashback from the Archives," http://www.nationalreview.com).

64. Philip Rieff, *The Feeling Intellect*, ed. Jonathan Imber (Chicago: University of Chicago Press, 1990), 354; *My Life among the Deathworks* (Charlottesville: University of Virginia Press, 2006), xxiii, 171–72.

65. Paul Greenberg, "Shrinking Lincoln," *Arkansas Democrat-Gazette*, February 12, 2001, 6B. The blankness of Presidents' Day is also distinguished by its widening commercialization. Brad Anderson depicts the mood of the day in a cartoon that associates Presidents' Day with Washington and Lincoln alone, the better to trivialize the lives of both. The transformation is occasioned by the substitution of the language of commerce for the language of statesmanship and nationalism. Panel 1: Hi! I'm George! / And I'm Abe. Panel 2: George Washington (GW): "Tomorrow is Presidents' Day. It's a national holiday for the observance of our birthdays." Panel 3: Abraham Lincoln (AL): "Right, George. But more important is the humongous SALE we're having at . . ." Panel 4 (AL): ". . . George 'N' Abes's Mart" / (GW): "Yessiree, Abe . . . Panel 5: (GW): "Prices are slashed!" / (AL): We've got bargains galore!" Panel 6: (GW, AL): SO, COME ON DOWN! (Illinois State Historical Library, Springfield, Illinois.) The 1967 Congressional committees had something different in mind when they conceived the Uniform Holiday Bill, but the tone of Presidents' Day advertisements conform to the spirit of their plan: the promotion of commerce.

66. Max Weber, *The Theory of Social and Economic Organization* (New York: Free Press, 1947), 341–58; Edward A. Shils, *Tradition* (University of Chicago Press, 1981), 9–10.

67. Weber, *The Theory of Social and Economic Organization*, 329–40.

68. Howard Schuman, "Two Sources of Antiwar Sentiment in America," *American Journal of Sociology* 54 (1972): 351–81.

69. For example, see Forgie, *Patricide in the House Divided.*

70. Herbert Mitgang, "The Mexican War Dove," *New Republic* (February 11, 1967): 23–24.

71. Library of Congress, *Yankel Collection,* 6-U.S. 1119.

72. Harold R. Collier, "Lincoln and the War with Mexico," *Congressional Record* (Senate), February 2, 1966, 1982.

73. Thomas J. Dodd, "The War in Vietnam and the American Civil War," *Congressional Record* (Senate), August 26, 1966, 20873.

74. Donald M. Kudrec, *National Review* 21 (November 18 1969): 1155.

75. *New York Times,* February 12, 1973, 26.

76. Ibid., February 26, 1973, 30.

77. Ibid., January 14, 1973, 1.

78. Ibid., January 20, 1973, 32.

79. Ibid., June 30, 1973, 15.

80. Ibid., February 12, 1974, 33.

81. Ibid, February 13, 1974, 1.

82. Ibid., February 20, 1974, 36.

83. Richard Harris, "Nixon and Lincoln," *New Yorker* 50 (April 15, 1974): 108, 113.

84. More than twenty years later, Nelson Mandela visited Congress and appeared beneath Abraham Lincoln's statue with Strom Thurmond. A black man imprisoned for twenty-seven years who forgave his captors, an ardent segregationist renouncing his past prejudice lifting the hand of that black man as one would a champion, and Lincoln's life-size image looking down on the scene could be read as an allegory of Lincoln's forgiving the South for slavery and segregation and restoring the Union. Instead, the writer saw the Mandela-Thurmond meeting as a frame for thinking about President Clinton's indiscretions. If Mandela bore no hard feelings toward Thurmond, and Lincoln bore no hard feelings toward the South, then why should not everyone forgive Clinton's trivial misstep (Frances X. Clines, *New York Times,* September 24, 1998, A18)?

85. According to Mike Musick, retired National Archives Civil War specialist, there exists no formal series of death warrants or pardons signed by Abraham Lincoln. Robert Alotta made use of an 1885 War Department compilation of U.S. military executions, but this information is far from complete. Many case file transcripts are located today in the Judge Advocate General's Office Record Group 153, but there are also many in Record Group 9. Also, not all executions were carried out as a result of general courts-martial. White House records consist of two volumes of court-martial cases from which 1861 and 1862 cases are missing. Thomas P. Lowry, on the other hand, provides the most extensive analysis of court-martial data. He took a 50 percent sample of Record Group 153, amounting to 40,000 cases, and found more than 500 files on which he could find Lincoln's signature or remarks. The chain of command and influence through which each case passed, Lowry shows, was lenient, and Lincoln tended to follow the recommendations made on the cases that came down to him. There is no way to determine from Lowry's work, however, which cases were capital cases. Private correspondence from Mike Musick, February 11, 2007. See Robert I. Alotta,

Civil War Justice: Union Army Executions under Lincoln (Shippensburg, PA: White Mane Publishing Company, Inc., 1989); Thomas P. Lowry, *Don't Shoot That Boy!: Abraham Lincoln and Military Justice* (Mason City, IA: Savas Publishing Company, 1999).

86. Edward L. Schnapsmeier and Frederick H. Schnapsmeier, "Gerald Ford and the Lincoln Legacy: A Time to Heal," in *Abraham Lincoln: Contemporary*, ed. Frank J. Williams and William D. Pederson (Campbell, CA: Savas Woodbury Publishers, 1995), 52.

87. Ibid.

88. Ibid., 58.

89. Ibid., 59–60.

90. Joshua Meyerowitz, *No Sense of Place: The Impact of Electronic Media on Social Behavior* (New York: Oxford University Press, 1985), 270.

91. That Roosevelt's paralysis was unknown to the majority of Americans strains credibility. On national holidays, including Lincoln Day, he stood at attention by leaning on a military aide, his picture appearing in all major newspapers. Roosevelt campaigned for office publicly on the back of trains and in the back seat of automobiles. In large cities he appeared at public rallies at sports stadiums, his car circling the playing field near the seats and driving up a ramp to a platform from which he spoke while sitting.

92. Daniel Boorstin, "From Hero to Celebrity: The Human Pseudo-Event," in *The Image: A Guide to Pseudo-Events in America* (New York: Harper and Row, 1964), 45–76.

93. Mark Feeney, *Nixon at the Movies: A Book about Belief* (Chicago: University of Chicago Press, 2004).

94. Related television themes include *Running Mates* (TNT, 2000), which has a double plot: (1) the president opposes special interests and (2) has affairs with his campaign manager, social secretary, and the alcoholic wife of a senator. One of the drama's highlights, advertised in previews, is an episode in which the president's wife and three lovers discuss his sexual prowess. The special interest plot is a mere vehicle for a sexcapade story. In the twenty-first-century television series, 24, President Charles Logan is part of a complex scheme to assassinate his predecessor, spread nerve gas throughout the United States, and commit other hideous crimes.

95. Stephen Holden, "Those Strange Bedfellows Haunt a Politician," *New York Times*, October 13, 2000, E1. In a 2006 film, *Sentinel*, the bedfellows are the president's wife and one of his secret service agents.

96. Rumor content expresses the same mentality. On April 2, 2001, the online magazine *Slate* distributed a *London Times* article, widely reproduced in the United States, stating that Doris Kearns Goodwin and Steven Spielberg were planning to portray Lincoln on film as "a manic depressive racist." Goodwin's Lincoln in *Team of Rivals: The Political Genius of Abraham Lincoln* (New York: Simon and Schuster, 2005) bears no resemblance to either a manic depressive or a racist, but the publicity's content reflects the public's receptiveness to the rumor.

97. Erosion of authority is apparent in other aspects of popular culture. From the 1930s to the 1950s, fictional heroes, no less than real heroes like Lincoln, possessed powers and performed deeds that commanded attention and respect. The most popular heroes, represented by Superman, shared three characteristics: extraordinary physical and mental powers, an ascetic life devoted entirely to the upholding of society's

ideals and destruction of its enemies, and a studied remoteness from the people they serve. Expressed in the form of a mask or disguised identity, this last characteristic was crucial. Unmasking the hero would not only make him vulnerable to evil forces but also transform powers sanctified by mystery into profane extensions of police authority. Constantly threatened, yet always surviving demystification, superheroes appeared in comic books, radio, and film, then on television, through the 1950s. After 1960, however, heroic adventures were converted into light comedies. Epic fantasies of Superman vanished as the Man of Steel tried to "fit in" with normal people. Romance, not justice, became his greatest challenge. The 1993 television series, *Superman and Lois,* as the title implies, focuses as much on the hero's relationship with reporter Lois Lane as on his feats on behalf of society. The television premier, showing his alias, Clark Kent, involuntarily rising from the floor (crudely suggesting an erection) at the first sight of Ms. Lane, extends the movie plot of *Superman II,* in which Superman and Lois Lane work up to a sexual liaison (which was seen before 1960 only in "two by fours" and similar pornographic comic strips.). Likewise, vanity replaces self-sacrifice as television's Superman tries on different uniforms and capes to see which makes him look best. Here is no super man at all; only a strong fellow who can fly—otherwise no different from anyone else. He performs the same feats as before, but the enchantment is gone.

98. Alexis de Tocqueville, *Democracy in America* (New York: Knopf, 1945), 2:105–6. Since democratic historians, as Tocqueville observed, see history driven by societal conditions and forces over which no one individual has control, political and military leaders attain respect but never the great veneration they know in aristocratic societies (90–93).

99. As heroes appear less heroic, villains appear less villainous. Fidel Castro, Che Guevarra, and Ho Chi-Minh remain respected by many on the left. The public's fascination with the Mafia, the godfather, John Giotti, Bonnie and Clyde, and Al Capone are equally instructive examples of "defining deviance down." The title of James Kirby Martin's biography, *Benedict Arnold, Revolutionary Hero: An American Warrior Reconsidered* (New York: New York University Press, 1997) defines deviance down by arguing that Benedict Arnold's heroism somehow compensates for his treason, makes it less malicious, more "understandable." New efforts to "humanize" and "understand" Hitler contribute to the same process (Maureen Dowd, "Swastikas for Sweeps," *New York Times,* July 17, 2002, A23), as does the "Genocide as Art" exhibition at New York's Jewish Museum. The display draws "unnerving connections between the Third Reich and today's consumer culture." The LEGO concentration camp set by Polish artist Zbigniew Libero makes for a fresh way of thinking about the Holocaust: an emaciated inmate holds a can of diet Coke above the slogan "It's the Real Thing—Self-Portrait at Buchenwald." "Giftgas Giftset" Zyklon B canisters bear the logos of Chanel, Hermes, and Tiffany's. "Goebbels and Geduldig" is a farce about Goebbels and a Jew who looks like him (*New York Times,* November 25, 2002, A11). The Holocaust is a wonderful teaching opportunity, declares a sarcastic George Will, because it allows a gendered approach that can be tied to victimization of any kind. Holocaust victims prefigure the Battered Woman (*Washington Post,* June 20, 2002, A23).

100. Mt. Rushmore T-Shirts & Company's Web site (http://www.mtrushmore tshirts.com/art.htm) advertises the image.

101. American Association of Colleges for Teacher Education, "On One Model American: A Statement on Multicultural Education," *Journal of Teacher Education* 24 (1973): 264–65. Twenty years later, proponents of the new National History Standards denounced prevailing American political history as a "traditional, elitist, and distorted view of the past that has eroded its once prominent place in college curricula, academic job markets, and the meeting programs of major historical associations"(Donald A. Richie. "Politics as Usual?" *Reviews in American History* 25 [1977]: 698). Twenty-seven years later, friends of the New York Historical Society began to worry that the organization's new emphasis on national history would stress "leaders rather than ordinary people: minorities, women, immigrants, for example." Casting history in light of "great white men" who left behind written documents, museums become "shrines where a patriotic fervor can be cultivated" (*New York Times*, July 19, 2004, B5). Such is the conviction of Richard Rabinowitz, president of the American History Workshop. The implication of Rabinowitz's statement is that museums that dwell on African Americans, Hispanics, Native Americans, and women mercifully *reduce* patriotic fervor.

102. Peter Novick, *That Noble Dream: The "Objectivity Question" and the American Historical Profession* (Cambridge: Cambridge University Press, 1988).

103. On the relation between post-1960 immigrant history and American historians' desire to emphasize the diversity and retention of immigrant values, see Rudolph Vecoli, *From the Melting Pot to Multiculturalism: The Evolution of Ethnic Relations in the United States and Canada*, edited by Valeria Gennaro (Rome, Italy: Bulzoni Editore, 1990).

104. The U.S. Mint's decision perfectly mirrors "a society preoccupied with the virtue of compassion and cynical about every other. In its careless sloughing off of America's founding figures and ideas, its substitution of sentimentality for any invocation of sacrifice, courage, or fortitude, and its nervous defaulting to the spurious democracy of focus groups, it is indeed a coin for our time." Michael J. Lewis, "Of Kitsch and Coins," *Commentary* 108 (October 1999): 36.

105. Basler, *Collected Works of Abraham Lincoln*, 1:279.

106. Cartoon commentary on Lincoln and the politics of recognition is hilariously shown in Mike Thomson's "If Bush and Clinton Speechwriters Had Worked for Lincoln." Lincoln's Gettysburg Address is redlined by comments about his referring to "fathers" and "men" but leaving out mothers and women. The word "conceived" might offend family values advocates. And why not change "civil war" to Operation Rebel Storm? (Newspaper unknown.)

107. Peter L. Berger, Brigitte Berger, and Hansfried Kellner, *The Homeless Mind: Modernization and Consciousness* (New York: Vintage, 1973), 77–80. Political erosion corresponded to changes occurring at other levels of the society. Robert Griswold points out that the authority of the father, driven to work outside the home by the Industrial Revolution, had deteriorated before industrialism matured in the early twentieth century. By the end of the Depression and World War II, child-rearing experts were encouraging fathers to be friends and playmates of their children rather than to impose moral values on them. Children should have lifestyle alternatives so they can participate in their own socialization. This pattern was manifested in the passing of the last remnants of the Victorian age which, Gertrude Himmelfarb shows, maintained low rates of illegitimacy and crime in England and the United States through World War I, the Great Depression, and World War II. During the 1960s, Victorian values

collapsed, releasing unprecedented volumes of moral and criminal deviance in both countries. Robert L. Griswold, *Fatherhood in America: A History* (New York: Basic Books, 1993); Gertrude Himmelfarb, "A De-Moralized Society," in *De-Moralization of Society: From Victorian Virtues to Modern Values* (New York: Knopf, 1995), 221–57.

108. The first set of four coins, bearing the likenesses of George Washington, John Adams, Thomas Jefferson, and James Madison, will be released at three-month intervals during 2007. Subsequent series will be circulated every year until 2016 (*New York Times*, November 20, 2006, A16).

109. So far, the U.S. Mint has failed to replace historical figures on regular currency; however, the U.S. Treasury has succeeded in representing minorities, or, rather, minority achievements, on its bonds. The present I-Bond series (the values of which reflect the consumer price index) portrays eight different Americans, of whom only one, General George Marshall, is a native born white male. The others are Marian Anderson, Helen Keller, Spark Matsunaga, Albert Einstein, Chief Joseph, Hector Garcia, and Martin Luther King Jr.

110. Michael S. Roth, "A Note on Kojeve's *Phenomenology of Right*," *Political Theory* 11 (1983): 447–50; *Knowing and History: Appropriations of Hegel in Twentieth-Century France* (Ithaca: Cornell University Press, 1988); S. B. Smith, *Hegel's Critique of Liberalism* (Chicago: University of Chicago Press, 1989); Allen D. Bloom, *Love and Friendship* (New York: Simon and Schuster, 1993).

111. Pierre Nora cited in Nancy Wood, "Memory's Remains: Les Lieux de Memoire," *History and Memory* 6 (1994): 135, 141.

112. Mick Hume, *The Times*, November 11, 2002. Article republished in http://www.spiked-online.com.

113. For further discussion of this "skeptical" conception of the past, see Anne-Marie Rosenau, *Post-Modernism and the Social Sciences* (Princeton: Princeton University Press, 1992), 63–65.

114. Stamps commemorating events and organizations are excluded.

115. Members of the Citizens' Stamp Advisory Committee as of August 2005 were Cary R. Brick, congressional staff adjunct; Michael R. Brock, graphic designer; David L. Eynon, science fiction writer; Jean Picker Firstenberg, American Film Institute; Dr. Henry Louis Gates Jr., Afro-American studies, Harvard University; Sylvia Harris, information design strategist; Michael I. Heyman, University of California, Berkeley; John M. Hotchner, American Philatelic Society; Karl Malden, actor; James Micho, design educator; Joan A. Mondale, patron of the arts; Richard F. Phelps, television sports commentator; Ronald A. Robinson of Cranford, Johnson, Robinson, Woods Company; Maria E. Santana of Parham/Santana, Inc.

116. These decisions include the production of increasingly popular postcards and stationery. Also, the postal service has provided new express mail services to compete with the private carriers, and these require new stamps. See U.S. Postal Service, *The Postal Service Guide to* U.S. Stamps (New York: HarperResource, 2000).

117. From the beginning to the end of the twentieth century, the percentage of white males drops from 90 percent to 80.6 percent; white females double from 6.9 to 14.6 percent. Nonwhite males and females make up zero and 3.4 percent of the total at the beginning of the century; 12.7 and 3.5 percent at the end.

118. The diffusion of reputation occurring between the beginning of the century, when a small number of individuals are represented, and the end of the century, when a large number of individuals are represented, can be summarized with a statistic (sum of the squares of the separate proportions) measuring the homogeneity of categories within each twenty-year period. This statistic decreases from 0.586 in 1900–1919 to 0.145 in 1980–99.

119. The latest and ultimate postal development is the personalized photo postage stamp. PhotoStamps, a California company, produced regular postage stamps for a dollar apiece, with a photo of one's choice engraved on the stamp decoration. Production stopped when individuals chose to post their letters with controversial figures: Ethel and Julius Rosenberg, Monica Lewinsky, Linda Tripp, New Jersey Governor McGreevy and his alleged gay lover, and baby Adolph Hitler. Photostamps has isolated these anomalies and is back in the business, licensed by the U.S. Postal Service, producing personalized stamps.

120. Fred I. Greenstein, "New Light on Changing American Values: A Forgotten Body of Survey Data," *Social Forces* 42 (1964): 445.

121. The Library of Congress list contains 56 and 12 percent white and nonwhite males respectively; 16 percent white and nonwhite females.

122. *Time*'s list contains 55 percent white males; 18 percent white females; 17 percent nonwhite males; and 9 percent nonwhite females.

123. *Dictionary of American Biography*, ed. Dumas Malone (New York: Scribner, 1928–36), 1:vii, xiv.

124. Ibid., 1:vii, xiv; *American National Biography*, 24 vols. ed. John A. Garraty and Mark C. Carnes (New York: Oxford University Press, 1999). The latter's Web site is http://www.acls.org/pro-anb.htm.

125. Ronald Reagan, Abraham Lincoln, Martin Luther King Jr., George Washington, and Benjamin Franklin respectively occupied the first five places.

126. Edward Tiryakian, "The Wild Cards of Modernity," *Daedalus* 32 (1997): 163.

127. Tom W. Smith, National Opinion Research Center, personal communication, December 3, 1996.

128. Robert Lerner, Althea K. Nagai, and Stanley Rothman, *Molding the Good Citizen: The Politics of High School History Texts* (Westport, CT: Praeger, 1995), 69–88 (see also 125–50); Peggy Noonan, "Patriots, Then and Now," wsj.com, March 30, 2006.

129. Trends for Eisenhower and Kennedy are harder to interpret because they reflect not only the presidency's reduced prestige but also the tendency for articles about presidents to diminish rapidly during the years immediately following their deaths. From the time Dwight Eisenhower left the presidency (1961) to the year before his death (1968), an annual average of 94 *New York Times* articles about him appeared. In the three years following his death, the volume dropped sharply to 34, 25, and 15 respectively, and has since then never exceeded 10. John Kennedy, who died in 1963, was the subject of 55 *New York Times* articles per year between 1965 and 1969, but only 17 per year in the early seventies, then 7 to 8 thereafter.

130. The fading and deconstruction of traditional heroes is widespread. Robert E. Lee, as recently conceived, favored slavery, was profligate in the use of his men, actively sought rank in the Union army, and chose to fight for the Confederacy

because the former denied it to him. Far from seeking reconciliation after the war, he was concerned simply to save his own reputation. Christopher Columbus personifies all the evils of Western civilization: he caused plunder, rape, colonialism, slave trade, and ecological crisis. Conor Cruise O'Brien represents a wide spectrum of opinion by denouncing Jefferson as a racist who envisioned a lily-white nation ("Thomas Jefferson: Radical and Racist," *Atlantic Monthly* [October 1996]: 53–74). Jefferson, a hypocrite and slave holder, is condemned for holding slaves and fathering children with a slave mistress, although the DNA evidence does not lead to Thomas Jefferson himself. The cowboy hero was actually a moral and economic basket case, dependent on the federal government for protection and land. The Wild West is now the cradle of Big Brother, big government, and big business. In this environment, legendary heroes have no place. Alan T. Nolan, *Lee Considered: General Robert E. Lee and Civil War History* (Chapel Hill: University of North Carolina Press, 1991); Herbert E. Sloan, *Principle and Interest: Thomas Jefferson and the Problem of Debt* (New York: Oxford University Press, 1995); Richard White, *It's Your Misfortune and None of My Own: A History of the American West* (Norman, OK: University of Oklahoma Press, 1991).

131. Zelinsky, *Nation into State*, 96, 102. U.S. Department of the Interior, National Park Service, *Public Use of the National Parks: A Statistical Report, 1904–1940*. See also the reports for 1941–53, 1954–64, 1960–70, 1971–80, and 1981–92.

132. *Atlanta Journal-Constitution*, January 17, 1999, F1, F3.

CHAPTER SEVEN

1. One week after the *Arkansas Democrat-Gazette*'s Lincoln's birthday edition, the *New York Post* editorial page published Mark Goldblatt's column on the left wing of American higher education: "Racist Abe? Horrid Charges Taken as Truth: Welcome to Modern Academia, a House Divided against Its Own Ideals," February 19, 2001, 25.

2. Ernest Renan, *Discours et Conférences* (Paris: Calman-Levy, 1887), 309–10.

3. The phrase "easy to track" does not mean the information in chapters 1 to 5 was easily obtained and analyzed; it means the information was available and analyzable.

4. *Webster's New Collegiate Dictionary* (Springfield, MA: G. and C. Merriam Co., 1977), 589.

5. Michael Schudson, "The Present in the Past versus the Past in the Present," *Communication* 11 (1989): 109.

6. Michael Frisch, "American History and the Structure of Collective Memory: A Modest Exercise in Empirical Iconography," *Journal of American History* 75 (1989): 1130–55.

7. Jeffrey K. Olick, "Genre Memories and Memory Genres: A Dialogical Analysis of May 8, 1945, Commemorations in the Federal Republic of Germany," *American Sociological Review* 64 (June 1999): 381–402. See also Howard Schuman, Barry Schwartz, and Hannah D'Arcy, "Elite Revisionists and Popular Beliefs: Christopher Columbus: Hero or Villain," *Public Opinion Quarterly* 69 (2005): 2–29.

8. "Once commemoration gets under way," Michael Schudson observes, "it picks up steam, it operates by a logic . . . of its own. Not only are records kept, diaries saved, and news accounts written, but statues are built, museums endowed, brass plaques are engraved and placed in sidewalks and the walls of buildings." "The Present in the Past," 108.

9. Knowledge of Lincoln must affect his reputation, and this knowledge, in absolute terms, is limited. In 1999, for example, a survey of college seniors at fifty-five elite colleges, from Princeton to Stanford, revealed that only 22 percent knew that the words "government of the people, by the people, for the people" are from the Gettysburg Address. Sixty percent could place the Civil War in the last half of the nineteenth century. Forty-four percent knew that Lincoln's presidency fell in the period 1860–80. Fifty-nine percent thought Reconstruction referred to repairing of physical damage caused by the Civil War (George F. Will, "Our National Memory Loss," *Washington Post*, December 23, 2001, B7). Given the increasing percentage of students graduating high school and attending college, however, knowledge of Lincoln, in relative terms, has never been greater. The general public's knowledge of history—or any academic subject, including physical science—is shallower, of course, than that of university students. Michael X. Delli Carpini and Scott Keeter, *What Americans Know about Politics and Why It Matters* (New Haven: Yale University Press, 1989).

10. Jacques Le Goff, "Mentalities: A History of Ambiguities," in *Constructing the Past: Essays in Historical Methodology*, ed. Jacques Le Goff and Pierre Nora (Cambridge: Cambridge University Press, 1985), 170.

11. Emile Durkheim, *The Elementary Forms of the Religious Life* (New York: Free Press [1915] 1965), 464.

12. Susanne K. Langer, "The Art Symbol and the Symbol in Art," in *Problems in Art* (New York: Charles Scribner's Sons, 1957), 133.

13. William Manchester, *The Death of a President* (New York: Harper and Row, 1967), 629.

14. *New York Times*, November 25, 1963, 1.

15. Manchester, *The Death of a President*, 466.

16. *New York Times*, December 2, 1963, 22.

17. Maurice Halbwachs, *Collective Memory*, ed. Mary Douglas, trans. Francis J. Ditter Jr. (New York: Harper and Row, [1950] 1980), 128–57.

18. Murray Edelman, *Constructing the Political Spectacle* (Chicago: University of Chicago Press, 1988).

19. Lt. Will C. Carlton and J. Aldrich Libbey, "History Has Given Us Another Lincoln" (San Francisco: John P. Broder, 1901).

20. Frank Murman, "America, America" (Mountain Top, PA: Airy Music Company, 1964).

21. For comparative discussion of public reaction to Lincoln's, Garfield's, McKinley's, and Kennedy's assassination, see Barry Schwartz, *Abraham Lincoln and the Forge of National Memory* (Chicago: University of Chicago Press, 2000), 58–63.

22. Bill Mauldin's image of Daniel Chester French's Lincoln Memorial statue bent over in grief is probably the most often reproduced of all the Kennedy mourning illustrations.

23. The assassination of Garfield would have probably provoked a more passionate public reaction if he rather than Lincoln had been the first presidential victim; however, the circumstances of Lincoln's death—the last days of a bitter, four-year war—probably did most to affect the public's mourning.

24. For the most comprehensive collection, see Raymond B. Rajski, ed. and comp., *A Nation Grieved: The Kennedy Assassination in Editorial Cartoons* (Rutland, VT: Charles E. Tuttle Co., 1967).

25. Corlus Walker and Andrew Spalding, "Four Sad Days" (Hollywood: Nordyke Songs and Music Publishers, 1964).

26. *New York Times*, December 23, 1963, 1.

27. Anonymous, "Lincoln-Kennedy: Coincidence?"

28. Roland Barthes, "Structure of the *Fait Divers*," in *Critical Essays*, trans. Richard Howard (Evanston, IL: Northwestern University Press, 1972), 191.

29. Robert P. Hay, "Providence and the American Past," *Indiana Magazine of History* 65 (1969): 79–101; "George Washington: American Moses," *American Quarterly* 21 (1965): 780–91.

30. Also, Booth fled to Maryland, not to a warehouse, after shooting Lincoln.

31. Buddy Starcher, "History Repeats Itself" (New York: Gleser Publications, Inc., 1965). Anthony Newly's musical *Tribute*, published in 1964, never mentions Lincoln's name, but the parallel with Kennedy is evident: "We never could appreciate a / good man 'til he's gone. And we have lost the greatest man our time will look upon." In solemn cadence the next line reveals that "he was much more than just a leader, he was really a Messiah. He / had a dream for all man-kind that set their hearts afire. That all men should be equal was the / dream he had in view. We recognized the message and we crucified him, too" (New York: Melody Trails, Inc., 1964). For the sake of equality, Lincoln saved a people and died for them. So did Kennedy. Now we know how history repeats itself.

32. For detail, see Carol Emmens, *Famous People on Film* (Metuchen, NJ: Scarecrow Press, 1977), 137–38.

33. *Washington Post*, July 7, 1993, 1A, 16A.

34. Ibid., July 11, 1993, 15A.

35. Ibid., 1B.

36. Ibid., July 17, 1993, 16A, 3C.

37. Stephan Thernstrom and Abigal Thernstrom, *America in Black and White: One Nation, Indivisible* (New York: Simon and Schuster, 1997), 69–97.

38. "The Night I Met Lincoln," extension of remarks by Walter H. Judd, *Congressional Record* (Senate), May 2, 1960, A3715.

39. David McCullough, *Truman* (New York: Simon and Schuster, 1992), 569–70.

40. *Chicago Defender*, February, 13, 1967, 1.

41. Ibid., February 12, 1964, 1.

42. Ibid., February 13, 1969, 12.

43. *Jet* 29 (February 1966), 36.

44. Taylor Branch, *Parting the Waters* (New York: Simon and Schuster, 1988), 589.

45. Ibid.

46. Thomas Fleming, "Presidents on Presidents," *American Heritage* (November 1992): 59.

47. *Chicago Defender*, February 12, 1975, 9; February 12, 1976, 15; February 12, 1980, 9; February 12, 1981, 11.

48. *Atlanta Daily World*, February 23, 1960, 1; Chicago *Defender*, February 13, 1961, 11, and February 12, 1968, 15; *New York Amsterdam News*, February 8, 1964, 5.

49. Cited in Don Fehrenbacher, *Lincoln in Text and Context* (Stanford: Stanford University Press, 1987), 100.

50. Alfred Schutz, *Alfred Schutz on Phenomenology and Social Relations*, ed. Helmut R. Wagner (Chicago: University of Chicago Press, 1970), 316.

51. James M. Fields and Howard Schuman, "Public Beliefs about the Beliefs of the Public," *Public Opinion Quarterly* 40 (1976–77): 435–42. See also Howard Schuman, "Attitudes, Beliefs, and Behavior," in *Sociological Perspectives in Social Psychology*, ed. Karen S. Cook, Gary Alan Fine, and James A. House (New York: Simon and Schuster, 1995), 68–89.

52. Charles Horton Cooley, *Social Process* (New York: Charles Scribner's Sons, 1918), 116.

53. Michael Schudson, *Watergate in American Memory* (New York: Basic Books, 1992), 205–21; Gary Alan Fine, "On the Macrofoundations of Microsociology," *Sociological Quarterly* 32 (1991): 161–77.

54. *New York Times*, February 2, 2007, 21.

55. Cited in Michael Kammen, *Mystic Chords of Memory: The Transformation of Tradition in American Culture* (New York: Knopf, 1991), 126–27.

56. Personal communication from Martin J. Moran, United States Historical Society, March 8, 2007. It was Mr. Moran who faced most of the anti-Lincoln hate mail, angry phone calls, and threats, including legal threats against the society's nonprofit status.

57. In February 2007, the Virginia General Assembly passed a resolution, 97–0, expressing "profound regret" for slavery and exploitation of Native Americans. The resolution anticipated the 400th anniversary of the first permanent English settlement in America, at Jamestown. Ironically, the Virginia Senate unanimously passed legislation to create a Virginia Commission on the Bicentennial of Abraham Lincoln, but the measure was tabled and killed by the House Rules Committee. The state of Virginia can cooperate with the federal Bicentennial Commission without a state body, but the symbolic force of the House Committee's action cannot be ignored.

58. Martin J. Moran, "Richmond's Lincoln Statue," first symposium of the Lincoln Society of Virginia, Bridgewater College, Bridgewater, Virginia, March 23, 2005.

59. Bell Irvin Wiley, "Lincoln and Lee," Speech delivered at Emory University, April 9, 1965. Reprinted in *Congressional Record*, May 4, 1965, 9401.

60. Michael Davis, *The Image of Lincoln in the South* (Knoxville: University of Tennessee Press, 1971). Reviewed by Christopher Dell, "Why They Spoke Well of Lincoln," *The Nation* (March 13, 1972): 348–49.

61. Howard Schuman, Charlotte Steeh, Lawrence Bobo, and Maria Kryan, *Racial Attitudes in America: Trends and Interpretations* (Cambridge, MA: Harvard University Press, 1997), 108–18, 125–26, 131–34.

62. *The Perfect Tribute* (air date: April 21, 1991). For details, see Maj Canton, *The Complete Guide to Movies and Miniseries Made for TV and Cable, 1989–91* (Santa Monica: The Hollywood Creative Directory, 1992), 44.

63. U.S. Library of Congress, *With Malice Toward None* (video), June 22, 1991.

64. Graham DuBois, *With Malice Toward None: A Play for Lincoln's Birthday, Plays* 31 (February 1972): 25–36. In a related case, Ken Burns's television series, *The Civil War* (1990), portrayed Robert E. Lee glowingly, devoted an inordinate amount of time to his surrender, and described the high regard in which Northern soldiers held him and his men.

65. Governor George Wallace to Joseph Garrera, president, Lincoln Group of New York. The communication included an engraving of Lincoln inscribed by Governor Wallace on November 10, 1994. On this same date the governor inscribed similar thoughts on a second engraving: "Your life being taken was a blow to the South. Had you lived the South wouldn't [have] undergone the horrors it did." Both statements are signed George C. Wallace. Personal communication from Joseph Garrera, January 15, 2006.

66. William Childs Westmoreland to Joseph E. Garrera, December 16, 1997. Personal communication from Joseph Garrera, January 15, 2006.

67. Gary Fine and Amy Champion's analysis of Sinclair Lewis's being embraced by the very community he condemned is one of the clearest cases of reputations sustained by inertia—in this case, inertia based on the interdependency of two reputations, Lewis's and Sauk Center, Minnesota's. Gary A. Fine, *Difficult Reputations* (Chicago: University of Chicago Press, 2001), 232–58.

68. The Louisiana Lincoln Group, Shreveport, Louisiana, the first such organization founded in the South, publishes the *Louisiana Lincolnator*, a journal of information relating to Lincoln.

69. Presidential rankings are also converging. In the most recent (1999) survey (chapter 4), Lincoln, Kennedy, and Roosevelt are named as the three greatest presidents by non-Southerners. Among Southerners, Kennedy ranks first, followed by Lincoln and Roosevelt.

70. Increased commemorative activities in the South accompany the convergence in statistical ratings. A civil war that kills or injures more men than all American wars combined, including World War I and World War II, is hard to forget, but to overlook all efforts to commemorate Lincoln in the South leads to a stunted view of the future. Philip Stone's activities are untypical in Virginia, but their occurrence might well prefigure later commemoration in the South of Lincoln's role in American history. The erection of statues of Lincoln in Vicksburg and Richmond warrant the speculation.

71. James Hunter, *Culture Wars* (New York: Basic Books, 1994), 200–201.

72. Mike Featherstone, "The Heroic Life and Everyday Life," in *Cultural Theory and Cultural Change* (London: Sage, 1992), 159–82.

73. Alex Callinicos, *Against Postmodernism: A Marxist Critique* (London: Polity Press, 1989), 171; Scott Lash and John Urry, *The End of Organized Capitalism* (Madison: University of Wisconsin Press, 1987), 296; Frederic Jameson, "Postmodernism; or, The Cultural Logic of Late Capitalism," *New Left Review* 146 (1989): 381; Anne-Marie Rosenau, *Post-Modernism and the Social Sciences* (Princeton: Princeton University Press, 1992), 54.

74. Lloyd Warner, *The Living and the Dead* (New Haven: Yale University Press, 1959), 428.

75. Robert Hewison, *The Heritage Industry* (London: Methuen, 1987); Jean Baudrillard, *Simulations* (Cambridge, MA: Semiotext, 1983); Zygmunt Bauman, "From Pilgrim to Tourist—or a Short History of Identity," in *Questions of Cultural Identity*, ed. Stuart Hall and Paul du Gay (London: Sage, 1996), 18, 29, 30, 35, 36; George Allan, *The Importance of the Past: A Meditation on the Authority of Tradition* (Albany: State University of New York, 1986), 227–43; Chris Rojek, *Ways of Escape: Modern Transformations in Leisure and Travel* (Lanham, MD: Rowman and Littlefield, 1993); *Decentering Leisure: Rethinking Leisure Theory* (London: Sage, 1995); David Lowenthal, *The Heritage Crusade and the Spoils of History* (New York: Free Press, 1991), 7; Marvin Trachtenberg, *The Statue*

of Liberty (New York: Allen Lane, 1976), 16; Pierre Nora, *Realms of Memory* (New York: Columbia University Press, 1996), 1:19.

76. Dana E. Dolsen, Margaret Littlejohn, and Gary E. Machlis undertook the study of the Lincoln Home Historical Site for the National Park Service (1990). Analysis of visitors' responses is based on copies of original data stored at the University of Idaho, Moscow, Idaho.

77. The Director of the Springfield, Illinois, Convention and Visitors Bureau supplied the original data from the *Springfield Visitors Survey* (1991, 1992).

78. Whether Springfield's self-selected universe can be considered part of the universe investigated by the national survey depends on whether (1) Gallup's well-educated respondents, who admire Lincoln the most (chapter 5, this volume), resemble Springfield visitors more closely than do Gallup's less educated respondents, who admire Lincoln the least, and (2) whether Springfield visitors are more similar to the Gallup survey's best-educated respondents than to its least educated respondents (see table 5.2). Neither of the two propositions can be tested here, but to reject them out of hand would be unnecessarily limiting. The reason for supposing that most Springfield visitors deem Lincoln a great president is, simply, that they have spent the time and money to visit his shrines. The reason for supposing that a significant percentage of Gallup's best-educated respondents match Springfield visitors' admiration for Lincoln and interest in his shrines is that they are most likely to consider him a great president.

79. On the other hand, Eugene Webb, *et al* have noted that "individually restricted and nonidentical universes can provide collectively valuable outcroppings for the testing of theory"–"outcroppings" being the points where available data and theoretical assertions meet (Eugene Webb, Donald Campbell, Richard Schwartz, and Lee Sechrist, *Unobtrusive Measures* [New York: Rand-McNally, 1966], p.28). The crossing of the Springfield data and the postmodern theory of the past define this point.

80. Edward A. Shils and Michael Young, "The Meaning of the Coronation," in *Center and Periphery: Essays in Macrosociology* (Chicago: University of Chicago Press, 1975), 135.

81. For detailed treatment of this image at another Lincoln site, see Edward Bruner, "Lincoln's New Salem as a Contested Site," *Museum Anthropology* 17 (1993): 14–25; "Abraham Lincoln as an Authentic Reproduction: A Critique of Postmodernism," *American Anthropologist* 96 (1994): 397–416.

82. Warner, *The Living and the Dead*, 111.

83. Dean MacCannell, *The Tourist* (New York: Schocken, 1976), 110–11.

84. For another example, the extraordinary reaction to the death of Princess Diana would be incomprehensible if she had not been a member of the royal family. Both cases qualify Daniel Boorstin's claim that media celebrities have totally replaced symbols of state as objects of admiration ("From Hero to Celebrity: The Human Pseudo-Event," in *The Image: A Guide to Pseudo-Events in America* [New York: Harper and Row, 1964], 45–76).

85. Peter Brown, *The Cult of the Saints: Its Rise and Function in Latin Christianity* (Chicago: University of Chicago Press, 1981).

86. U.S. National Park Service, *Visitation, Springfield, IL* (1990), 5.

87. Maurice Halbwachs, *Collective Memory*, 128–57; Barbie Zelizer, "Reading the Past Against the Grain: The Shape of Memory Studies," *Critical Studies in Mass Communication* 12 (1995): 223–24.

88. Brown, *The Cult of the Saints*, 86–87.

89. Katharine W. Hannaford, "'Now He Belongs to the Ages': The Legacy of Abraham Lincoln, Abstract and Concrete," *American Quarterly* 51 (1999): 876.

90. Hugh Sidey, *John F. Kennedy, President* (New York: 1964), 231.

91. Edward A. Shils, *Tradition* (Chicago: University of Chicago Press, 1981), 12–14, 31–32, 38.

92. See Emile Durkheim, *Elementary Forms of the Religious Life* (New York: The Free Press, [1915] 1965) and commentary by W. S. F. Pickering, *Durkheim's Sociology of Religion: Themes and Theories* (London: Routledge and Kegan Paul, 1984), 352–54, 408, 358–61, on the transcendent (*la vie serieuse*) and the mundane (*la vie legere*). See also Wilbur Zelinsky, *Nation into State: The Shifting Symbolic Foundations of American Nationalism* (Chapel Hill: University of North Carolina Press, 1988), 100, 101, 277.

93. Schudson, *Watergate in American Memory*, 14.

94. Roger A. Fischer, "The 'Monumental' Lincoln as an American Cartoon Convention," *Inks* 2 (1995): 22.

95. *Atlanta Constitution*, April 22, 1990, G2; *USA Today*, August 18, 1994, A10. The cartoonist depends on his audience to assume, as he does, that Lincoln planned to emancipate all slaves instantaneously. In fact, Lincoln's second address to Congress, delivered a few weeks before he signed the Emancipation Proclamation, asked for legislation compensating slaveholders for each slave freed between the bill's passage and the year 1900.

96. John Gillis, ed., *Commemorations* (Princeton: Princeton University Press, 1994), 20.

97. Jean-Francois Lyotard, *The Postmodern Condition* (Minneapolis: University of Minnesota Press, [1979] 1984), 14, 37.

98. Raymond Williams, *Marxism and Literature* (New York: Oxford University Press, 1977), 122.

99. Personal communication, Grant DiCianni, May 3, 2007. For detail, see Heroes Series at http://www.tapestryproductions.com/products.

100. Mircea Eliade, *Myth and Reality* (New York: Harper and Row, 1963), 34; Edward A. Shils, "Tradition," in *Center and Periphery: Essays in Macrosociology*, 198.

CONCLUSION

1. George Forgie, *Patricide in the House Divided* (New York: W. W. Norton, 1979).

2. David W. Blight, *Race and Reunion: The Civil War in American Memory* (Cambridge, MA: Harvard University Press, 2001). See also David W. Blight, *Beyond the Battlefield: Race, Memory, and the American Civil War* (Amherst: University of Massachusetts Press, 2002). David Blight has dominated current thinking on the memory of the Civil War.

3. Edward L. Ayres, "Worrying about the Civil War," in *What Caused the Civil War? Reflections on the South and Southern History* (New York: W. W. Norton, 2005), 118.

4. This phase began with the Montgomery bus boycott, continued through the Birmingham and Selma confrontations, and concluded in the Northern cities, where economic and social goals were superimposed upon the goal of political justice. During the latter part of this period the Vietnam War protests grew, Martin Luther King Jr. and Robert Kennedy were assassinated, and urban disorders spread.

5. David Harlan, *The Degradation of American History* (Chicago: University of Chicago Press, 1997), 157.

6. Robert Lerner, Althea K. Nagai, and Stanley Rothman, *Molding the Good Citizen: The Politics of High School History Texts* (Westport, CT: Praeger, 1995), 69–87.

7. Ayres, *What Caused the Civil War?* 120.

8. Mary Douglas, *Natural Symbols* (New York: Vintage, 1973), 77–92.

9. Bruno Bettelheim, *The Uses of Enchantment: The Meaning and Importance of Fairy Tales* (New York: Knopf, 1977).

10. For a general discussion, see Reinhard Bendix, *Max Weber: An Intellectual Portrait* (Garden City, NY: Doubleday, 1962).

11. Representative readings in labeling theory can be found in one of the popular readers of the period: *Deviance: The Interactionist Perspective*, ed. Earl Rubington and Martin Weinberg (New York: Macmillan, 1978).

12. Academic disciplines changed directions. "The New History" reached down beyond "the ruling class" and its elites to explore experiences of the ordinary man and the underdog. This new history had no place for Lincoln or any other hero; its concern was to describe the past "from the bottom up, in retaliation for years of history from the top down." Meanwhile, the "new sociology" turned away from "consensus" theories of society and formulated "conflict" theories that justified opposition to the established order and sympathy for its "victims." Central to the conflict program since the 1960s has been the documentation of unequal opportunities, unequal rewards, unequal penalties, unequal deference, unequal obligations, unequal rights, and the relentless effort to construct theories of how these inequalities are sustained. In the classroom, the office, store, and street, America's culture of distinction and exclusion rapidly became a culture of egalitarian inclusion. See, for example, Eric Foner, *The New History* (Philadelphia: Temple University Press, 1990); Ralf Dahrendorf, *Class and Class Conflict in Industrial Society* (Stanford: Stanford University Press, 1959); Alvin Gouldner, *The Coming Crisis of Western Sociology* (New York: Basic Books, 1970). For critique of sociology's left-oriented politicization, see Irving L. Horowitz, *The Decomposition of Sociology* (New York: Oxford University Press, 1995) and Stephen Cole, *What's Wrong with Sociology?* (New Brunswick: Transaction Publishers, 2001).

13. Moisés Naim, "Our Inequality Anxiety," *Foreign Policy* (May 2006), http://www.foreignpolicy.com.

14. Kenneth Gergen, *The Saturated Self* (New York: Basic Books, 1991), 202–6.

15. John O'Neill, "Religion and the Postmodern: The Durkheimian Bond in Bell and Jameson," in *Postmodernism/Jameson/Critique*, ed. Douglas Kellner (Washington DC: Maisonneuve Press, 1995), 197.

16. Edward Bruner, "Abraham Lincoln as Authentic Reproduction: A Critique of Postmodernism," *American Anthropologist* 96 (1994): 413. The continuing relevance of metanarratives and commemorative symbols is evident in ongoing debates over cultural diversity. Products of postmodernity's aversion to boundaries and differentiation, multiculturalists see the cultivation of national memory alienating people from their particular ethnic communities, traditions, and histories. Critics charge that multiculturalism promotes alienation by discouraging shared traditions and undermining the shared history that once unified and inspired an ethnically diverse nation (Arthur M.

Schlesinger Jr., *The Disuniting of America: Reflections on a Multicultural Society* (New York: W. W. Norton, 1993).

17. Pierre Nora, *Realms of Memory* (New York: Columbia University Press, 1996), 3.

18. Jean-Francois Lyotard, *The Postmodern Condition* (Minneapolis: University of Minnesota Press, [1979] 1984), 66.

19. Alan Wolf, "Out of the Frying Pan into What?" in *America at Century's End*, ed. Alan Wolf (Berkeley: University of California Press, 1991).

20. Emile Durkheim, *The Division of Labor in Society* (New York: Free Press, [1893] 1964), 80. See also Seymour Martin Lipset, "A Changing American Character?" in *The First New Nation* (New York: W. W. Norton, 1964), 80; Barry Schwartz, "The Democratization of George Washington," *American Sociological Review* 56 (1991): 221–36.

21. Stjepan Mestrovic, *Durkheim and Postmodern Culture* (New York: Aldine de Gruyter, 1992), 91, 263.

22. Sigmund Freud, *Group Psychology and the Analysis of the Ego* (New York: Bantam, 1960), 46–53. Sociologist Talcott Parsons later redefined identification as "the process by which a person comes to be inducted into membership into a collectivity . . . in accord with the pattern of values governing the collectivity." *Social Structure and Personality* (New York: The Free Press, 1970), 91.

23. *Congressional Record* (HR), H9265.

24. Barry Schwartz, "The New Gettysburg Address: Fusing History and Memory," *Poetics* 33 (2005): 63–79.

25. *Congressional Record* (HR), April 15, 1999, to be acted upon by the Congress and its Commission, S14943.

26. Jennifer Rosenfeld to members of the Abraham Lincoln Bicentennial Commission Advisory Committee, "Announcement of April 15, 2007 Meeting," March 1, 2007.

27. Abraham Lincoln Bicentennial Commission (ALBC) Advisory Committee Meeting, *ALBC Public Awareness Committee Programs*, February 13, 2006, 2.

28. Cited in Francis Fukuyama, *The End of History and the Last Man* (New York: Avon, 1992), 306.

29. Ibid., 307.

30. For evidence, see Alan Wolfe's survey, *One Nation, After All* (New York: Viking, 1998).

31. Peter H. Gibbon, *A Call to Heroism: Renewing America's Vision of Greatness* (New York: Atlantic Monthly Press, 2002), 167, 178.

APPENDIX A

1. Richard Hofstadter, *The Age of Reform: From Bryan to F.D.R.* (New York: Vintage Books, 1955), 3–22.

2. John Steinbeck, *Grapes of Wrath* (New York: Penguin, 1991), 536–37, 542.

3. Michael Deming, *The Cultural Front: The Laboring of American Culture in the Twentieth Century* (New York: Verso, 1997). Conservatives gave this myth a peculiar twist in their mass-produced inventory of Lincoln's pre-presidential failures. Lincoln lost a bid for the Illinois legislature; failed in business; lost a race for the U.S. House of Representatives; was passed over for a land office appointment; ran unsuccessfully for his party's vice presidential candidacy; then lost a U.S. Senate race to Stephen Douglas.

The message: "tough out" the Depression. In 1939, a short film, *A Failure at Fifty*, shows an unemployed man being told about Lincoln's overcoming a succession of setbacks through hard work. Such narratives, however, were rarely produced on film and few paid attention to those that were. Hard work seemed feeble advice for people who could find no work to perform. Nevertheless, the narratives were influential because they portrayed Lincoln as an ordinary man injured by circumstances rather than a super man who defies them.

4. Lewis A. Coser, ed., *Sociology Through Literature* (Englewood Cliffs, NJ: Prentice-Hall, 1963), 2.

5. Charles Horton Cooley, *Human Nature and the Social Order* (New York: Schocken, [1902] 1964), 116–17.

6. *Abraham Lincoln* was produced by D. W. Griffith, who had achieved fame a decade earlier with *Birth of a Nation*—a film that also portrays President Lincoln reverently.

7. See also Richard J. S. Gutman, "Three Outstanding 'Abes': Lincoln's Image in the Cinema, Part II, 1931–1977," *Lincoln Herald* 80 (Fall 1978): 122–31. The racehorse Seabiscuit (subject of the film *The Story of Seabiscuit*, with Shirley Temple and Barry Fitzgerald) reflects the same pattern of traits. Seabiscuit, the most popular racehorse of the 1930s, was ugly, clumsy-looking, and moved with an awkward gait. He lost most of his early races and was ridiculed by the Eastern racing establishment. Yet, he later defeated War Admiral and other horses better bred than he. In short, to think of Seabiscuit and to think of Lincoln is to think of the same ideals: Seabiscuit was "a hard-luck horse for a troubled nation." "He looked like America." "A sunrise to a Depression-hit people." "The triumph over hardship, which is the theme of the American story" (Laura Hillenbrand, *Seabiscuit: An American* Legend (New York: Random House, 2001). See also the PBS Web site "American Experience: Seabiscuit" for visual documentation.

8. *North American Review* 206 (December 1938): 374.

9. Euphemia Wyatt, "At Last a Great American Play!" *Catholic World* 48 (December 1938): 341.

10. Ibid.

11. Lord Goeffrey R. B. Charnwood, *Abraham Lincoln* (Garden City, NY: Garden City Publishing Co., 1917).

12. This statement is true notwithstanding Robert Sherwood's Canadian background.

13. Susanne K. Langer, "The Art Symbol and the Symbol in Art," in *Problems of Art* (New York: Charles Scribner's Sons, 1957), 133.

14. Portrayals of prominent leaders during the late nineteenth and early twentieth centuries inclined strongly toward neoclassical convention. Of the eleven statues unveiled before 1899, ten are neoclassical, one unclassifiable. Conversely, the "genrified" (realist) and mixed-form statues' (excluding two unclassifiables) increase from 0 percent before 1900 through 52 percent between 1900 and 1929 to 78 percent after 1930. Barry Schwartz, "Iconography and Collective Memory: Lincoln's Image in the American Mind," *Sociological Quarterly* 32 (1991): 313.

15. Barry Schwartz, *Abraham Lincoln and the Forge of National Memory* (Chicago: University of Chicago Press, 2000), 256–92. See also Barry Schwartz, "Newark's Seated Lincoln," *New Jersey History* 113 (1995): 23–60.

16. Examples include statues by George Grey Barnard, 1917; Gutzon Borglum, 1911; Merrell Gage, 1918; Alonzo Lewis, 1918; and Andrew O'Connor, 1918.

17. Barry Schwartz, "Iconography and Collective Memory," 303–8.

18. Frederic L. Bullard, *Lincoln in Marble and Bronze* (New Brunswick: Rutgers University Press, 1952), 279.

19. Three years later, the city of Indianapolis dedicated a simple statue of Lincoln in University Park, its most beautiful public place. Lincoln sits upon a massive chair of state, his left elbow resting upon the chair's arm, his right hand raised as if expressing a critical point. He would appear Zeus-like if the sculptor, Henry Hering, had not draped a shawl over the back of the chair and placed a tall hat by its side. The shawl and hat symbolize a humanity with which all can identify.

20. Joseph F. Booton and Jerome Ray, *Record of the Restoration of New Salem* (Springfield, IL: State of Illinois Department of Public Works and Buildings, 1934).

21. Barry Schwartz, "Ann Rutledge in American Memory: Social Change and the Erosion of a Romantic Drama," *Journal of the Abraham Lincoln Association* 26 (2005): 1–27.

APPENDIX C

1. Richard Curtin, Stanley Presser, and Eleanor Singer, "The Effects of Response Rate Changes on the Index of Consumer Sentiments," *Public Opinion Quarterly* 64 (2000): 413–28; Scott Keeter, Carolyn Miller, Andrew Kohut, Robert M. Groves, and Stanley Presser, "Consequences of Reducing Nonresponses in a National Telephone Survey," *Public Opinion Quarterly* 64 (2000): 125–48.

2. Howard Schuman and Jacqueline Scott, "Generations and Collective Memories," *American Sociological Review* 54 (1989): 359–81.

3. Ibid., 372–74.

APPENDIX G

1. Michael Kammen, *Mystic Chords of Memory: The Transformation of Tradition in American Culture* (New York: Knopf, 1991), 465–73, esp. 470.

2. Wilbur Zelinsky, *Nation into State: The Shifting Foundations of American Nationalism* (Chapel Hill: University of North Carolina Press, 1988), 100–104.

APPENDIX K

1. E. Wayne Ross and Perry M. Marker, "Social Studies: Wrong, Right, or Left? A Critical Response to the Fordham Institute's *Where Did Social Studies Go Wrong?*" *The Social Studies* 96 (August 2005): 139–42. Ross and Marker are criticizing a report on civics and social science education by the conservative Fordham Institute (J. Leming, L. Ellington, and K. Porter Magee, *Where Did Social Studies Go Wrong?* (Washington, DC: Thomas B. Fordham Institute, 2003). Walter Berns, an eminent conservative scholar, is equally critical of the "blind tolerance" characteristic of American civic education (*Making Patriots* [Chicago: University of Chicago Press, 2001]; see esp. 65–80). James D. Hunter uses a different language ("culture war") to restate Berns's point: by relativizing culture, "multicultualism undermines the authority of cultural norms and cultural institutions, unwittingly teaching students that culture should not be taken very seriously" (*Before the Shooting Begins* [New York, The Free Press, 1994], 208; see also 190–211). William Backus Guitteau (*Preparing for Citizenship: An Elementary*

Textbook in Civics [Boston: Houghton Mifflin Company, 1913], 13) would appear a "blind patriot" to many twenty-first-century scholars, but during the 1920s, he along with David Saville Muzzey, was considered an un-American libertine with no commitment to the nation he described. See Sidney Brown, "The Textbook Furor in the 1920s," *Paradigm* 2 (October 2000), 12–18.

2. Julian C. Aldrich and Marlow A. Markert, *We, the Citizens: Senior Problems in Civic Responsibilities* (New York: Inor Publishing Co., Inc., 1948). Mark S. Mathews, *Guide to Community Action: A Sourcebook for Citizen Volunteers* (New York: Harper & Brothers, 1954), 239–52; Guitteau, *Preparing for Citizenship*, 233; see also more generally 229–38.

3. James D. Hunter, *Culture Wars: The Struggle to Define America* (New York: Basic Books, 1991), 120.

4. Woodrow Wilson's address to newly naturalized citizens and U.S. Bureau of Education's *Americanization Bulletin* are cited in Hunter, *Before the Shooting Begins*, 195.

5. For additional examples of earlier civics writing, see R. O. Hughes, *Elementary Community Civics* (Boston: Allen and Bacon, 1922); *Community Civics* (Boston: Allen and Bacon, 1921); William O. Penrose, *Freedom Is Ourselves: Legal Rights and Duties of the Citizen as a Basis for Civic Education* (Newark: University of Delaware Press, 1952); William S. Vincent, *Roles of the Citizen: Principles and Practices* (Evanston, IL: Row, Peterson and Company, 1959). Not all texts written before the 1960s conformed to the patriotic "indoctrination" model. See Ralph Barton Perry, *The Citizen Decides: A Guide to Responsible Thinking in Time of Crisis* (Bloomington, IN: Indiana University Press, 1951).

6. Rogers M. Smith, *Civic Ideals: Conflicting Visions of Citizenship in U.S. History* (New Haven: Yale University Press, 1997). Ironically, if ascriptive Americanism is defined in terms of identity rather than rights, a sharp rise characterizes its late twentieth-century trend. In mass media and academic publications, minority experiences are represented at the expense of nonminority experiences.

7. Joy Elmer Morgan, *The American Citizens Handbook* (Washington DC: National Education Association, 1941).

8. For examples of more recent civics writings, see James E. Davis and Phyllis Fernlund, *Civics: Participating in Government* (Upper Saddle River, NJ: Prentice Hall, 2003); Ralph L. Mosher, Robert A. Kenny, and Andrew Garrod, *Preparing for Citizenship: Teaching Youth to Live Democratically* (Westport, CT: Praeger, 1994); Lee Arbetman and Edward L. O'Brien, *Street Law: A Course in Practical Law* (New York: Glencoe/McGraw Hill, 2005); John Marciano, *Civic Illiteracy and Education: The Battle for the Hearts and Minds of American Youth* (New York: Peter Lang, 1997); James D. Carroll, Walter D. Broadnax, and Gloria Contreras, "What Do U.S. Government and Civics Textbooks Teach?" *Education Digest* 53 (September 1987): 36–38. Description and analysis of other recent texts appear in Allen Quist, *FedEd: The New Federal Curriculum and How It's Enforced* (St. Paul: Maple Education Coalition, 2002); Patricia G. Avery and Annette M. Simmons, "Civic Life as Conveyed in United States Civics and History Textbooks," *International Journal of Social Education* 15 (Fall/Winter 2000/2001): 105–30; Sharareh Frouzesh Bennett, "An Analysis of the Depiction of Democratic Participation in American Civics Textbooks," available at http://www.civiced.org. See also Michael Schudson, *The Good Citizen: A History of American Civic Life* (New York: The Free Press, 1998). The only participation anyone can expect from the busy citizen, according to Schudson, is to

monitor the behavior of his representatives in government. The good citizen is the "monitorial citizen" (310–12).

9. The power of diversity, Richard Merelman explains, is evident in the very existence of the 1994 National Standards for Civics and Government. But Merelman's argument is subtle. Nowhere do these standards explicitly define diversity a threat, but Merelman believes they do so implicitly: "the proposed national civic standards are mainly a symbolic ritual masked as an educational policy for reinforcing cultural hegemony." Because such rituals are ineffectual, however, diversity will continue to flourish—in the nation and in its textbooks. Richard Merelman, "Symbols as Substance in National Civics Standards," *Political Science and Politics* 29 (March 1996): 56.

10. Ulrich Beck, *The Cosmopolitan Vision* (Cambridge: Polity Press, 2006); Davis and Fernlund, *Civics*, 521–39.

11. Barry Schwartz, "George Washington and the Whig Conception of Heroic Leadership," *American Sociological Review* 48 (1983): 18–33.

Index

Page references in italics refer to illustrations and tables.